The Bible Speaks Today

Se⟨...⟩)

I⟨...⟩)

The Message of
the Cross

Titles in this series

OLD TESTAMENT

The Message of the Cross

Wisdom unsearchable, love indestructible

Derek Tidball
Principal of London Bible College

Inter-Varsity Press

Inter-Varsity Press
P.O. Box 1400, Downers Grove, IL 60515-1426
World Wide Web: www.ivpress.com
E-mail: mail@ivpress.com

Inter-Varsity Press
38 De Montfort Street, Leicester LE1 7GP, England
World Wide Web: www.ivpbooks.com
E-mail: ivp@uccf.org.uk

InterVarsity Press® is the book-publishing division of InterVarsity Christian Fellowship/USA®, a student movement active on campus at hundreds of universities, colleges and schools of nursing in the United States of America, and a member movement of the International Fellowship of Evangelical Students. For information about local and regional activities, write Public Relations Dept., InterVarsity Christian Fellowship/USA, 6400 Schroeder Rd., P.O. Box 7895, Madison, WI 53707-7895.

Inter-Varsity Press is the book-publishing division of the Universities and Colleges Christian Fellowship (formerly the Inter-Varsity Fellowship), a student movement linking Christian Unions in universities and colleges throughout the United Kingdom and the Republic of Ireland, and a member movement of the International Fellowship of Evangelical Students. For information about local and national activities write to UCCF, 38 De Montfort Street, Leicester LE1 7GP, England.

USA ISBN 0-8308-2403-0
UK ISBN 0-85111-543-8

Typeset in Great Britain by The Midlands Book Typesetting Company.

Printed in the United States of America ∞

British Library Cataloguing in Publication Data

A catalogue record for this book is available from the British Library.

Library of Congress Cataloging-in-Publication Data

Tidball, Derek.
    The message of the cross/Derek Tidball.
        p. cm.—(The Bible speaks today—Bible themes series)
    Includes bibliographical references.
    ISBN 0-8303-2403-0 (pbk.: alk. paper)
    1. Holy Cross. 2. Evangelicalism. I. Title. II. Series.
    BT465.T53 2001   2001024409
    232.96—dc21

| 18 | 17 | 16 | 15 | 14 | 13 | 12 | 11 | 10 | 9 | 8 | 7 | 6 | 5 | 4 | 3 | 2 | 1 |
| 16 | 15 | 14 | 13 | 12 | 11 | 10 | 09 | 08 | 07 | 06 | 05 | 04 | 03 | 02 | 01 |

To my son
RICHARD
Galatians 6:14

Contents

General
preface

THE BIBLE SPEAKS TODAY describes three series of expositions, based on the books of the Old and New Testaments, and on Bible themes that run through the whole of Scripture. Each series is characterized by a threefold ideal:

- to expound the biblical text with accuracy
- to relate it to contemporary life, and
- to be readable.

These books are, therefore, not 'commentaries', for the commentary seeks rather to elucidate the text than to apply it, and tends to be a work rather of reference than of literature. Nor, on the other hand, do they contain the kind of 'sermons' which attempt to be contemporary and readable without taking Scripture seriously enough.

The contributors to *The Bible Speaks Today* series are all united in their convictions that God still speaks through what he has spoken, and that nothing is more necessary for the life, health and growth of Christians than that they should hear what the Spirit is saying to them through his ancient – yet ever modern – Word.

ALEC MOTYER
JOHN STOTT
DEREK TIDBALL
Series Editors

Author's preface

The writing of any book is a collaborative effort, even though the author bears the ultimate responsibility alone for what is published. I would like to thank the team of people who have made this book possible.

My conversation partners about the cross, as will be obvious from the bibliography, have largely been biblical commentators rather than systematic theologians. I am grateful for the rich insights they have offered. Many of them are excellent advertisements for the value of scholarly research for Christian living. Other conversation partners have been audiences to which I have presented parts of this material in very draft form, including the Free Methodist Easter Conference, Preston, the Chinese Church Summer School, London, and the Ridley College Preaching School, Melbourne. I have been thankful for all their feedback and encouragement.

London Bible College granted me a sabbatical term, for which I am grateful. It was an excellent way to commence the new millennium, but not, I am told, a precedent for the rest of it. The absence of a college principal puts extra responsibilities on others, and I am grateful to all my colleagues for their helpfulness in making my leave possible. Special thanks go to those on the college executive, to several who undertook particular duties to cover for me and, as always, to my personal assistant, Jenny Aston, who steadfastly protected me from disturbance and helped in so many other ways. The college has proved a congenial environment in which to write, not least because of its excellent library facilities. I am grateful as well for the many students who have encouraged me with their prayers, showed an interest in my progress and spurred me on to reach the goal.

Once again I am indebted to my friend Andy Partington for working through the draft for me and making a multitude of wise comments. I am also grateful to David Kingdon and Alec Motyer, who read the manuscript and made many helpful suggestions. It was a privilege to be asked by IVP to edit The Bible Speaks Today Bible

Themes series, and to contribute this particular volume myself. It is a delight to work in partnership with Colin Duriez on both enterprises. His gentle and experienced editorial support has been a great asset.

Traditionally, authors thank their spouses and families for putting up with their long absences while they write. In my case, the reverse is the case. Writing at home means we have seen much more of each other than we do when I am engaged in the usual demands of leadership and preaching. It has been one of the real bonuses of the project, and I am grateful even more for the love of my wife Dianne, and son Richard, which has been enriched during these months. The book is dedicated to Richard, our much-loved son, in the hope that as he grows to manhood he will come to glory in the cross of Jesus, and in the cross alone.

I am all too aware of what a foolish ambition it is to think that one can write adequately about such a magnificent theme as the cross of Christ. When I had finished writing I was left with a renewed sense of awe at the splendour of God's grace and his wonderful plan of redemption. To think that the Son of God 'loved me and gave himself for me' is almost more than I can grasp. I hope that, for all the faults and inadequacies of what follows, as you 'survey the wondrous cross' with me, from the many different angles which the Bible reveals, you too will be encouraged to love him 'who laid down his life for us' more.

DEREK J. TIDBALL
London Bible College
Easter 2000

Abbreviations

AB	The Anchor Bible
AV	The Authorized (King James) Version of the Bible, 1611
BAGD	Walter Bauer, *A Greek-English Lexicon of the New Testament and Other Early Christian Literature*, translated and adapted by William F. Arndt and F. Wilbur Gingrich (University of Chicago, 1957)
BSC	Bible Student's Commentary
BNTC	Black's New Testament Commentaries
BST	The Bible Speaks Today
CBG	Crossway Bible Guides
CC	Communicator's Commentary
CGTC	The Cambridge Greek Testament Commentary
DJG	*Dictionary of Jesus and the Gospels*, ed. Joel B. Green, Scot McKnight and I. Howard Marshall (IVP, 1992)
DNTT	*Dictionary of New Testament Theology*, ed. Colin Brown, 3 vols. (Paternoster, 1975–78)
DPL	*Dictionary of Paul and his Letters*, ed. Gerald F. Hawthorne, Ralph P. Martin and Daniel G. Reid (IVP, 1993)
DSB	Daily Study Bible
EB	*The Expositor's Bible*
EBC	The Expositor's Bible Commentary
ET	English translation
IBC	Interpretation Bible Commentary
ICC	International Critical Commentary
Int	*Interpretation*
LXX	The Old Testament in Greek according to the Septuagint, 3rd cent. BC.
mg.	Margin
NAC	The New American Commentary
NCB	New Century Bible Commentary

NICNT	New International Commentary on the New Testament
NICOT	New International Commentary on the Old Testament
NIGTC	New International Greek Testament Commentary
NIV	The New International Version of the Bible (Inclusive Language Edition, 1996)
NLCNT	New London Commentary on the New Testament
NRSV	The New Revised Standard Version of the Bible (1995)
NTCS	New Testament Commentary Series
OTL	The Old Testament Library
PC	Pelican Commentaries
TCS	Torah Commentary Series
TDNT	*Theological Dictionary of the New Testament*, ed. G. Kittell and G. Friedrich, translated by G. W. Bromiley, 10 vols. (Eerdmans, 1964–76)
TDOTTE	*Theological Dictionary of Old Testament Theology and Exegesis*, ed. William A. van Gemeren, 5 vols. (Paternoster, 1996)
TNTC	Tyndale New Testament Commentaries
TOTC	Tyndale Old Testament Commentaries
WBC	Word Biblical Commentary
WEC	Wycliffe Exegetical Commentary

Select bibliography

Works listed here are referred to in the footnotes by author's surname, or surname and abbreviated title.

Alexander, T. D., 'The Passover sacrifice', in Beckworth and Selman (eds.), *Sacrifice in the Bible*, pp. 1–24

Anderson, A. A., *The Book of Psalms*, NCB 1 (Marshall, Morgan and Scott, 1972)

Arnold, Clinton, *The Colossian Syncretism* (Mohr, 1995)

—————— *Powers of Darkness* (IVP, 1992)

Aulén, Gustaf, *Christus Victor* (SPCK, 1931)

Aune, David, *Revelation 1 – 5*, WBC (Word, 1997)

Baillie, D. M., *God was in Christ: An Essay on the Incarnation and the Atonement* (1956; Faber and Faber, 1961)

Baldwin, Joyce, *The Message of Genesis 12 – 50*, BST (IVP, 1986)

Barnett, Paul, *The Second Epistle to the Corinthians*, NICNT (Eerdmans, 1997)

Barrett, C. K., *The First Epistle to the Corinthians*, BNTC (A. and C. Black, 1968)

—————— *The Second Epistle to the Corinthians*, BNTC (A. and C. Black, 1973)

Bauckham, Richard, and Hart, Trevor, *At the Cross: Meditations on People who were There* (Darton, Longman and Todd, 1999)

Beasley-Murray, George R., *John*, WBC (Word, 1987)

—————— *The Book of Revelation*, NCB (Oliphants, 1974)

Beckwith, Roger T., and Selman, Martin J. (eds.), *Sacrifice in the Bible* (Paternoster, 1995)

Blomberg, Craig L., *The Historical Reliability of the Gospels* (IVP, 1987)

—————— *Matthew*, NAC (Broadman, 1992)

Boice, James M., and Ryken, Philip G., *The Heart of the Cross* (Crossway, 1999)

Boring, M. Eugene, *Revelation*, IBC (John Knox, 1989)

Brown, Raymond, 'The saving message of the cross', in Porter (ed.),

The Cross and the Crown, pp. 55–122.

Brown, Raymond E., *The Death of the Messiah*, 2 vols. (Geoffrey Chapman, 1994)

———— *The Gospel According to John 2*, AB (Doubleday, 1970)

Bruce, F. F., *Commentary on the Epistles of Ephesians and Colossians*, NICNT (Eerdmans, 1957)

———— *1 and 2 Corinthians*, NCB (1971; Marshall, Morgan and Scott, 1980)

———— *The Epistle to the Hebrews*, NLCNT (Marshall, Morgan and Scott, 1964)

Brueggemann, Walter, *Genesis*, IBC (John Knox, 1982)

———— *Theology of the Old Testament* (Fortress, 1997)

Burridge, Richard, *Four Gospels, One Jesus? A Symbolic Reading* (SPCK, 1994)

Caird, G. B., *The Revelation of St John the Divine*, BNTC (A. and C. Black, 1966)

Calvin, John, *A Commentary on Genesis* (ET Banner of Truth, 1965)

———— *The Gospel According to St John 2* (ET St Andrew Press, 1961)

Carroll, John T., and Green, Joel B. (eds.), *The Death of Jesus in Early Christianity* (Hendrickson, 1995)

Carson, D. A., *The Cross and Christian Ministry: An Exposition of Passages from 1 Corinthians* (IVP, 1993)

———— *The Gospel According to John* (IVP, 1991)

———— 'Matthew', in EBC 8 (Zondervan, 1984)

Clines, David J. A., *I, He, We, They: A Literary Approach to Isaiah 53* (JSOT Press, 1976)

Clowney, Edmund P., *The Message of 1 Peter*, BST (IVP, 1988)

Cole, Alan, *Exodus*, TOTC (Tyndale Press, 1973)

Craigie, Peter C., *Psalms 1 – 50*, WBC (Word, 1983)

Cranfield, C. E. B., *The Gospel According to Mark*, CGTC (Cambridge University Press, 1963)

———— *Romans 1*, ICC (T. and T. Clark, 1975)

Creed, J. M., *The Gospel According to St Luke* (Macmillan, 1930)

Demarest, Gary W., *Leviticus*, CC (Word, 1990)

Denney, James, *The Death of Christ*, ed. R. V. G. Tasker (1902; Tyndale Press, 1951)

Dodd, C. H., *The Epistle of Paul to the Romans* (1932; Fontana, 1959)

Dray, Stephen, *Exodus*, CBG (Crossway, 1993)

Dunn, James D. G.,*The Epistle to the Colossians and to Philemon*, NIGTC (Paternoster, 1996)

———— *Romans 1 – 8*, WBC (Word, 1988)

Durham, John I., *Exodus*, WBC (Word, 1987)

Eaton, Michael, *1, 2, 3 John* (Christian Focus Publications, 1996)

Ellingworth, Paul, *The Epistle to the Hebrews*, NIGTC (Paternoster,

1993)
Ellison, H. L., *Exodus*, DSB (St Andrew Press, 1982)
Fee, Gordon D., *Paul's Letter to the Philippians*, NICNT (Eerdmans, 1995)
————— *Philippians*, NTCS (IVP, 1999)
————— *The First Epistle to the Corinthians*, NICNT (Eerdmans, 1987)
Fiddes, Paul S., *Past Event and Present Salvation: The Christian Idea of Atonement* (Darton, Longman and Todd, 1989)
Forsyth, P. T., *The Cruciality of the Cross* (1909; Paternoster, 1997)
France, R. T., *Jesus and the Old Testament* (1971; Baker, 1982)
————— *Matthew*, TNTC (IVP, 1985)
————— *Matthew: Evangelist and Teacher* (Paternoster, 1989)
Fretheim, Terence E., *Exodus*, IBC (John Knox, 1991)
George, Timothy, *Galatians*, NAC (Broadman and Holman, 1994)
Gibson, John C. L., *Genesis 2*, DSB (St Andrew Press, 1982)
Goldingay, John, *God's Prophet, God's Servant: A Study in Jeremiah and Isaiah 40 – 55* (Paternoster, 1984)
————— 'Old Testament sacrifice and the death of Christ', in Goldingay (ed.), *Atonement Today*, pp. 3–20
————— 'Your iniquities have made a separation between you and your God', in Goldingay (ed.), pp. 39–53
————— (ed.), *Atonement Today* (SPCK, 1995)
Gordon, James M., *Evangelical Spirituality: From the Wesleys to John Stott* (SPCK, 1991)
Green, Joel B., 'The death of Christ', in *DPL*, pp. 201–209
————— 'The death of Jesus and the ways of God: Jesus and the Gospels on Messianic status and shameful suffering', *Int* 52 (1998), pp. 24–37
————— *The Gospel of Luke*, in NICNT (Eerdmans, 1997)
Greidanus, Sidney, *Preaching Christ from the Old Testament* (Eerdmans, 1999)
Grudem, Wayne, *1 Peter*, TNTC (IVP, 1998)
Guillebaud, H. E., *Why the Cross?* (IVF, 1937)
Gundry, Robert H., *Mark: A Commentary on his Apology for the Cross* (Eerdmans, 1993)
————— *Matthew: A Commentary on his Literary and Theological Art* (Eerdmans, 1982)
Gunton, Colin, *The Actuality of the Atonement: A Study in Metaphor, Rationality and the Christian Tradition* (T. and T. Clark, 1988)
Hagner, Donald A., *Matthew 1 – 13*, WBC (Word, 1993)
Hanson, A. T., *The Wrath of the Lamb* (SPCK, 1959)
Hanson, Paul D., *Isaiah 40 – 66*, IBC (John Knox, 1995)
Harrison, R. K., *Leviticus*, TOTC (IVP, 1980)
Hartley, John E., *Leviticus*, WBC (Word, 1992)

Hawthorne, Gerald F., *Philippians*, WBC (Word, 1983)

Hengel, Martin, *The Atonement. The Origin of the Doctrine in the New Testament* (1980; ET SCM, 1981)

Hooker, Morna D., *Not Ashamed of the Gospel: New Testament Interpretations of the Death of Christ* (Paternoster, 1994)

————— *The Message of Mark* (Epworth, 1983)

Hughes, Philip Edgcumbe, *The Book of Revelation* (IVP, 1990)

————— *A Commentary on the Epistle to the Hebrews* (Eerdmans, 1977)

————— *Paul's Second Epistle to the Corinthians*, NLCNT (Marshall, Morgan and Scott, 1961)

Hyatt, J. P., *Exodus*, NCB (1971; Marshall, Morgan and Scott, 1980)

Jackman, David, *The Message of John's Letters*, BST (IVP, 1988)

Jenson, Philip P., *Graded Holiness: A Key to the Priestly Conception of the World* (JSOT Press, 1992)

————— 'The Levitical sacrificial system', in Beckwith and Selman (eds.), *Sacrifice in the Bible*, pp. 25–40

Kaiser, Walter C., 'Exodus', in EBC 2 (Zondervan, 1990)

Kidner, Derek, *Genesis*, TOTC (IVP, 1967)

————— *Psalms 1 – 72*, TOTC (IVP, 1973)

Lane, William L., *The Gospel of Mark*, NICNT (Eerdmans, 1974)

————— *Hebrews 1 – 8*, WBC (Word, 1991)

Levenson, Jon D., *The Death and Resurrection of the Beloved Son* (Yale University Press, 1993)

Levine, Baruch, *Leviticus*, TCS (Jewish Publication Society, 1989)

Lindars, Barnabas, *The Theology of the Letter to the Hebrews* (Cambridge University Press, 1991)

Lloyd-Jones, D. Martyn, *Romans: An Exposition of Chapters 3.20 – 4.45, Atonement and Justification* (Banner of Truth, 1970)

Long, Thomas G., *Hebrews*, IBC, (John Knox, 1997)

Longenecker, Richard N., *Galatians*, WBC (Word, 1990)

McGrath, Alister E., *The Enigma of the Cross* (1987; Hodder and Stoughton, 1996)

McIntyre, John, *The Shape of Soteriology* (T. and T. Clark, 1992)

Marshall, I. Howard, *The Gospel of Luke*, NIGTC (Paternoster, 1978)

————— *The Epistles of John*, NICNT (Eerdmans, 1987)

————— *1 Peter*, NTCS (IVP, 1991)

Martin, Ralph P., *2 Corinthians*, WBC (Word, 1986)

————— *Reconciliation: A Study in Paul's Theology* (Marshall, Morgan and Scott, 1981)

Mays, James L., *Psalms*, IBC (John Knox, 1994)

Michaels, J. Ramsey, *1 Peter*, WBC (Word, 1988)

Milgrom, Jacob, *Leviticus 1 – 16*, AB (Doubleday, 1991)

Milne, Bruce, *The Message of John*, BST (IVP, 1993)

Moberly, R. W. L., 'Christ as the key to the scripture: Genesis 22 reconsidered', in R. S. Hess, P. E. Satterthwaite and G. J. Wenham (eds.), *He Swore an Oath: Biblical Themes from Genesis 12 – 50* (Tyndale House, 1993) pp. 143–173

Moltmann, Jürgen, *The Crucified God* (1973; ET SCM, 1974)

Moo, Douglas, *Romans 1 – 8*, WEC (Moody, 1991)

Morris, Leon, *The Apostolic Preaching of the Cross* (1955; Tyndale Press, 1965)

———— *The Atonement: Its Meaning and Significance* (IVP, 1983)

———— *The Cross in the New Testament* (Paternoster, 1965)

———— *The Cross of Jesus* (Paternoster, 1988)

———— *The Epistle to the Romans* (IVP, 1988)

———— *The Gospel According to John*, NICNT (Eerdmans, 1971)

Motyer, Alec, *Isaiah*, TOTC (IVP, 1999)

———— *The Prophecy of Isaiah* (IVP, 1993)

Moule, Handley C. G., *The Epistle of St Paul to the Romans*, EB (Hodder and Stoughton, 1894)

Mounce, Robert H., *The Book of Revelation*, NICNT (Eerdmans, 1977)

Nolland, John, *Luke 3:18:35 – 24:53*, WBC (Word, 1993)

Noordtzij, A., *Leviticus*, BSC (Zondervan, 1982)

North, Christopher R., *The Second Isaiah* (Oxford, 1964)

————*The Suffering Servant in Deutero-Isaiah* (1948; Oxford University Press, 1956)

O'Brien, Peter T., *Colossians, Philemon*, WBC (Word, 1982)

———— *Commentary on Philippians*, NIGTC (Eerdmans, 1991)

———— *The Letter to the Ephesians* (Apollos, 1999)

Packer, J. I., *Knowing God* (Hodder and Stoughton, 1973)

———— *A Passion for Holiness* (Crossway, 1992)

———— 'What did the cross achieve?', in *Celebrating the Saving Work of God: The Collected Shorter Writings of J. I. Packer* 1 (Paternoster, 1998), pp. 85–123. Originally delivered as the Tyndale Biblical Theology Lecture at Tyndale House, Cambridge, 1973, and published in *Tyndale Bulletin* 25 (1974), pp. 1–43

Pickett, Raymond, *The Cross in Corinth: The Social Significance of the Death of Jesus* (Sheffield Academic Press, 1997)

Porter, David (ed.), *The Cross and the Crown* (OM Publishing, 1992)

Rad, Gerhard von, *Genesis*, OTL (1961; ET SCM, 1972)

Sailhamer, John H., 'Genesis', in EBC 2 (Zondervan, 1990)

Sawyer, John F. A., *Isaiah* 2, DSB (St Andrew Press, 1986)

Seifrid, M. A., 'Death of Christ', in R. P. Martin and P. H. Davids (eds.), *Dictionary of the Later New Testament and its Developments* (IVP, 1997), pp. 267–287

Senior, Donald, *The Passion Narrative According to Matthew: A Redactional Study* (Leuven University Press, 1975)

———— *The Passion of Jesus in the Gospel of John* (Michael Glazier,

1991)

————— *The Passion of Jesus in the Gospel of Luke* (Michael Glazier, 1989)

————— *The Passion of Jesus in the Gospel of Mark* (Michael Glazier, 1984)

Smail, Tom, 'The cross and the Spirit', in Tom Smail, Andrew Walker and Nigel Wright, *Charismatic Renewal: The Search for a New Theology* (SPCK, 1993)

————— *Once and for All: A Confession of the Cross* (Darton, Longman and Todd, 1998)

————— *Windows on the Cross* (Darton, Longman and Todd, 1995)

Spurgeon, C. H., *Sermons on the Blood and Cross of Christ*, ed. C. T. Cook (Marshall, Morgan and Scott, 1961)

Stein, Robert H., *Luke*, NAC (Broadman, 1992)

Stibbs, A. M., *The Meaning of the word 'Blood' in Scripture* (Theological Students Fellowship, 1954)

————— *The First Epistle General of Peter*, TNTC (Tyndale Press, 1959)

Stott, John R. W., *The Cross of Christ* (IVP, 1986)

————— *The Epistles of John*, TNTC (IVP, rev. ed. 1988)

————— *The Message of Romans*, BST (IVP, 1994)

Sweet, John, *Revelation*, PC (SCM, 1979)

Tomlin, Graham, *The Power of the Cross* (Paternoster, 1999)

Wallace, Ronald, *The Atoning Death of Christ* (Marshall, Morgan and Scott, 1981)

Watts, John D. W., *Isaiah 34 – 66*, WBC (Word, 1987)

Webb, Barry, *The Message of Isaiah*, BST (IVP, 1996)

Weiser, Artur, *The Psalms*, OTL (1959; ET SCM, 1962)

Wenham, Gordon, *Genesis 16 – 50* WBC (Word, 1994)

————— *The Book of Leviticus*, NICOT (Hodder and Stoughton, 1979)

Westermann, Claus, *Genesis 12 – 36* (Augsburg, 1985)

————— *Isaiah 40 – 66*, OTL (1966; ET SCM, 1969)

Whybray, R. N., *Isaiah 40 – 66*, NCB (1975; Marshall, Morgan and Scott, 1981)

Witherington III, Ben, *Conflict and Community in Corinth: A Socio-Rhetorical Commentary on 1 and 2 Corinthians* (Paternoster, 1995)

Wright, N. T., *The Challenge of Jesus* (SPCK, 2000)

————— *Colossians*, TNTC (IVP, 1986)

————— *The Crown and the Fire: Meditations on the Cross and the Life of the Spirit* (Eerdmans, 1992)

————— *Jesus and the Victory of God* (SPCK, 1996)

————— *What Saint Paul Really Said* (Lion, 1997)

Wright, N. T., and Borg, Marcus, *The Meaning of Jesus: Two Visions* (SPCK, 1999)

Introduction:
The cross in evangelical spirituality and theology today

The National Gallery in London decided that the most appropriate way to celebrate the advent of the new millennium was to mount an exhibition of art on 'The Image of Christ'. It was presented in the belief that even secular audiences could engage with the artists' portrayals of the life and death of Jesus and see the continuing truth and importance they depicted. Towards the end of the exhibition the visitor encountered Salvador Dali's *Christ of St John of the Cross*, painted in 1951. When first displayed, it met with considerable criticism from the experts. Yet within the first two months, fifty thousand people of all types queued to see it, and a press report commented, 'Men entering the room where the picture is hung instinctively take off their hats. Crowds of chattering, high-spirited school children are hushed into awed silence when they see it.'[1]

Before the cross of Christ countless men and women of every generation and culture have stood in adoring wonder and humble penitence. The cross stands at the very heart of the Christian faith, manifesting the love of God, effecting salvation from sin, conquering the hostile forces of evil and inviting reconciliation with God. This book invites us to stand at the foot of the cross once more and gaze at it in gratitude and faith through the eyes of the varied witnesses of Scripture.

The cross is a wonderfully wrought and complex work of God which cannot be captured in its fullness from one standpoint alone, and even less in one theory. Ronald Wallace has warned:

If we are to do full justice to the varying witnesses, and let them fully illuminate the meaning of the Gospel, we shall require now one 'theory' of the atonement and now another to help us in our exposition. Often we shall see some new aspect of the cross that

[1] *Scottish Art Review*, quoted in G. Finaldi, *The Image of Christ* (National Gallery, 2000), p. 198.

does not quite fit into any kind of dogmatic system at all. We must be prepared for this. We must allow our thinking to be dominated by the shape and dynamic of the biblical text rather than by our theological preferences. The Bible allows us a large area to move in, with many different levels and standpoints from which we can look at the death of Christ.[2]

Consequently, we shall walk through the pages of the Bible, stopping to look first at one and then at another of the portraits of the cross it presents. We begin with the sketches drawn by the Old Testament writers, centuries before it ever became a historical reality. We shall linger over the eye-witness masterpieces of the Gospels, before moving on to the more reflective pieces of Paul and the other New Testament interpreters of the cross. In selecting the particular passages for consideration, I have sought to make a representative choice but lay no claim to its being exhaustive.

Readers anxious to begin the journey may quite legitimately wish to go ahead to the initial portrait from Genesis 22, in chapter 1. For others, however, gaining some preliminary orientation on the place of the cross in evangelical spirituality and theology may be beneficial. The cross has always been at the heart of both,[3] defining our doctrine, dominating our preaching, inspiring our devotion and motivating our mission. Today, though, there are some signs that it no longer occupies the central place that once it did, at least as traditionally interpreted. While this book does not permit an extensive treatment of the subject, a brief review may be in order.

1. Evangelical spirituality and the cross today

a. The traditional importance of the cross in evangelical spirituality

'Spirituality' refers to our experience of God rather than mere knowledge about God; to the inner life of the believer in relation to God; to the devotional life and practice which provide the motivating power for our transformation and our action; and, therefore, to one's central orientation around which all else revolves. At the heart of evangelical spirituality lies the atoning work of Christ. The Christian life is viewed primarily as a life that finds its origin in the cross and is lived in grateful response to it and humble imitation of it.

The hymnwriters and preachers of previous generations show it to

---

[2] Wallace, p. 93.
[3] So much so that D. Bebbington convincingly makes 'crucicentrism', along with conversionism, activism and biblicism, one of the four distinguishing hallmarks of evangelicalism: *Evangelicalism in Modern Britain: A History from the 1730s to the 1980s* (Unwin Hyman, 1989), pp. 14–17.

be so. Isaac Watts' invitation to 'survey the wondrous cross' is classic evangelical spirituality, as is Charles Wesley's celebration of the cross in his hymn 'And can it be, that I should gain / An interest in the Saviour's blood?', with its exclamation, 'Amazing love! How can it be / That thou, my God, shouldst die for me?' A multitude of hymns and songs about the cross testifies to its importance for spirituality.

The faith of the eighteenth-century evangelical leader Charles Simeon is described as 'the religion of a sinner at the foot of the cross'.[4] And one of his most important sermons was entitled, 'Christ Crucified, Or Evangelical Religion Described', in which he argued that the atonement is the only adequate basis for Christian spirituality.[5] In another sermon he announced: 'A sense of Christ's love in dying for us must be inculcated as the mainspring and motive for all our obedience.'[6] Bishop J. C. Ryle, in a passionate prayer based on the cross, stated that without substitutionary atonement 'your religion is a heaven without a sun, an arch without a keystone, a compass without a needle, a clock without a spring or weights, a lamp without oil'.[7] C. H. Spurgeon stated, 'The cross is the centre of our system.'[8] Campbell Morgan, of Westminster Chapel, said that 'every living experience of Christianity begins at the cross', which he had found to be 'the fulcrum of the spiritual life'.[9] Today, the same understanding of the cross is seen in the writings of John Stott, J. I. Packer and Martyn Lloyd-Jones.[10]

It is true to say that, contrary to some of evangelicalism's critics, the cross has never exhausted evangelical spirituality. But it has defined its centre.

b. The cultivation of evangelical spirituality

Evangelical spirituality is often assumed to be word-centred and associated with preaching, or even mistakenly identified with the practice of the 'quiet time' and thought to consist of little else. The 'quiet time' is the practice of reading daily and privately a portion of Scripture, often with brief explanatory notes, and of personal, probably extempore, prayer. It can too easily become a sort of magic ritual,

[4] Gordon, p. 96.
[5] Ibid., pp. 96–97.
[6] C. Simeon, *Evangelical Preaching* (Multnomah, 1986), p. 53.
[7] Gordon, p. 219.
[8] Quoted in D. Bebbington, *Holiness in Nineteenth-Century England* (Paternoster, 2000), p. 38. The book contains a number of other insights into the centrality of the cross in evangelical spirituality.
[9] Gordon, p. 314.
[10] Stott, *Cross of Christ, passim.* Stott's work is no dry academic treatise, but one which frequently bursts into doxology. See Packer's works in the bibliography. There is no single statement about the cross in Lloyd-Jones's writing, but the theme is to be found in numerous places.

disconnected from real life, which, once performed, somehow protects Christians but does not transform them. How barren such an understanding of spirituality appears to be in comparison with the rich contemplation involved in other traditions, often aided by colourful icons and symbols, or other visual helps, and involving more costly disciplines such as fasting, retreats or silences! In the visual surroundings of our lives the word-orientation of evangelical spirituality often seems sterile.

But if we think evangelical spirituality is reducible to listening to sermons or to the mechanical practice of the 'quiet time', we have been misled and are mistaking the husk of evangelical method for the kernel of evangelical truth and experience. There can be no richer spirituality than that based on the contemplation of God's amazing grace and on submission to his living word. It is not the spirituality that is at fault, but our practice of it, and perhaps the frenetic pace at which we live.

Evangelical spirituality calls on us to contemplate the cross. Not for nothing did Isaac Watts talk of 'surveying' the wondrous cross. Not for nothing did George Whitefield exult in the cross in his numerous letters, and urge readers to 'Forget not a bleeding God'. He hoped, he wrote, that one of his converts would 'know what it is to feast on a crucified Jesus'; he pointed out 'how mean and contemptible does every creature appear, when the soul gets a near view of the crucified Redeemer', and he encouraged meditation on 'the agony and bloody sweat of an incarnate God'.[11]

The Methodist leader Samuel Chadwick adopted Lenten disciplines dominated by the passion of Christ: 'Usually the days are with "set face" towards the Cross.' Catholic devotional manuals, books on the atonement and carefully chosen Bible passages were vehicles for meditation on the passion. James Gordon comments: 'The critical reverence of the Bible student gave way to the humble research of a soul seeking illumination, "turning leisurely and prayerfully from one great passage to another, to track out words and trace their unfolding in the book of God".'[12]

Bishop Handley Moule, in his book *The Call of Lent*, taught that prayer was the prerequisite to assurance, and that to reflect upon the love of the Crucified was to strengthen the sense of being loved. 'The love of the Crucified, that love which He IS, turns the word "redemption", "possession", "servitude" into the inmost voice of an infinite affection.'[13]

It is meditation and prayer, based firmly on scriptural revelation

[11] Gordon, p. 57.
[12] Ibid., p. 260.
[13] Ibid., p. 212.

rather than on private imagination, that lead to a deepening sense of wonder at God's grace at Calvary. 'Meditation', as the Singaporean evangelical theologian Simon Chan has recently written, is 'the main link between theology and praxis. It is the way to make truth come alive as it courses from mind to heart to daily living.'[14] Meditation, he argues, is no recent invention, but traces its root back to John Calvin, who saw it as central to our union with Christ.

c. The outworking of a crucicentric evangelical spirituality

Evangelical spirituality centred on the cross *expresses itself in song*, because the love of God is experienced ('felt', as older evangelicals might say) through the cross. It is founded not on a formal assertion of truth but on a living experience of grace. So it finds expression in joy and thanksgiving, and hence in song. Many of the great evangelical hymns have been about the cross, from Isaac Watts, Charles Wesley, and John Newton, down to Graham Kendrick and Matt Redman in our own day. Though the early period of contemporary hymnwriting and song-writing, which had its origins in the efflorescence of the charismatic movement in the 1970s, saw little written about the cross, this has now been corrected. The excessive preoccupation with a theology of glory, victory and triumphalism has given way to a better balance that mirrors the dying-and-rising motifs of New Testament Christianity. Graham Kendrick's hymn 'Meekness and majesty',[15] and his song 'The price is paid', both contain rich expositions of the cross, and will surely be remembered for generations to come. Similarly, Matt Redman's 'Jesus Christ, I think upon your sacrifice', which invites us to respond with our 'ev'ry breath', and his song 'The cross has said it all', stand in the classic evangelical tradition although very contemporary in musical and verbal idiom. Evangelical spirituality still expresses itself in song.

It expresses itself in action. One of the heroic episodes of my youth was the martyrdom of five young American missionaries by Auca Indians. Motivated by the cross, they felt unable to stay at home while tribal people elsewhere were in ignorance of the gospel. They went to make God's love known, and paid for it with their lives. But the cross meant that they always believed themselves to be expendable.[16]

The self-giving love Christ has for us leads in turn to believers'

---

[14] S. Chan, *Spiritual Theology: A Systematic Study of the Christian Life* (IVP [USA], 1998), p. 167. Packer asks, 'How can we turn our knowledge *about* God into knowledge *of* God? The rule for doing this is demanding but simple. It is that we turn each truth that we learn *about* God into a matter of meditation *before* God, leading to prayer and praise *to* God.' *Knowing God*, p. 18.

[15] The subtitle of this book comes from 'Meekness and majesty', verse 3.

[16] The story is told by Elizabeth Elliot, the widow of one of those murdered, in her *Through Gates of Splendour* (Hodder and Stoughton, 1957).

giving themselves for the world in preaching the gospel, in social action, in peacemaking and through acts of self-giving and self-denial. John Stott has written that our 'insistence on security is incompatible with the way of the cross'. Referring to James and John, he continues: 'It is the glory of Christ's cross which shows up their selfish ambition for the shabby, tatty, threadbare thing it was. It also highlights the choice, which faces the Christian community in every generation, between the way of the crowd and the way of the cross.'[17] Service and mission, of all kinds, are cross-shaped.

It expresses itself in perseverance. Charles Simeon was much opposed for his evangelical ministry in Cambridge, and James Gordon writes that 'In the message of the suffering Christ, Simeon found a paradigm for his own cross-bearing. It is impossible to separate his passionate loyalty to Christ crucified from the opposition, ridicule and hostility he encountered for prolonged periods at Cambridge.'[18] Simeon noted that Simon, who carried Christ's cross, had the same name as he. 'What a blessed hint of encouragement!' Simeon wrote. 'To have a cross laid upon me, that I might bear it after Jesus – what a privilege! It was enough. Now I could leap and sing for joy as one whom Jesus was honouring with a participation in his sufferings ... I henceforth bound persecution as a wreath of glory round my brow.'[19]

Although some evangelical writers and composers speak of the cross in terms of romanticism or of an amorous experience,[20] the dominant evangelical strain about the cross is one of rigorous realism. It is one that, far from being privately indulgent, compels disciples to enter into all the muck and pain of the world and to embrace it with arms stretched out as wide and fastened as steadfastly as the arms of Jesus to his cross.

It expresses itself in holiness. Simeon serves as our spokesperson again. In one sermon he said,

> Finally let us show the wisdom of our intent by the holiness of our lives. The doctrine of Christ crucified has and always will appear foolishness in the sight of the ungodly ... There is only one way that we can display its excellence in such a manner that we effectively 'put to silence the ignorance of foolish men'. This is 'by well-doing'. That is to say we show the sanctifying and transforming efficacy of this doctrine.[21]

[17] Stott, *Cross of Christ*, p. 288.
[18] Gordon, p. 97.
[19] Ibid.
[20] The impact of the Romantic movement is seen in evangelicalism especially in the teaching of the early Keswick movement. See Bebbington, *Evangelicalism*, pp. 80–81, 167–169, and *Holiness*, pp. 73–90.
[21] Simeon, *Evangelical Preaching*, p. 57.

It expresses itself in community. We do not stand as individualists at the foot of the cross. It brings us into reconciled relationships with others and it forms a community in which we come together in the breaking of bread, serve one another in love, and find solidarity with one another as the reproach of the world is borne.

The Christian life has its beginning and its continuance in the work of the cross as Christ died for the forgiveness of our sins and to impart new life to us. The Christian life is cruciform as we die to sin, to selfish individualism, to our own desires and ambitions, to the mindset of the world and to the life dictated by the old nature, and become like Christ himself in his death.[22]

d. The dangers of evangelical spirituality

There are certainly dangers in cross-centred evangelical spirituality. There is the danger of morbidity and of an excessive dwelling on the darkness of Calvary. William Cowper, for example, who had a depressive personality, penned what some see as 'a grimly forensic description of the atonement in which he painted the peril of the soul and the efficacy of Christ's death in the starkest possible colours,'[23] in hymns such as 'There is a fountain filled with blood / Drawn from Immanuel's veins'. 'Few can have known more intimately than Cowper', comments Newey, 'the inner wilderness created by guilt and self-hatred … the terrifying vision of an unappeased God.'[24] But this is just the sort of conscience the cross was designed to alleviate.

There is the danger of leaving Christ on the cross and failing to appreciate the significance of the incarnation, the resurrection and the day of Pentecost. There is the danger of trivializing this world and becoming world-denying in a distorted way. There is the danger of unhealthy attitudes to oneself and to people in general, as in Elizabeth Clephane's otherwise beautiful hymn 'Beneath the cross of Jesus'. It includes the words, 'Two wonders I confess – / The wonder of redeeming love, / And *my own worthlessness.*' In view of the doctrine of creation and the cost of our redemption, it is surely wrong to speak of our 'worthlessness'. We should readily sing of our 'unworthiness', but not of our 'worthlessness'. The one too easily slides into the other, giving a quite wrong estimation of human life and creation.

e. Contemporary developments in evangelical spirituality

There is evidence that the cross is being displaced from the centre of evangelical spirituality today. For example, a recent book on evangelical

---

[22] Phil. 3:10.
[23] Gordon, p. 73.
[24] Quoted in ibid., pp. 73–74.

spirituality, which in other ways is excellent, says little on the cross, and an examination of 'cross' and related words in the Index yields almost as many references to St John of the Cross as to the cross of Jesus. At a popular level, an evangelical spirituality is developing which, in its search for self-affirmation and comfort, can only be described as cross-avoiding rather than cross-carrying.

Two particular trends which have affected contemporary evangelicalism are worthy of comment.

First, for some, *Calvary has been replaced by Pentecost.* Tom Smail, a leading thinker of the charismatic movement, recently wrote, 'Experience of the Spirit has for many become more central than faith in the Crucified, so that the Christian centre has moved from Calvary to Pentecost.'[25] One can understand why. The charismatic movement arose partly in reaction to a Christianity that was defeatist and binitarian, living too much in the reality of this world and not enough in the light of the kingdom *present* as well as future. It had a theology of the cross but not of glory, and tended to be too complacent about the work of Satan. The rediscovery of the Spirit brought a fresh confidence and a greater questing after God in our experience. So much was good.

But Tom Smail has critiqued this move in his essay 'The cross and the Spirit: Towards a theology of renewal'. Pentecostal theology, he says, like all theologies, has limitations. 'Chief among these … is the fact that the basic structures of Pentecostal theology make it difficult to recognise the close and intimate relationship between the renewing and empowering work of the Spirit and the centre of the gospel in the incarnation, death and resurrection of Jesus Christ.'[26] It tends to forget that 'The way to Pentecost is Calvary; the Spirit comes from the Cross'. The power department and the pardon department may be under the same roof, but in charismatic theology, unless we are careful, they do not necessarily relate to each other. Smail advises that this may well lead to a two-stage Christianity, with the cross being Stage 1, from which one graduates to charismatic experience. It can also lead to a preoccupation with power. But power needs to be critiqued. Do we, Smail asks, have a love of power or know the power of love? 'When we take our bearings from the cross, we can see that the only power with which Jesus works is the power of that utterly self-giving love that was itself weak and helpless on Calvary. He overcame all the violent force and violence of evil that fell upon him there, not by exercising greater force and violence, but by renouncing them altogether.'[27] The division between power and pardon can further lead to a concern for healing and various manifestations. 'What heals is not esoteric techniques, or

[25] Smail, *Once and for All*, p. 17.
[26] Smail, 'Cross and Spirit', p. 54.
[27] Ibid., p. 62.

even supernatural endowment as such; what heals is Calvary love.' 'A church in which healing, renewal and effective evangelism can happen is a church that is open to receive Christ's Calvary love ...'[28] The division can also contribute, says Smail, to a failure to provide an adequate pastoral theology of suffering and failure, and, I would add, to a failure to provide genuine assurance of acceptance by God as people constantly seek 'more love and more power' and forget to stand on the completed work of Christ and confidently appropriate what is already available to them through him.

Secondly, for some, *atonement has been replaced by incarnation or creation* as the centre of their theological perspective. Several evangelical teachers, rightly concerned about the relationship between the church and postmodern culture, have recently suggested that we need to move from the cross to a more creation-centred and incarnational approach to spirituality if we are to reach the world in which we live. Their major concern is to recognize the spiritualities of people found outside the church rather than writing them off as illegitimate. Our mission, they say, should start where people are – as Jesus himself did and as Paul modelled[29] – entering their world and having a much more positive orientation towards creation and culture than evangelicals have traditionally espoused.

The curious revival of Celtic spirituality in the UK, which many evangelicals, among others, find enticing with its creation-centred ethos, illustrates the trend. To the Celtic preachers God was a down-to-earth God who was intensely real and showed himself in the ordinariness, goodness and majesty of his creation. He could be discerned in the wind and the waves, as well as in the eucharist and the prayer cell. Such a spirituality resonates with a world concerned about matters of ecology and stops us from indulging in building a spirituality that is irrelevant. And yet contact with it makes some begin to feel that the cross is remote from the real world and less significant.

f. Reclaiming the cross today

These trends have much to teach us, but they must not be uncritically accepted, for they can lead too easily to a spirituality devoid of the cross and deficient in terms of God's revelation to us in Christ. From the standpoint of spirituality, as well as of theology, there is a need to restore the cross to its central position among evangelicals. To do that, we must explore its depths and dimensions more and discover its sufficiency, not turn our back on it and assume that the solution to our ills lies elsewhere. How many evangelicals today, one wonders, can truthfully say with Paul, 'May I never boast except in the cross of our

[28] Ibid., p. 63.
[29] Acts 14:8–20; 17:16–34; 1 Cor. 9:19–23.

Lord Jesus Christ, through which the world has been crucified to me, and I to the world'?[30]

2. Evangelical theology and the cross today

a. The classic evangelical position

Evangelicals have always recognized that no single interpretation of the cross is adequate to explain it all,[31] but the classic evangelical understanding of atonement is found in the idea of penal substitution. J. I. Packer maintains that it is this notion that 'takes us to the very heart of the Christian gospel'.[32] Leon Morris argues similarly: 'One thing I am concerned to contend for is that, while the many-sidedness of the atonement must be borne in mind, substitution is at the heart of it.'[33]

That Jesus died in our place to pay the penalty for our sin has been the gospel to which evangelicals have testified down the centuries. Martin Davie, in his recent Tyndale Doctrine Lecture,[34] for example, quoted the testimony of Charles Simeon from 1779: 'Like a flash it came to him, "I can transfer all my guilt to another! I will not bear them on my soul a moment longer."' He pointed out the similarity of that to David Watson's testimony in the 1950s. When Watson was a student, John Collins introduced him to the meaning of the cross one morning over breakfast, using cold toast as an analogy. According to Isaiah 53:6, our sin and guilt could be transferred from us and laid on Jesus Christ as completely as the toast could be transferred from one hand to the other. 'In my heart', Watson commented, 'I was beginning to see it, even though my mind wanted something much more intellectually profound. Perhaps that was the meaning of the cross. Perhaps Jesus did somehow take upon himself the sin and guilt of us all so that we, sinners though we are, could be free to know the love and forgiveness of God without any barrier at all.'

This interpretation of the cross, it is contended, not only can be clearly seen in Scripture but also assumes a privileged position with regard to other interpretations of the atonement. Historically, it was the

---

[30] Gal. 6:14.

[31] Other views of the cross emphasize it as a ransom to Satan; as an example; as a moral influence on us; as a demonstration of God's moral government; as victory over the forces of evil; or as satisfaction to the Father. See M. J. Erickson, *Christian Theology* (1983; Baker, 1998), pp. 798–817, W. Grudem, *Systematic Theology* (IVP, 1994), pp. 581–586, and McIntyre, pp. 26–52.

[32] Packer, 'What did the cross achieve?', p. 85.

[33] Morris, *Cross in the New Testament*, pp. 404–405. By 'substitution' Morris means 'penal substitution'.

[34] M. Davie, 'Dead to sin and alive to God', Tyndale Doctrine Lecture, 1999. Unpublished paper, p. 1.

Reformers who brought it to the fore and, in doing so, tended to eclipse other explanations. Martin Luther, in his *Lectures on Galatians* (1531), spoke of

> ... the unspeakable and inestimable mercy and love of God towards us unworthy and lost men: to wit, that our most merciful Father, seeing us to be oppressed and overwhelmed with the curse of the law, and so to be holden under the same that we could never be delivered from it by our own power, sent his only Son into the world and laid upon him the sins of all men, saying: Be thou Peter that denier; Paul that persecutor, blasphemer and cruel oppressor; David the adulterer ...[35]

And John Calvin wrote in his *Institutes of the Christian Religion*:

> Thus we perceive Christ representing the character of a sinner and a criminal, while at the same time his innocence shines forth, and it becomes manifest that he suffers for another's and not for his own crime. He therefore suffered under Pontius Pilate ... Our acquittal is in this – that the guilt which made us liable to punishment was transferred to the head of the Son of God (Is. 53:12). We must specially remember this substitution in order that we may not be all our lives in trepidation and anxiety, as if the just vengeance, which the Son of God transferred to himself, were still impending over us.[36]

Many have expounded the doctrine since then, notably James Denney in *The Death of Christ*, Archdeacon H. E. Guillebaud in *Why the Cross?* and, most recently and skilfully of all, John Stott in *The Cross of Christ*.

In a redoubtable and clear defence of the model, J. I. Packer, in the Tyndale Biblical Theology Lecture of 1973, pleads for us to set aside our 'speculative rationalism' and attend to the inspired biblical witnesses, learning to hear and echo what they say about the cross.[37] If we do so, we shall arrive not at some cold formula that explains it all, but at a framework that helps us to discern the fundamental features of its mystery. We shall find a dynamic, dramatic and 'kerygmatic picturing of divine action'[38] which shows that Christ died as our substitute to pay the penalty for our sins, not to satisfy some impersonal demand of justice but to restore our personal moral relationship with a

---

[35] Quoted in ibid., pp. 2–3.
[36] *Institutes* 2.16.5. Quoted in ibid., p. 3.
[37] Packer, 'What did the cross achieve?', p. 115. See also pp. 94–97.
[38] Ibid., p. 97.

holy God. Though the notion of penal substitution can be presented crudely, it is anything but 'forensic' or 'legal', as some suggest. It is about relationships – the relationship between a holy and loving God and a sinful and undeserving people, which God in his grace moves to restore by bearing the cost of the severance himself.[39]

Substitution, Packer reminds us, 'is a broad idea that applies whenever one person acts to supply another's need, or to discharge his obligation, so that the other no longer has to carry the load himself'.[40] The adjective 'penal' is added to it to anchor the substitution 'within the world of moral law, guilty conscience and retributive justice'.[41]

Packer goes on to draw out four key insights in this interpretation of the cross:

1. The retributive principle has his sanction, and indeed, expresses his holiness, justice and goodness reflected in his law, and that death, spiritual as well as physical, the loss of the life of God as well as that of the body, is the rightful sentence which he has announced against us, and now prepares to inflict.

2. Standing under this sentence, we are helpless to undo the past or to shake off sin in the present and thus have no way of averting what threatens.

3. Jesus Christ ... the God-man ... took our place under judgment and received in his own personal experience all the dimensions of the death that was our sentence, whatever these were, so laying the foundation for our pardon and for our immunity.

4. Faith is a matter first and foremost of looking outside and away from oneself to Christ and his cross as the sole ground of present forgiveness and future hope.[42]

b. Unease with the classic evangelical doctrine

In recent days there has been growing unease about this classic evangelical interpretation of the atonement. In spite of John Stott's careful exposition of it, a number of evangelical writers remain unconvinced, thinking it not only too restrictive but actually flawed.[43] Alastair Campbell, for example, wrote recently that

Evangelical thinking about the atonement has long resembled a man o'war that has stuck fast on a reef. It is still capable of

---

[39] Ibid., p. 107.
[40] Ibid., p. 98.
[41] Ibid., p. 105.
[42] Ibid., pp. 109–110.
[43] The critics include Martin Davie, John Goldingay, Tom Smail and Stephen Travis, whose writings will be referred to subsequently. Another critique is found in Nigel Wright, *The Radical Evangelical: Seeking a Place to Stand* (SPCK, 1996), pp. 58–72.

defending itself and will if necessary go down with all guns blazing, but it is not able to make any further progress and is afraid that if pulled off it will begin to sink below the waves. The reef in this case is the doctrine of penal substitution to which we cling in sermon and song but which we no longer truly believe in our hearts.[44]

Several reasons for the unease are mentioned:

1. Penal substitution can too easily be presented as a legal transaction, even a legal fiction, that seems to alter nothing in reality. "Tis done, the great transaction's done,' we sing.[45] But what has changed? The sinner pridefully believes his or her sins to be forgiven and continues to live an unholy life. The relational dimension is virtually absent and the transaction purely forensic.

2. Penal substitution can too easily be presented as driving a wedge between God the Father and God the Son, thus dividing the Trinity. An angry God needs to take it out on a unwilling Son. A submissive Son has to persuade an unwilling Father to forgive.

3. Penal substitution focuses on the problem of sin, whereas many today have little consciousness of sin and feel instead a need for healing and wholeness. While the answer may lie in making people aware of their guilt before God, can the cross not speak more directly to the condition experienced by men and women today?

4. Penal substitution is built on the idea of retributive justice, which is out of fashion in a world that believes that all justice should be restorative but not retributive. The New Testament, some claim, does not speak of the wrath of God nearly as much as was once thought, and when it does, it does not mean by it what we once thought.

5. Penal substitution is based on the questionable morality of God's punishing a substitute rather than the real offenders. Is that really just? 'What kind of justice is it', Smail asks, 'that lets anyone but the guilty criminal be punished for what he has done?'[46]

6. Penal substitution is based on the idea of 'propitiation', which many find to be a primitive idea that portrays God as a savage being in need of appeasement. Many transpose the language of 'propitiation' into that of 'expiation', or even into softer vocabulary still.

7. Penal substitution tends to isolate the work of the cross from that of the resurrection, rather than holding them together as inseparable sides of the same coin of salvation. The resurrection is reduced to a mere affirmation that the sacrifice on the cross was accepted by God. In so far as this is true, it is a just criticism, for Scripture does not separate them. Even so, there is a proper place for focusing on the cross alone.

[44] Review of Smail's *Once and for All* in *Baptist Times*, 8 April 1999.
[45] Hymn, 'O happy day that fixed my choice', by Philip Doddridge.
[46] Smail, *Windows*, p. 48.

8. Penal substitution is, at the most, only one model of the atonement in the New Testament, and perhaps not the most significant one. No evangelical of whom I am aware would dissent from the view that there is more than one model or metaphor of the cross in Scripture, even if many would hold on to penal substitution as the most fundamental of all.

These criticisms should be borne in mind as we examine the biblical passages chosen for exposition in this book. Many of them are 'men of straw', easily open to criticism themselves, and are over-reactions to the crudeness with which the penal-substitutionary view of the cross can be preached, rather than a valid and mature evangelical understanding of it. Some reflect the changing cultural attitudes of our time. In every generation the message of the cross needs to be expressed anew for effective communication. But great care needs to be taken in doing so, so that our reinterpretation does more than merely reflect the culture of our day. Our preaching of the cross will often be necessarily counter-cultural, and must faithfully represent the revelation of our God rather than gratify the fashions of society. Our task is not to mirror our culture but to convert it, and the cross calls us to do that in the most radical of ways.

c. Shifts in current evangelical thinking

Given the discomfort with the classic evangelical understanding of the cross, it is possible to discern that a number of evangelicals are shifting their emphasis and refashioning the model of atonement. The shifts can be outlined, in a very rudimentary way, by a series of dichotomies.

There is a move from the stress on the cross as retributive justice to a stress on it as restorative justice. The cross is seen less as a punishment of wrongdoing than as the setting right of the wrongdoer. Hand in hand with this goes the move from the cross as a punishment for sin, meted out by a wrathful God, to the cross as the inevitable consequence of our sin. A strong motivation on the part of many is to ensure that the cross is taken out of a legal framework and interpreted instead from a relational viewpoint. The judicial is replaced by the personal. Christ is seen less as our substitute than as our representative, even our example. The cross is therefore not so much an act of propitiation as one of identification – of God's being with us in our pain. With that, the Christ of the cross is portrayed less as a villain who dies the deserved death of the sinner than as a victim who bears the suffering of the world. His self-offering is, then, not so much a punitive bearing of the cost of sin as an exemplary model of obedient self-giving. Jesus is not so much a sacrifice demanded by a broken covenant as the fulfilment of the covenant and the model of a life lived in total obedience to it.

Michelangelo is said once to have encouraged one of the students engaged in painting the Sistine Chapel with the single word *amplius*, that is, 'fuller'. Evangelicals in past times have sometimes stood in need of a fuller, more variegated, understanding of the work of the cross. The prism through which the cross has been viewed has sometimes been too restrictive, and its narrowness has not been warranted by Scripture. In so far as some of these debates lead us to a richer understanding of the biblical revelation of the cross, we should welcome them. In so far as they lead to an impoverishing or trivializing of the work of Christ, of the holiness of God or of the awfulness of sin, we should resist them. If they complement the notion of penal substitution, provided they are satisfactory on other grounds, they are wholly positive. But if they seek to do away with the notion and replace it as either unbiblical or no longer appropriate, we must view them with extreme suspicion. For while the classic evangelical perspective on the cross may not be all that there is to say about it, any honest examination of the text of Scripture makes it unavoidable – or so it seems to me – as the expositions that follow will suggest.

In his little book *The Cross of Jesus*, no less a champion of the classic evangelical view than Leon Morris confesses that he does not see the traditional theories saying all that needs to be said about the cross. There are new avenues of understanding and new depths of interpretation yet to be explored.[47] Consequently he sets about exploring the relationship of the cross to victory, futility, ignorance, loneliness, sickness and selfishness. With him, however, we must strive to be careful that the metaphors we develop and the perspectives we adopt are not only consonant with Scripture but rooted in Scripture. Contemporary metaphors have the advantage of being alive, of overcoming the sterility and barrenness of propositional statements, and of giving fresh insights when dead analogies inherited from the past no longer communicate. But all metaphors need anchoring. So, for example, as Tom Smail warns, 'A theory of the atonement that is out of relation to the historical record of what Jesus did and saw himself to be doing in his death is disqualified by the fact.'[48] Our understanding must match that of Scripture, and our beliefs must fit the facts.

Conclusion

The object, of course, is not to engage in theorizing about the cross, but to reap its benefits, live its life and proclaim its gospel. We shall have failed in our journey through the major passages of the Bible that speak of it if all we can do afterwards is argue about doctrine. Our aim as we 'survey the wondrous cross' must be to deepen our appreciation of the miracle of God's grace and strengthen our resolve to preach the good

[47] Morris, *Cross of Jesus*, p. 116.
[48] Smail, *Once and for All*, p. 19.

news of 'Christ crucified' in all its breadth and with all its implications for creation as well as for individuals. I trust we shall be led again to stand beneath it and in humble awe to thank God for his manifold mercy shown to us through the cross of Jesus.

PART 1
THE CROSS ANTICIPATED

Genesis 22:1–19
1. The Lord will provide

It is both the most exquisitely told and the most profoundly shocking story in the Old Testament. Our modern minds revolt against the command of God to Abraham to offer his son Isaac in sacrifice, and yet we cannot be other than moved by the depth and tenderness of relationships that this barbaric demand uncovers. The story speaks of love and sacrifice, of trust and obedience, of perplexity and loyalty, of giving and receiving, of faithfulness and reward.

Before ever it was sheathed in layers of Christian interpretation, Abraham's sacrifice of Isaac was a story for God's elect people, Israel. The two key words in the story, according to R. W. L. Moberly, are the verbs 'test' (1) and 'fear' (12). Through it God's people were given a model to imitate and an encouragement always to fear God, not in the sense of being in awe of him, but in the sense of obeying him no matter what test he chose to apply to them, for he would always prove to be a God worthy of their trust.[1]

As the centuries passed, Christians could not fail to see in this event, in addition to its original significance, a number of other features which they felt compelled to connect to the cross of the Son of God. Without detracting from its earlier meaning, they developed the imagery of the story 'in a very striking way',[2] or rather in a number of striking ways, all of which consistently unfold the original episode as it is recorded. In other words, they engaged in exegesis (*reading out of* the text what is there), not eisegesis (*reading into* the text what is not there).

The story is told with sublime simplicity. Three times a voice is heard, providing the narrative with its shape. The first voice is that of God, who makes a demand (1–2). The second is that of Isaac, who asks a question (7). The third is the voice of the angel (11–12, 15–18), who provides a solution both to the demand God makes and to the question Isaac asks. It gives us 'the barest essential facts and no more. It is', as

[1] Moberly, p. 155.
[2] Wenham, *Genesis*, p. 117.

John Gibson comments, 'completely devoid of the kind of circumstantial detail a modern author would delight in.'[3] The timing of it is vague and the landscape minimalist, and one searches in vain for the motives and feelings of those involved. But the narrator's strategy only heightens the sense of drama as the story reaches its climax.

Why did God demand the life of Isaac from Abraham with such cold cruelty? What was his purpose? What insight into his character can be gleaned? What understanding of his ways can be grasped? The answers emerge as one focuses first on Abraham the father, secondly on Isaac the son, and thirdly on God the Lord, before finally noting Moriah, the place.

1. The costly sacrifice of the father (22:1–10)

The harsh tone of verse 1, which soon gives way to the more tender tones of verse 2, places Abraham squarely in the centre of the picture and bids us look carefully at what he is to be subjected to and how he handles it.

a. The testing ordeal Abraham faced (22:1–2)

God is to submit Abraham to a test in an honest desire to find out how genuine his faith was and to discover how far he would be obedient to the covenant stipulation to 'walk before me and be blameless' (17:1). As far as the covenant God and Abraham had entered was concerned, it was, notes Deryck Sheriffs, 'the most specific test of loyalty and obedience that could be devised'.[4] Significantly perhaps, the personal name for God is avoided in the story until 22:11, which, Franz Delitzsch says, suggests that it is God speaking as the creator, the sovereign one, who requires Abraham to surrender Isaac, as opposed to God speaking as 'the LORD', the personal and covenant God, who later spares the life of Isaac and provides the ram as a substitute.[5]

From Abraham's standpoint, the test is real. There is nothing to suggest to him that 'it is only a test' and that it is bound to end happily ever after. The readers are made aware of the full situation, like viewers of a TV quiz programme who are shown answers kept hidden from the contestants. But Abraham is ignorant of the full situation, and we should not be too quick to soften the horror of the demand or its impact on Abraham, as some are in danger of doing.[6]

---

[3] Gibson, p. 111.
[4] D. Sheriffs, *The Friendship of the Lord: An Old Testament Spirituality* (Paternoster, 1996), p. 51.
[5] Cited by Wenham, *Genesis*, p. 103.
[6] For example, Sailhamer, p. 167: 'the writer quickly allays any doubt about God's real purpose. There is, then, no thought of an actual sacrifice of Isaac in the narrative ...'

The test required that Isaac should be killed as a sacrifice. Worse still, Abraham himself was to put his son to death.[7] One can sense the pathos in verse 2 as a fourfold description of the sacrificial victim is given. Abraham had two sons, Isaac and Ishmael, but, so that there can be no mistake about the identity of the one to be offered up, God says it is to be *your son, your only son, Isaac, whom you love.* It was his favoured, uniquely precious son who was to be sacrificed. Abraham must have felt, as Joyce Baldwin perceptively describes it, like an airline passenger when the reverse thrust of the engine brings the plane to a halt: 'God's promises appear to have been put in reverse gear.'[8] 'There was a danger that the entire pilgrimage from 11:30 has been for nought.'[9] The child of promise for whom Abraham and Sarah had waited interminably, and whom they eventually received well past the time when any child could possibly, let alone reasonably, have been expected – the child on whom the future fulfilment of the promise that Abraham would be 'the father of many nations' (17:4–6) depended – was suddenly placed in jeopardy. As the father myself of an only child who almost did not survive to full term and whose life for some weeks was precarious, I can identify a little with the human feelings of Abraham. But to have a child of such promise as he had when he was already over 100, given by the Lord, and then potentially removed by the Lord in such a manner, puts Abraham's problem into a league altogether different from any that others such as I have faced. What was God doing?

The idea of child sacrifice is one that today we rightly find repulsive. So it is important to understand God's command in the context of Abraham's time in order to grasp God's purpose. It was axiomatic to Israel that all life belonged to God and was his to grant or dispose of as he chose. The firstborn children were particularly marked out as belonging to the Lord. The law stated, 'You must give me the firstborn of your sons',[10] meaning that they were entirely at God's disposal, for him to do what he wanted with them. But, as Claus Westermann points out, as soon as this command is given, 'it is simultaneously abolished' by a law that makes it usual for the firstborn to be redeemed.[11] Israel practised child sacrifice (which was common in the surrounding nations) vary rarely indeed, and for the most part it was

---

[7] 'Yet not only is the death of his son announced to him, but he is commanded with his own hand to slay him; as if he were required, not only to throw aside, but cut in pieces, or cast into the fire, the charter of his salvation, and have nothing left to himself but death and hell.' Calvin, *Genesis*, p. 563.

[8] Baldwin, p. 90.

[9] Brueggemann, *Genesis*, p. 188.

[10] Exod. 22:29.

[11] Exod. 34:20. Westermann, *Genesis*, pp. 357–358.

expressly forbidden among them.[12] But they would not have questioned God's right to ask for such a sacrifice, and 'it is precisely because of this ambivalence that the command to Abraham is a particularly suitable test'.[13]

In reading this passage, we should be careful not to superimpose modern child-centred attitudes on Abraham's patriarchal age. Children were not then seen to the same extent as individuals in their own right, but only as extensions of their fathers. So, in spite of his love for Isaac, Abraham would have approached the ordeal with a less sentimental perspective than we would adopt now.

None of this really diminishes the severity of the test Abraham faces. He is called to offer Isaac as a burnt offering, the most common of all the sacrifices. In the burnt offering, as opposed to some other offerings, the sacrificial victim is wholly consumed by fire in an act which symbolized total consecration to the Lord as well as being a means of atonement.[14] Again, we can see the special suitability of this offering: Abraham is being asked whether he is wholly devoted to the Lord. It presents him with the stark choice as to whether he loves Isaac more than God, and forces him to make visible the answer he cannot sidestep. Abraham does not have the luxury of professing his commitment in words without having to demonstrate it in action, as we so often do. If this was at the heart of the test Abraham faced, it is not, in principle, any different from one that every child of God is called to undertake. All believers are to love the Lord their God with all their hearts, souls and minds, and to put him above all other things, possessions, persons or ambitions, in daily and total consecration.

b. The trusting obedience Abraham showed (22:3–10)

If the test was severe, the response was superb. Abraham not only obeyed, but obeyed in an exemplary manner. Phrase after phrase delineates the dimensions of his obedience until the cumulative picture has reached completion, and Abraham stands before us as a man of total, trusting obedience.

His obedience was prompt (3). *Early the next morning* Abraham began to put his obedience into action. He did not delay his response in the hope that God would reconsider his demand. This is not the first time Genesis has told us that Abraham set about a difficult task early in the morning, giving rise to Derek Kidner's observation that 'it seems safe to infer a habit of facing a hard task resolutely'.[15] Henry Law generalizes

---

[12] Lev. 18:21; 20:2–5; 2 Kgs. 17:17; 23:10; Jer. 32:35. The very rare exceptions appear to relate to times of national crisis: Judg. 11:31–40; 2 Kgs. 3:27.

[13] Westermann, *Genesis*, p. 358.

[14] Lev. 1:3–17; 6:8–13.

[15] Kidner, *Genesis*, p. 140.

from Abraham's example and advises that 'prompt obedience is the surest wisdom', before issuing this graphic warning: 'To linger is to court ruin. Delay is the craftiest net of Satan. It is the terrible pitfall, out of which there are rare escapes.'[16]

His obedience was conscientious (3). He took with him all the things his mission would need, although the Hebrew original seems to make a point of saying that he did things the wrong way round. Curiously, he left the cutting of the wood that would be needed for the sacrifice until after he had saddled the donkey and gathered his companions. Was he trying to conceal the reason for their journey until the latest possible moment, so that not too many questions would be asked, or was it that his mind was in a whirl of confusion?[17]

His obedience was firm (3–4). The destination God had given him was some forty-five miles away, so it took three days to reach it. To obey God in every detail was going to require perseverance and resolution. There had to be a steady determination on Abraham's part if he were not to deviate from the path. Obedience was not accomplished overnight.

His obedience was solitary (5). Once they reached the foot of the mountain, he had to go on alone, except for Isaac. The servants were left at the foot of the mountain. Since Isaac carried the wood and Abraham carried the rest of the supplies, it seems likely that the servants were left to look after the donkey because the mountain would have been too steep for it to climb. Calvin's forthright explanation was different, however. He says Abraham left them there so that when he raised the knife to Isaac, they might not lay their hands upon him (to prevent him), as upon a delirious and insane old man.[18] The narrative, while paradoxically saying that Abraham went on with Isaac (6), really serves to stress the loneliness of the test Abraham faced. His family was three days away and his servants were at the bottom of a steep mountain. He had to work this one out on his own, neither supported nor dissuaded by any human companions.

His obedience was trusting (5). The most thought-provoking comment in the whole story comes when Abraham, in taking leave of his servants, said, *'We will worship and then we will come back to you.'* Commentators argue over whether Abraham was confused about what was happening, lying to hide the truth from them, or expressing hope, perhaps even catching in confident faith 'a first glimpse of the resurrection'.[19] While Gordon Wenham is right to admit that 'white lies, prophecy, hope, even disobedience, can surely co-exist in the

[16] H. Law, *The Gospel in Genesis* (1854; Banner of Truth, 1960), p. 139.
[17] Wenham, *Genesis*, p. 106.
[18] Calvin, *Genesis*, p. 576.
[19] Kidner, *Genesis*, p. 142.

believer, especially in times of crisis',[20] it is surely more consistent with all else that is said of Abraham to view it as a statement of faith, even if his words 'have more truth in them than Abraham originally knew'.[21] Abraham had, after all, earlier expressed his faith in the justice of God (18:25), and Hebrews 11:17–19 certainly interprets his statement as an act of faith. Calvin comments on this verse:

> But when he came to the conclusion that the God with whom he knew he had to do, could not be his adversary; although he did not immediately discover how the contradiction might be removed, he nevertheless, by hope, reconciled the command to the promise; because being indubitably persuaded that God was faithful, he left the unknown issue to Divine Providence.[22]

Even when Abraham did not understand all, he trusted all to the God who would do right.

His obedience was humble (5). Abraham made the unqualified statement, '*We will worship …*' – a statement that speaks of his submissive heart and rings all the more authentic because it was spoken by one who was wounded by the cost of his obedience.

His obedience was total (9–10). As the story reaches its climax it seems to go into slow motion. The closer the denouement, the slower the pace, with every movement now specified to add to the pathos. But when the moment of execution came, Abraham's obedience was absolute. Having prepared the altar and the sacrifice, he *took the knife to slay his son*. Not even his precious son was to come between him and his complete, unwavering obedience to the Lord.

c. The typical significance Abraham has

One purpose of the story, as mentioned earlier, was probably to teach Israel that the sort of worship that pleased God was obedience to his word rather than the ritual offering of sacrifices regardless of whether the rest of the law was obeyed or not. In later days, when some were tempted to prise the temple worship of Mount Zion apart from the spoken word of Mount Sinai, this story would bring them together and insist that they should not be separated. In Abraham they were provided with the perfect model, as Moberly suggests.[23] But that does not exhaust the significance of the passage. For centuries, Christians have seen in it deeper meanings that foreshadow the work of the cross.

We need to exercise care in reading Christian meanings back into

[20] Wenham, *Genesis*, pp. 107–108.
[21] Von Rad, p. 244.
[22] Calvin, *Genesis*, p. 563.
[23] Moberly, p. 155.

the Old Testament, since there is a long history of Christians' discovering in the ancient texts, by the use of a variety of enterprising tools, all sorts of spiritual meanings which are almost certainly not there and, therefore, of treating those texts as if they had no message for the people of God prior to the coming of Christ. Yet there is a place for a disciplined re-reading of the Old Testament from a Christian perspective, and we must insist that the unified message of the whole Bible finds its focus in Christ.

In his excellent book *Preaching Christ from the Old Testament*, Sidney Greidanus judiciously sets out several roads that lead from the Old Testament to the New. They consist of the progressive unfolding of redemptive history, promise and fulfilment, typology, analogy,[24] longitudinal themes, New Testament references, and contrast.[25] It is true that often more than one category of interpretation can be used, and, in his examination of Genesis 22, Greidanus judges that all but the way of contrast applies. 'I favour', he concludes, 'a blend of the typology of the substitute offering (ram–Christ), of the longitudinal theme of substitute offerings (ram, Passover lamb, temple sacrifices, Christ), and the New Testament references regarding God himself offering his only Son (John 3:16; Rom. 8:32).'[26] But even this does not exhaust the possible legitimate links between Abraham's action and the work of Christ.

At this point, we note the significance of Abraham's action in surrendering his son to death. Gerhard von Rad thought God's command to Abraham concerned 'something much more frightful than child sacrifice. It has to do with a road out to Godforsakenness, a road on which Abraham does not know that God is only testing him.'[27] Thus he sees Abraham as prefiguring Christ on his cross, abandoned by his Father, crying, 'My God, my God, why have you forsaken me?'[28] But to do this assumes an understanding of Abraham's psychological state which we are not given (and which he himself had earlier cautioned against).[29] It fractures any coherence in the interpretation of the story as we seek to understand it in the light of Calvary. It would mean, as we shall see, that Abraham, Isaac and the ram all become symbols of Christ.

---

[24] Greidanus cites Walther Eichrodt's definition of typology: 'Types "are persons, institutions, and events of the Old Testament which are regarded as divinely established models or prepresentations of corresponding realities in the New Testament salvation history".' Analogy, by contrast, 'while based on the unity of redemptive history', is a much more popular and freer method of comparison which relates the Old to the New Testament and both, beyond them, to the Christian life. Greidanus, pp. 254–255, 262–263.

[25] Ibid., pp. 182–225.

[26] Ibid., p. 314.

[27] Von Rad, p. 244.

[28] Mark 15:34.

[29] Von Rad, p. 241.

It is better to go with the more straightforward view that observes how willingly the father goes to sacrifice his son as an offering that will make atonement. That approach connects to the majestic words of John 3:16: 'God so loved the world that he gave his one and only Son, that whoever believes in him shall not perish but have eternal life.' There is, of course, one immense difference between the father of Isaac and the Father of Jesus. At the last moment Abraham was not required to kill his son, but there was no such reprieve for God.

Paul almost certainly alluded to this incident and pushed its image even further. In writing to the Christians in Rome, he used words that seem to echo the thought that Abraham had not withheld his son. 'If God is for us,' he asked, 'who can be against us? He who did not spare his own Son, but gave him up for us all – how will he not also, along with him, graciously give us all things?'[30] If God has done the greater thing of sacrificing his Son, he would surely do the lesser thing and give himself to supplying the daily and more trivial needs of discouraged disciples. God is the Father who willingly paid the ultimate cost in sacrificing his Son, and the Father who still willingly pays the daily cost of caring for his children.

2. The willing submission of the son (22:2, 6–9)

Isaac is not a bright star in the firmament of Scripture, but in this moving episode of his life he 'comes briefly into his own – not by what he does but by what he suffers'.[31] At each phase of the unfolding drama he serves as an unmistakable picture of Christ.

a. The son Isaac was (22:2)

Isaac is described as an *only son*, who was much loved by Abraham. In the river of baptism[32] and on the mount of transfiguration[33] a voice from heaven echoes this description and says of Jesus, 'This is my Son, whom I love.'[34] Both occupy a unique place in their fathers' families and their fathers' affection.

b. The burden Isaac bore (22:6)

At the foot of the mountain where the sacrifice was to take place, *Abraham took the wood for the burnt offering and placed it on his son Isaac.* The words inevitably remind later readers of the way in which Jesus went to the hill of Golgotha, according to John, 'Carrying his

[30] Rom. 8:31–32.
[31] Kidner, *Genesis*, p. 143.
[32] Matt. 3:17.
[33] Matt. 17:5.
[34] Cf. John 1:14.

own cross'.[35] Moberly, in searching for a more original Christological interpretation of this passage, dismisses this link as 'imaginatively suggestive', but one which 'has no bearing on the issue of the moral or theological importance of the text'.[36] But that is the comment of an over-neat academic mind. Many have heard the echo of these words in John's Gospel, and they should not be dismissed so readily. If it is objected that no Jewish mind would have applied the words about Isaac to the idea of carrying a cross to the place of execution, and that consequently this interpretation should not be read into it here, that is a more serious objection. But it is easily refuted, for *Genesis Rabbah*, the Jewish Midrash, 'comments that Isaac with the wood on his back is like a condemned man, carrying his own cross'.[37] Evidently, even those who are not believers in Jesus could see the parallels.

c. The question Isaac asked (22:7)

As father and son together made their way up the mountain, Isaac asked his father where the lamb of the sacrifice was. Most find it difficult to know whether Isaac asked the question because he was naïve (and should by now have deduced the answer), genuine (thinking that his father may have unintentionally missed something), or sharp (hoping to indicate to his father that he was aware of what was happening, or alternatively to draw from his father the truth about what was to happen). It can be taken in any of the three ways.

It is equally difficult to be sure how Isaac would have taken his father's reply. To Gerhard von Rad it was merely a reply of 'tender love not intuitive hope'.[38] Or perhaps, as Gordon Wenham suggests, it sounded to Isaac 'like an evasion'.[39] But if it disturbed Isaac, the text does not tell us so. Rather, he went on trudging up the mountain with his father.

There are no exact parallels to this in the New Testament, but it is worth observing some similarities. The Midrash referred to above mentions that Isaac requested to be bound, because he was afraid that despite his 'informed consent' there was a possibility that he might lose his resolve as the moment of sacrifice approached.[40] The questions Jesus asked of his Father indicated the same mixture of consent and apprehension. If there was a difference, it was twofold. The small hint of bewilderment found in Isaac[41] becomes a loud cry of anguish in Christ. But then, Christ knew for certain what his Father was doing

---

[35] John 19:17.
[36] Moberly, p. 162.
[37] Wenham, *Genesis*, p. 108.
[38] Von Rad, p. 240.
[39] Wenham, *Genesis*, p. 115
[40] Levenson, p. 135.
[41] Gibson, p. 112.

and what his fate was going to be. But, whatever their apprehensions, both went willingly on their way and each submitted to his father's will.

d. The submission Isaac showed (22:9)

The most remarkable point of similarity between Isaac and Jesus is the voluntary submission they showed as they were bound and prepared for sacrifice. In a remarkable reversal of verse 6, where Isaac had the wood laid on top of him, he himself was now laid on top of the wood.[42] Although we cannot be sure, it is reasonable to assume that when this event happened Isaac would have been a teenager, and it would have been easy for him to resist his father and escape, should he have chosen to do so. The aged Abraham would have been quite unable to overpower him and subject him to ritual execution unless young Isaac had co-operated. But he did not resist. He submitted.

A comment made earlier in the story perhaps hints that Isaac might submit to his father in this way. Verse 6 mentions that when they left the servants behind, *the two of them went on together*. This evocative clause suggests a perfect harmony between father and son, and perhaps prepares the way for the climax. This is not a picture of a sadistic father imposing punishment on a reluctant son, but a picture of father and son working together in ready agreement to ensure that obedience might be perfectly rendered and a perfect sacrifice offered to God.

So Isaac foreshadows Jesus' perfect obedience and submission to God; Jesus relinquished his life into the hands of his Father,[43] becoming the ultimate sacrifice that renders all other sacrifices obsolete. In demonstrating such obedience, Jesus did what we are quite unable to do. He kept the law of God perfectly and so was able to undo all our disobedience towards God.

Derek Kidner's epitaph for Isaac is astute. Suffering 'it seems is his role, undistinguished though he may be in himself. Others will do exploits; it is left to this quiet victim, in a single episode, to demonstrate God's pattern for the chosen "seed": to be a servant sacrificed.'[44]

e. The 'resurrection' Isaac experienced

There is one further aspect of Isaac's experience we must examine, and that is his 'resurrection'. If, to us, it seems tenuous to refer to Isaac's return from Mount Moriah alive as a resurrection, it apparently did not seem forced to the writer of Hebrews to see the outcome of the event as a symbol of the resurrection. He insists that, 'figuratively speaking, he

---

[42] Levenson, p. 136.
[43] Luke 23:46. See ch. 8, below, for Luke's portrait of Jesus as a trusting son.
[44] Kidner, *Genesis*, p. 143.

[Abraham] did receive Isaac back from death'.[45] Unlike the 'resurrection' of Isaac, the resurrection of Jesus was not figurative but actual, since he died. The New Testament refuses to drive a wedge between the death of Christ and his resurrection. Both are aspects of the one movement of God in gaining our salvation. So it is fitting that this early paradigm of the salvation obtained for us by Christ should dwell not only on his voluntary suffering but also on his triumphant return from the dead.

3. The gracious provision of the Lord (22:11–19)

With split-second timing, it seems, the angel of the Lord urgently called Abraham's name for a second time in the drama. And, with a quickened pace, the story goes into reverse.

a. The purpose of God is served (22:12)

Abraham passed the test with flying colours. *'Now I know that you fear God, because you have not withheld from me your son, your only son.'* He proved his total obedience to God and showed, by graduating with first-class honours from the ordeal, that he put God before all else. The test need not continue. Consequently, the original command was now decisively revoked.

b. The provision of God is discovered (22:13–14)

Then comes the pivotal moment in the story. Abraham discovered that God is the Lord who provides.

Abraham's 'evasive' reply to Isaac that *'God himself will provide the lamb for the burnt offering'* (8) proved prophetic. Startled by the angel, at just the right moment Abraham saw *a ram caught by its horns* in a nearby bush. He released it from its temporary prison only to exact from it the ultimate penalty. The ram died. God indeed provided, precisely on time, and more 'completely and exactly'[46] than Abraham had ever envisaged. 'The ram had not wandered there accidentally, but had been placed there by God,' comments Calvin.[47] Walter Brueggemann makes a similar observation, and then points out how counter-cultural the belief is:

> ... the alternate ram did not appear by accident, by nature or by good fortune (v. 13). They (that is, v. 8, and v. 14) mean, rather, that the same God who set the test in *sovereignty* is the one who resolves the test in *graciousness*. In a world beset by humanism,

[45] Heb. 11:19.
[46] Wenham, *Genesis*, p. 115.
[47] Calvin, *Genesis*, p. 571.

scientism, and naturalism, the claim that God alone provides is as scandalous as the claim that he tests.[48]

And yet, here is a key revelation of God's character. He is generous and gracious in providing for us, and never more so than when it concerns the problem of our sin.

The ram God provided, we should note, was much more suitable as an alternative for a young man than a little lamb would have been. And Abraham instinctively used it as a substitute for Isaac. It is interesting, as Joyce Baldwin notes, that 'no-one had to tell Abraham to substitute the animal for his son'.[49] The principle of substitution, it seems, was being taken for granted even at this very early stage in Israel's history.

God's provision, then, was available exactly when needed and exactly matched the need. God provided the material with which Abraham was to worship him satisfactorily. This was not only a true revelation of God in its own time – for God in his grace always has provided for his people – but a pointer to a fuller revelation of God yet to come, for God has provided for us supremely in Christ.

The New Testament picks up the story of God's provision of the sacrificial ram and applies it to Jesus. Whatever happened there at Moriah, it says, happened once more in an even greater way in the coming of Christ, for he is 'the Lamb of God who takes away the sin of the world'.[50] The lamb God provides, the lamb who is his Son, is the only one who can remove the sin of the world by offering himself in sacrifice.

The sacrifice Abraham offered that day was, no doubt, bathed in joy. The ritual of consecration and atonement inherent in the burnt offering must have been overwhelmed by the voicing of thanksgiving. God's provision of a substitute sacrifice meant that Abraham's own son could go free and that they could go back home together. The freedom the Lamb of God has won for us on Calvary still bids us join in exuberant thanksgiving and offer 'a sacrifice of praise'.[51]

c. The promise of God is confirmed (22:15–18)

At the start of the story, Abraham's offering of Isaac threatened to bring to nothing all the promises of God for his life. In what way was God blessing him by removing his much-loved son from him? How could he bless others if he returned alone, a broken and frail old man, to his aged and infertile wife? How could he be 'the father of many nations' if his only son lay burnt to a crisp on a bloody altar? Were God's calling and

[48] Brueggemann, *Genesis*, p. 191.
[49] Baldwin, p. 91.
[50] John 1:29.
[51] Heb. 13:15.

covenant all for nothing? At the end of the story, God repeats his promises and the prospect of bleak barrenness is replaced by the promise of abundant fruitfulness.

God, then, was not even so unkind as to leave Abraham quaking at the thought of his near miss and to send him home still quivering. He spoke to him a third time, through the voice of the angel, and restated his promises. If there is little in these promises that is new, they were spoken 'in a uniquely emphatic way'.[52] Abraham did not go home with nothing to show for his 'purposeless suffering'.[53] He went home with renewed and surer promises. Gordon Wenham draws attention to the fact that here, 'For the first and last time in Genesis, the LORD swears an oath in his own name guaranteeing what he is about to say.'[54] If he had promised to bless Abraham in the past, he now *really* promised to bless him. The promises of God, which were always certain, have been strengthened by Abraham's own obedience. Although the fulfilment of God's promise did not depend on Abraham's obedience, 'Abraham's obedience has been incorporated into the divine purpose'.[55]

4. The abiding significance of the place

More than the usual amount of attention seems to be given to the site where Abraham's offering of Isaac took place. One way or another, it is referred to in verses 2, 3, 4, 9 and 14. The place God told him about (2) was one of the mountains in the region of Moriah, three days away from home. The call to worship God on a mountain would have not caused any particular surprise. Mountains, whether because of the beauty of their loftiness[56] or some other awe-inspiring characteristic, were often considered fitting places for the worship of God.[57] But why this particular one? Part of the answer lies in its name, and part in its location.

a. The name of Moriah
Abraham called that place The LORD Will Provide (14). Abraham's choice of this name is, in Hebrew, a clear pun on the name 'Moriah'. In Hebrew, the word 'provide' may equally mean 'see'. If that sounds confusing, it is not as odd as at first appears. As Brueggemann points out, it is not so difficult to understand the connection. The Latin word for 'provide' is *provideo*, 'see beforehand'.[58] Our understanding of God's

[52] Moberly, cited by Wenham, *Genesis*, p. 112.
[53] Wenham, *Genesis*, p. 111.
[54] Ibid., p. 115.
[55] Moberly, p. 161.
[56] Ps. 48:2.
[57] For Mount Sinai, see Exod. 19.
[58] Brueggemann, *Genesis*, p. 191.

providence, which is key to this event, is that God sees our need in advance and supplies it. So here, in a constellation of ideas that are fluid, God sees the need and 'sees to it'[59] that it is met, while at the same time God himself is seen[60] (revealed) in his gracious act of providing the sacrifice. Moriah, then, is the place where God is to be seen in the beauty of his generous grace and provision.

b. The location of Moriah

For several good reasons tradition identified Moriah with Jerusalem. Moberly lists three of them.[61] First, Jerusalem is the place where God sees and is seen. After David had arrogantly numbered his troops and provoked God's anger, the plague God sent was halted when it reached 'the threshing-floor of Araunah the Jebusite', which David purchased and on which he offered a burnt offering to the Lord.[62] It was the site of the future temple.[63] It was there that Isaiah saw the Lord 'seated on a throne, high and exalted'.[64] And it was there that the pilgrims appeared before God in Zion.[65] Secondly, Genesis 22:14 uses the phrase *the mountain of the LORD*, which numerous other texts use of Jerusalem.[66] And, thirdly, Abraham's offering of Isaac 'resonates' with the *raison d'être* for the Jerusalem temple. They are both about sacrificial worship.

There seems, then, no serious reason for doubting that Abraham's ancient Moriah was the location of the future Jerusalem. Given this, it is an intimation of the far more wonderful sacrifice that would one day take place on that mountain, at Golgotha,[67] when another Son, provided by God, would be offered in total dedication to the Lord as a sacrifice of atonement.

Conclusion

Glimpses of Calvary can be seen repeatedly in Genesis 22. If the picture that emerges is not fully developed, neither is it superficial. Like one of those children's puzzles where a tangled web of lines has to be sorted out to reveal the connection between the objects, so here complex connections emerge which New Testament writers about the death of Christ want to trace back to this story. A constellation of clues bursts

---

[59] Kidner, *Genesis*, p. 144.
[60] Von Rad comments, 'The reader is here summoned to give free rein to his thoughts' (p. 242).
[61] Moberly, pp. 157–158.
[62] 2 Sam. 24:1–25.
[63] 2 Chr. 3:1.
[64] Is. 6:1.
[65] Ps. 84:5–6.
[66] Ps. 24:3; Is. 2:3; Zech. 8:3.
[67] Matt. 27:33; Mark 15:22; John 19:17.

from the story like the shower of lights that explodes skywards from a splendid firework.

Here, the father gives. The son surrenders. The Lord provides. The ram dies. And the people profit. Here, for sure, the cross is anticipated.

Joyce Baldwin says it well:

> The Genesis record of Abraham's testing, then, is rather like the first drawing of a great artist, who has in mind a master work. The pencil sketch is perfect in its own right, yet the finished painting far surpasses the original drawing in the which the same hand can be seen to have been at work.[68]

One day, centuries later, on a mountain called Golgotha, the masterpiece was fully unveiled in all its glory.

[68] Baldwin, pp. 262–263.

Exodus 12:1–51
2. It is the Lord's Passover

Throughout history, Israel's exodus from Egypt has been an inspiring symbol for movements of political revolution and people seeking emancipation. It was employed by Oliver Cromwell and the English radicals who overthrew Stuart oppression,[1] owned by the civil-rights movement in 1960s America[2] and adopted widely as a motif by liberation theologians in Latin America.[3] The transformation of the sovereign action of God on behalf of Israel into a common metaphor for any movement towards freedom, however, is dangerous. Too often people want the exodus without the Passover, liberation without the blood, salvation without the sacrifice and freedom without the cross. In the historic understanding of Israel, the exodus and the Passover are inseparable. The one would not have happened without the other.

The events of Passover night, when Israel was set free from their 'cruel bondage' in Egypt (Exod. 6:9), were the defining events of their history. That night was to them the beginning of nationhood. It fashioned their understanding of God, framed their worldview, configured their laws, moulded their social life and pervaded their worship. In Walter Brueggemann's characteristically refreshing way of speaking, 'At the core of Israel's God-talk is the persistent claim that Israel knows no God except the One who in ancient, remembered time acted in a way that made the life of Israel as a people a genuine historical possibility.'[4]

Critical scholars have been doubtful about the historical basis of the exodus and have therefore sought to explain the account of it in other

[1] C. Hill, *The English Bible and the Seventeenth Century Revolution* (Allen Lane, 1993), pp. 113, 125, 144. Michael Walzer quotes Oliver Cromwell as saying that the exodus was 'the only parallel of God's dealing with us that I know in the world'. *Exodus and Revolution* (Basic Books, 1985), pp. 3–4.

[2] Walzer, ibid., pp. 3–4. His own view is: 'We can think of the Exodus as an example of what is today called "national liberation". The people as a whole are enslaved, and then the people as a whole are delivered' (p. 32).

[3] E.g. G. Gutiérrez, *A Theology of Liberation* (ET SCM, 1974), esp. pp. 155–159.

[4] Brueggemann, *Theology*, p. 176.

ways. The prevailing scholarly view of the Passover is that it did not begin in the way and for the reasons Exodus 12 states, but that it was probably an older agricultural ceremony that expressed thankfulness for fruitful flocks and herds, sought protection from hostile forces or solicited prosperity for their livestock. But these imaginative reconstructions fail for a number of reasons. They are entirely speculative (they depend on assumptions about literary sources for which there is no evidence), theologically impoverished (the biblical account is far richer than the alternative proposed) and historically dubious (Israel's defining memory could not have been based on a work of fiction).[5] The account given in Exodus 12, complex though it is, makes greater sense, historically and theologically, as it stands.

The account is complex because it is not a straight reporting of the introduction of the Passover. It weaves instructions about observing subsequent Passovers (14, 24–28, 43–49) into the instructions about the first Passover, and it inserts other instructions about the related, yet distinct, Feast of Unleavened Bread (14–20) into the middle. Even if we look only at those elements to do with the original Passover, the chapter doubles back on itself halfway through. The sacrifice is outlined in verses 1–13, launched in verses 21–23, consummated in verses 29–42 and concluded in verses 50–51.

1. God's initiative: the origin of the Passover

The greatest danger of using the exodus as a metaphor for any movement of human liberation is that it moves the centre of the action from where it lay in the original exodus story (that is, with God) to where we smugly think the action lies today (that is, with us). Neither the exodus nor the Passover was a human initiative. Moses' earlier, self-motivated attempts at liberation had failed (2:11–15). Now the initiative is located firmly in the hands of God. From the opening words of chapter 12, *The LORD said to Moses and Aaron in Egypt*, to its concluding sentence, *And on that very day the LORD brought the Israelites out of Egypt by their divisions*, the chapter is alive with the sovereign activity of God. Its fulcrum lies in verse 11, with its declaration that *it is the LORD's Passover*. Above anything else, the Passover story is a self-disclosure of God.[6]

It reveals *the faithfulness of God* to his word.[7] Generations before, God had warned Abraham that his descendants would endure a prolonged period of slavery, at the end of which God promised him, 'I

---

[5] Alexander provides an excellent critique.
[6] Stott, *Cross of Christ*, p. 139. Stott, however, limits himself to God's self-disclosure as Judge, Redeemer and Covenant God, whereas the story reveals God in other roles too.
[7] Alexander, p. 16.

will punish the nation they serve as slaves, and afterwards they will come out with great possessions.[8] It was a promise that the book of Exodus recalls more than once,[9] speaking of it in a very deliberate manner as a covenant God entered and an oath God swore, as well as a promise God made. God can be trusted not to go back on his word. And, indeed, he did not, for now, after 430 years (40), through the leadership of Moses, the time had come to fulfil his promise.

It reveals *the compassion of God* for his people. The Lord heard their groans, listened to their cries for help, saw the misery they were in and had pity on them (2:23–24; 3:7). They were held in slavery, and were forced to submit to hard labour, to suffer unrestrained beatings and to make bricks without straw (2:11; 5:1–21). The unjust denial of their liberty and the oppressive behaviour of their captors could not fail to move the God of justice, love and mercy, so he came down to rescue them from the hand of the Egyptians (3:7).

It reveals *the justice of God* among the nations. By his actions God revealed himself to be sovereign over all nations, not just the covenant God of Israel, and still less the puny tribal deity of a second-rate people. As a sovereign, righteous God, he moves against all unrighteousness wherever it is found in his creation.

Finally, the Passover reveals *the power of God* over his world. He did not enter into delicate negotiations with Pharaoh as if he were a politician on equal terms with him and as if each had some right on his side. He moved against Pharaoh with 'an outstretched arm and with mighty acts of judgment' (6:6). He raised his 'mighty hand' against this totalitarian ruler without any fear that he might be entering a contest he might not win. He acted in prevailing and transforming power.

Walter Brueggemann points out what an astonishing variety of 'verbs of deliverance' Exodus uses of God.[10] He 'brings out',[11] 'rescues' (3:8), 'delivers', 'saves' (14:30) and 'redeems' (6:6) his people. Each verb has its own nuance. In Hebrew, they come from different spheres of life and evoke images of a geographical exit, of being pulled out of danger, of transforming a situation, of decisive military action and of being released from slavery. But the remarkable thing is that God 'is the subject of all these verbs'. The exodus was his initiative, and he carried it through successfully to completion. The covenant God of Israel and sovereign Lord of creation acted in faithfulness, compassion, justice and power to grant his people liberty.[12]

---

[8] Gen. 15:13–14.
[9] Exod. 2:24; 3:17; 6:5; 13:5, 11.
[10] Brueggemann, *Theology*, pp. 174–176.
[11] Exod. 13:3 and a further seventeen occasions.
[12] Brueggemann, *Theology*, p. 176.

2. God's instructions: the substance of the Passover

The Passover lies at the heart of this great redemptive and transformative act of God. He carefully instructed his people as to how they were to celebrate it immediately prior to the exodus. While the deliverance was undoubtedly due to the action of God, his action cannot be divorced from his word.[13] Their freedom came as much through Israel's obeying God's word as from their observing his power. In obeying his instructions they became participants in the drama of salvation. Their escape from slavery was not merely prefaced by their celebrating the Passover meal; it was symbolized, interpreted and activated by their doing so. *All the Israelites did just what the LORD had commanded* (50).

Just what was it that the Lord had commanded, and why?

a. A time is set

God instructed his people to commence preparations for the Passover meal on the date of the spring moon, that is, on the tenth day of Abib, known later in Babylonian times as Nisan (2–3).[14] The corn would be newly ripe, and so would serve as a fitting marker that what the Passover stood for was a new beginning, a fresh start for Israel as a nation.[15] By making it the first of months in their calendar, and numbering everything from it, the reminder of Israel's beginning would be routinely reinforced.

The victim was to be killed four days later, at twilight – literally, that is, 'between the two evenings', which the rabbis took to mean 'between 3 o'clock in the afternoon and when the sun set'.[16] This timing, as we shall see, was to prove significant. That night they were to eat the roasted flesh of their sacrifice at a family meal (8). Sacrifices were usually offered during the day, but this one was presumably to be offered and consumed at night, as Desmond Alexander suggests,[17] because the Egyptians would have kept them busy during the day. The later setting would also be necessary if, following the visit of the destroying angel, they were to make a hasty exit from Egypt under cover of darkness.

b. A victim is chosen

Careful instructions are given about the nature of the sacrificial animal

---

[13] Fretheim, p. 138.
[14] March-April in our calendar
[15] Cole, p. 104.
[16] Hyatt, p. 132.
[17] Alexander, p. 7.

they were to choose. Either a *lamb* or *young goat is permitted*,[18] the difference between them not being too great (3,[19] 5). But it is not any old lamb or goat that is permitted. The selected animal had to conform to certain specifications. It had to be sufficient to feed a family, but not more than necessary, so as to avoid waste, since the sacrifice had to be consumed completely (4, 10). If one animal proved too much for one family, they were encouraged to share it with other families so that this instruction could be observed to the letter. The sacrifice was precious and not to be discarded as rubbish.

While the fact that the animal may be taken from among either the sheep or the goats, and the permission to share it with other families, make it as easy as possible for the Israelites to obtain their sacrificial offering, the next instruction proves restrictive. *'The animals you choose must be year-old males without defect'* (5). The stress falls on the need for the sacrifice to be perfect, which they thought was more likely to be achieved if the animal was in its prime and, remembering their patriarchal context, male. The Israelites were being told that they must offer God the best of the flock, not a cheaper animal suffering from illness or old age. The designated animal must then be kept for four days (6), to ensure either that it was ritually pure at the time of its death[20] or that it reached the standard of perfection God required. Others would be able to inspect it in that time,[21] so those who wished to cheat on God would soon be found out. Nothing less than perfection would be adequate as an offering to God.

c. The blood is smeared

When the time came for the animal to have its throat slit, its blood was to be caught in a basin (22) and, using a hyssop plant[22] as a primitive paint brush, the blood was to be smeared around the sides and top of the door-frame. The blood had to be not only shed but applied – not just drained from the victim but appropriated by those who wished it to save them from death. The same point was conveyed in later sacrificial rituals by the sprinkling of the blood on the altar, in front of the curtain in the tabernacle or on persons seeking healing.[23]

This blood was to be the sign that would ward off the destroying angel as he visited Egypt later that night on his dreadful errand, and the means by which the Israelite families would gain protection. Terence

[18] See NIV mg.
[19] Cole, p. 105.
[20] Alexander, p. 7.
[21] Ellison, p. 65.
[22] An aromatic plant of the mint family, found in the Sinai desert, which had a woody base and a straight stalk, and formed a small bush at the top (Kaiser, p. 376). The connection with John 19:29 is not to be missed.
[23] E.g. Lev. 1:5, 11; 3:2, 8, 13; 4:6, 17; 7:2; 8:19, 24; 9:12, 18; 14:7.

Fretheim rightly draws attention to the importance of the choice of blood as the sign because of the crucial meaning attached to it in Scripture. 'The sign', he writes, 'is not simply a "marker," as if any colorful substance that caught the eye would do. In the blood was life; it is the vitality of the living (Lev. 17:11, 14 cf. Dt. 12:23, Ps. 72:14) ... It is the *life given* that provides life for Israel, not simply the blood as a marker for protection.'[24] Luminous paint, neon lights and laser beams would not have met the necessary criteria. They may have attracted the angel of death, but they would not have repelled him. Life had to be sacrificed if life was to be preserved. Hence the significance of blood.[25]

d. The flesh is eaten

Once the blood had been applied to the door-frames, the dead animal was to be roasted and then totally consumed by the family (8), thus further strengthening the union between them. The meal meant that life was not only laid down but imparted. The sacrificial animal bequeathed life to the family not only by being a substitute that shed its blood, thus gaining the freedom of the firstborn, but by being a nutriment that supplied its energy to all the family.

Instructions about the meal are given in meticulous detail. The meat was to be accompanied by *bitter herbs* (probably wild lettuce) and unleavened bread (8). The herbs were later taken by the Israelites as a savoury reminder to the palate of the bitterness they had experienced in Egypt. Leaven or *yeast* later became a symbol of corruption, but originally the fact that they ate unleavened bread probably had more to do with the fact that 'Israel left in such haste that their dough had no time to rise'.[26] A further sign of their haste was the unusual dress they were required to wear for this meal. They were to wear their outdoor, travelling clothes (11), ready for departure from Egypt without delay, as soon as the signal was given. These instructions may imply a joyful family gathering, but even so, the people were meant to be neither lethargic in eating the meal nor indolent in responding to the command to depart when it came.

As we shall see, all these details gained greater significance as they were applied to the work of Christ. But, before tracing the meaning invested in them later, our description must give way to explanation. We must examine more fully why God acted in the way he did, and what was accomplished on the night of that first Passover.

---

[24] Fretheim, p. 138.
[25] See further below, p. 76.
[26] Cole, p. 109.

3. God's intention: the achievements of the Passover

In that one remarkable event, five distinct yet related outcomes were accomplished by God. They were works of both judgment and salvation, for the one is the inevitable corollary of the other. Each was another revelation of God, displaying further some aspect of the excellence of God's awesome and wondrous character.

a. Judgment for a sinful people: God is judge

The same night that was to bring tremendous joy to the Israelites was to bring deep grief to the Egyptians, for it was then that *the destroyer* (23) did his work among them. The destroyer, an angel mentioned again in 2 Samuel 24:16, is not a demonic power that God is unable to control,[27] but an agent of God himself – an angel of judgment.

The penalty to which God sentenced Pharaoh was that every firstborn person and animal would be struck down (12). In view of Pharaoh's earlier intention to commit genocide against the Israelites (1:16), it was no more than he deserved. Pharaoh's sin was catching up with him; or, rather, rebounding on him. He who had laid claim to the lives of the Israelites now came face to face with God's counter-claim. He who had sought to reduce God's created order to chaos now finds that 'the moral order has "boomeranged"'[28] on him and the avenging angel is reducing his world to chaos. No-one is exempt, unless sheltered by a blood-marked house. *At midnight the LORD struck down all the firstborn in Egypt, from the firstborn of Pharaoh, who sat on the throne, to the firstborn of the prisoner, who was in the dungeon, and the firstborn of all the livestock as well* (29). High-born and low, rich and poor, human and animal were all trapped in the web of Pharaoh's evil, and paid for it with the price of young life. The grief was tangible, the *wailing* universal and the effect catastrophic (30).

The venting of God's anger against Egypt seems to have taken the form of a plague (13).[29] While our mechanistically oriented western minds seek an explanation in the natural realm, Scripture expresses little interest in doing so and says little about the means God used to bring his judgment about. It is more interested in explaining the events in terms of the powerful anger of God against sin. Psalm 78:49–50, for example, uses not just one but four different words for his anger, while commenting only momentarily on the techniques God used to accomplish his righteous will:

---

[27] Ibid., p. 110. 'The destroyer' does not indicate a belief in dualism, as if a power for good and a power for evil were fighting it out in the cosmos, with the outcome uncertain. 'The destroyer' is under God's control.

[28] Fretheim, p. 141.

[29] Cf. Ps. 78:50.

> He unleashed against them his hot anger;
> his wrath, indignation and hostility –
> a band of destroying angels.
> He prepared a path for his anger;
> he did not spare them from death
> but gave them over to the plague.

Such an approach does not fit comfortably with our world, not just because we prefer natural to supernatural explanations of events, but also because our image of God does not permit us easily to think in terms of his anger. Tolerance is now considered to be the outstanding virtue, so a picture of a God of wrath provokes disbelief or embarrassment rather than fear or wonder. We like somehow to soften the blow of his judgment and remove the scandal of indignation. In an illuminating comment, Terence Fretheim reveals our unease by comparing the judgment meted out on Pharaoh to the judgment involved in dropping bombs on Hitler. We may fully understand why it is necessary, even good, to do so. But, he writes, 'It is one thing to speak of American bombs, but it seems almost blasphemous that God is the one who "drops the bomb".' Yet, he adds, 'The text does not back off from identifying the subject of this judgment. God smote all the firstborn in Egypt ...'.[30] But the holy exactness of God's judgment is a matter altogether different from a humanly devised bombing campaign. Given this, the Bible does not share our embarrassment in identifying God as one who is angry at evil. Indeed, it is part of the glory of God that he exercises his wrath against wrong-doing.

If God permitted the human beings he has created to do whatever they wanted by way of wickedness and destruction, and to perpetrate inhuman acts against others, without ever calling them to account or expressing his revulsion at what they were doing, how could he be worthy of our worship? As J. I. Packer has written:

> The truth is that part of God's moral perfection is His perfection in judgment.
> Would a God who did not care about the difference between right and wrong be a good and admirable Being? Would a God who put no distinction between the beasts of history, the Hitlers and Stalins (if we dare use the names), and His own saints, be morally praiseworthy and perfect? Moral indifference would be an imperfection in God, not a perfection. But not to judge the world would be to show moral indifference. The final proof that God is a perfect moral Being, not indifferent to questions of right and wrong, is the

[30] Fretheim, p. 141.

58

fact that he has committed Himself to judge the world.[31]

God's retribution against Pharaoh 'verifies that the God of Israel is a relentless opponent of human oppression, even when the oppression is undertaken and sponsored by what appear to be legitimate powers'.[32] It speaks with warning to those who preside over the houses of bondage that exist today, as much as it spoke then, and brings hope to those who suffer at the hands of oppressors. One day the oppressors will be dethroned and the captives will go free, as happened within recent memory when the communist dictatorships of Eastern Europe fell and the racially unjust regime in South Africa was displaced. For God still remains a God who answers 'with awesome deeds of righteousness'.[33]

b. Defeat for an idolatrous people: God is living

Coupled with the judgment against Pharaoh is the judgment God brings *on all the gods of Egypt* (12). The contest between Egypt and Israel, Pharaoh and Moses, was a contest not only of strength but of spiritual power. It was a contest between the living God of Israel and the impotent gods of Egypt. Virtually every political ideology in the world has sought legitimation by reference to a spiritual, and usually transcendent, source of authority greater than itself, and Egypt was no exception.[34] So, if God was to set his people free, he not only had to defeat Pharaoh but also had to show that the gods who held up his regime were impotent as well.

The plagues inflicted on Egypt (7:14 – 11:10) had demonstrated God's power and were chosen specifically to undermine the credibility of the gods of Egypt. The Nile, for example, was deified, and Hapi, the god of the Nile, was thought to bring fertility to Egypt. So turning the Nile to blood (7:14–24) was not merely a spectacular act but a threat to their whole economic and religious system. Or take the second plague, of frogs (7:14 – 8:15). 'Frogs were associated with the goddess Heqt, who helped women in childbirth, but they were unclean for the Egyptians.'[35] So a plague of them would defile the whole land and suggest that the goddess had lost control. Although at first the Egyptian magicians had been able to reproduce some of the sensational works of power (7:11), they reached their limits when it came to the gnats. 'When the magicians tried to produce gnats by their secret arts, they could not' (8:18). Then they began to realize that Moses and Aaron were not producing magical

---

[31] Packer, *Knowing God*, p. 130.
[32] Brueggemann, *Theology*, p. 180.
[33] Ps. 65:5.
[34] P. L. Berger, *The Social Reality of Religion* (1967; Penguin, 1977), pp. 44–48, 95–96.
[35] Ellison, p. 46.

tricks but demonstrating that the powerful presence of God was with them. The Egyptians gods were facing a power that was far greater than they were and that would inevitably spell their defeat.

The power struggle escalates until the ultimate plague (the death of the firstborn, 11:1–10) is reached. When God inflicts this final blow on Egypt, which he does at the stroke of midnight by releasing his angel of death as the Passover meal is enjoyed (29), the record tells us that it was not only the firstborn of the Egyptian people but the firstborn of the animals too that were struck down. This is no incidental reference. The animals were included because many of them – bulls, cows, goats, jackals, lions, baboons and rams, among them – represented deities. 'With the sudden death of these sacred representatives,' as Walter Kaiser says, 'there could be little doubt that it would be interpreted as a direct blow to the gods of Egypt themselves.'[36] The gods of Egypt, already impotent, were routed and unmasked for the futile, empty and worthless idols they really were. They were thoroughly debunked.

At one point in his first letter, Peter writes of 'the precious blood of Christ, a lamb without blemish or defect'.[37] Most consider it a clear allusion to the Passover lamb. Significantly, he says that that blood has redeemed people 'from the empty way of life handed down to you from your ancestors'.[38] This highlights a further connection between the work of Christ and the events of Passover night. Just as Christ redeems us from futility and unmasks idolatry for what it is worth, so in Egypt, centuries before, Passover night exposed the empty gods of Pharaoh to defeat and ridicule. As Paul was to put it later, 'having disarmed the powers and authorities, [Christ] made a public spectacle of them, triumphing over them by the cross'.[39]

c. Protection for a threatened people: God is redeemer

There are two ways in which the Passover provides protection for a threatened people: one is general, and the other particular.

The children of Israel were not automatically safe from the avenging angel on Passover night by virtue of their ethnic origin. They were secure only if they painted the blood of the Passover lamb on their door-frames and then remained within their blood-marked houses. 'None of you', they were warned, 'shall go out of the door of your house until morning' (22). It was the death of the lamb that meant they were provided with the protection they needed in the face of the judgment of a holy God.[40]

---

[36] Kaiser, p. 372.
[37] 1 Pet. 1:19.
[38] 1 Pet. 1:18.
[39] Col. 2:15.
[40] J. A. Motyer, *Look to the Rock* (IVP, 1996), pp. 45–51. Motyer points out 'that on

Some have sought to find the thought of atonement here. Stephen Dray,[41] for example, points out that 'Israel were no less sinners than Egypt' (5:21; 6:5, 9), and that if they were to escape God's fatal judgment they had to offer sacrifice and make provision to remove their guilt. The fact of Israel's sinfulness is beyond dispute and therefore their need for atonement is clear, but that is not the emphasis here, and such an approach runs the danger of pressing the many and varied achievements of the cross into too narrow a framework. It is more true to say that really there is not even a fully developed idea of sacrifice here (even though we have been using the word loosely to refer to the Passover lamb), in the sense of the later atonement offerings.[42] The focus here is on the power of the blood to ward off evil destruction.

It was an embryonic way of portraying the protection the blood of Christ would offer subsequent believers, such as those mentioned in Revelation who faced the wrath of 'the great dragon', the 'ancient serpent called the devil, or Satan', who was intent on their destruction. But, John triumphantly declares, 'They [Christian brothers and sisters] overcame him by the blood of the Lamb.'[43]

The general picture of protection by blood comes into sharper focus when applied to the redemption of the firstborn in Israel. If blood protected them all, it saved the lives of the eldest children in particular. Except for the blood, their lives would have been forfeited to God alongside those of the firstborn in Egypt. All the firstborn belonged to him.[44] But their redemption, that is, their release from the obligation they owed God by the payment of a suitable price, was one of the primary purposes of the Passover sacrifice and governed its design (12–13). If their lives were to be spared, another life had to be forfeited in their place. So God graciously arranged for a lamb to be substituted and for its life-blood to be spilled instead of theirs. Hebrews 11:28 sums it up concisely: 'By faith he [Moses] kept the Passover and the sprinkling of blood, so that the destroyer of the firstborn would not touch the firstborn of Israel.'

As a result, then, of the lamb's death, when the avenging angel visited Egypt he did not enter any houses marked with blood, but

---

Passover night there was a death in every house in Egypt without exception'. It was the death either of the firstborn or of the lamb that afforded protection to those who sheltered beneath the victim's blood.

[41] Dray, p. 75, and Alexander, p. 17. Morris points to the Midrash, which says that the Israelites were under God's condemnation because of idolatry: *Apostolic Preaching*, p. 132.

[42] Cole, p. 106. Morris's overall position concurs: 'In the original Passover, although there is no mention of atonement, there is mention of blood as a means of averting destruction.' *Apostolic Preaching*, p. 121.

[43] Rev. 12:9, 11.

[44] See Exod. 22:29 and the discussion in ch. 1, above.

'passed over' them to other houses. Many ingenious attempts have been made to trace the origin of the word 'Passover'. Some connect it with words for 'limping', or perhaps 'leaping', and conjure up the idea of a limping dance which was used to keep evil spirits at bay.[45] But the more straightforward explanation, that it comes from the angel's 'passing over' (perhaps, 'leaping over') the houses of the Israelites, is much to be preferred. When, in later generations, children asked their parents the meaning of the Passover meal, the answer they gave was unequivocal: *'It is the Passover sacrifice to the LORD, who passed over the houses of the Israelites in Egypt and spared our home when he struck down the Egyptians'* (27).

The message is crystal clear. The blood of the lamb prevented the righteous judgment of God from falling on those who deserved it. God the judge is also God the redeemer and protector. The sacrifice of a perfect offering drew the sting of his wrath. The death of the substitute guaranteed the life of the firstborn. The God who promised to redeem them 'with an outstretched arm and with mighty acts of judgment' (6:6) does so through the Passover meal, through the visit of the angel and by changing the mind of Pharaoh.

d. Deliverance for an oppressed people: God is saviour

The dreadful events of Passover night led to the urgent expulsion of the children of Israel from Egypt (33, 39), carrying Egyptian gold with them (34–35), by a terrified people who until that moment had been their oppressors. Freedom had come at last. Deliverance had finally arrived. Liberation Day was here. It came, the text is anxious to remind us, not because of some political settlement or even because of the genius of Moses, their leader, but because *the LORD brought the Israelites out of Egypt by their divisions* (51). God is the one who saved them by exacting the death penalty from the Egyptian firstborn, following the offering of the Passover lamb.

The act of exodus became central to Israel's understanding of its identity, and was regularly retold in the annual Passover celebrations.[46] When they experienced exile once more, this time in Babylon, it was to the exodus that they looked for a paradigm of deliverance, even though they intensified the imagery and believed that their second exodus would be even more glorious.[47] Still today, the Jews celebrate God's goodness in saving them from the house of bondage as they observe the Passover meal.

[45] For details see Durham, p. 155, and Cole, p. 108.

[46] Apart from other references to the Passover in the Pentateuch, it is mentioned in Josh. 5:10–11; 2 Kgs. 23:21–23; 2 Chr. 30:1–20; 35:1–19; Ezra 6:19–20; Ezek. 45:21–24.

[47] Is. 35:8; 52:11–12.

The words of the Passover Haggadah (liturgy) are instructive. At one point it says:

> How many are the claims of the Omnipresent upon our
>   thankfulness!
> Had he taken us out of Egypt,
>   but not executed judgments on them,
>   We should have been content!
> Had he executed judgments on them,
>   but not upon their gods,
>   We should have been content!
> Had he executed judgments on their gods,
>   but not slain their first-born,
>   We should have been content!
> Had he given us their substance,
>   but not torn the Sea apart for us,
>   We should have been content!
> Had he brought us through it dry,
>   but not sunk our oppressors in the midst of it,
>   We should have been content![48]

And so the liturgy continues, giving thanks to God for his provision of food and the law in the wilderness until they were brought into the Promised Land. In every generation, they proclaim, the Jewish people must live as if they themselves had come out of Egypt. And then they recite these words:

> Therefore, we are bound to thank, praise, laud, glorify, exalt, honour, bless, extol, and adore him who performed all these miracles for our fathers and for us. He has brought us forth from slavery into freedom, from sorrow to joy, from mourning to festivity, from darkness to great light, and from bondage to redemption. Let us then recite before him a new song; Hallelujah.[49]

The King of the Universe is indeed Saviour.

e. Creation of a holy people: God is Lord

'When bondage goes, pilgrimage starts,' Alec Motyer says succinctly.[50] The meal was to be eaten by people ready to make a journey, and once they experienced deliverance they became a pilgrim people on a journey

---

[48] N. N. Glatzer, *The Passover Haggadah* (1953; Shocken, 1989), pp. 53–55.

[49] Ibid., p. 61. The word 'festivity', used in some versions, has been substituted for the word 'holiday' in the text quoted.

[50] Motyer, *Prophecy of Isaiah*, p. 420.

to the Promised Land. The Passover and exodus led to their formation as a free, but holy, nation. They were a people set apart for God.

Desmond Alexander argues that the Passover meal closely parallels the account of the consecration of Aaron and his sons as priests, found in Exodus 29 and Leviticus 8.[51] There, too, a ram was slaughtered, blood was sprinkled, the ram was cooked and eaten, along with unleavened bread. No others were permitted to eat it (cf. Exod. 12:43–49), and any meat left in the morning had to be destroyed in the fire (cf. 12:10). On the basis of these similarities he argues[52] that the Passover may have served the same purpose as the sacrificial meal which consecrated the priesthood. By consuming the meal, Israel is being consecrated as a holy nation and a kingdom of priests. The absence of any reference to the necessity of a priesthood to sacrifice the Passover lamb, and the fact that each family was required to offer its own lamb, only serve to underline the point. From now on they were all involved in the calling to be 'a kingdom of priests and a holy nation' for God (19:6). They were to serve him through their worship in the tabernacle, by their obedience to his law and by distinctive living in his world. In all things, he was to be Lord and they were to be his, and his alone.

The Passover, then, signalled not only the redemption and liberation of Israel, but its consecration too, as they were thrust out of Egypt into the wilderness and eventually beyond to the Promised Land.

The achievements initiated by this one Passover meal were remarkably complete. They involved salvation and judgment, for where the one is available the other must be found too. They included judgment of human sin, the propitiation of God's holiness and the unmasking of useless idols. For God's elect people they embraced protection from evil, redemption from sin, release from oppression and dedication for service. The sacrificial ritual was exquisitely designed to achieve its end and to serve as a mirror which would reflect the many-sided splendour of almighty God. It reveals him to be judge, victor, redeemer, protector, saviour and Lord.

4. God's instrument: the fulfilment of the Passover

a. An explicit statement

While other Old Testament images of the death of Jesus are alluded to, more or less clearly, in the New Testament, that of the Passover lamb is made explicit. Paul says, 'Christ, our Passover lamb, has been sacrificed.'[53] The Passover lamb sacrificed in Egypt is a forerunner of the Christ sacrificed at Calvary. The remarkable thing about the statement,

---

[51] Alexander, p. 8.
[52] Ibid., pp. 8, 17, 18.
[53] 1 Cor. 5:17.

as Joachim Jeremias points out, is the 'casual way' in which Paul says it, as if the comparison was already familiar to the Corinthian church. The tone of it, as well as the way the image is frequently used elsewhere in the New Testament, leads Jeremias to propose that the analogy 'probably goes back to Jesus himself'.[54] What is being claimed here is astonishing. It is saying that all that happened through the Passover lamb in Israel's experience happens now through Jesus in our experience. His sacrifice on the cross brings sinners to judgment, principalities and powers to destruction, those under sentence of death to redemption, the oppressed into freedom and its participants into membership of a consecrated people.

In Paul's statement, in context, it is the last of these that is highlighted. How can the people of God go on living in a sinful state, with the old yeast of pride and immorality evident among them, if the Passover lamb has been killed? If the lamb is already sacrificed, it means that the old yeast should already have been removed in accordance with God's instructions. So those who trust in the sacrifice of Christ for salvation must join to their trust the removal of all sinful behaviour from within their ranks. Only then can the Passover festival be celebrated with genuine joy and sincere hearts.

b. A frequent image

The image of Christ as a sacrificed lamb is common in the New Testament. Not every use of the image will necessarily mean that the Passover lamb is in mind. People differ over whether 'the Lamb of God' in John 1:29 and 36 is the Passover lamb or one of the other lambs mentioned in the Old Testament.[55] The hesitancy about relating it to the Passover lamb derives simply from the statement that this Lamb 'takes away the sin of the world'. The focus on sin, as we have seen, is not a major emphasis of the Passover story. But the image is less than precise, and it may well be intended to build a bridge between Jesus and the Passover.

1 Peter 1:18–19 reveals the blood of the lamb as the purchase price of redemption – the price paid to secure the freedom of those who are in slavery, just as the original Passover lamb did. Then, too, the Lamb mentioned in Revelation 5:6, 8, 12, 13, and 12:11, fits the Passover lamb in a fairly obvious way.[56] This Lamb, though slain, is a figure of power who purchases people for God with his blood and defeats the dragon by his death. Two vital achievements of God's activity through the Passover lamb, therefore, are attributed to Christ as well.

[54] J. Jeremias, 'pascha', TDNT 5, p. 900.
[55] For the other suggestions, see below, p. 178.
[56] Rev. 1:5 also speaks of Christ as having 'freed us from our sins by his blood', without specifically referring to the lamb.

c. An implied comparison[57]

Further indications that the early Christians readily understood Jesus to be the new and greater Passover lamb are found in the timing and words of Christ himself at the last supper, the Christians' Passover meal. Luke is quite definite that the last supper was the Passover meal.[58] He records Jesus as saying to his disciples, 'I have eagerly desired to eat this Passover with you before I suffer',[59] and as calling what they were doing a fulfilment of the Passover and 'a banquet of the age of salvation'.[60] Jesus' reference to the cup as his 'blood of the covenant, which is poured out for many',[61] similarly echoes the language of the Passover, while at the same time transforming it, as Jesus claims that he himself is the lamb whose blood was being spilled. John makes the same identification between Christ and the Passover, but in a different way. According to his timetable, Jesus is condemned to death 'between the two evenings', just at the time when the Passover lambs were being killed in the temple precincts.[62]

John observes two more detailed links between the death of the Passover lamb and of Christ. The first is that hyssop is employed in both cases, though to different ends.[63] The second is that the legs of neither were to be broken, although, again, probably for different reasons.[64] The echoes of the original Passover heard in the later one are, however, unmistakable.

In all these ways, the early Christians saw in the Passover lamb a foreshadowing of the work of Christ. Just as, through the shedding of the blood of the original lamb, God was able to move in judgment on Egypt and to provide salvation for Israel, so, through the death of Christ, God acts to destroy sin and Satan and to bring salvation to all those held in slavery.

The Passover lamb was an early pattern for Christ, our Passover lamb. The Passover meal was a model for our Lord's Supper of bread and wine. The Passover sacrifice was a paradigm of the cross. Wonderful though the original was, it differs from the real thing as much as a manual typewriter differs from the latest word processor. Its work was limited to Israel, whereas the blood of the great Passover Lamb purchases 'members of every tribe and language and people and

[57] For more detailed comments on the setting and sayings of the last supper, see the appropriate pages in chs. 6–9 below.
[58] Luke 22:13.
[59] Luke 22:15.
[60] Jeremias, pp. 900–901.
[61] Mark 14:24.
[62] John 19:14.
[63] Exod. 12:22; John 19:29.
[64] Exod. 12:46; John 19:33, 36.

nation' to be righteous kings and liberated priests in the service of God.[65]

When the Jewish Passover meal today reaches the point at which the great acts of God have been recited, the leader urges the people on with these words: 'Then how much more, doubled and redoubled, is the claim the Omnipresent has upon our thankfulness.'[66] In view of the great accomplishments of the cross, how much more, doubled, trebled and quadrupled, is the claim the Christ, the Lord's Passover, has on our thankfulness!

[65] Rev. 5:9–10.
[66] Glatzer, *Passover Haggadah*, p. 57.

Leviticus 16:1–34
3. 'This day atonement shall be made for you'

Everything about the Day of Atonement indicates that it was a day of supreme importance. It was celebrated on the tenth day of the seventh month,[1] the most sacred of all months.[2] The high priest wore special dress and underwent very careful preparation, heightening the sense of its importance. The rituals undertaken were unique, their effect was unequalled and their significance unrivalled. It was celebrated but once a year. The whole community was instructed to observe it by denying themselves and abstaining from work.[3] Instructions about it are placed at the very centre of Leviticus, underlining its pivotal importance for the whole book. Given all this, it is easy to understand why the rabbis came to refer to it simply as 'The Day'.

The fullest account of the day, found in Leviticus 16,[4] gives the people of Israel a comprehensive guide to its conduct. It provides instructions for priest and people alike. It is introduced with a solemn warning (1–2), which is followed by personal instructions to the high priest (3–5), a brief overview of the rite (6–10) and the expanded details of the ceremony (11–28), before concluding with instructions to the people (29–34).

1. The awesome holiness of God

Right from the start we are made aware that this sacrifice requires extra care. Every element of it demonstrates that the God with whom Israel has to do is awesome in holiness. His majestic presence has to be entered with extreme caution, and his offended righteousness has to be propitiated with blood sacrifices.

---

[1] Lev. 23:26.

[2] Hartley, p. 387. Its sacredness lay in the importance Israel attached to the number seven.

[3] This instruction comes not just in Lev. 16:29 but three times in Lev. 23 (vv. 28, 31–32), with the severest penalties for those who disobey (vv. 29–30).

[4] It is also mentioned at Exod. 30:10; Lev. 23:26–32; 25:9; and Num. 29:7–11.

68

a. Divine warning

The day is set in a fear-inducing context. *The LORD spoke to Moses after the death of the two sons of Aaron who died after they approached the LORD* (1). Shortly after they began their priestly ministries, Nadab and Abihu 'offered unauthorised fire before the LORD, contrary to his command', and were consequently struck dead by God as 'fire came out from the presence of the LORD and consumed them' (10:1–2). Aaron had already learned from painful personal experience that God had to be approached with care, but the reminder of it at this point adds solemnity to the instructions about to be given.

b. Personal preparation

Aaron is given directions as to how to prepare himself for the task ahead. To us, the NIV translation of verse 3 reads straightforwardly enough. But as Baruch Levine comments, the Hebrew is emphatic: 'only in this way shall he enter …' 'Strict adherence to the prescribed procedures' is required.[5] As far as Aaron himself is concerned, the instructions involve what he is to wear, how often he is to wash and his need to offer a sin offering and burnt offering. His dress is unusual. On this day he is to lay aside the splendid and ornate garments of the high priest's office, described in Exodus 28, and clothe himself in a *sacred linen tunic* (4). The simple white linen garment may say something about the degree of purity needed[6] to officiate in the Most Holy Place,[7] but most agree[8] that it is more likely to stress the humility and penitential attitude Aaron requires as he performs his duties. The garment is that of a slave – 'a significant reminder that when the high priest enters the very presence of God he is nothing more than a simple servant'.[9]

Before the high priest puts on these clothes, he is to bathe himself. In fact, the rabbis tell us that on the Day of Atonement the high priest bathes himself five times altogether, that is, every time he changes his clothes, in addition to washing his hands and feet ten times.[10] Complete physical cleanliness is required before entering the heart of God's sanctuary, symbolizing the complete inner purity required of the priest of God and matching the total spiritual cleansing the offerings will obtain for Israel.

---

[5] Levine, p. 101.

[6] Jenson, *Graded Holiness*, p. 200. Others see it as a reference to the dress of angels: Milgrom, p. 1016.

[7] The 'Most Holy Place' is the NIV's translation of what is traditionally known as the Holy of Holies, and will be used here.

[8] Hartley, p. 235; Levine, p. 101; Wenham, *Leviticus*, p. 230.

[9] Demarest, p. 174.

[10] Morris, *Atonement*, p. 76. For details see Milgrom, p. 1047.

Finally, before entering the Most Holy Place he has to offer a sin offering *to make atonement for himself and his household* (6, 11). There is to be no presumption that the high priest is already fit to undertake his responsibilities that day. He might well have have become ritually unclean, either because of his own actions or as a result of contamination by a member of his family. So the first thing he has to do is to ensure that he is ritually qualified to minister in the way God requires.

These numerous demands would have a powerful impact on both the high priest himself and on all Israel. Aaron must take special care to approach with due reverence. The God whom he is to encounter in the Most Holy Place is a God of commanding might and absolute purity.

c. Ritual arrangements

Aaron has to prepare not only himself but the materials needed in the ceremonies. He needs a *bull* for his own *sin offering and a ram for a burnt offering* (3).[11] He also needs two *goats* and a *ram* to offer respectively as a *sin offering* and *burnt offering* on behalf of the whole *Israelite community* (5). Once all the sacrificial animals had been gathered, Aaron was to cast lots over the two goats to determine which of them would be slain on the altar as a sacrifice to the Lord and which would be set free in the desert as a *scapegoat* (7–8). Aaron's own sin offering is to be offered first (11), followed by the sin offering for Israel (15). The climax of the liturgy would be the release of the scapegoat, the unique element in the ceremony (20–22). Even then, further sacrifices were to be offered (24). This time they were the burnt offerings – offerings of dedication – again for Aaron personally and then for the whole community. Having been cleansed, the renewed community was to consecrate itself again to its Lord.

d. Necessary protection

Still the careful preparation is not complete. On this day, and on this day alone, the high priest is to enter the Most Holy Place and officiate in the very presence of God himself, who had chosen to take up residence there. His holiness, emanating from his seat on the lid of the covenant ark, is a tangible force. As the high priest goes behind the curtain, which hid it even from the priests who served in the Holy Place, he is entering dangerous territory. He does not dare enter it as if he had a right to be there; still less in a casual manner. He does not dare enter at all without protection. So God thoughtfully commands him to bring fire and high-quality, *finely ground fragrant incense*[12] with him

[11] For details of the sin offering, see Lev. 4:1–35; and for the whole or burnt offering, Lev. 1:1–17.
[12] Verse 12 refers to the quality of the incense offered rather than merely, as in NIV, to the quality of its grinding. Hartley, p. 239, and Milgrom, p. 1025.

and, before he does anything else, to create a smoke-screen to serve as a wall of protection. Aaron wisely obeys. Israel knew that 'to look on God meant certain death'.[13] The smoke ensures that God's holiness is bearable by a sinful man; God's being remains shrouded in mystery and his servant is safeguarded.

The combination of these initial instructions leaves one with a powerful impression of God as majestic in holiness. They thus begin to suggest the problem the Day of Atonement was designed to address. This holy God, for whatever reason and in whatever way, has been offended by his people; and the offence cannot simply be ignored, for that would compromise his purity and his character. The offence must be removed. It won't just go away; it must be taken away. But exactly what is the offence the ceremonies are designed to cleanse?

2. The alienating nature of sin

John Goldingay writes:

> Scripture has a telling range of terms for sin: to list the most common of these, sin means failure, rebellion, transgression, trespass, turning from the right road, stain, infidelity. Each of these terms is a symbolic expression – it takes some deeply significant human experience and utilizes it to illumine aspects of the nature of our relationship with God.[14]

He is right. Sin is complex. No single word can capture the full range of its meaning; hence the variety of metaphors used to convey its pervasive, varied and serious nature. In Leviticus 16 four words are used to express the offence caused by human beings to God.

a. Sin is spiritual pollution

The first word, in verse 16, is *uncleanness* (*ṭumâ*). The behaviour of the children of Israel has, somehow or other, polluted the dwelling-place of God, making it an increasingly uncomfortable place for him to live. Unless cleansing takes place, there is a danger that God will be forced out of his dwelling and cease to live in their midst. The causes of pollution are not mentioned, but almost certainly include their neglecting to offer all the sacrifices they should, offering them in some unintentionally less than correct manner, accidentally permitting some impurity to enter the sanctuary or acting in ignorance.[15] Whatever the cause, their failure to match the standard of holiness required by God

---

[13] Noordtzij, p. 165. Cf. Exod. 20:19; 33:20; Judg. 6:22–23; 13:22.
[14] J. Goldingay, 'Your iniquities', p. 39.
[15] Jenson, *Graded Holiness*, p. 207. See also his 'Sacrificial system', p. 35.

has filled his dwelling-place with spiritual pollution, and he is repelled by it.

This is why one strand of this passage speaks not about making atonement for people but about making *atonement for the Most Holy Place* (16). It is not just the children of Israel who need cleansing (though they do, 17), but the tabernacle of God too. And the cleansing agent that God has selected to accomplish the task is blood. Usually blood is only sprinkled in front of the curtain or applied to the relevant altar in the Holy Place or the outer court. But on this occasion it is showered on everything. The *atonement cover* in the Most Holy Place (14–15), *the Tent of Meeting*, which included the altar of incense (16) and the *altar* of burnt offering in the outer court (18–19) are all sprinkled *seven times*[16] *to cleanse it and consecrate it from the uncleanness of the Israelites* (19). This is the most comprehensive act of blood cleansing that existed in Israel's sacrificial system.[17]

Just as the physical pollution of our natural environment is rendering some cities almost uninhabitable, so the spiritual pollution of Israel rendered the Tent of Meeting uninhabitable to God. It is a vivid metaphor for sin. Whether by unintentional spiritual neglect, more conscious spiritual indifference or outright spiritual rebellion, sin drives God out of his world and alienates him from his creatures with whom he delights to live and to relate.

b. Sin is outright rebellion

If the accent of the first picture fell towards the unintentional end of the spectrum of sin, the accent of the second most definitely does not. Sin is not only spiritual pollution but wilful transgression. The word 'rebellion (*peša'*, 16, 21) basically refers to a legal offence.[18] It was the word used of the rebellion of a vassal against an overlord. It occurs when men and women know what they are doing and deliberately, brazenly, fly in the face of God's law.

Until recently, this understanding of sin has dominated evangelical preaching and has been complemented by the stress on the cross as a work of penal substitution and on salvation as a work of legal justification. Thus it is said that Christ died because he bore the lawful sentence of God the judge on our sin, so that we might be declared innocent and be set free from the dock in God's lawcourt. Many (as this book explores more fully elsewhere) have sought to move away from this picture and stress that 'rebellion' or 'transgression' is a relational term rather than a legal one. They emphasize that we rebel against a person, causing his anger, rather than transgress a law,

---

[16] Seven is a symbol of completeness.
[17] Jenson, *Graded Holiness*, p. 204.
[18] E. Carpenter and M. A. Grisanti, '*pesaḥ*', in *TDOTTE* 3, p. 707.

provoking its forensic reaction against us. This is where John Goldingay, for example, puts the emphasis. It is, he writes, 'Our infidelity to God as lover, our disloyalty to God as friend, and our ignoring of God as generous father [that] place a barrier of conflict, anger and enmity between us which we as the people in the wrong can hardly attempt to overcome'.[19] He goes on to stress that anger is an emotion that arises within the context of human friendship, and is associated with jealousy, pain and grief, as distinct from general judicial wrath.

I readily wish to agree with what such writers affirm. Sin is about a disruption of relationships. It alienates us from a generous, loving, gracious Father. But some use this stress on relationships to argue that the law of God is not the issue here. They oppose relationships and law. But law is, in part, what enables good relationships to exist. The relational view of sin and atonement, far from negating the place of the law, confirms it. The God who is Father is also the God who is holy, judge and lawgiver. To deny that fact is to fly in the face of a substantial amount of Scripture's teaching about God's nature, and, not least, to draw the sting of his holiness as it is graphically represented in the ritual of the Day of Atonement. The law we break by our transgression is his law, and so we alienate ourselves from him. But we are still law-breakers. The anger we face is his, measured out to us neither in the flawed and temperamental way in which we are given to express our anger, nor with the impersonal inevitability about it that some, who wish to distance God from his wrath, would describe. It is the perfect anger of a righteous judge and an offended father, who has given us himself and his law and longs for us to be both his children and his subjects. Sin is rightly described, among other things, as transgression against his law.

c. Sin is conscious wickedness

A further word for the problem resolved on the Day of Atonement is used in verses 21–22. It is the word *wickedness* (NIV), or 'iniquities' (NRSV) (*'āwôn*). Jacob Milgrom argues that it is 'the key term', because it is the only category of sin chosen for use in the summary statement and confession of verse 22 (translated *sins*),[20] where it carries the idea of the perversion of our fallen human nature. With the rabbis, he defines it as 'deliberate wrongdoing ... whose gravity is one notch below that of "transgressions"'.[21] It relates primarily to the religious and ethical sphere,[22] and lays the responsibility for wrong clearly at the feet

[19] Goldingay, 'Your iniquities', p. 49.
[20] Milgrom, p. 1043.
[21] Ibid.
[22] A. Luc, ''āwôn', *TDOTTE* 3, p. 351.

of human beings as moral agents accountable to God, without attributing to them the degree of wilfulness inherent in the word 'transgression'.

d. Sin is any wrongdoing

The fourth word is simply the word *sins* (*ḥaṭṭā't*, 16, 21, 30, 34), the catch-all word for any wrongdoing, serious or trivial, deliberate or unintentional, conscious or unconscious, visible or invisible, an act or a disposition, consisting of commission or of omission.[23]

Using an analogy from baseball, John Hayes sums it up well. With all these definitions of sin, he says, 'all bases are covered'.[24] During the year many 'sins' would have accumulated in the course of routine worship, which means that the sanctuary needed to be purged from its pollution and the people needed to be cleansed from their wrongdoing. The Day of Atonement was the great day of the spiritual 'spring clean', when all the sins of the people were removed and their relationship with God was repaired, allowing him to be at home among them, in his sanctuary, once again.

John Hartley points out that all four words for 'sin' are used in the plural, to indicate 'the frequency and totality of humans' sinning'.[25] Together they provide a remarkably comprehensive analysis of human wrong. Any of the first three, used in isolation from the others, might present only one dimension of the nature of sin. But together they show something of the spectrum of sin and, in doing so, convey something of its seriousness. Sin is spiritual pollution that needs cleansing; wilful disobedience that needs putting right; explicit wrong that needs pardoning, and manifold failure that needs forgiveness. None of this can happen on the cheap. Sin has its price. The cleansing, righting, pardoning and forgiving we need cost something. It is to the payment of that price that we now turn.

3. The essence of the atonement

The initiative for overcoming the problem of sin, which has alienated God from his covenant people, comes from God himself. He commands Moses to instruct the priests how to make amends.[26] Four aspects of the ritual require attention. First, it was sacrificial in nature,

---

[23] Milgrom, p. 1034.

[24] J. H. Hayes, 'Atonement in the book of Leviticus', *Int* 52 (1998), p. 13.

[25] Hartley, p. 241.

[26] Moses rather than Aaron is addressed because Leviticus 16, as Hartley has pointed out, is almost certainly a general guide for the laity rather than a manual for the priests, for whom it would be insufficiently detailed. Since it was addressed to all, it was appropriate that the instructions came through Moses, who led all, rather than through Aaron, who primarily led the priests.

placing it within the mainstream of Israel's worship. Secondly, it was substitutionary In approach. Thirdly, it was atoning in significance. Fourthly, it was sufficient in design and effect to accomplish its twofold task, putting it into a category all of its own.

a. It is sacrificial in character

At this stage of its history, the worship of Israel was essentially sacrificial in nature. The opening chapters of Leviticus detail five sacrifices that were to be offered for different purposes and in various ways. They were the whole or burnt offering (1:1–17; 6:8–13), a general act of worship and atonement; the grain offering (2:1–16; 6:14–23), an expression of covenant commitment; the fellowship or peace offering (3:1–17; 6:11–21), a celebratory and communion meal in the presence of God; the sin or purification offering (4:1–5; 6:24–30), which dealt with unintentional sins; and the guilt or reparation offering (5:14 – 6:7; 7:1–10), which involved making restitution for wrong. They could initiate a new relationship between God and his people, remedy a damaged one or strengthen an existing one.[27] As is evident, not all of them involved making atonement for sin. Sacrifices were also means of offering a gift to God, removing stains, paying debts, enjoying communion and connecting this ordinary, mundane world with the world of the holy.[28]

With the exception of the grain offering (a voluntary act which usually accompanied one of the other sacrifices),[29] all involved the slaughtering of an animal and the ritual handling of its blood. Philip Jenson has identified six stages they typically went through, although he admits to several variations.[30] Worshippers approached the sanctuary with the animal to be sacrificed, laid hands on it and slaughtered it; the priest sprinkled the blood, poured it out or applied it to various objects and then prepared and burnt the sacrifice on the altar; after which the flesh was eaten and the remainder removed.

Most of these steps are evident on the Day of Atonement. The duties involved the sacrifice of a sin offering and a burnt offering for Aaron and his family, and of sin and burnt offerings for the whole community. But on this day a change was made to the normal ritual. Two goats were to be chosen for the people's sin offering, but only one of them was to be slaughtered as a sacrifice. The other was to be set free in the wilderness. This novel aspect of the sacrifice will be examined in

[27] Jenson, *Graded Holiness, passim.*
[28] A full, somewhat enterprising, exposition of these purposes is found in Goldingay, 'Old Testament sacrifice'. He adds sacrifice as a way of handling the fact of violence in the community.
[29] Lev. 23:13; Num. 15:1–12; cf. 5:15.
[30] Jenson, 'Sacrificial system', p. 27.

a moment. For now, our interest lies in what the sacrifices of this day have in common with the other sacrifices.

The death of the sacrificial victims and the manipulation of their blood were essential components of the sacrificial system. The blood is drained from the dead animal, and then, in the case of the Day of Atonement, sprinkled first on the surface of the *atonement cover* ('the mercy seat', NRSV) and then in front of it *seven times* (14), before being applied to items in the rest of the Tent of Meeting and its surrounds.

Leviticus 17:11 helps us to understand the significance of this. It reads, 'For the life of a creature is in the blood, and I have given it to you to make atonement for yourselves on the altar; it is the blood that makes atonement for one's life.' The shedding of blood symbolizes a life laid down on behalf of others, and the sprinkling of blood serves to cleanse the unclean. Many have sought to switch the focus of this verse away from the death of the victim to its life. They have argued that the important factor in the sacrificial offerings is that, by shedding the animal's blood, a life is released and presented to God as a perfect offering, and thereby life is bestowed on the worshipper. Paul Fiddes, for example, says, 'The idea seems to be that the tainted and unclean life of the offending community is renewed by the pouring out of the fresh life present in the blood of the animal.'[31] The result of such a view is that the death of the sacrifice is incidental, no more than an unfortunate means of obtaining life.

This view has been challenged by Leon Morris, who, after a detailed examination of the use of the word in Scripture,[32] concludes with Alan Stibbs that the shedding of blood does not stand for 'the release of life from the burden of the flesh, but for the bringing to an end of life in the flesh. It is evidence of physical death, not spiritual survival.'[33] The focus rests, then, on the death of the victim as the significant aspect of the sacrifice: that is, a life is given in exchange for a life which, through wrongdoing and uncleanness, had become forfeit. Blood was the price to be paid if cleansing and forgiveness were to be available.

b. It is substitutionary in approach

The purpose of the sacrifice is to make atonement for the one who offers it. The straightforward interpretation of the ritual is that the sacrificial offering takes the place of the sinful worshipper and dies as his or her substitute. The sacrifices required the offerers to lay their hands on the animals before slaughtering them[34] in a symbolic act which appears to transfer the total dedication (in the case of the burnt

---

[31] Fiddes, p. 69.
[32] Morris, *Apostolic Preaching*, pp. 114–118.
[33] A. M. Stibbs, *Meaning of Blood*, p. 11.
[34] Lev. 1:4; 4:4, 15, 24, 29, 33.

offering) or the sin (in the case of the guilt offering) to the victim. The victim then serves as a substitute by becoming either the perfect gift of worship to God (in the burnt offering) or the perfect payment of a ransom to God (in the guilt offering). On the Day of Atonement, the same act of transference takes place not only with the offerings but also with the goat that would be led away into the wilderness (21).

Again, in recent times, people have questioned whether the sacrifice really is a substitute. Their objections relate more specifically to the idea of the sacrifice as a penal substitute. How just of God is it, they ask, to punish a substitute for wrongdoing? How would punishment of any kind, but especially substitutionary punishment like this, right the situation? They have been happy to use the word 'representative', to say that the death is vicarious or that the victim is identified with the worshipper, because these ideas do not relate to the payment of a penalty for sin; but they wish to stop short of using the word 'substitute' because it has been monopolized by those who advocate the penal theory of the atonement.[35]

The sophisticated objections of contemporary men and women sometimes seem to arise more from pride than from anything else. They stand against the long and forceful current of the church's history. C. H. Spurgeon, a champion of the view of sacrifice as a penal substitution,[36] once said, 'We have heard sometimes foolish persons ask, "Where is the doctrine of substitution in Scripture?" to which I would answer, "Where is it not?" Take it out of the Scriptures, and there is positively nothing left.'[37]

The Day of Atonement, it must be remembered, is about the removal both of uncleanness from God's sanctuary and of sin from God's people. At the very least, the use of 'transgression' (NIV, *rebellion*, 16, 21) to describe part of the problem that needs to be remedied implies that here is a legal offence that needs to be confronted and that will be dealt with in a judicial context. So shades of punishment and, therefore, of penal substitution are found here.

When applying this argument to Leviticus,[38] we must remember that

---

[35] For an exposition of these positions see C. A. Baxter, 'The cursed beloved: a reconsideration of penal substitution', in Goldingay (ed.), pp. 54–72.

[36] 'It is the curse of God. God who made the law has appended certain penal consequences to the breaking of it, and the man who violates the law, becomes at once the subject of the wrath of the Lawgiver. It is not the curse of the mere law itself, it is a curse from the great Lawgiver whose arm is strong to defend his statutes. Hence ... let us be assured that the law-curse must be supremely just, and morally unavoidable. It is not possible that our God, who delights to bless us, should inflict an atom of curse upon any one of his creatures unless the highest right shall require it; and if there be any method by which holiness and purity can be maintained without a curse, rest assured the God of love will not imprecate sorrow upon his creatures.' Spurgeon, p. 118.

[37] Ibid., p. 169.

[38] The issues will be revisited in ch. 10.

we have here only a shadow of the reality to come. Here is a preliminary sketch of what God would one day do for his world through the offering of Christ as our substitute. When we get the full picture, it makes more sense. For then, as Christina Baxter suggests, those who advocate this substitutionary approach to atonement are like people who have to deal with a broken window. They know there is a cost to be paid for its repair. In the cross, she says, God bears the cost himself. 'But the cost of forgiveness is cost to God; the cross is God's declaration of the payment of the cost.'[39] There he not only expresses wrath against sin, but bears the penalty of it himself, and graciously substitutes himself for us.

c. It is atoning in effect

The wonderful achievement of the sacrificial ritual, whatever its precise mechanisms may be, is *atonement*. But what exactly does 'atonement' mean? Since the fourteenth century the English word has had its roots in being 'at one'; that is, of being in a state of friendship, reconciliation or harmony. John Wycliffe translated the word in his New Testament as 'onement'. But some regard that understanding as unfortunate because, however reasonable a translation, it is not, for them, a sufficiently precise definition.[40]

The word used in Leviticus for 'atonement' comes from the Hebrew root *kpr*, and three different meanings lie behind it. It might mean 'to cover', as, for example, when a piece of wood is covered over with pitch[41] or a debt is covered by payment. Secondly, it might mean 'to ransom', having its origin in connection with bribery or the payment of a price to achieve a favourable result. Or thirdly, it might mean 'to wipe away' or 'purge'.[42]

Traditionally it was the second of these ideas that was thought to get to the heart of atonement; that is, atonement was the paying of a ransom price. Many now, however, prefer the third idea –'to wipe away' – as a more accurate translation.[43] The setting of the word in the context of the Day of Atonement's cleansing of the sanctuary favours this meaning, it is said, quite apart from any other considerations. To choose this meaning does not diminish the other function of the Day of Atonement. It can – and does – apply as much to the wiping away of the people's sin as to the purging of the Tent of Meeting from uncleanness.

---

[39] Baxter, 'The cursed beloved', p. 72.
[40] E.g. Brueggemann, *Theology*, p. 193, who objects that this makes it a relational term instead of one that suggests 'a containment of the material threat in the form of uncleanness'.
[41] Gen. 6:14.
[42] R. E. Averbeck, '*kpr*', in *TDOTTE* 3, pp. 689–710.
[43] Ibid., p. 696.

Some fear that adopting this interpretation of atonement in place of the traditional one will weaken our view of God's holiness, trivialize the horror of sin and cheapen the value of the sacrifice. It need not. Other parts of Scripture will provide a robust defence for those concerns. It may simply broaden our appreciation of the depth of the atonement act which God has provided for us.

Even so, it must be said that the arguments in favour of the meaning 'to wipe away' are not conclusive. There are good grounds for accepting the idea of atonement as a penalty paid or sin covered. The word may well mean 'to pay the covering price'. It would fit the context, even if not quite as well as 'to wipe clean' does. So it should not be lightly cast aside.

d. It is comprehensive in scope

From the complexities of recent theological debates we emerge into the clarity of the scapegoat ritual. It feels like moving from the theological half-light of dusk to the transparent clarity of a sun-filled noonday. The unique thing about the Day of Atonement was the role of the scapegoat. The rituals find their focal point here.

Aaron is instructed *to take two goats and present them before the LORD at the entrance of the Tent of Meeting* (7). There is nothing unusual about that. But what follows next is unprecedented. He is told to *cast lots* for them to determine which will be slaughtered and offered to the Lord as a sin offering, and which will be presented alive and then released into the wilderness as a *scapegoat* (8–10). Aaron obeys, first sacrificing the one designated as the *sin offering* (15) and then, after cleansing the sanctuary with its blood (16–19), turning his attention to the goat that is to be released (20). This goat is brought forward. Aaron lays *both hands* on its *head*, confesses all the sins of Israel over it, and then dispatches it to a solitary place in the desert, where it is released (21–23).

As Gordon Wenham comments, 'the symbolism of this ceremony is transparent'.[44] The sanctuary having been cleansed with blood, the sins of the people are now being carried away, removed as far as possible outside the camp and done away with. It involves what Baruch Levine refers to as 'rites of riddance'.[45] The transgressions of Israel and their priests 'are dramatically transferred to the scapegoat, which is driven into the wilderness, never to return'.[46] It is a wonderful picture of God's grace. It is what Psalm 103:11–12 celebrates in these words:

---

[44] Wenham, *Leviticus*, p. 233.
[45] Levine, p. 99.
[46] Ibid.

> For as high as the heavens are above the earth,
>   so great is his love for those who fear him;
> as far as the east is from the west,
>   so far has he removed our transgressions from us.

In spite of the clarity of the overall picture, however, there are some details that deserve closer examination. When the two goats are brought forward for their fate to be determined by lot, the text says, 'one lot [was] for the LORD and the other lot for Azazel' (8, NRSV).[47] Just who or what Azazel was remains, in the end, a mystery. It could be a word for a 'goat that departs', a phrase meaning 'fit for removal', a rocky precipice or the name of a demon, even the devil himself, which haunted the wilderness.[48] The most popular interpretation is that it is the name for a desert demon. Gordon Wenham explains that not only does it then balance the name for God in the verse, but that this is how it was used in later Jewish literature, and it fits with the people's perception of the wilderness as a place haunted by demons.[49]

The ritual is evocative. Sin is being removed from the camp and taken back to its source. It belongs not among the covenant people of God but among the demons and wild spirits of the desert. In sending sin back to Azazel, God is confronting and mocking him. He is saying, in effect, 'Here are all the sins you have engineered. You can have them back. They have power over us no longer.'[50]

The rabbinic writings tell us that in later history, to ensure that the scapegoat did not return to the camp, on reaching their destination the escort tied the goat to a rock and then pushed it from behind over a precipice. 'It rolled over and over and was broken in pieces before it had gone half-way down.'[51] There was, for sure, no way back. Sin had been irretrievably banished and irrevocably forgiven.

The scope of the cleansing achieved on the Day of Atonement is remarkable. Jacob Milgrom believes that it involved two acts of atonement for two different categories of sin. The guilt offering, which Aaron offers in the Most Holy Place, and the sprinkling of blood that follows, deal with the cleansing of the Tent of Meeting. The scapegoat ritual, he suggests, deals with the sins of the people.[52] But this is to be more precise either than the priests would have imagined or than the text demands. Most interpreters feel that the ritual should not be

---

[47] NIV refers to Azazel only in mg., but chooses to translate the main text by the alternative of scapegoat, meaning 'goat of removal or dismissal'. See Harrison, p. 170. The juxtaposition of 'for the Lord' and 'for Azazel' is, however, to be preferred.

[48] Hartley, p. 237, Wenham, *Leviticus*, p. 234.

[49] E.g. Lev. 17:7. The 'goat idol' (NIV) is a demon who lives in the wilderness.

[50] Demarest, p. 179.

[51] Morris, *Atonement*, p. 78.

[52] Milgrom, pp. 1060ff.

fragmented, but rather treated as a unified ritual. Each part of it contributes to a comprehensive solution to the problems Israel faces, whether uncleanness that arose from breaking ritual law and defiled the dwelling-place of God, or personal and social sin that transgressed God's other laws and merited his disapproval and wrath.

The geographical movements involved in these rituals were wider than those involved in any comparable act of sacrifice. And these, too, serve to underline the comprehensive scope of the forgiveness made available on the Day of Atonement. The sacrificial drama was usually played out in the courtyard of the Tent of Meeting and in the Holy Place. The drama of this day reaches into the innermost core of the Tent of Meeting, the Most Holy Place, and is not completed until the scapegoat is let loose in the region beyond the camp. The layout of Israel's camp may be envisaged as consisting of five concentric zones. Zone 1 is the Most Holy Place. Zone 2 is the Holy Place. Zone 3 is the courtyard. Zone 4 is the camp itself that surrounds the Tent of Meeting. Zone 5 is 'outside the camp,' the place of evil spirits, where the unclean and those who have been expelled are condemned to live. Only the rituals of Atonement Day cover the complete geography of holiness in Israel, from the most sacred spot of all to the uncleanest place in their world.

Philip Jenson points out that the two goats begin the day 'by being indistinguishable'. Both are designated for the atonement sacrifice. Only the lots differentiate them. After that, their futures are very different. 'By the end of the day they have embraced the extreme reaches of significant space.'[53] Atonement reaches right into the heart of God and ejects sin to the nethermost part of the world. We learn from the drama that cleansing comes from an act of God in his dwelling-place and leads to the removal of the problem as far away from us as it is possible to conceive.

4. The infinite superiority of Christ

The rituals of this great day effected a real atonement. But they were only shadows of the reality to come. They pointed to one who would be the high priest who would offer the perfect sacrifice once for all, the lamb of the burnt and the guilt offerings whose life would be surrendered to death, and the scapegoat who bore away the sins of the world, all in one. It is curious that the New Testament does not identify the work of Christ with that of the scapegoat in any overt and exclusive way.[54] That was left to the *Epistle of Barnabas* around the year

[53] Jenson, *Graded Holiness*, p. 202.
[54] In some places, e.g. John 1:29 and 1 Pet. 2:24, the idea of Passover lamb and the Day of Atonement seem to be combined.

AD 130, after which the parallel became more popular in the early church. But, in spite of the absence of any direct reference, the New Testament allusions to aspects of the Day of Atonement are numerous, and are especially considered in Hebrews 9. The allusions all go to prove the infinite superiority of the sacrifice of Jesus Christ over the sacrifices of that day.

The superiority of his work is seen both in points of comparison and in points of contrast.

a. The superiority demonstrated by way of comparison

By comparison, the blood of Jesus Christ was poured out as a 'sacrifice of atonement',[55] just like a sin offering, and justifies those who have faith in him. Like the scapegoat, the cross of Jesus bears away the sins of the world and utterly removes the burden of sin from those who are responsible for it. In the words of 2 Corinthians 5:21, 'God made him who had no sin to be sin for us.' In the words of 1 Peter 2:24, 'He himself bore our sins in his body on the tree.' According to Hebrews 9:28, 'Christ was sacrificed once to take away the sins of many people.' He was the greatest 'rite of riddance', removing people's sins far from them.

Another allusion to the scapegoat is found in Hebrews 13:12. Just as the scapegoat was sent outside the camp, so Jesus died outside the city.

A further similarity (though not precise) lies in the idea of going into the wilderness. Peter tells us that, after his death, Christ went into his own sort of wilderness and 'preached to the spirits in prison'.[56]

Finally, Jesus continues to practise the ministry of earlier high priests in one respect. As our great high priest, he continues to be our 'advocate with the Father'.[57]

b. The superiority demonstrated by way of contrast

Although the similarities help us to interpret the death of Christ as a sacrifice of atonement, it is the contrasts with the sacrifices of the earlier time that point to the greatness of Christ. The high priest of old was a sinner and had to offer sacrifices for his own sin, whereas Jesus, our high priest, is unblemished in his perfection and has no such need.[58] Aaron had to offer the sacrificial blood of goats and bulls, whereas Jesus offers his own blood.[59] The old priests sacrificed annually and repeatedly, whereas Jesus had to offer his perfect sacrifice only 'once for

---

[55] Rom. 3:25.
[56] 1 Pet. 3:19.
[57] 1 John 2:1, NRSV.
[58] Heb. 7:26–28.
[59] Heb. 9:12.

all'.[60] The old sacrificial system could make people ceremonially clean on the outside but do nothing to cleanse people's consciences. But the sacrifice of Christ is able to cleanse the conscience.[61] Under the former system, the Israelites were repeatedly reminded of their failure, since they had to offer their sacrifices repeatedly to gain atonement. But the work of Christ releases us from such a depressing treadmill. His single death was the ultimate act in the drama of atonement and won for us a permanent forgiveness.[62]

The wonderful result of Christ's atoning death is that now 'we have confidence to enter the Most Holy Place by the blood of Jesus'.[63] Every believer has direct and unimpeded access into the presence of his or her holy God and loving Father because Christ died. In this way, the letter to the Hebrews is only making explicit what the Gospels had stated implicitly as they recorded the events around the death of Christ. When Christ was crucified, the curtain of the temple was ripped in two,[64] providing all who trusted in him with unhindered access into the Most Holy Place. No longer is the privilege of being in the immediate presence of God limited to the high priest and to his annual encounter in a smoke-filled room. It is a daily experience for all God's children, and one in which they have an unclouded vision of him, for he 'made his light shine in our hearts to give us the light of the knowledge of the glory of God in the face of Christ'.[65]

Under the old covenant, the Day of Atonement was a great annual festival, solemnly observed (30) and joyfully concluded.[66] But it was far exceeded by the day of Calvary, a unique event which we both solemnly remember and joyfully celebrate. For if the Day of Atonement was a means by which the children of Israel could be made clean from all their sins (30) until the next time, the day of Calvary is the means by which the disciples of Christ are made clean from all their sins for ever. And if the Day of Atonement cleansed them from uncleanness, transgressions, iniquities and sins, the blood of Christ is even more effective. As Spurgeon preached, 'the blood of Christ, *it is all-sufficient.* There is no case which the blood of Christ cannot meet; there is no sin which it cannot wash away. There is no multiplicity of sin which it cannot cleanse, no aggravation of guilt which it cannot remove.'[67]

[60] Heb. 7:27; 9:12, 26, 28.
[61] Heb. 9:9, 13–14.
[62] Heb. 10:11–12.
[63] Heb. 10:19.
[64] Matt. 27:51; Mark 15:38; Luke 23:45.
[65] 2 Cor. 4:6.
[66] The rabbis tell us that in later Jewish tradition the arrival of the scapegoat in the wilderness 'was signalled all the way back to Jerusalem by the waving of towels': Morris, *Atonement*, p. 78.
[67] Spurgeon, pp. 112–113.

Jesus is both priest and sacrifice, both the lamb who dies as the sin offering and the scapegoat who goes into the wilderness bearing away sin. He lived and died in total submission and dedication to God, becoming for us the perfect burnt offering. He removed the defilement of our sin and paid the price for our iniquity. He ripped open the curtain and gave us constant access to the intimate presence of God. In him, our alienation from God and his from us are overcome, and we are reconciled. Every aspect of the work of atonement discerned in the complex model of that ancient annual festival finds fulfilment in him. He is indeed the all-sufficient one.

Psalm 22:1–31
4. 'My God, my God, why?'

'No Christian can read this', Derek Kidner writes of Psalm 22, 'without being vividly confronted with the crucifixion.'[1] Certainly the Gospel writers could not read it without thinking of the cross of Christ. Not only did its opening words form the wrenching cry of dereliction that came from the lips of Jesus as he died,[2] but also the manner of his death, in detail after detail, seems to be prophesied here. Thirteen Old Testament texts are quoted in the passion narratives of the Gospels, of which nine come from the Psalms. Of these nine, five are found in this psalm.[3] So exactly does it portray the suffering of our Lord that it has aptly been called 'the Fifth Gospel'.[4]

Before we seek to apply it to the crucifixion, however, we must endeavour to understand the psalm in its own right. To do so will lead to a richer and deeper appreciation of the light it sheds on the cross.

The psalm comprises two parts, which are remarkably dissimilar. The first part, verses 1–21, is a psalm of lament, and the second, verses 22–31, a song of praise. This simple analysis, however, belies its 'finely wrought compositional design',[5] for it expresses jumbled, even conflicting, emotions. In the first part, despair alternates with hope, and in the second, the immediate and personal joy of an individual gives way to the distant and universal worship of the cosmos. The lament that dominates the beginning is found in verses 1–2, 6–8 and 12–18. Each time it is countered by an expression of trust, recorded in verses 3–5, 9–11 and 19–21. The praise that concludes the psalm begins with a personal testimony to answered prayer and ends with a crescendo declaring the universal sovereignty of God. The psalm is like a musical

---

[1] Kidner, *Psalms 1 – 72*, p. 105.

[2] Matt. 27:46; Mark 15:34.

[3] Mays, p. 105. Mays recognizes that others might identify seventeen Old Testament quotations in the passion narratives.

[4] Quoted in Craigie, p. 202. Cf. S. B. Frost, 'Psalm 22: an exposition', *Canadian Journal of Theology* 8 (1962), p. 113.

[5] Mays, p. 108.

composition in two movements, in which major and minor melodies strive with each other throughout until they are brought to a fitting and climactic resolution at the end.

The psalm gives voice to one who is suffering. Although it has sometimes been taken as an expression of the suffering of Israel, most accept that it is the anguished cry of an individual. The heading refers to it as 'a psalm of David', but no particular incident in his life seems to match it entirely. It could, in fact, reflect several of his experiences.[6] He speaks, however, not exclusively for himself but as a representative of others who find themselves in extreme trouble, perhaps facing ill health or the prospect of very near death. It confronts us mostly with the isolation and loneliness of the sufferer. But in one respect the sufferer does not suffer alone, for he expresses both his complaint and his praise in the congregation of God's people, where he first seeks comfort and later enjoys companionship. The psalm, then, is not so much a private prayer as a public liturgy.[7]

1. The trouble he faces (22:1–2, 6–8, 12–18)

Shakespeare wrote, 'When sorrows come, they comes not single spies, / But in battalions.'[8] That was certainly how the psalmist felt. He voices his complaint because his powerful God seems all too distant, his tormenting friends all too near and his sickly body all too feeble.

a. The first lament: a longing for God (22:1–2)

When we are in difficulty most of us cry out, 'Why me?' The psalmist's cry is that and more. Whatever the experience is that he faces, it is not only physically extreme and emotionally demanding but spiritually intense. It is a crisis of faith. In the moment when he needs God and seeks his comforting presence, fully expecting to receive it, he is faced with the total absence of God. God is *so far* away, utterly distant. God neither steps in to deliver him from his affliction nor seems even to hear his prayer. The heavens are silent, and his gloomy words rebound on him, exacerbating his pain. There is a vast abyss between him and the God in whom he has trusted.

The Godforsakenness he feels is made worse by the massive tension between his belief and his experience. His theology tells him he ought not to be ignored by God at such a time as this. His experience tells him he is being deserted by God. The God whom he has trusted until now is, he believes, a God of power who answers prayer and saves people in need (3–5). So what has happened to his power? Why has he

---

[6] Frost, 'Psalm 22', pp. 108–109.
[7] Ibid., p. 198.
[8] *Hamlet*, Act 4, Scene 5.

not stepped in to rescue him now? The problem he faces, then, is more than the mystery of suffering alone. It is a mystery rooted in a contradiction between what he has been taught (and has most firmly believed) and what he knows from his own experience. Many believers, even the most godly, experience such tensions at some time or other in their Christian lives. David Watson wrote frankly about his struggle with terminal cancer, and at one point honestly confessed:

The worst times for me were at two or three o'clock in the morning. I had preached the gospel all over the world with ringing conviction. I had told countless thousands of people that I was not afraid of death since through Christ I had already received God's gift of eternal life. For years I had not doubted these truths at all. But now the most fundamental questions were dragging away insistently, especially in the long hours of the night. If I was soon on my way to heaven, how real was heaven? Was it anything more than a beautiful idea? What honestly would happen when I died? Did God himself really exist after all? How could I be sure? Indeed how could I be certain of anything apart from cancer and death? I literally sweated over these questions, and on many occasions woke up with my pyjamas bathed in cold sweat! Never before had my faith been so ferociously attacked.[9]

He continued,

My own doubts and questions did not last for very long, although in the middle of the night I was not sufficiently awake to counter the sense of fear and foreboding that at times overcame me. Those were times of seeming abandonment by God. 'My God, my God, why have you forsaken me?'[10]

The silence of God sometimes seems most unyielding precisely when we feel we most urgently need him to speak to us.

b. The second lament: loathed by others (22:6–8)

The psalmist's sense of God's absence is grossly aggravated by the presence of others. If God seems unreal, they seem all too real. Their derisory comments and scornful body language undermine any sense of self-worth he otherwise might have, making him feel less than human and more like an animal; and not a very significant animal at that – just a *worm* (6). The very people on whom he should be able to rely are part of his problem. They strike him where it hurts most, for they mock

---

[9] D. Watson, *Fear No Evil* (Hodder and Stoughton, 1984), p. 43.
[10] Ibid., p. 44.

him for having apparently been abandoned by God and placed under some sort of curse. They pour sarcasm on his faith, and this serves only to underline his problem with God and make it worse.

If God is his primary problem, those around him come a close second. They certainly do nothing to help. In fact, they compound his problem with God.

c. The third lament: lamenting for himself (22:12–18)

In his third expression of lament, the psalmist returns to describe what the attack to which he is subject feels like. He pictures his tormentors as 'hidden behind the animal masks they wear'.[11] Using metaphors from the animal kingdom, he says he feels surrounded by bloodthirsty, baying beasts that will not be satisfied with anything less than his total destruction inflicted in the most terrifying way. He feels surrounded by the *bulls of Bashan* (12) who were well known for their size and strength derived from the fertile pastures on which they grazed east of Jordan. He feels mauled by *lions*, mercilessly *tearing* the flesh off their *prey* (13). He feels hemmed in by *dogs*, snarling, growling and ready to pounce and destroy their prey (16). 'The words', writes Peter Craigie, 'evoke the abject terror of one who is powerless, but surrounded, with no avenue of escape.'[12]

The psalmist gives full rein to his feelings of self-pity. He is as spent as poured out *water*, as smashed up as a body full of dislocated bones and as limp as melted wax, while his strength has evaporated like moisture out of a baked clay pot. He is like a corpse ready to be laid out for burial. Those who have attacked him are already dividing his property between them. He is 'merely a bag of useless bones';[13] no longer a living human being.

These verses give us a moving picture of his emotional and physical condition, to add to what we already know about his desperate spiritual state. His constant thirst, the *tongue* sticking *to the roof of* his *mouth* (15), suggests an advanced state of nervous exhaustion. Physically he is drained and at the end of his reserves. Socially he is isolated, with no-one to share with him the ordeal of cruel mockery or the terror of inevitable mortality. His life is smashed and shattered. Others count it as over, dividing his clothes among them. As far as he is concerned, his life might just as well be finished and laid to rest.

---

[11] Mays, p. 110.
[12] Craigie, p. 200.
[13] Ibid.

2. The trust he shows (22:3–5, 9–11, 19–21)[14]

And yet he is not prepared to give up. Battling with the dominant, haunting melody of trouble is the irrepressible music of trust. Terrified though he is at the mystery of God's desertion of him, he does not allow himself to lapse into unbelief. His 'restlessly searching mind'[15] hunts through his experience and places his immediate situation in a broader context of what he knows and has experienced about God. From the shaky ground on which he now stands he reaches out to surer ground. He brings the reality of his suffering into contact with another reality – the reality of his covenant God. He operates on the basis of the wise advice not to doubt in the dark what he knew to be true in the light. What is it, then, that he calls to mind about God?

a. He affirms God's position (22:3)

Yet you are enthroned as the Holy One. God's sovereign position in the universe, confirmed by the praises of his people Israel, is not to be doubted. The psalmist has received no news that God's royal throne has been demolished. God still presides over his world. But he presides as the Holy One, of whom it is said that 'the LORD Almighty will be exalted by his justice, and the holy God will show himself holy by his righteousness'.[16] He is, then, at the same time both perfectly righteous (and so likely to come to the aid of the one under attack) and altogether transcendent (and therefore not at the psalmist's beck and call).

b. He affirms God's power (22:4–5)

The psalmist looks back to history. For sure, God had once delivered the whole nation from bondage in Egypt. The great historical event of the exodus, which had so profoundly shaped their identity, was not to be doubted. If God could deal with Pharaoh and defeat the Egyptian armies, the psalmist's own problem could not be so difficult for God, could it? Others, before him, had trusted in God and had not been let down. Why should it be different for him?

c. He affirms God's purpose (22:9)

His birth was not a random happening, a purposeless result of the forces of evolution or even the planned result of the sexual drives of his parents. It was more significant than that. God had *brought* him *out* of his mother's *womb*. He was no accident of nature, but the object of God's loving design and purpose.

[14] In the Hebrew, each of these sections begins with the same word, 'yet', which is not brought out in the NIV translation of v. 19.
[15] Weiser, p. 221.
[16] Is. 5:16.

d. He affirms God's providence (22:10–11)

As he reflects further on his personal life, he recalls the signs of God's care for him in a myriad ways since his birth. The words *cast upon you* are placed to give them emphasis: 'Upon *you* was I cast.' It is as if the psalmist has been assigned to God's special care and custody.[17] In view of all that he has experienced of God up to this point, could he do other than trust in God now? He believes that when others are unable or unwilling to help, God will still be his helper. As Peter Craigie comments, the sense of distance between himself and God would certainly disappear if he were healed, but that is not his primary concern here. He longs for a restoration of the intimate presence of God in the situation he is in, so that he can face sickness and death 'squarely in the presence of God, who would be a *helper*'.[18] More than anything, he longs for a renewed sense of God's providential care.

e. He affirms God's promise (22:19–21)

In spite of having just reached his lowest point, in the third part of his lament, the sufferer still affirms that God is his God. Having said that his *strength is dried up* (15), he now calls God his *Strength* (19). He has none left in himself, but he still clings to the belief that God can be an abundant source of strength to people like himself in need of rescue. God had promised to rescue Sarah from the shame of barrenness, and did so. He had promised to rescue Israel from the tyranny of Egypt, and did so. He had promised to rescue the weak and defenceless, the poor and needy. Would he not do so?

He pleads for God to remove the distance between them (19) and to reverse the litany of ruin he has just recited. The list of enemies he wishes to see God defeat on his behalf is the same as the list in verses 12–18, only in reverse order. There it was *bulls, lions, dogs* and death. Here it is death, *dogs, lions* and *oxen*. Everything his enemies and his life experiences are doing to him can be undone by God. He has no doubt that God is likely to come to the rescue, in the sense that he is both able and willing to do so.

Even in the most lamentable situations, then, the psalmist's faith will not let him give in to unbelief or give up in despair. As Artur Weiser says, 'A spark of faith kindles in him; through prayer he has gradually drawn near to God. At this very moment, too, in the hour of his direst need, he feels himself thrown upon God as the One who alone is able to help.'[19]

This psalm contains in concentrated form the tension between what

---

[17] Mitchell Dahood, cited by Anderson, p. 189.
[18] Craigie, p. 199.
[19] Weiser, p. 222.

Walter Brueggemann has called 'the core testimony' and the 'countertestimony' of Israel. They are condensed into the life of one individual.

> The core testimony, rooted in the great transformative verbs,[20] ends in an affirmation of Yahweh's faithful sovereignty and Yahweh's sovereign fidelity. The countertestimony, rooted in Israel's lived experience of absence and silence, ends in an articulation of Yahweh's hiddenness, ambiguity and negativity.[21]

Or, as he says elsewhere, with experiences such as the exile and writings such as the book of Lamentations in mind:

> Israel's testimony to Yahweh has proposed a God who in majestic sovereignty provides a viable life-order in the world through decisive, transformative interventions, a God who in generous compassion attends to the needs of Yahweh's own. But Israel's experience appears to deliver neither viable life-order nor generous compassion – certainly not by highly visible, nameable acts of intervention.[22]

The tension between the testimony and the countertestimony is never permanently resolved until it is resolved, as we shall see, in the cross. For Israel it was an ongoing tension, for they refused to be other than honest about the enigmatic nature of their experience. As well as seeing the faithful hand of God at work on their behalf, 'Israel unflinchingly saw and affirmed that *life as it comes, along with joys, is beset by hurt,* betrayal, loneliness, disease, threat, anxiety, bewilderment, anger, hatred and anguish.'[23] It is this same ambiguity to which the psalmist, from his individual viewpoint, gives expression.

3. The transformation he knows (22:22–31)

What it is that causes the psalmist to change so dramatically from lament to praise, to move from countertestimony to core testimony, we

---

[20] The verbs Brueggemann has in mind are to 'create', 'give life', 'deliver', 'redeem', 'save', 'bring out', etc.

[21] Brueggemann, *Theology*, p. 400.

[22] Ibid., p. 318.

[23] Brueggemann, *Psalms*, pp. 67–68 (italics his). He goes on to suggest: 'The study of the lament may suggest a corrective to the euphoric, celebrative notions of faith that romantically pretend that life is sweetness and joy, even delight. It may be suggested that the one-sided liturgical renewal of today has, in effect, driven the hurtful side of experience either into obscure corners of faith practice or completely out of Christian worship into various forms of psychotherapy and growth groups.'

are not told. But the shift is startling. In verses 19–21 he turns the corner, and from then on he is consumed not by his problems but by God's honour. It may just be that his affirmations of trust in God have led him to see things in a new perspective. But it is likely that there has been some active intervention by God that brought relief. Whatever the cause, he now confidently asserts his faith in God as the God who hears and answers the cries of the suffering for help. He not only testifies to the goodness of God in the worshipping community, but spurs them on to augment their own praise and thanksgiving.

a. The vow he keeps (22:22–26)

At some time during his suffering he must have vowed that if he recovered he would offer a voluntary sacrifice as an act of thanksgiving.[24] Now he is delivering on his promise. Such occasions often lasted two days, and although they were very personal in nature, they would be shared not only with the wider family but with servants and other people in need (26).[25] It would have been a joyful celebration that included toasting his guests in the words *may your hearts live for ever!* (26), as well as a sacrifice to the Lord.[26]

The thanksgiving begins very personally: *I will declare your name ... I will praise you* (22). It catches up others in its train: *You who fear the LORD, praise him!* (22). It reaches its high point as it focuses on God (24). Great party and warm fellowship though it was, the camaraderie they experienced was not permitted to crowd God out, as so often happens in contemporary, people-centred 'worship celebrations'. The reason for the thanksgiving was that God had totally reversed the psalmist's predicament, as the contrast between verse 2 and verse 24 shows. He had thought God had written him off, but now he knows that God never despised him. He had thought God had forsaken him, but now he knows that he never did anything of the sort. He had thought God was not listening, but now he realizes that his cry has been heard.[27] God has proved himself worthy of trust in the dark, and now deserves reverent submission in the light.

The psalmist's approach to God at the end of the psalm is altogether different from his approach at the beginning. There is an emphasis here on honouring God and revering him (23), rather than on holding him to account. It reminds one of Job's parallel experience of suffering. For when Job emerged from his long, dark night of the soul, he came out with a deeper understanding of God and a more, not less, profound reverence for him. Job confessed that he had muttered his lament in

---

[24] Lev. 7:16.
[25] Kidner, *Psalms 1 – 72*, p. 108.
[26] Craigie, p. 201.
[27] Ibid.

ignorant haste, and consequently he humbly submitted himself to God again, with a new sense of his own unworthiness.

Then Job replied to the LORD:

'I know that you can do all things;
  no plan of yours can be thwarted.
You asked, "Who is this that obscures my counsel
    without knowledge?"
  Surely I spoke of things I did not understand,
  things too wonderful for me to know.

'You said, "Listen now, and I will speak;
  I will question you,
  and you shall answer me."
My ears had heard of you
  but now my eyes have seen you.
Therefore I despise myself
  and repent in dust and ashes.'[28]

So, in the worshipping community, the erstwhile sufferer gives voice to his thanksgiving and instructs his fellow-worshippers in the deeper arts of praise. But it does not end there.

b. The vision he sees (22:27–31)

This joyful banquet, where the needs of the poor are fully met (26), prompts the psalmist to look into the future and capture a vision of a time when all will worship the Lord. His vision extends geographically out from Jerusalem to *the ends of the earth*, and encompasses all nations and social classes in its embrace (27, 29). It extends chronologically from the immediate present to future generations *yet unborn* (30–31). He envisages a future when *all the ends of the earth*, to the furthest reaches of space and time, will submit to the dominion of the Lord and he will reign all in all.

What began as a personal song of praise, then, moves out in ever-increasing circles until the whole world is caught up in worship. 'The voice of the one', writes Patrick Miller, 'becomes a choir of many.'[29] It is a far-sighted vision, amplified later by Paul, who looked forward to the day when every knee in the universe would bow in recognition and every tongue confess that 'Jesus Christ is Lord'.[30]

[28] Job 42:1–6.
[29] P. D. Miller, *They Cried to the Lord: The Form and Theology of Biblical Prayer* (Fortress, 1994), p. 192.
[30] Phil. 2:10–11.

4. The template he created

Psalm 22 served as a template for the crucifixion of Christ. Even those who resist the idea that it was intended as a predictive prophecy of his death[31] (often on the grounds of their more general scepticism about the ability of prophecy to predict) cannot but acknowledge the real points of contact that exist between this psalm and Christ's passion. Even if there is nothing more to it than this, they recognize that Jesus was a righteous person who endured extreme suffering, holding on to his faith as he bore it, just like the narrator in Psalm 22. But it does seem a remarkably apt portrayal of the suffering Christ was to experience, and it is remarkably accurate, not just in its general thrust, but in its details, leading many to believe that it is indeed a prophecy of the cross of Jesus.

To say that Jesus fits the template of Psalm 22 is not to say that he deliberately manipulated his situation to fit it. He could not have done so even if he had tried. The specific points of contact, to which we will shortly turn, were beyond his control when he hung on the cross. It is, however, quite possible to say that the New Testament writers saw the fit and interpreted what Jesus said and suffered in the light of it. In doing so, some things about his death which might have been left hazy from other perspectives were illuminated and given greater clarity.[32]

a. Jesus and the silence of God
i. The words of Christ from the cross
As Jesus hung dying on the cross it was to Psalm 22 that his mind turned, perhaps instinctively,[33] to declare his agony and implore for help. Matthew[34] and Mark[35] both record that Jesus cried out, 'My God, my God, why have you forsaken me?' In using these words Jesus identified himself with the suffering psalmist and with Israel as a whole.[36] The God with whom Jesus had enjoyed close intimacy throughout his life, and from whom he had received visible affirmation, now seemed, in the hour of his extreme need, to have deserted him. The agony of Calvary was more than that of physical torture, public humiliation and painful death. It was the torment of separation from God – the God whom he knew, and whom he knew to be powerful, now seemed so very far away. In entering his own 'dark night of the soul', Jesus was one with the many who struggle with severe suffering

[31] Anderson, p. 185.
[32] Mays, p. 106.
[33] Lane, *Mark*, p. 572.
[34] Matt. 27:46.
[35] Mark 15:34.
[36] Craigie, p. 202.

and affliction. The tension they face between, on the one hand, the reality of their knowledge and experience of a good and loving God and, on the other, the reality of the hurt, betrayal, bewilderment and suffering they are undergoing, is the tension he experienced to the full on the cross. More completely than any other person ever will, he entered into the very human experience, not only of suffering, but of the hiddenness and silence of God just when we need him most.

ii. The experience of Christ on the cross

If Jesus identified himself with the suffering psalmist in this way, the Gospel writers make the identification even more clearly. The experiences of the psalmist and of Jesus touch one another at any number of points, as the Gospel writers are keen to highlight.

The hiddenness of God passed no more quickly for Jesus than for the psalmist. It was a real, deep and complex agony that he endured. Unlike those who witnessed the total eclipse of the sun in the summer of 1999, which, after months of hype, was over in a moment, they both experienced a genuine and prolonged sense of darkness. The Gospel writers point out in detail the close connection between their experiences. The psalmist endured the cynical derision of the crowds and had to listen to their insulting taunts (7), just as Jesus did.[37] The mockers scorned the psalmist's trust in God (8), just as they did that of Jesus. Quoting Psalm 22 almost word for word, they cried, 'He trusts in God. Let God rescue him now if he wants him, for he said, "I am the Son of God."'[38]

Three other details are common to both experiences. First, John notes Jesus' thirst on the cross[39] which recalls the psalmist's tongue sticking to the roof of his mouth (15). Secondly, both sufferers have their hands and feet pierced (16), which seems a very appropriate allusion to crucifixion as the form of execution.[40] Thirdly, the dispersal of the victim's garments among his persecutors by the casting of lots, mentioned in the psalm in verse 18, is a remarkably prescient detail on which all the Gospel writers comment.[41]

If anyone fitted the description of a righteous man who struggled with the absence of God as he endured the suffering others inflicted on him and which led him to his death, it was Jesus. The psalm was certainly written about others, but it was supremely written about him. It is a human composition and a divine inspiration. It is a moving

[37] Matt. 27:39; Mark 15:29.
[38] Matt. 27:43.
[39] John 19:28.
[40] Ps. 22:15 is uncertain in the Hebrew, and may be translated: 'like lions they maul my hands and feet', rather than as in NIV. Kidner, *Psalms 1 – 72*, p. 107, sees it on linguistic grounds as an apparent prediction of the cross.
[41] Matt. 27:35; Mark 15:24; Luke 23:34; John 19:23–24.

portrayal of the anguish of suffering, but it is a supreme portrayal of the anguish of Christ's cross.

In it all Jesus gave full vent to his experience of Godforsakenness, and yet, like the psalmist, never let go of God. Derek Kidner sees the cry, not as a lapse of faith or of a broken relationship, but as 'a cry of disorientation as God's familiar protective presence is withdrawn and the enemy closes in'.[42] Whether that takes the terror of the cry seriously enough is a moot point. For, as Maynard Smith claimed, 'the awful cry which startled the onlookers cannot be reconciled with a devotional exercise'.[43] But it is true that the note of trust remained. The God who had apparently deserted Jesus was still his God. The cry of dereliction was a reaching out to God and a cry for help. It is a cry which, both for the psalmist and for the Christ, was eventually answered, if in different ways.

b. Jesus and the deliverance of God

i. Jesus' intention

If we knew what was in Jesus' mind as he uttered his cry of dereliction, it would be easier to determine what degree of faith in God was inherent in it. In quoting only the first verse of Psalm 22, was he saying all that he intended to say? Was he using the familiar words of the psalm simply to give voice to the pain of rejection, without intending to imply more? Or was he using the opening verse of the psalm to signal his identification with the whole psalm? Was he putting not so much a metaphorical full stop after the saying as a comma, intending us to recall the rest of the psalm?

Our answers to these questions will lead us to very different understandings of his cry. If his intention was to isolate verse 1 from the rest of the psalm, it becomes a cry of despair, albeit tinged with trust. But if he was using this verse as a means of launching us into the rest of the psalm, which ends not with defeat but with deliverance, it becomes a cry of hope, albeit tinged with agony. It then becomes a sign that he knew that his God would in the end step in and vindicate him.

Unfortunately, the evidence that might help us to come down on one side or the other is mixed. James Mays, for example, adopts the second, more traditional view, and believes that 'it is not just the opening words that are involved. Citing the first words of a text was, in the tradition of the time, a way of identifying the entire passage.'[44] John Reumann, by contrast, speaks for many when he says that though Jesus' words might have become commonly used in this way, we lack the

---

[42] Kidner, *Psalms 1 – 72*, p. 106.
[43] Quoted in Morris, *Cross of Jesus*, p. 71.
[44] Mays, p. 105.

evidence to prove that this is how the Jews of Jesus' day used Scripture.[45] Leon Morris thinks that 'we cannot assume that his use of the opening words implies that he was reciting the whole', and argues that if Jesus had wanted to include the more comforting words of the latter part of the psalm, 'it is fair to ask why he did not use them'.[46]

We cannot be sure what was in the mind of Christ. But we can be sure what was in the mind of God. For whether or not Jesus intended us to hear him say, at this particular time,[47] that he would go through death to deliverance, that was exactly what God had planned.

ii. Jesus' experience
Whatever Jesus intended, the identification of his experience with that of the psalmist does not end with the lament section of the psalm. Their experiences touch one another as much in the latter part of the psalm as in the first. Both experience the deliverance of God. Both the psalmist and Jesus come through their times of suffering and are restored to full life and health. But there is a difference we should note. As Peter Craigie says, 'The psalm concludes with praise because the sufferer escaped death; Jesus died.' The psalmist is delivered *from* death, whereas Jesus is delivered *through* death.[48] The deliverance experienced by Jesus, then, was total. For the psalmist, death was merely postponed. One day it would come knocking on his door again. For the Christ, death was defeated. It could never return to knock on his door.

When fulfilled through the resurrection of Jesus, the testimony of the psalmist in verse 22 takes on an altogether different complexion. What was merely a hint about the resurrection becomes a reality in Christ. What the psalmist could only strive towards and see dimly by faith, the Christian believer can see with greater clarity. The death and resurrection of Christ provide us with a much firmer basis on which to build the eschatological vision with which the psalm ends than the writer could have conceived. The cross and the resurrection are proof that God is still the God of the exodus, that he still rescues from enemies, delivers from wild beasts, comes quickly to help, and saves his people from death. For 'having disarmed the powers and authorities, [Christ] made a public example of them, triumphing over them by the cross'.[49]

It is the cross that finally resolves the tension between Israel's testimony and countertestimony (to use Brueggemann's terminology).

[45] J. H. Reumann, 'Psalm 22 at the cross', *Int* 28 (1974), pp. 48–49.
[46] Morris, *Cross of Jesus*, p. 71.
[47] On other occasions Jesus is certainly confident of his vindication, so it could have been in his mind: e.g. Mark 8:31; 9:31; 10:34; John 2:19.
[48] Craigie, p. 203.
[49] Col. 2:15.

For on the cross God's chosen one, his only Son, entered into the negative experience of Israel's countertestimony to the full. He suffered the full impact of the hiddenness of God. But in his resurrection he entered into and established Israel's positive testimony, once and for all. It was their testimony that was to have the final say. Having drunk the bitter cup of countertestimony to its dregs, he replenished it with the new wine of God's deliverance. Our experience may still sometimes lead us into the paths of hiddenness and uncertainty about God. But his cross and resurrection give us the final answer, and tell us that if we trust in God we shall not be disappointed (5).

In his moving account of his struggle with terminal cancer David Watson writes at one point:

> William Temple once put it like this: 'There cannot be a God of love,' men say, 'because if there was, and he looked upon the world, his heart would break.' The Church points to the Cross and says, 'It did break.' 'It is God who made the world,' men say. 'It is he who should bear the load.' The Church points to the Cross and says, 'He did bear it.' Although Christ has suffered once for all on the cross for our sins, he still today weeps with those who weep, he feels our pain and enters into our sorrows with his compassionate love.[50]

Psalm 22 anticipates the cross of Christ at exactly this point. Christ did indeed enter into our sorrows with his compassionate love. But the psalm goes beyond it too. It suggests to us that beyond the cross there is a resurrection. When we see it fulfilled in the passion and resurrection of Jesus, it is as if all the pieces of the jigsaw fit into place and at last make sense. It is through his entering into our suffering and his rising from the dead that all enemies, including death itself, are overcome. What God wrought in the life of this one individual establishes 'the universal, comprehensive, everlasting kingdom of God'.[51] So the cross and resurrection are 'a summons to the world (in the most inclusive sense of that term) to believe in the reign of the Lord'.[52] We are invited to join the community of praise whose ranks will go on swelling until *all ... bow down before him* and acknowledge that *dominion belongs to the LORD and he rules over the nations* (27–28).

James Mays draws attention to the way many churches use this psalm during Holy Week as a clue to how we are to understand it. The role we are given, he says, is the role of the listener. 'We do not identify,' he writes, 'either as individuals or community, with the person who prays and praises, as in the use of many other psalms.' Why

[50] Watson, *Fear No Evil*, p. 136.
[51] Mays. p. 113.
[52] Ibid., p. 115.

not? Because 'that role is claimed for and explicated by Jesus alone'.[53] It is not that we cannot identify with the suffering of the psalmist. Indeed we can. And many have found it helpful in their own struggles to use his words to express the ambiguities of faith and to work towards their resolution in praise. But Jesus alone perfectly fits the words and completely fulfils their meaning. In his willingness to be forsaken by God, he reversed the power of suffering and death and released a chorus of praise which will reach its grand crescendo when 'the earth will be filled with the knowledge of the glory of the LORD, as the waters cover the sea'.[54]

[53] Ibid., p. 113.
[54] Hab. 2:14.

Isaiah 52:13 – 53:12
5. Man of sorrows

When an important treasury official from Ethiopia, who was reading Isaiah 53 as he returned home from a religious festival in Jerusalem, asked Philip the evangelist to explain to him who the prophet was talking about, Philip had no hesitation in applying Isaiah's words to the good news about Jesus.[1] By this time it was commonly accepted among the early Christians that this passage in Isaiah's prophecy spoke about him. Their interpretation was not a belated discovery, foisted on the ancient prophet long after Christ's death, but went back to the understanding Christ himself held and taught. He saw himself as fulfilling the role of Isaiah's suffering servant.

Isaiah's portrait gives us the richest understanding of the work of Christ to be found in the Old Testament. Even within its own context, Isaiah stretches the boundaries of understanding about the ways of God. Of the four servant songs,[2] this final one is more poignant than the others and has an urgency and passion about it that exceed the others.[3] But its chief characteristic is that it says something daringly new about God. Though the work of the servant is modelled on the familiar sacrifices of the Day of Atonement and the guilt offering,[4] it far surpasses anything we see in them. Here the sacrifice offered is a human being. And though human sacrifices were known and offered by Israel's neighbours, they were forbidden in Israel itself.[5] Abraham had been prevented from offering Isaac, though he had gone to do so,[6] and Moses' offer to die in the place of the sinful children of Israel was refused by God.[7] Here, then, is an unheard-of innovation.[8]

---

[1] Acts 8:32–35.
[2] Is. 42:1–4; 49:1–6; 50:4–9; 52:13 – 53:12.
[3] P. D. Hanson, p. 158.
[4] Lev. 5:14 – 6:7; 7:1–10; 16:1–34.
[5] Goldingay, *God's Prophet*, pp. 147–148.
[6] Gen. 22.
[7] Exod. 32:30–33.
[8] Whybray calls it 'an unheard of and inexplicable innovation ... contrary to the principles of justice constantly reiterated in the OT' (p. 171). 'Unheard of', yes;

This song takes us to the heart of the human problem and the heart of the divine mind. It offers a bold and daring answer to the question, 'How is God going to deal with sin and, without detriment to his own righteous character, break the pattern of sin and punishment and replace it with forgiveness and compassion?' His answer 'revolves around the servant of the Lord whose surrender to God's will was so total that he took the consequences of the sin of the community upon himself, even though he was innocent of any wrongdoing'.[9] It is an audacious approach, not only because the answer involves the unprecedented sacrifice of a human being, but because the solution it proposes involves a 'perversion of justice', since the human being is innocent of any transgression.[10] It tells us something of God's passionate commitment to his people, and of his willingness to take whatever steps were necessary to achieve the solution the sacrificial system had failed to provide and to pay whatever it cost to do so himself.

Here, then, is one of the peaks of the Old Testament's revelation of God. From its summit, we can look across the intervening centuries and see the distant coming of Christ. From our vantage point, we obtain a clear view of his work on the far-off summit of Calvary and gain a definitive perspective on its meaning.

Of course, the prophecy was not just written about the work of Christ. Prophecy functions like the coming in of the tide. Waves build and crash until the tide reaches its high point and begins to ebb. In a similar way, prophecy is often capable of multiple fulfilment. It is fulfilled progressively until it is fulfilled definitively – the high tide – with the coming of Christ.[11] Scholars differ over the original setting of this song, but many relate it to the suffering borne by Israel in the period of the Babylonian exile.[12] Such suffering, they argue, had a purpose. It was redemptive, and, when sin had been paid for (40:1–2), it led to their deliverance and restoration. This, however, ignores the emphasis on the sinlessness of the sufferer.

Just who is the suffering servant? Some identify him with the nation of Israel, while others identify him with Jeremiah, with the writer of Isaiah 53 or with one of the other prophets or key figures of salvation history.[13] Some opt for a combination of these. The image is fluid, spoken of sometimes as a collective plural and sometimes as an indi-

---

'inexplicable', surely not. There were hints which anticipated such a development, as in the passages quoted above, even if as yet a human sacrifice had not been accepted.

[9] P. D. Hanson, pp. 156–157.

[10] Ibid., p. 158.

[11] See Greidanus, pp. 242–244.

[12] Watts, pp. 219–221.

[13] For an authoritative, if dated, survey, see North, *Suffering Servant*.

vidual, and can be made to fit several interpretations. As C. R. North concludes, however: 'We have, then, when we have done our best with the historical interpretations, to deal with a plus, a plus to any one of them taken singly, a plus to any selection of them, a plus even to all of them taken together. That plus is a unique individual who obviously has not yet appeared.'[14]

What is it about the role of the servant that makes him so crucial in the history of salvation, both for Israel and for the church, the new Israel? To that the text gives a detailed answer which, overall, most regard as transparently clear. There are debates about its meaning in parts. It is fond of using pronouns such as 'he', 'they', 'we' and 'I' without any antecedents, leading to some lack of clarity as to who is speaking at various stages. Some even wish to challenge the obvious and literal interpretation that the servant dies as a substitute for others, or even that he dies at all.[15] But their arguments seem like tortuous special pleading and fail to appreciate the allusive nature of the language of poetry. There is no convincing reason for not accepting the traditional view that this song speaks of the shameful and unjust death of a suffering individual through whom justification and life are brought to many. The thrust and depth of the text draw the reader in to perceive the mystery of God's grace at work.

The song is composed of five stanzas. Viewed as three concentric circles, the outer circle contains the introduction (52:13–15) and the conclusion (53:10–12). The next circle in reflects on the life of the suffering servant (53:1–3) and on his death (53:7–9). The central circle, the heart of the song, reflects on the purpose of his mission and meaning of his sacrifice (53:4–6). The song is structured so as to draw our attention in to its centre.

1. The enigma of the servant (52:13–15)

In the overture to the song, themes are introduced that will be picked up again in the conclusion. It gives us a broad view of the one who is the subject of the song, starting, as it were, with the last page of his life before leading us back to the earlier chapters of his biography. It presents to us one whose life is an enigma.

a. His personal dignity (52:13)

We are commanded to look carefully at the servant, who will 'act wisely' (NIV) or 'prosper' (NRSV). The word (śākal) normally means 'to be wise', but may also mean 'to be successful'. Here both seem to be

---

[14] Ibid., p. 214.
[15] Notably Whybray, pp. 171–172, 177.

intended. The one seems to be the outcome of the other, for the person who is successful is usually the person who has acted with wisdom.[16] Either meaning is a remarkable claim to make for this servant, in view of all that is subsequently said of him.

The next claims are even more remarkable. The servant is presented to us as one who, in the future, *will be raised and lifted up and highly exalted.* He is destined to occupy a position of supreme dignity, superior to all others, although none would have guessed it in view of what he was in himself and what he endured in his life. The exalted language suggests that the servant will one day receive 'a share in the dignity of Yahweh himself'.[17] Alec Motyer takes the threefold phrase more specifically – surely with some justice – and sees it as a significant clue to the servant's identity, for it reminds us of the resurrection, ascension and enthronement of Jesus.[18]

b. His shocking appearance (52:14)

The dignity the servant will enjoy in the future stands in marked contrast to the people's response to him earlier. When the writer traces the servant's earlier life he paints a picture of extreme suffering. He was physically so disfigured that people instinctively turned away from him, as we usually do, sadly, when we suddenly come face to face with someone whose features are badly deformed or whose limbs are severely damaged. John Watts believes that the words imply that 'the executed body was mutilated'.[19] It may have been, but whether it was or not, people wondered whether it was a human being whose body they were observing.

The striking contrast between the opening two verses drives us to ask how it was that the servant was to undergo such a massive change in his fortunes. How could he who had been so blemished and hurt in his life become so highly exalted after his death?

c. His startling effect (52:15)

Our surprise is shared by others. Nations and kings are driven to silence as they try to work out the enigma. How can it be that this person who was written off and treated with such rancour can rise to a height of power and authority that far exceeds theirs? Their cleverest advisors are unable to explain it, since it is beyond human wisdom to understand what was taking place. Only when the matter is revealed by God can it be understood.

This verse contains one of the many conundrums in the text. Will

[16] Ibid., p. 169.
[17] D. R. Jones, quoted in Goldingay, *God's Prophet,* p. 151.
[18] Motyer, *Prophecy of Isaiah,* p. 424; idem, *Isaiah,* p. 332.
[19] Watts, p. 230.

this disfigured yet transformed servant *sprinkle* (NIV) the nations and kings, or will he 'startle' (NRSV) them? 'Sprinkle' is certainly the usual way to translate the Hebrew word (*nāzâ*), and there should be good grounds for rejecting it before we do so. Many reject it because the Septuagint speaks of many being 'astonished' at the servant, and they believe 'startle' fits the context better.[20] 'Sprinkle' is used in connection with the manipulation of blood in religious sacrifices. It is the vocabulary of purification, and leads us to see the work of the servant as that of a priest, cleansing sinful people. If this is the correct interpretation, then, as Barry Webb says, 'The one the people regarded as unclean ... will turn out to be the one who cleanses others. It is a paradox so astounding that it will dry up every accusation and cause every mouth to be stopped.'[21] One way or another, the life of the servant is enigmatic in the extreme.

2. The rejection of the servant (53:1-3)

After the overture, the writer takes us back from the servant's future success to consider his past rejection: one side of the coin of paradox.

a. Divine revelation (53:1)

The opening lines of this stanza link back to the last lines of the previous one. They reinforce the perception that the message about the servant is quite unheard-of and beyond human understanding. What was happening in the servant's suffering was that *the arm of the LORD* was being made known. His strength and power were at work. But who would have guessed it? His work could not be judged by any of the normal measurements of power. It was not speaking a language they were used to speaking. It was not valued in a currency they were used to handling. People's minds are so distorted by sin that they would never come to the right conclusions about the servant except by divine revelation.

As Alec Motyer comments:

> ... to see the Servant and find *no beauty* in him (2cd) reveals the bankruptcy of the human emotions; to be one with those who despise and reject him (3ac) exposes the misguidedness of the human will; to appraise him and conclude that he is nothing condemns our minds as corrupted by, and participants in, our sinfulness. Thus every aspect of human nature is inadequate; every avenue along which, by nature, we might arrive at the truth and

---

[20] For opposite sides see Whybray, p. 170, and Motyer, *Prophecy of Isaiah*, pp. 425–426.

[21] Webb, p. 210.

respond to God is closed. Nothing but divine revelation can make the Servant known to us and draw us to him.[22]

b. Human reflection (53:2)

The people looked at the servant and saw a wasted human person rather than God's power at work. His lamentable state gave them a number of reasons for writing him off. Using stock language of the day, Isaiah lists them. He had an unpromising beginning; *he was a root out of dry ground*. It was a miracle that he grew up at all, since he lacked the vital nutriments he needed to develop healthily. To his unpromising beginning they added his unimpressive appearance. They applied the usual tests. Was he good-looking (*beauty*)? Did he have an impressive personality (*majesty*)? What overall impression did he make (*appearance*)? He seemed to fail on all counts.[23] He may have been *a tender plant* from God's perspective, but there was nothing at all impressive about him from a human perspective. 'The more he grew the less impressive he became.'[24]

c. Total rejection (53:3)

His unimpressive appearance led to his social ostracism and eventually to his outright rejection. It was not simply that he withered away because of some feeble constitution or because he received no recognition and encouragement from others. It was more than that. They deliberately rejected him and caused his suffering by their conscious repudiation of him. To say that *we esteemed him not* is to use the language of accounting. When they reckoned up the value of his life, they considered him worthless. His life was reckoned to contribute nothing to the balance sheet of humanity.

The psychologist Abraham Maslow has taught us that human beings have a hierarchy of needs. Once the physical needs for air, food and water are satisfied, people look for the fulfilment of four levels of psychological need: namely, for safety; love and belonging; esteem and feelings of worth; and self-actualization.[25] In Maslow's terms, all the psychological essentials of life were withdrawn from this 'man of sorrows'. He was anything but safe; he was an isolated person who was refused love; he received no esteem from others; and he walked the path of self-destruction rather than of self-fulfilment. The viability of his life was highly questionable, and he was left exposed and vulnerable without out a shred of protection amid intense suffering.

[22] Motyer, *Prophecy of Isaiah*, p. 429.
[23] Motyer, *Isaiah*, p. 333.
[24] Webb, p. 211.
[25] A. H. Maslow, *Motivation and Personality* (1954; Harper and Row, 1987), pp. 15–31.

3. The mission of the servant (53:4–7)

What brought about this situation? What lay behind it? Is there any deeper meaning to be found in the rejection and suffering of this man of sorrows? The answer is an emphatic 'Yes'. The next stanza in the song develops the explanation. His suffering and death have a significance unparalleled by any ordinary suffering and death. It is one in which 'he', God and 'we' all have our parts to play, and it is in the roles we play that the meaning of his death becomes apparent.

a. Their view (53:4)

Yet we considered him stricken by God, smitten by him and afflicted. And they were right, but not in the way they thought. The *we* here are probably the Jewish onlookers who observed the life of the original suffering servant and misinterpreted it. But later, as the song progresses, it becomes apparent that all of us take our stand in the crowd of spectators along with them.

When they tried to make sense of this wasted life of the servant, they came to the conclusion that God was punishing this man for sin. His suffering was actively caused by God, and his pain deliberately inflicted by the Almighty. Since many Jews assumed a connection between sin and suffering, they assumed that the servant had done something dreadfully wrong to merit God's opprobrium to this extent. He had obviously deserved what God was meting out to him. But their view of him was a dangerous half-truth. The true half was that God was involved: God was the active agent in the suffering. The untrue half was that this man had done something to deserve punishment from God.

b. God's purpose (53:4–5)

Repugnant though it may be to think in these terms today, the song attributes the affliction of the servant to God. His suffering was not the outworking of some impersonal, inevitable consequence of sin; still less the result of some unfortunate series of mistakes. It was inflicted by God. Verse 10 returns to the theme, putting it in stark, even shocking, terms: *Yet it was the LORD's will to crush him and cause him to suffer.* Why should a righteous God engineer such an unjust and horrifying act?

The rest of verse 4 tells us that in being *smitten* by God, and *afflicted*, the servant *took up our infirmities and carried our sorrows*. The language comes right out of the sacrificial experience of Israel and, in particular, from their practices on the Day of Atonement. Here, as there, the scapegoat victim is loaded down with the misfortunes, sins and failures of the people and, once atonement has been made through the offering of a substitutionary sacrifice, deals with them by carrying them away into the wilderness, so that they trouble the people no more.

Just what is it that this scapegoat removes? The burden the servant bears is the burden of pain and of sickness, according to the vocabulary of verses 3 and 4.[26] The word *stricken* is used sixty times in Leviticus 13 – 14 to describe the infliction of the 'blow' of leprosy.[27] The choice of these particular words suggests that the full breadth of the human problem is being dealt with here. The servant's suffering deals not only with our deliberate rebellion against God but with all that blights our lives: physical, moral and spiritual.

Some strive to maintain that the image here is not that of substitution but rather that of identification: the servant identifies with Israel in their suffering, or even just exchanges their suffering for his.[28] But the emphatic nature of the interplay between *he* and *our* in these verses suggests that substitution, already well known in Israel's worship, is in mind. As Claus Westermann says, substitution is not new. 'But the thing that was new and revolutionary for the present speakers was the fact that in this case suffering which gave power to be a substitute and to atone was found residing in a quite ordinary, feeble and incon- siderable person ...'[29]

Others argue that the traditional understanding of neither expiation (that is, of making amends for our sin) nor propitiation (that is, of removing God's wrath), as an objective act, is to be found in these verses. Rather, they say, the emphasis lies not in what the servant accomplished by his action in relation to sin or to a holy God, but in what he accomplished in changing the minds of the onlookers. Commenting on Isaiah 53 from the perspective of its fulfilment in Christ, Paul Fiddes states this position with conviction:

> ... the sacrifice of Christ *enables* and *creates* our gift-offerings and communion-offerings. Since the offering of ourselves to God and to others is the denial of sin, the overcoming of an attitude of self- centredness and rebellion against God, then we can call the offering of Christ which produces this effect a 'sin-offering'. In this sense the sacrificial death of Christ expiates sin; it expiates sin by changing sinners.
>
> Thus, if the cross of Christ has power to turn the sinner towards good, we may truly say that it 'wipes away' sin.
>
> In fact the Song of the Suffering Servant *shows* us the power of sacrifice to transform other human lives when it is made in a person rather than in animals, fruit or cereal ... If we enter imaginatively into the scene which the song portrays we find a drama of expiation,

[26] Sawyer, p. 146.
[27] Motyer, *Prophecy of Isaiah*, p. 430.
[28] Whybray, p. 175.
[29] Westermann, *Isaiah*, p. 263.

in which the suffering of the servant brings other people to a realisation of their own state, and to a healing repentance.[30]

True enough, the element of repentance is to be found here. The onlookers did discover that they had been mistaken about the servant. They confessed their error and revised their opinion about him (52:13 – 53:3). His action would have brought them to their senses, enough for them to see the folly of their ways and that they were the ones straying from God (6). But to conclude that the full extent of God's purpose was to bring sinners to repentance by influencing them through the example of the servant is grossly deficient. It does no justice to the totality of the sacrificial system, which included not only acts of thanksgiving, commitment and communion, but acts of propitiation as well. It disregards the objective accomplishments of the sin offering and the rituals of the Day of Atonement. It puts human beings at the centre of the transaction, rather than God. And it makes God guilty of a much greater injustice than the one of which he is usually accused – that of punishing a substitute in place of the real culprits. Would God really resort to such measures and inflict such suffering on a righteous individual merely to persuade people to revise their attitudes? Surely not. Something greater than that must have been taking place through the suffering of the servant if we are to account for its horror. Sinners were being justified (12), not just influenced. Sin was being disposed of by a gracious act of God, not just renounced by its perpetrators. And God's righteous character was being appeased; it was not just that people's sinful attitudes were being transformed so that they might do better.

Here is God's merciful design for dealing with our sins and our sicknesses and for propitiating himself. He lays the burden and guilt of all our ills on the suffering servant, who was *pierced for our transgressions* and *crushed for our iniquities* (5). Like the scapegoat on the Day of Atonement, which carried 'on itself all their sins to a solitary place',[31] this despised and rejected, stricken and smitten, pierced and crushed servant bears them all away.

c. His role (53:4–5)

The role of the servant was to suffer as a substitute and hence to carry away sin. It was a demanding role that cost him everything. He was pierced, as Rahab was when the 'arm of the LORD' dealt the monster her death blow.[32] He was crushed, as people are crushed when trampled to death. Nothing remained of his life. He was wounded and left with

[30] Fiddes, pp. 79–80.
[31] Lev. 16:22.
[32] Motyer, *Isaiah*, p. 335; Is. 51:9.

open lacerations to which no-one attended. There was nothing pleasant about the role he was called upon to play.

And yet it was a role he undertook willingly and without complaint (7). 'The Servant', Paul Hanson comments, 'did not submit to affliction through pathetic resignation but as a bold choice to participate with God in an act aimed at breaking the stronghold that sin had maintained for countless ages over the human family.'[33]

The outcome of his complete surrender to the will of God is the most rewarding result conceivable. For by taking the full brunt of God's punishment for sin on himself, he brought us peace. And by his bearing the suffering for others, they are healed.

d. Our part (53:6)

It is not possible to leave the meaning of verse 6 trapped in history. Whoever the *we* were originally, it surely now broadens in its embrace and becomes inclusive of us all. What is the part we play in the intense drama of suffering? All we can contribute is our sin, the cause of the Servant's misfortune. *We all ... have gone astray, each of us has turned to our own way; and the LORD has laid on him the iniquity of us all.* Whether we have merely meandered from the path or have deliberately chosen a wrong direction, the death of this suffering servant will bring us back, enabling us to change direction and to be released from sin. In him our sinful state finds forgiveness, our alienation from God is overcome and our broken personhood finds healing.

4. The death of the servant (53:7–9)

The next stanza concentrates on the death of the servant, and in so doing develops some of the ground already covered concerning its purpose and meaning.

a. His submission was voluntary (53:7)

The writer is struck by the fact that the victim was unprotesting as he went on his way to death. He therefore informs us twice that, when unjustly accused, *he did not open his mouth.* That, as George Adam Smith remarked, is something absolutely new. 'In the Old Testament the sufferer is always either confessing his guilt to God, or, when he feels no guilt, challenging God in argument.' It makes us ask, 'Why was this Servant the unique and solitary instance of silence under suffering?'[34]

The answer must be that the servant voluntarily chose to let the tragedy be played out as already decided. It was a conscious choice on

---

[33] P. D. Hanson, p. 159.
[34] Quoted in Goldingay, *God's Prophet*, pp. 145–146.

his part, a deliberately selected option. He 'does nothing and says nothing but lets everything happen to him'[35] by his own resolution.

The voluntary nature of his death distinguishes it from all Israel's animal sacrifices offered up to this point. The victims selected for slaughter had had no choice in the matter. Their complaints would not have been heard or understood by their executioners, even if they could have expressed them. The animals were incapable of understanding what was going on. For all they knew, they might as well have been on their way to new pasture, or to shearing, as to death. Their calmness, if such it was, was the calmness of ignorance rather than of control. But here was a human being in full possession of all his faculties, who knew what the outcome was going to be, yet who permitted others to victimize him and hound him to death.

As Alec Motyer (whose insights are drawn on here) mentions, there is something terribly significant about this aspect of the servant's suffering. The earlier sacrifices of Israel were good as far as they went, but suffered one 'fatal flaw': '... sin involves the will. But this is precisely the point at which animals can only picture the substitute we require and cannot actually be that substitute: they have no consciousness of what is afoot nor of any deliberate, personal, self-submissive consent to it. Ultimately only a Person can substitute for people.'[36] Here was a sacrifice that surpassed the earlier guilt or atonement offerings; a sacrifice that exposed the fatal flaw and overcame it in one stroke.[37] Rams, sheep, goats and bulls had only approximated to our condition. They could do no more than that. But here was a substitute that exactly fitted our need.

b. His death was violent (53:8)

Although some question it, 'everything in this chapter points to his having died a violent death'.[38] His execution was the result of *oppression*. In other words, it was a miscarriage of justice. In being subjected to an unjust trial, in which no defence was offered on his behalf, his civil rights were violated – and not merely his civil rights, but his divinely decreed rights, for God had commanded that all should be able to find justice in the courts, and here his word was blatantly being disregarded.

Having been tried, he was now led in procession from the court to execution. It was a lonely walk. He went to death enduring total isolation, as the line *And who can speak of his descendants?* indicates. That sentence is one of the many difficult phrases in this verse. It may mean that his life was cut short, his line came to an end and his family

[35] Clines, quoted in Motyer, *Prophecy of Isaiah*, p. 432.
[36] Motyer, *Isaiah*, p. 336.
[37] Motyer, *Prophecy of Isaiah*, p. 433.
[38] North, *Second Isaiah*, p. 241.

was cut dead. He was a childless person without any future, and before long no-one would remember him. But David Clines offers this translation: 'And against his generation who protested?'[39] In other words, no-one was there to stand up for him and protest his innocence. Either translation yields the same meaning. Here was one who died alone.

The verbs in the rest of the verse, *cut off* and *stricken*, imply a violent and awful death. His death was extraordinary as much for the manner of it as for what led to it.

c. His burial was ambivalent (53:9)

Israelites would normally anticipate being buried in their family grave so that they would be reunited with their ancestors. But even this was denied the servant, who, like any common criminal, was *assigned a grave with the wicked*. The loss of this privilege adds one last indignity to the sadness of the story.[40]

But here the tale takes a curious twist, for although he was predictably assigned a grave with the wicked, the song immediately goes on to add *and with the rich in his death*. How can both be true? Do they not contradict each other? The contradiction appears so plain to many that they have sought to remove it by amending the text. Some, such as David Clines, translate it as 'He was assigned a grave with the wicked, a burial place with criminals', not because, as he admits, the word 'criminals' is a satisfactory translation of the Hebrew, but simply because some parallel to the word *wicked* (in the first line) seems necessary.[41] The words 'evildoers', 'rabble' and 'demons' have all been suggested, but they seem forced. Other scholars resolve the tension in a different way. They accept that the word means 'rich', but assume that any rich person would have gained his wealth by wrongdoing, so the phrase is simply another way of saying that he was buried among the wicked.

It is admittedly a difficult statement, and there is no certainty as to its meaning. But why are we so keen to amend the text? Is it really impossible that it is hinting at the burial that the ultimate suffering servant would one day receive in the garden of a rich disciple called Joseph of Arimathea?[42] Certainly Matthew thought not. The prophet would not have clearly foreseen the burial of Christ, and would have been speaking of a mystery he could not himself unravel. But in the ambiguity of this verse there seems to be a suggestion that, though wicked men were involved in putting the servant to death, and though

[39] Clines, p. 18.
[40] Goldingay, *God's Prophet*, p. 143.
[41] Clines, pp. 19–20.
[42] Matt. 27:57.

the death of a common criminal would be expected to result in burial on the scrap heap among the corpses of others reprobates, somehow that is not the scenario. Somehow, this man is buried in an unexpected place. And, at last, jolting us out of the gloom of the chapter, a chink of light breaks in.

5. The deliverance of the servant (53:10–12)

A glimmer of light has dawned and, in the final stanza, goes on growing into the full light of day. In the song's finale the writer both recapitulates familiar themes, bringing them all together to a coherent conclusion, and introduces some new elements that bring his music to a climax. Joy and thanksgiving enter the song where, until now, all has been gloom and doom. The writer reaches his conclusion by reminding us of the hand of God in the suffering, informing us of the outcome for the servant, and summarizing for us the meaning of his suffering.

a. The servant fulfils the will of God (53:10)

None of this happened by the design of human beings, even if, to the superficial glance, they were the ones who brought it about. The servant suffered because of the will of the Lord. He planned it in order to provide a new and more satisfactory sacrifice that would deal with sin once and for all. In executing his plan, he enjoyed the willing co-operation of his servant, who voluntarily surrendered his life to bear sins that were not his own.

If the earlier allusions to sacrifice had been to the Day of Atonement, the writer now states explicitly that the life of the suffering servant was sacrificed as a guilt offering. This offering involved both restitution and atonement. Offered for deliberate sin, it was the means by which the offender would get right with God. The rubric for the sacrifice makes it plain that it was the Lord who had been offended and needed to be propitiated, even when the sin was self-evidently against one's neighbour.[43] The sin was expiated by the offering of a blood sacrifice as well as by the offer of recompense. The suffering servant is 'a new kind of guilt offering that will utterly surpass anything that has gone before',[44] because never before has the sacrifice been that of a perfect human being.

b. The servant is vindicated by God (53:10–11)

We now learn that the servant, having offered his life in such a fashion, and having faced the prospect of being not only *cut off from the land of the living* personally, but of being cut off without any possibility of

---

[43] Lev. 6:1–7.
[44] Webb, p. 213.

future offspring to perpetuate his name, in fact experienced a massive reversal of fortunes.

He who had no *descendants* (8) *will see his offspring* (10). He who was *cut off* in the midst of life (8) will now *prolong his days* (10). He who was *stricken* (8) will now *prosper* (10). He who was dead (9) will come alive (11). He who was unjustly condemned (9) will *be satisfied* (11). He who *was despised and rejected* (3) will become the centre of a great throng (11–12), and he who was a helpless victim (7) will become a triumphant victor (12). This unanticipated and massive reversal of his situation is what causes the consternation of the *kings* and *nations* with which the song began. None of them would have foreseen that this is how the story would end.

The previous stanza had left the question of his vindication a little ambiguous. Perhaps he was buried in a rich man's grave, and, if so, perhaps this gave the first intimation that God might vindicate him. But now the writer leaves us in no doubt. Following death, the servant's future is glorious, proving beyond doubt that God had accepted his sacrifice and that it had done its work.

c. The servant meets the needs of the people (53:11)

From the vindication of the servant, Isaiah's thought turns to its effect on the people. *By his knowledge my righteous servant will justify many, and he will bear their iniquities.* At first sight the reference to the servant's knowledge seems odd. But in the context of Old Testament thought, it is not as strange as it appears. His knowledge was not academic learning but the personal knowledge that grows in relationships. It is his knowledge of God and his ways that has led him to act sacrificially and thereby to *justify many*. The wise, knowledgeable ones, as Daniel noted, are those who have a positive effect on others. They are the ones who resist evil, take positive action and instruct others.[45]

The wise one of 52:13 is *my righteous servant*, and this is what enables him, through the offering of himself, to *justify many*. This phrase, a construction unique in the Old Testament, means that he will 'provide righteousness for' or 'bring righteousness to' many.[46] His own righteousness, then, is exchanged for their unrighteousness. He bears the unrighteousness of many and transfers his righteousness to them.

All that people need, they find in this servant. He removes their guilt by offering an unprecedented guilt offering. What they could never be in themselves – that is, a perfect sacrifice – he is. He identifies with them in their suffering. But, more than that, he bears their sins and sorrows away. He suffers to the very core of his being; it was a suffering

[45] Dan. 11:32–33.
[46] Motyer, *Prophecy of Isaiah*, pp. 441–442.

of his soul, not just in thought but in reality. And so he makes an unrighteous people righteous.

Alec Motyer's summary is worth quoting in full:

> Isaiah 53:11 is one of the fullest statements of atonement theology ever penned. (i) The Servant knows the needs to be met and what must be done. (ii) As 'the righteous one, my servant', he is both fully acceptable to the God our sins have offended and has been appointed by him to the task. (iii) As righteous, he is free from every contagion of our sin. (iv) He identified himself personally with our sin and need. (v) The emphatic pronoun 'he' underlines his personal commitment to this role. (vi) He accomplished the task fully. Negatively, in the bearing of iniquity; positively, in the provision of righteousness.[47]

d. The servant conquers the enemy, sin (53:12)

The song ends by celebrating the total supremacy of the servant and presenting him as a victorious general returning from the battle. Again, the text is difficult. But the thought seems to be that just as a conquering hero is feted with honours on exhibiting the spoils of his war, so is the servant. He is given *many*,[48] that is, those he has redeemed, as an award for his victory. And he parades the *strong*, who sought to do away with him, as his prisoners to show that they are defeated and that he has conquered all.

Of all the powers that march vanquished in his victory parade, the strongest is sin. Bearing the weight of sin in his sufferings means that he has borne it away for ever. And an oppressed people are set free.

Some time ago in Timisoara, Romania, I stood at the cross erected as a memorial to the victims of those who fell in the revolution that overthrew the tyranny of Ceausescu. It was a moving experience as I and others paid our respects and offered thanks for those who had sacrificed their lives for the cause of liberty. But the sacrifice of the suffering servant goes much deeper than theirs. Here was a totally innocent victim who became not a martyr for a cause but a sacrificial offering before a righteous God, and who became the means by which full salvation could be made available to a sinful and undeserving people.

6. The identity of the servant

Just who was this suffering servant? Given the amount of suffering that has been the lot of the Jews down the centuries, it is not surprising that they have often cast themselves in the role of the suffering servant.

[47] Ibid., p. 442.
[48] NIV mg.

Many see it as their calling to suffer and so somehow to bring redemption to others as a result. Since suffering has been so much a part of Israel's experience, John Goldingay is right to say that 'it is in some ways distasteful for a gentile to refuse to allow her to find herself in this passage'.[49] It must in some measure speak of the people of Israel – even if only a remnant of Israel, as some would suppose.

Others have tried to identify an individual who fits. The suggestions have been numerous, and range from Moses to Zerubbabel via the prophets of Israel (Isaiah, Jeremiah and Ezekiel), the kings of Israel (Uzziah, Hezekiah and Jehoiachin), and even the ruler of the Medo-Persian empire, Cyrus. None fits exactly, and the possibility of identifying the servant with any such individual remains uncertain.

One person alone fits the role of the suffering servant exactly: Jesus of Nazareth. The identification of Jesus with the suffering servant was obvious to the Christian church from the beginning. Jesus himself saw the relevance of the figure for his own work. On one occasion he quoted Isaiah 53:12, 'And he was numbered with the transgressors', and added, 'I tell you that this must be fulfilled in me. Yes, what is written about me is reaching its fulfilment.'[50] On two other occasions he clearly alludes to the passage[51] and, in R. T. France's considered view, there are two further 'possible verbal allusions'.[52] In addition, France claims, there is 'a whole series of predictions of which Isaiah 53 is the most probable source'.[53] After examining the evidence, he concludes 'that Jesus saw his mission as that of the Servant of Yahweh, that he predicted that in fulfilment of the role he must suffer and die, and that he regarded his suffering and death as, like that of the Servant, vicarious and redemptive'.[54]

His followers quickly adopted the servant figure as a framework for understanding the death of Christ. Philip the evangelist had no hesitation in making the connection,[55] as we have mentioned. But it is Peter, the chief apostle, who expounds the connection most fully.[56] Martin Hengel points out that in some ways it was surprising that the early disciples should see such a link, for there is no clear evidence that before their time anyone spoke of the vicarious suffering of the Messiah in connection with Isaiah 53.[57] But the fit was so exact that the comparison could not be avoided. If others approximated to the role, it

[49] Goldingay, God's Prophet, p. 154.
[50] Luke 22:37.
[51] Mark 10:45; 14:24.
[52] Mark 9:12, Matt. 3:15.
[53] France, Jesus and the Old Testament, p. 130.
[54] Ibid., p. 132.
[55] Acts 8:32–33.
[56] See ch. 16 below.
[57] Hengel, The Atonement, p. 59.

is the Jesus of the cross who fulfils it supremely.

The servant continues to take our infirmities upon himself and to carry our diseases. Since this is so, to what extent can we expect him to remove from us our physical sicknesses, as implied by Matthew's application of Isaiah's words to the healing ministry of Christ?[58] In using them like this, Matthew is telling us first of all that 'what heals is Calvary love'.[59] There is no healing apart from the suffering of the servant. Secondly, he is setting before us a full revelation of the extent of Christ's saving work, which will one day culminate in the complete healing of all our sicknesses and infirmities, including our physical ones. But in doing so, he is not promising physical healing now for every sickness or disease. The focus of the total New Testament witness to Christ as the suffering servant is repeatedly on his healing of our *sins*.[60]

John Goldingay summarizes the position in these wise words:

> But as long as we see that our need of forgiveness remains our deepest need, we can go on to rejoice that because Jesus died for us the rest of our ills can be dealt with precisely because sin, atonement and forgiveness are the root matters. We can bring our sins to the cross and leave them there; we can also bring our pains, our griefs and our sorrows to the cross and leave them there too. We need not hang on to them. The Servant suffers both for our rebellion and for our pain and suffering.[61]

Here, then, we have the fullest anticipation of the cross in the Old Testament. It is a vision that moves us one stage away from the animal sacrifices of Israel and one step nearer to the ultimate sacrifice of Calvary. It causes us to stand humbly before the cross of the one who so willingly suffered in our place, and to contemplate his sacrifice with adoring wonder. That he should have done so much for me! It is a beautiful song, blending tragedy and hope in its meditation on the one who is its central figure. As Barry Webb has written, 'Many, many facets of the Servant's character are revealed in this song. He is sage, priest, sacrifice, servant, sufferer, conqueror and intercessor. He is the channel of God's grace to sinners. In him the holiness and mercy of God are perfectly reconciled.'[62]

---

[58] Matt. 8:17.
[59] Smail, 'Cross and Spirit', p. 63.
[60] See France, *Matthew*, pp. 158–159.
[61] Goldingay, *God's Prophet*, p. 156.
[62] Webb, p. 214.

PART 2
THE CROSS EXPERIENCED

Matthew 26:1 – 27:56
6. Crucified Messiah

'It was manifestly the most famous death in history. No other death has aroused one-hundredth part of the interest, or been remembered with one-hundredth part of the intensity and concern' as the death of Jesus of Nazareth.[1] Although the Romans put hundreds to death by the cruel and degrading method of crucifixion around the time of Jesus, it is remarkable that we know virtually nothing of their deaths. Somehow the death of this man is different. His death has exercised an unparalleled hold and fascination over the minds and imaginations of men and women of so many cultures and ages. This man's death has never been forgotten; rather, it has exercised 'a unique effect on world history', as Martin Hengel points out, because of the way it came to be interpreted.[2] The early Christians quickly came to realize that his death was singularly special because through the cross of Christ God was at work, demonstrating his love, acting to save sinners and working to inaugurate a new era in human history.

Although, on a cursory reading, the Gospels seem to offer little by way of an interpretation of the death of Jesus, they leave us in no doubt about its importance. It is unusual for biographies to be so preoccupied with the death of their subject as the Gospels are. Not only do they devote so much space to recounting the events of Jesus' betrayal, arrest, trial and crucifixion (describing them all in minute detail, even if in a restrained and remarkably matter-of-fact way), but early in his life they also foresee his passion. From the start, there are hints about the pain his life would involve,[3] and several clear predictions of the manner of his death are woven into the story of his ministry.[4] There was 'something tragic in his destiny'[5] of which Jesus was aware from the beginning.

Granted the importance of the death of Christ in the Gospels, why

---

[1] Malcolm Muggeridge, 'The crucifixion', *The Observer*, 26 March 1967.
[2] Hengel, *Atonement*, p. 1.
[3] Luke 2:35.
[4] Mark 8:31; 9:31; 10:45.
[5] Denney, p. 19.

is it that they appear to say so little by way of its significance? Why did this teacher of love, teller of truth and worker of miracles die so undeservedly? Why did he not die in an accident or of old age in his bed? Why did he die so young? Why did he die so monstrously, so cruelly on a cross? Why did the Roman and Jewish authorities uncharacteristically conspire to be rid of him?

In fact, the Gospels do much more than simply recount for us the facts of his death. By the very way in which they tell the story they offer us an interpretation of the cross of Christ. They do so implicitly, in their choice of words and details, and in the emphases they each bring to the writing of their accounts. All four report, with an eye to historical accuracy, the occurrence of the one, same event. They have a great deal in common with each other, and the differences between them should not be overstated. It is easy to harmonize the accounts even where they differ in detail. Yet each brings a distinctive perspective to bear.[6]

In Tom Smail's words, 'the dark stage of Calvary is swept by four penetrating gospel searchlights, each of which picks out a series of sometimes coinciding and sometimes diverging details in a way that builds up the kind of picture of the crucified Christ that each evangelist wants us to see'.[7] And he rightly warns: 'We defeat their intention if, in the interests of constructing a unified story, we too quickly try to superimpose these pictures upon each other.'

To the Gospel writers the scene at the crucifixion is like an act being played out in a public square. They witness the identical event. But from high above, four people throw open the windows, one on each side of the square, and describe what they see. Their reports have plenty in common, but each records what he sees as he views it from his own angle. One Gospel writer allows his eye to linger over a detail his fellow-evangelists miss, and another strains his ear to pick up a saying to which the others are deaf. No doubt each is alert to those aspects of the scene that fit his own interests and strike him as particularly relevant to the audience for whom he writes.

The sharp focus into which each Gospel writer brings the events of Calvary is without detriment to the historical reliability of their accounts. There is no need to doubt their historical veracity.[8] Indeed, as

---

[6] Burridge, p. 92. See also R. W. L. Moberly, *From Eden to Golgotha: Essays in Biblical Theology* (University of South Florida Press, 1992), pp. 83–104. He argues against the traditional evangelical approach to harmonizing the Gospels in favour of maintaining their distinctive accounts, believing not only that the facts about the death of Christ are true, but that their interpretations also are true, authoritative and divinely inspired. See esp. p. 97.

[7] Smail, *Once and for All*, p. 20.

[8] On the questions of historicity see I. H. Marshall, *I Believe in the Historical Jesus*

has often been pointed out, there would be more reason to doubt their reliability if they all merely parroted one another, for that, as in any court of law where witnesses agree in every detail with one another, would give rise to the suspicion that they had all been carefully coached about the evidence they provided. Rather, the differing perspectives on the cross which each Gospel writer provides gives us a complete and multifaceted view of what happened on that first Good Friday.

The starting-gun of hostility that would eventually lead Jesus to the cross is fired early in Matthew's Gospel. When Herod heard that wise men from the east were searching for 'one who has been born king of the Jews' (2:2), he immediately sensed a threat to his reign and took steps to remove it (2:16–18). In ordering the massacre of the baby boys of Bethlehem, Herod was both acting in character and signalling a conflict between his way of doing things – typical of power-obsessed worldly rulers – and the way of King Jesus. This conflict grew in intensity until Jesus was arrested, tried and executed by those worldly rulers.

Three times Matthew records Jesus as predicting his own death to his bemused disciples (16:21–27; 17:22–23; 20:17–28). On the mountain of transfiguration, Jesus had once more spoken of his future suffering (17:11–13). The events of passion week itself commenced as Jesus again predicted, with tragic accuracy, that *the Passover is two days away – and the Son of Man will be handed over to be crucified* (26:2). The growing conflict with the chief priests and elders was about to reach its climax. The time for the showdown had come.

The shadow of the cross is to be discerned falling across the whole of Matthew's Gospel, even if it is not as noticeable as in Mark, where the same predictions stand out more starkly. The reason is the nature of each Gospel rather than the significance of the predictions. Matthew's Gospel is longer than Mark's. His interests are wider and his agenda fuller. Mark concentrates on the actions of Jesus; Matthew interleaves his actions with concentrated blocks of his teaching (chs. 5 – 7; 10 – 13; 18; 23 – 25). Inevitably, therefore, the portrait of Jesus Matthew paints is more crowded. But the colour of blood, as we shall see, remains the primary colour of the Gospel.

Whatever the precise details (and scholars differ over them),[9] it is evident that Matthew has a special interest in the relationship between the Christian faith and the Jewish faith.[10] His original readers may well have experienced a particularly difficult time in their relations with the Jewish community. Hence, questions of how faith in Jesus Christ fulfils the Old Testament Scriptures, together with the place of the law, the

(Hodder and Stoughton, 1977), and more recently Blomberg, *Historicity*, and Wright, *Jesus and the Victory* and *Challenge*.

[9] For a good introduction see Hagner, pp. lix–lxxi.

[10] See esp. Gundry, *Matthew*, pp. 5–10.

nature of the church, the place of the Gentiles and the legitimacy of evangelizing, all come to the fore, and most of these come into focus in Matthew's account of the crucifixion.

Greater than any of these concerns, however, is his interest in setting out a full understanding of Jesus as the Christ. Matthew has a fuller, more developed, sense of the doctrine of Christ than one finds in Mark. So it is not surprising that his account of the crucifixion focuses on who it was that was crucified on Calvary. Matthew delights in reminding his readers that the one put to death in this most degrading fashion is none other than the Son of God, the Son of Man, the King of the Jews, and the Christ (26:63–64; 27:37–44). In writing of the death of Jesus, Matthew speaks to us as much about who he was as about what he did.

Five themes emerge in Matthew's passion narrative, each of which sheds light on the person of the crucified one.

1. The anticipated Messiah: he fulfils prophetic Scripture

The life of Jesus sees the fulfilment of God's plans and purposes. Ten times Matthew introduces an aspect of his birth or ministry with the formula: 'this took place to fulfil what the Lord had said through the prophet', or some such words.[11] Using many other strategies and quotations from the Old Testament, Matthew sees history as coming to a climax in the ministry of Jesus.[12] Jesus' death, no less than his life, took place in fulfilment of the Old Testament prophecies about the Messiah.

a. The scriptures he quotes

Before the final act of his life, Jesus placed himself in the line of the godly prophets of previous generations who had been rejected by their peers. He told the parable of the son, the last of a long line of messengers from the owner of a vineyard, who was ejected and killed by the tenants – with the consequence that they brought down judgment on their own heads (21:33–44). No Jew would have mistaken the thinly disguised allusion. The vineyard, according to the familiar imagery of Isaiah,[13] was Israel; the owner was God; the messengers were the prophets; and the son was Jesus himself. The judgment, clearly foreshadowed in Psalm 118:22–23, with which he concluded the story, was about to fall. In this way Jesus announced that 'he saw his death as the culmination of centuries of Jewish rejection of God's message, and foretold that God's judgement would bring Jewish national privilege to an end'.[14]

---

[11] Matt. 1:22–23; 2:5–6, 15, 17–18, 23; 4:14–16; 8:17; 12:17–21; 21:4–5; 27:9–10.
[12] For a full discussion see France, *Matthew: Evangelist and Teacher*, pp. 166–205.
[13] Is. 5:1–7.
[14] Stott, *Cross of Christ*, p. 28.

Later, In pronouncing judgment on the teachers of the law and the Pharisees, Jesus again placed himself in the succession of the prophets and righteous ones whom their ancestors had killed. He rejected their plea that they would not have acted in such a way had they lived in the days of the prophets, and told them that their actions proved that they were 'the descendants of those who murdered the prophets'. He goaded them into filling up 'the measure of the sin of your ancestors' (23:30–35).

It was widely believed at the time (and it certainly seems to have been deep within Jesus' own consciousness) that if God was to initiate a new era of redemption and to forgive Israel her sins, such redemption would come only through the intense suffering of the righteous.[15] Jesus, then, placed his conflict with the Jewish leaders in this wider context. Through it, God was bringing to a head the battle between two kingdom powers, and would engineer the downfall of the misguided religious system of the Jews and the true liberation of Israel. He willingly stands in the shoes of the righteous ones, up to and including John the Baptist, who had endured suffering before him.

This consciousness of fulfilling the prophets pervades the final drama of Jesus' life. When the crowd came to arrest him in the garden of Gethsemane, Jesus surrendered to them without calling on celestial protection, so that *the Scriptures* could *be fulfilled that say it must happen in this way* (26:54). He did not do so without a challenge. *'Every day'*, he said, *'I sat in the temple courts teaching, and you did not arrest me.'* Then he added, *'But this has all taken place that the writings of the prophets might be fulfilled'* (26:56). He probably had no particular prophetic scripture in mind, but he did have a clear appreciation that in many places, not least in the servant passages of Isaiah, it was envisaged that God's servant would suffer.

Only twice does Matthew directly quote Old Testament Scripture in the passion narrative. In warning his disciples that they would desert him at the end, Jesus quoted Zechariah 13:7:

> '"I will strike the shepherd,
>   and the sheep of the flock will be scattered "' (26:31).

The second quotation falls in the account of the Pharisees' purchase of the Field of Blood after Judas had tried to return the thirty pieces of silver he had earned for betraying Jesus to them (27:6–10). They would have none of it, since the money was considered to be unclean. Their action in buying a potter's field, Matthew tells us, fulfilled the prophecy of Jeremiah. Matthew's reference is problematic. It seems to fit the prophecy in Zechariah 11:12–13 more easily. But a good case can be

---

[15] See Wright, *Jesus and the Victory*, pp. 579–592.

made out for its derivation from Jeremiah 19:1–13.[16] The point Matthew makes is clear. No aspect of the drama of the death of Jesus is there by chance. Every detail of it – the details of the betrayal, no less than those of the death itself – had been anticipated and foretold.

b. The scriptures he omits

Given Matthew's penchant for quoting the Old Testament, there are some unexpected omissions from his repertoire when it comes to the crucifixion itself. Although, for example, he quoted from Isaiah 53:4 in 8:17, he fails to refer directly to Isaiah 53 during his passion narrative, which Christians today would consider an obvious point of reference. Even so, the Old Testament is never far below the surface of his writing. As John Carroll and Joel Green assert, 'Although the crucifixion scene lacks any explicit Scripture citations, it is replete with biblical echoes and allusions.'[17]

In fact, in telling the story of Christ's death Matthew makes a great deal of use of the Psalms of Lament, where the righteous cry to God for vindication – especially Psalms 22 and 69. Thus, when wine *mixed with gall* is offered him (27:34), Psalm 69:21 is alluded to. When the soldiers cast *lots* for *his clothes* (27:35), Psalm 22:18 is in mind. And when they mock him (27:43), they use the words of Psalm 22:8. Furthermore, when *darkness came over all the land* (27:45), there is an allusion to Amos 8:9. The cry of dereliction directly echoes Psalm 22:1.

c. The significance he conveys

There are several reasons Matthew chooses to highlight the fulfilment theme in telling of Christ's death. First, it suggests that Christ's death was no accident, no mere working out of an unfortunate coincidence of circumstances beyond anyone's control. It was all in accordance with God's divine plan and his unfolding purpose. His death must be seen as the outworking of God's will.

Secondly, the prophecies highlight Jesus' prophetic knowledge.[18] What happened did not catch him unawares. He did not manipulate his life or engineer his death to play a predetermined role. Nevertheless, his life fits the prophecies concerning the one who would deliver Israel and confirms him as the messianic deliverer. Jesus himself, steeped in the Scriptures as he was, knew both that his death was inevitable and that its effect would be redemptive.

Thirdly, Matthew uses the theme of fulfilment to point out that there is continuity in the work of God as well as discontinuity. Although, as we shall see, the cross inaugurates a new era in the history

---

[16] See Carson, 'Matthew', pp. 562–563. Others connect the quotation with Jer. 32:6–9.
[17] Carroll and Green, p. 51.
[18] Senior, *Matthew*, p. 337.

of salvation, it is not to be seen as an unexpected development. Christ's death is part of the unfolding of the plan God had announced generations before, for which many had thirsted and longed. Jewish Christians who questioned the legitimacy of this departure from Judaism would find assurance in understanding this truth. God was not double-minded, nor was his plan of salvation inconsistent. What happened at Calvary was foretold long before.

2. The sacrificial victim: he sheds sacrificial blood

The awfulness of Calvary has long since been muted in the minds of Christians and non-Christians alike. Christians have become too familiar with it, seeing the cross nicely polished and displayed in their churches, wearing it round their necks or in their lapels, and 'talking about it, hearing about it all the time'.[19] Those with no particular Christian commitment often see it as no more than 'a fashion accessory'.[20] For the original eye-witnesses it was altogether different. The cross was an instrument of inhuman and degrading torture.

Matthew needs no reminding of this, and gives expression to it by frequently speaking of blood. The cross had to do with blood. It wasted the blood of its victim. It smelt of blood. It splattered blood on those involved. And it meant that someone was responsible for the shedding of blood.

Matthew draws our attention to the blood of Christ more than any of the other Gospel writers. Indeed, 'the motif of the blood of Jesus weaves its way as a bright red thread through the Matthean passion account'.[21] The theme was signalled early in the Gospel when the blood of the innocent children of Bethlehem was shed (2:16–18). And it reaches its climax when Jesus dies. In Matthew's version of the last supper Jesus says, *'This is my blood of the covenant, which is poured out for many for the forgiveness of sins'* (26:28).[22] Judas protested in remorse that he had *betrayed innocent blood* (27:4), while the chief priests refused to accept the lucre Judas tried to return, because it was *blood money* (27:6) and therefore unclean. Appropriately enough, they purchased a *Field of Blood* with it (27:8). When Pilate washed his hands to divest himself of the guilt of Jesus' death, it was to the image of blood he turned. *'I am innocent of this man's blood,'* he vainly protested (27:24). By contrast, the people willingly accepted responsibility for Jesus' death, crying, *'Let his blood be on us and on our children!'* (27:25). An awareness of blood is inescapable as one reads Matthew's Gospel.

[19] Boice and Ryken, p. 137.
[20] Ibid.
[21] Carroll and Green, p. 39.
[22] Cf. Luke 22:20.

Matthew's purpose is more than mere reporting, more than the use of a shorthand expression to speak of a violent and ugly death. He speaks of blood both factually and, at a deeper level, symbolically. Its symbolism involves three dimensions.

a. The blood of the innocent

Judas was right when he cried that he had betrayed *innocent blood* (27:4). But in admitting it, he connects the death of Jesus with the long line of righteous ones whose blood had been unjustly shed by the religious leaders of their day, from *righteous Abel* to murdered *Zechariah* (23:35). [23] The priests firmly laid the responsibility for the betrayal of Jesus at the feet of Judas (27:4). But all know that that is an inadequate, if not totally misguided, answer. The reader is drawn in to probe the question of guilt more deeply. Who is it that is responsible for the shedding of this innocent blood? The Roman procurator, the Jewish authorities, the Jerusalem crowd? It is a question to which we shall return as we look more deeply at the injustice of Jesus' death. For the moment, our interest lies not on who is responsible for it, but on the saving, if unintended, effects of the shedding of his blood.

b. The blood of the covenant

As the third of the four cups of the Passover meal (the common cup from which all drank) was being passed around his disciples, Jesus referred to it as *my blood of the covenant* (26:28). As Craig Blomberg remarks, 'Each of the four cups was linked to one line of Exodus 6:6–7a. This one tied in with God's promise, "I will redeem you," in v. 6c and hence specifically to his original liberation of the Israelites from Egypt.'[24] But the words of Jesus invested it with a new meaning. The cup, he said in effect, no longer symbolizes the blood of the original Passover lamb, but his own blood which was to be the new means of liberation. The shedding of his blood would inaugurate a new covenant between God and humanity. His words also echo Exodus 24:8, where Moses sprinkled blood on the people of Israel to confirm the covenant of Sinai. As then, so now: blood was to be shed to inaugurate a new and greater covenant, the covenant envisaged by Jeremiah,[25] through which the law would no longer be an external reference point but an inner motivation, and in which God would be known by all his people and sin would be dealt with once and for all. The twin ideas of

---

[23] Jesus' point in addressing the 'snakes' and the 'vipers' in this verse (see v. 33) is that the righteous will always receive hostility and persecution – his disciples no less than he himself – until the culmination of God's judgment against the nation of Israel is reached, as it was with the destruction of the temple in AD 70.

[24] Blomberg, *Matthew*, pp. 390–391.

[25] Jer. 31:31–34.

emancipation and covenant come together in his words.

Another phrase in Jesus' statement deserves attention. The blood of the covenant, he says, *is poured out for many for the forgiveness of sins* (26:28). His words, then, echo not only Exodus 6:6 and 24:88, but also Isaiah 53:12, where the servant of the Lord is said to bear 'the sin of many'. This new covenant will be inclusive, embracing those outside Israel, as well as the unclean and the outcasts within it. It would provide forgiveness for clean and unclean, rich and poor, male and female, Jew and Gentile alike. For some of Matthew's readers this was a moot point. They were not sure that Christ intended to be so inclusive. So Matthew not only states the inclusive nature of the new covenant here, but underscores it as he reports the events that follow. While Jews mocked the dying Christ in disbelief, a Roman centurion confessed, *'Surely he was the Son of God!'* (27:54). Matthew's Gospel had begun with wise men from the east seeking the king of the Jews. It ends with a hardened Gentile from the west finding the Son of God. The good news of the death of Jesus is for all. His new covenant overcomes the racial segregation and cultural discrimination inherent in the former covenant and reaches out to all in forgiveness.

c. The blood of cleansing

In the mindset of any Jew, the shedding of blood was associated with the sacrificial system. Animals were offered to God for a number of purposes: to confirm covenants, to cement fellowship, to offer thanksgiving, to attest a vow, but most of all to secure atonement.[26] Any Jew would have taken for granted the claim of Hebrews 9:22: 'In fact, the law requires that nearly everything be cleansed with blood, and without the shedding of blood there is no forgiveness.' In the death of Jesus, then, covenant blood and sacrificial blood blend to make forgiveness from a just and holy God available to all, for, as James Denney put it, 'Covenant blood is sacrificial blood, and we have every reason to believe that sacrificial blood universally, and not only in special cases, was associated with propitiatory power.'[27]

The shedding of the blood of Jesus was the most special case of all, and wins wonderful atonement for those who avail themselves of its benefits. It may have been left to Paul and Hebrews to spell out more explicitly than Matthew does the meaning of the shed blood of Christ, but they are not saying anything other than he does. They simply use their insights to bring to full flower the bud seen in his Gospel.

John Carroll and Joel Green aptly sum up the theme and highlight the wonder of the blood of Jesus:

[26] Lev. 1:4; 4:20, 26, 31, 35; 5:6, 10, 13, 16, 18; 6:7; etc.
[27] Denney, p. 37.

If Matthew rivets our attention on the blood of Jesus ... it is not simply to point the finger at the responsible parties. No, the irony is thick here. The death of Jesus – precisely because it is the shedding of innocent sacrificial blood – creates the possibility of forgiveness even for the persons who bear the responsibility of putting him to death.[28]

3. The innocent servant: he accepts unjust suffering

Why did Jesus die? To some he is a martyr to a cause, not a victim of injustice. Marcus Borg has recently written:

> For me, the most persuasive answer is his role as a social prophet who challenged the domination system in the name of God ... he was also a God-intoxicated voice of religious social protest who had attracted a following.
>
> In Jesus' world, this was enough to get arrested and executed by authorities who did not care for criticism and who feared popular unrest, as the execution of Jesus' mentor, John the Baptizer, not long before demonstrates. To make the point yet one more way, Jesus died as a martyr, not as a victim. A martyr is killed because he or she stands for something. Jesus was killed because he stood against the kingdoms of this world and for an alternative social vision grounded in the kingdom of God. The domination system killed Jesus as the prophet of the kingdom of God. This is the political meaning of Good Friday.[29]

It is difficult to disagree with what Borg asserts. In his upside-down teaching in the Sermon on the Mount, his attitude to ritual washing, to eating with 'sinners', to the observance of the Sabbath, to patronage and, above all, to the temple, Jesus threw down the gauntlet again and again to both the Jewish and the Roman authorities.[30] Yet Borg does not go far enough in his explanation of Christ's death. The Gospels portray Jesus as more than a martyr. To Matthew, no matter how much Jesus had provocatively challenged the conventional view of things, his was the death of an innocent victim and a deeper reason for it must be sought.

Matthew highlights the innocence of Jesus by describing a trial which was full of 'apparent illegalities'.[31] No trial should have been held at night, or during a festival. No sentence of death should have been

---

[28] Carroll and Green, p. 47.
[29] Wright and Borg, p. 91.
[30] Green, 'Death of Jesus and ways of God', pp. 27–30.
[31] Blomberg, *Matthew*, p. 400.

reached in a single day, and a counsel for the defense should have been provided. The chief priests and members of the council actively looked *for false evidence against Jesus so that they could put him to death. But they did not find any, though many false witnesses came forward* (26:59–60). Eventually they secured two satisfactory witnesses to back up the allegations, and railroaded the trial to a conclusion from then on. It was a travesty of justice. For Matthew the Jew, concerned about the law and righteousness, this was the most unrighteous act of all.

Matthew emphasizes Christ's innocence by including material the other evangelists omit, and which points up not only Christ's innocence but, correspondingly, whose guilt it was that sentenced him to death.

a. The betrayal of Judas (27:1–10)

Matthew seems to interrupt the flow of events to speak of Judas' remorse and suicide after he had betrayed Jesus. Only he records it. Why did Judas come to realize that he had betrayed 'innocent blood', and why did he not see the true situation before he made his fateful way to the high priests to arrange the betrayal? We can only speculate. Perhaps he naïvely thought that Jesus might be restrained but not executed, and so when events turned out for the worse, he tried, all too late, to make amends. Perhaps he thought Jesus' hand would be forced and he would bring in his kingdom in power. Perhaps the truth just dawned on him too late.

Judas' remorse fell short of full repentance. Matthew uses the word *metamelomai* rather than *metanoia*, the more usual word for 'repentance', to describe his state of mind. It speaks of regret without implying 'a resulting forgiveness'. 'It is thus appropriate', writes R. T. France, 'to convey the idea of remorse without suggesting Judas' salvation.'[32]

It is clear that Matthew held Judas in some measure responsible for the death of Jesus. The fact that he played out a role in the divine plan and was fulfilling the ancient Scriptures in doing so (as verse 9 stresses) in no way lessens his personal responsibility for the free decision he took to betray his Master.[33] He had his own sordid motives for doing what he did, even though he was, all unknown to him, serving as an instrument in the fulfilment of God's plan. As Donald Hagner comments, 'we can pity Judas, but we cannot make a hero out of him, nor alas even a believer'.[34] He pays the price for his betrayal of one who was innocent.

[32] France, *Matthew*, p. 385.
[33] Cf. Mark 14:21.
[34] Hagner, p. 815.

b. The intervention of Pilate's wife (27:19)

A second episode that Matthew alone records is the intervention of Pilate's wife during the trial of Jesus by the governor. She urged her husband, *'Don't have anything to do with that innocent man, for I have suffered a great deal today in a dream because of him.'* In those days dreams were considered an important means by which the gods communicated with people. Whether she believed this dream to be from some fictitious god of Rome or from the living God of Israel is unknown. Either way, Matthew inserts these words of Pilate's wife to stress that Jesus is innocent, or just *(dikaios)*. Matthew then lets the spotlight roam more widely until it rests on those who were acting unjustly and so truly were responsible for his death.

It is often said that, in the interests of blaming the Jews, Matthew plays down the role of Pilate in sentencing Jesus to death: the trial scene is brief, and this cameo shows Pilate and his wife in a good light. But this view cannot be right. For all his weak vacillation and understandable frustration, Pilate permitted an injustice to be done. Try as he might, he could not wash his hands of the crime in which he was about to be implicated. His protestation of his own innocence (27:24) is drowned by the baying crowd. It is heavy with irony. Only one person in the drama was innocent – the one about to be condemned as guilty. Pilate could not disclaim responsibility for passing the death sentence on Jesus.

c. The response of the Jews (27:24–26)

Pilate did, however, throw out a challenge to others to accept responsibility for the death of Jesus, since he did not want to do so. The Jerusalem crowd, or a section of it, whipped up, no doubt, into a frenzied mob by the *agents provocateurs* of the Jewish Sanhedrin, willingly took on themselves the culpability. *'Let his blood be on us and on our children!'* they cry (27:25).

The Jewish authorities had choreographed the drama to this point, and now they moved in for the kill. They had looked for evidence against Jesus. They had forced him under oath to reveal his messianic identity and so, in their view, to commit blasphemy (26:63–65). They had transposed the charge of religious blasphemy into one of political sedition in order to secure a conviction in Pilate's court. Now they took back on their own heads, and on those of their children, the responsibility for his death.

Commenting on this verse, Morna Hooker writes:

These words (found only in Matthew) are attributed to the whole people, and not just to their leaders. Matthew thus lays the blame for Jesus' death squarely upon the Jews. There is tremendous irony here: the High Priest has pronounced Jesus guilty of blasphemy, which means that he falls under the curse of God; the Sanhedrin has engineered Jesus' death, and demanded that he be crucified, the form of death which branded him accursed. But he is innocent, and in shouldering responsibility for his death the people bring down the curse upon their own head.[35]

In fact, there are several ironies wrapped up in the part the high priest plays. In forcing Jesus to speak under oath and so, from the high priest's viewpoint, to convict himself of blasphemy, Jesus revealed his true identity, at least by his compliance ('*Yes, it is as you say*', 26:64). '*In the future*' (better translated as 'From now on'), he continued, '*you will see the Son of Man sitting at the right hand of the Mighty One and coming on the clouds of heaven.*' He is the heavenly figure, spoken of in Daniel 7:13–14, who is given divine power to establish a kingdom 'that will never be destroyed'. The kingdom over which Jesus presides is altogether different from the nationalistic and militaristic kingdoms the high priest had in mind. So, ironically, the judge became the guilty one, and the man on trial the innocent one. Ironically, God used this travesty of justice and this false accusation of blasphemy as means of establishing justice, truth and freedom. Ironically, in accepting responsibility for the judgment of Jesus, the Jews did, indeed, bring down judgment upon themselves and the next generation, their children. In rejecting God's Son they committed the ultimate act of refusing God and his word, and so unleashed forces that led, eventually, to the sack of Jerusalem, the destruction of the temple and the end of the Jewish nation as it had been constituted.

Over the years this reference to the Jews' accepting the blame for the death of Jesus has led to shameful acts of anti-Semitism on the part of Christians. But there can be no justification for such behaviour on the basis of Matthew's supposed bias towards blaming them. We have seen that Matthew does not intend to suggest that they bear the blame alone. Nor does he necessarily implicate the whole of the Jewish nation (any more than the rest of us) in placing on their shoulders the responsibility for his death. To be strictly accurate, as Craig Blomberg points out, it is only 'one segment of the uncommitted populace' that are implicated by Matthew's words.[36] To use these words as a rationale for anti-Semitism is 'absolutely indefensible',[37] since the blame is widely distributed in the Gospels, and also because 'we ourselves are also guilty. If we were in their place, we would have done what they did. Indeed, we *have* done it. For whenever we turn away from Christ, we

---

[35] Hooker, *Not Ashamed*, p. 73.
[36] Blomberg, *Matthew*, p. 414.
[37] Stott, *Cross of Christ*, p. 59.

"are crucifying the Son of God all over again and subjecting him to public disgrace".[38]

d. The meaning of the gospel

By stressing Jesus' innocence, Matthew is pointing to the deeper reasons that underlay his death. The servant songs of Isaiah bring the vocation and passion of Jesus into focus. Jesus died, like the suffering servant of Isaiah 53, not for his own sins but because the sins of others were laid on him. It is as he bore their guilt and the weight of their sin, by suffering the death they deserved, that their oppression and judgment are taken away and healing can come. The wonder of it all is that 'the death of Jesus – precisely because it is the shedding of innocent, sacrificial blood – creates the possibility of forgiveness even for the persons who bear responsibility for putting him to death'.[39]

4. The sovereign king: he demonstrates supreme control

The idea that Christ was an innocent victim as he wended his way to Calvary must not mislead us into thinking that he was a hapless casualty of forces too powerful for him and beyond his control. Matthew is at pains to point out that the truth is otherwise. Whereas Mark presents Jesus as a passive and silent hostage, Matthew portrays Jesus as a figure of commanding dignity. He took charge of events, as one might expect a king to do. He is the King Messiah, whose authority never diminished throughout the ghastly final phase of his earthly life.

His words were the chief demonstration of his sovereign control. Whereas in Mark[40] and Luke[41] Jesus sent his disciples to *ask* the house owner if he might observe the Passover at his house, in Matthew he sent his disciples to *tell* him that he was going to do so, in words remarkably reminiscent of the language John's Gospel uses. He told them to explain, *'My appointed time is near. I am going to celebrate the Passover with my disciples at your house'* (26:18). Jesus seems to have been not only aware of his timetable but in charge of it. During the supper itself, *he* disclosed to Judas that he, Judas, was the betrayer (26:25), whereas in the parallel accounts in Mark and Luke the identity of the betrayer is undisclosed.

In Gethsemane, Jesus gave Judas permission, even perhaps an instruction (as the NIV would have it), to betray him. *'Friend,'* he said, using a term not of endearment but one that expresses coolness

[38] Heb. 6:6; see ibid.
[39] Carroll and Green, p. 48.
[40] Mark 14:14.
[41] Luke 22:11.

between them, *do what you came for* (26:50).[42] Having been arrested, he left his captors in no doubt that he could have called twelve legions of angels (72,000 angels) to his defence and escaped their hands, but he chose not to do so and voluntarily limited his freedom in order to fulfil the prophecy of Scripture (26:53–54). Angels had come to his rescue before (4:11), and would have come again at his command. It is clearly Jesus who was calling the tune. He was giving them permission to arrest him; it is not that they were forcing him to surrender.

On trial, both before the high priest and before Pilate, Jesus stood with royal dignity unbowed. He did not condescend to answer the charges of those who accused him of blasphemy in the court of Caiaphas, but countered him by declaring that the events about to unfold would reveal him to be Daniel's Son of Man (26:59–64). Before Pilate, *to the great amazement of the governor*, he seems similarly unconcerned to defend himself once he has affirmed, in a qualified way, that he is Messiah, the king of the Jews (27:14). Elsewhere the reason for Jesus' caution becomes clear. Both Pilate and Jesus may have spoken the common language of kingship, but they meant radically different things by it. Jesus did not want to give Pilate the impression that their claims to authority implied that they ruled in the same way, for Jesus' kingdom is 'not of this world'.[43]

Commenting on John's account, Tom Smail has written that 'The cross is no tragedy passively endured but an action deliberately undertaken and successfully completed.'[44] The comment fits Matthew's record too. The one who is about to be spread-eagled naked on a cross is truly the one who is Lord of all.

5. The epoch-maker: he inaugurates a new era

The dying Christ cried in agony, *'My God, my God, why have you forsaken me?'* (27:46). Both Matthew and Mark[45] record the saying, but whereas in Mark the cry went unanswered and Jesus was left to struggle with the absence of God, according to Matthew the cry received the most spectacular and supernatural of replies.[46] In Matthew, Jesus experienced the real presence of God in the darkness, and an unmistakable affirmation that the sacrifice of his life was accepted.

---

[42] As the marginal reading of the NIV indicates, the original words are somewhat unclear. Literally they read, 'for which you are here'. They could express a wish or simply be a statement. They could also perhaps be a question. But, as France comments, 'Jesus is well aware of Judas' errand, but none the less he does not resist, even encourages, its completion.' France, *Matthew*, p. 375.

[43] John 18:34–37.

[44] Smail, *Once and for All*, p. 58.

[45] Matt. 27:46; Mark 15:34.

[46] I owe this point to Burridge, p. 95.

Matthew ends his account of Jesus' crucifixion not with the darkness of despair but with a series of 'apocalyptic fireworks'.[47] The events his death immediately activated do not lessen the reality of his agonized suffering. Even so, they cannot but cast it all in a different light. Cosmic signs appear to denote that powerful events were happening behind the scenes through the death of Jesus of Nazareth. The sky was darkened from noon until mid-afternoon. The curtain of the temple was ripped in two. An earthquake ensued and, most sensationally of all, the tombs of the righteous dead were opened and they were resurrected. Subsequently, these holy people appeared in Jerusalem and were seen by many people (27:45–53).

Puzzling as these events may seem to us, their meaning is clear. There is a potency in the cross of Christ which is well beyond any potency involved in the playing out of the politics of human governments. Greater forces are at work than are evident to the human eye. His death was not really to do with the interplay of the power élites of imperial Rome and downtrodden Israel. It was to do with the plan of almighty God, who, through the death of his Son, inaugurated a new age, a new beginning, for all men and women. It is about the power of God defeating the powers of sin and death.

a. Darkness covers the land

Amos had looked forward to the day of the Lord, 'when the sun' would 'go down at noon and darken the earth in broad daylight'.[48] Calvary said the day of the Lord had arrived – the day on which judgment would be meted out and mercy poured out, so that Israel might be set free and restored to God's gracious intention for them.

b. The temple curtain is torn

The temple had two curtains. One separated the Court of the Jews from the Court of the Gentiles. The other separated the Holy Place from the Most Holy Place. We cannot be sure which curtain was split in two. The rending of either would be deeply symbolic. The former would mean that the distinction between Jew and Gentile had been abolished by the cross, as Paul explains in Ephesians 2:13–19. Consequently, from then on there would not be separate ways for Jews and Gentiles to approach God, but only one way, and one new humanity would be created in Christ. The latter would mean that the severe restrictions on access to God had been abolished. The curtain that had prevented any human being entering the presence of God (except the high priest annually on the Day of Atonement) was no longer a barrier. All men and women could now have access to God at

[47] Carroll and Green, p. 48.
[48] Amos 8:9.

any time through the death of Christ. It is the destruction of this curtain that Hebrews assumes[49] and which is almost certainly intended. Whichever curtain is meant here, the implied effect is the same. All now have access to God, and, correspondingly, a means of having their sins forgiven, because Jesus died on a cross. The ultimate sacrificial offering has been presented to God and sin has been dealt with once and for all. The temple is past history in the economy of God, together with all the sacrificial ritual for which it stood. Indeed, not many years after this, it would no longer even exist.

c. The righteous are resurrected

The resurrection of the righteous is the most intriguing event of all. Rational western minds want to ask all sorts of questions about it. Did it really happen? Who came out of the tombs? Were they just resuscitated or did they experience lasting resurrection? What kind of bodies did they have? Why don't the other evangelists comment on this? Why don't we hear more about it? But no matter how much we wish to interrogate the text, it will yield nothing to satisfy our rationalism or our scepticism. Using the imagery of Ezekiel, who prophesied that the Sovereign Lord would open graves and resurrect people to life in the valley of dry bones,[50] Matthew is content to let the event stand unadorned because its symbolic meaning is clear. The raising of these holy ones is a foretaste of the resurrection to which all believers can look forward. Through the death of Jesus a new day has arrived, a day when death has been defeated by death, and resurrection to life eternal has been made possible.

This happening points to the future more than any other. It is the bridge to the good news of the resurrection of Jesus, as well as heralding the new age which will one day climax in the resurrection to life of all believers in Christ.[51] The cross of Christ was an apocalyptic event. The future has already arrived. Or, in R. T. France's more measured words, 'In his coming a new age has dawned; nothing will ever be quite the same again.'[52]

Conclusion

Morna Hooker[53] conjectures that because Matthew's Gospel was written later than Mark's, there is a difference in tone. The brooding darkness of Mark's crucifixion account, matching the ordeal of

[49] See Heb. 4:16; 6:19–20; 9:11–28; 10:19–22.
[50] Ezek. 37:11–14.
[51] 1 Cor. 15; 1 Thess. 4:13 – 5:11.
[52] France, Matthew, p. 38.
[53] Hooker, Not Ashamed, p. 76.

persecution experienced by Mark's readers, has been replaced, she suggests, by a more positive acceptance of Christianity. The scandal of the cross has begun to recede into the background, and more positive interpretations, which involve God working through it in powerful ways, come to the fore. But it is not necessary to resort to such situational theology to explain the difference between Matthew and Mark. Both provide true insights into the multifaceted cross of Christ.

For Matthew it is the cross of a crucified Messiah. He wants our attention to be held by who it was that was pinned in such a humiliating and fatal way to a stake on the hill of Golgotha. It is a portrait which in a myriad ways tells us about the real identity of the central figure and so of his mission. He wants us to look at Christ with those who passed by or lingered at the cross, such as the Jewish leaders who mocked him there (27:39–43). They insulted him, but in doing so they ironically spoke the truth about him. Matthew invites us to make the same affirmations, not in mockery but in submissive faith. He invites us to stand with the outsider, the Roman centurion, and offer our confession of who Christ is (27:54). The man on the cross is the true Son of God, the heavenly Son of Man, the real king of the Jews, the anointed one, the Christ, the fulfiller of prophecy, the one who can satisfy Israel's longings for deliverance, the Saviour of men and women, the instigator of a new way to God and the pioneer of a new temple and a new humanity. He is the agent of a new era.

Mark 14:1 – 15:47
7. Suffering servant

The preacher and theologian P. T. Forsyth once asserted: 'Christ ... is to us just what his cross is. You do not understand Christ till you understand his cross.'[1] No-one can read Mark's Gospel without coming to the same conclusion. To say that the shadow of the cross casts itself over the whole Gospel is perhaps too mild, for 'the death of Jesus broods over the entire Gospel'.[2] Not for nothing has the Gospel famously been described as 'a passion narrative with a long introduction'.[3]

Dismissing those who would mystify Mark's Gospel by attributing to it hidden meanings and symbolic enigmas, Robert Gundry, a recent commentator, has persuasively argued: 'Mark's meaning lies on the surface. He writes a straightforward apology for the Cross, for the shameful way in which the object of Christian faith and the subject of Christian proclamation died, and hence for Jesus as the Crucified One.'[4]

Given that Mark's is the shortest and the most energetic[5] of the Gospels, it is all the more surprising that the cross dominates in the way it does. Jesus is presented as a worker of miracles, a performer of exorcisms and a teacher of wonders.[6] And yet, from the start, it is the impending cross that dominates. The reader's eye is inescapably drawn to it.

Mark's Gospel is a Gospel in a hurry. He has no time to dwell on the birth of Jesus, but launches straight into the preaching of John the

[1] Forsyth, *Cruciality of the Cross*, p. 26.
[2] E. Best, *Mark: The Gospel as Story* (T. and T. Clark, 1983), p. 66.
[3] M. Kähler, *The So-called Historical Jesus and the Historic, Biblical Christ* (ET Fortress, 1964), p. 80.
[4] Gundry, *Mark*, pp. 1, 15.
[5] One of Mark's favourite words is 'immediately', which occurs eleven times in the Gospel, contributing to the sense of non-stop and breathtaking action on the part of Jesus.
[6] By comparison with the other Gospels, little of Jesus' teaching is presented: for example, only eleven of his parables are included, in comparison with Matthew's twenty-seven and Luke's thirty-three.

135

Baptist and the start of Christ's public ministry. And one only reads fourteen verses before meeting the first hint of the trouble to come. 'John', we read, 'was put in prison.' The word Mark chooses in the Greek is *paradidomi*, which has sinister overtones. The Greeks used it as a technical word for 'handing over prisoners to judgement',[7] but it is often translated 'betrayed'. The word weaves its way through the Gospel[8] until we all too quickly come to the climax and read that Pilate *handed him* (Jesus) *over to be crucified* (15:15).

From the start, conflict between Christ and the authorities is evident. It is as if, in Denney's words, 'The Christ sees two paths that lie before him, and he chooses at the outset, in spiritual conflict, that which he knows will set him in irreconcilable antagonism to the hopes and expectations of those to whom he is to appeal.'[9] After Jesus claims to be able to forgive the sins of a paralysed man, the scribal teachers contemptuously dismiss him as 'this fellow' (2:7). His working of miracles and demonstration of his right to forgive do nothing to overcome their opposition, and it is not long before 'the Pharisees went out and began to plot with the Herodians how they might kill Jesus' (3:6). The die was cast early in the ministry of Jesus.

From the midpoint of the Gospel – the point at which Peter confesses Jesus to be the Christ (8:29) – the cross comes to dominate the scene even more. Three times Jesus explicitly predicts his own sufferings.[10] Immediately Peter acknowledged Jesus as the Messiah, 'He began to teach them that the Son of Man must suffer many things and be rejected by the elders, chief priests and teachers of the law, and that he must be killed and after three days rise again' (8:31). After healing a boy with an unclean spirit (9:14–29), Jesus takes his disciples away for further training, the thrust of which concerns his suffering. 'The Son of Man is going to be betrayed into human hands. People will kill him, and after three days he will rise' (9:31). Then, most significant of all, in 10:45, in teaching his disciples about the true nature of leadership he remarks, 'For even the Son of Man did not come to be served, but to serve, and give his life as a ransom for many.'

Several common threads are found in these solemn predictions. Each is made as the disciples are arguing about leadership and what it means to be great. Jesus, as we shall see, has to reconstruct their understanding of greatness radically. Two of them point forward to the resurrection. All carry a note of inevitability about the cross: 'the Son of Man *must*

---

[7] R. E. Brown, *Death* 1, p. 211.

[8] The most significant references in relation to the Son of Man are 9:31; 10:33; 14:10, 21, 41; 15:1, 15.

[9] Denney, p. 20.

[10] France points out that there are many other passages in which Jesus shows a consciousness that his suffering and death were inevitable: namely 2:20; 9:12; 10:38; 12:1ff.; 14:8, 21–23, 25, 49: *Jesus and the Old Testament*, p. 125.

suffer'; 'The Son of Man is going to be betrayed'; 'The Son of Man [came to] give his life.' However strange or mysterious it may be, the death of Jesus 'is part of the divine purpose'.[11] But, as John Stott points out, 'More impressive still is the determination he both expressed and exemplified', in these sayings, to set his face towards the cross.[12]

Given that the cross dominates the portrait Mark paints of Christ, what particular features does he highlight? What is it about the cross that he brings into sharp focus? Four significant themes may perhaps be discerned. Without assigning priority to any of them, we might say that the cross is the cross of the suffering servant, of the conquering king, of the rejected son, and of the exemplary disciple.

1. The suffering servant[13]

By any measure, Jesus' prediction of his death in 10:45 is a key statement in the Gospel. Christians have been quick to claim that, given its emphasis on serving, it alludes to Isaiah 53 and presents Jesus as the suffering servant. Although it is certainly 'appropriate to find an allusion to the Servant of the Lord in Isaiah, who vicariously and voluntarily suffered and gave his life for the sins of others',[14] others question, on linguistic and conceptual grounds, how close the parallels are.[15] Isaiah 53 refers not to a ransom but to a guilt offering. Mark 10:45 does not mention sin, although it presupposes the need for people to be set free. The closest verbal correspondence is found in the words 'for many', which occur as the climax of Jesus' saying and in Isaiah 53:11. That same inclusive note is sounded again at the last supper, when Jesus spoke of the cup as his *blood of the covenant, which is poured out for many* (14:23) – a clear echo of Isaiah 53:11.

In spite of the objections, there is a wide consensus that Jesus is here referring to Isaiah 53 and casting himself in the role of the suffering servant. According to R. T. France,[16] it is the cumulative effect of the parallels, both in word and in thought, especially the idea of the servant's giving himself in redemptive suffering, that suggests that Jesus is deliberately alluding to it. The whole thrust of the saying resonates with the calling of the servant. The background to the saying may well lie more widely in the Old Testament as well. Exodus 6:6 and 16:13

---

[11] Hooker, *Mark*, p. 90. She notes also 9:12; 10:33.

[12] Stott, *Cross of Christ*, p. 27.

[13] Senior (*Mark*, p. 141) claims that 'Mark does not seem to give a strong emphasis to Jesus as the Suffering Servant of Yahweh in the passion story ...', but then immediately adds, 'yet the motif is present', and proceeds to give evidence of it from the last supper, Jesus' silence at the trial and the mocking of the soldiers.

[14] Lane, *Mark*, p. 384.

[15] See Gundry, *Mark*, pp. 591–592, and Hooker, *Mark*, pp. 248–249.

[16] France, *Jesus and the Old Testament*, pp. 116–121, 127.

(LXX) speak of God's ransoming Israel from Egypt. And in Isaiah 43:3–5, God promises to ransom his people from exile. Christians have not been misled in understanding the work of Jesus from the standpoint of Isaiah's suffering servant.

a. Servant suffering

In our concern to unpack the redemptive significance of Jesus' statement, it is important not to miss the obvious. His comment comes as the climax of his rebuke to James and John for wanting the seats of honour when he enters his kingdom (10:35–45). They have still to grasp that the kingdom of Jesus functions not according to the normal criteria but in a deeply counter-cultural way. In this 'ransom saying, Jesus profoundly subverts status-seeking practices'.[17] In his kingdom the first are last, the powerful are weak, the rich are poor, the insiders are outsiders and the greatest are the least. Significantly, each time Jesus predicts his death it is, in fact, in the context of arguing about power, leadership, glory and greatness. His disciples are taking some time to reconstruct their worldview and grasp that greatness comes through servanthood. His death would provide the ultimate proof of the truth of his teaching and be the unsurpassed example of what it meant to serve to the last degree.

b. Silent suffering

One of the unavoidable impressions of Isaiah's servant is of his uncomplaining acceptance of what others were doing to him; his unprotesting nature and his voluntary silence in the face of the scornful nature of the crime being perpetrated against him.

> He was oppressed and afflicted,
> yet he did not open his mouth;
> he was led like a lamb to the slaughter,
> and as a sheep before her shearers is silent,
> so he did not open his mouth.[18]

Mark observes the same feature in Christ as he records the final events of his life. Chapters 14 and 15 speak of Jesus being 'handed over' down a chain of guilt. Judas hands him over to the chief priests, the chief priests hand him over to Pilate, and Pilate hands him over to the soldiers to be crucified.[19] The strong impression given is that the action appears to lie with others. Jesus is portrayed as somewhat passive, allowing events to unfold around him. We see it even in the Garden of

---

[17] Green, 'Death of Jesus and ways of God', p. 31.
[18] Is. 53:7.
[19] R. E. Brown, *Death* 1, p. 211.

Gethsemane, where Jesus speaks with a sense of perplexity, almost of resignation, when they come to seize him. *'Every day I was with you, teaching in the temple courts, and you did not arrest me. But the Scriptures must be fulfilled'* (14:49). The commanding presence that Matthew observes gives way to the silent lamb being led to the slaughter.

The notes of innocence and acquiescence are heard clearly during the trial scenes. The Jewish authorities search for evidence against him, but the only evidence they can find is inconsistent and contradictory (14:55–57). Jesus remains silent while this charade of a trial happens around him, and briefly interjects to confirm his identity only when confronted directly by the high priest and left with little choice (14:60–62). Similarly, as he stands before Pilate he provokes amazement by his silent reluctance to defend himself (15:1–5). Truly Jesus was 'led like a lamb to the slaughter, and as a sheep before his shearers is silent, so he did not open his mouth'.

c. Saving suffering

The servant suffers, according to Isaiah 53:6–7, to bear away the iniquities of others and to bring them peace and healing. In numerous ways, Mark also conveys that the suffering of Jesus was redemptive. The life of the servant is given as a ransom, the price paid to secure emancipation for those in captivity. His death, then, was more than that of a martyr, or than an example of God's love. It was a death that accomplished, achieved and effected salvation.

The idea of the ransom leads to a consideration of three questions. Why is it needed? Who is going to pay it? And to whom is it paid?

The early ministry of Jesus has provided ample illustration of why a ransom was needed. People needed to be saved from slavery to sin and from Satan, whose handiwork was everywhere to be seen, creating havoc and destroying lives. In a typically breathtaking passage, 4:35 – 5:43, Mark gives us a taste of the need for emancipation. Jesus delivers his disciples from the destructive forces of a fallen nature, a man from the disintegrating forces of demonic possession, a woman from the degrading impact of a crippling disease and a family from the devastating force of the final enemy, death. Elsewhere it is the enslaving rules of the religious leaders, or the corrupting forces of sin lurking within their own natures, or even the captivating seduction of materialism from which people need to be emancipated. The whole of Mark's Gospel cries out for a liberator. People were oppressed, and by more than the might of Rome.

Colin Brown points out:

> Whenever men by their own fault or by some superior power have come under the control of someone else, and have lost their freedom to implement their will and decisions, and when their own

resources are inadequate to deal with that other power, they can regain their freedom only by the intervention of a third party.[20]

Jesus himself is the third party, the ransom, willing and able to pay what they could not pay and what we also cannot pay ourselves – for the need for liberation continues in our time as in theirs. The price was his life given in suffering and death. Paradoxically, in ways later writers will explore, the way to freedom was found in Jesus' voluntarily surrendering to those same forces he came to defeat, and through his weakness he brought their power to an end.[21]

The third question need not detain us. Although at various stages theologians have speculated about to whom the ransom was paid, the answers reached show how absurd the question is. Origen mused that the ransom was paid to the devil.[22] But surely the Lord of all glory is not in debt to the corrupter of his creation and pretender to his throne. To ask the question is to make the metaphor of ransom bear more weight than it can carry. Metaphors of atonement, like ransom, are 'incomplete symbols',[23] and it is wrong to press them exhaustively to their logical conclusion. To ask who receives the ransom is to shift the focus away from where it belongs. A precious ransom has been paid and a glorious emancipation has been won.

That the death of Jesus was to effect salvation does not hinge on the ransom statement alone. The whole manner of Christ's trial and execution shows him to be the servant crushed in bearing the sins of others. The way Mark reports the last supper, for example, indicates that Jesus is our Passover lamb.[24] Mark mentions that the meal took place on the evening of *the first day of the Feast of Unleavened Bread, when it was customary to sacrifice the Passover lamb* (14:12). Matthew omits the reference to the Passover lamb. As the meal proceeded, it was evident that Christ saw himself in that role and as establishing a new covenant of liberation by shedding his blood, *which is poured out for many* (14:24).[25] His act of liberation would bring benefits not only for the Jews, inheritors of the old covenant, but to men and women of every race.

As he hung bleeding and dying on the cross, 'hung up between

---

[20] C. Brown, 'Redemption', in *DNTT* 3, p. 177, quoted in Smail, *Windows*, p. 56.

[21] The theme will be explored further below, in chs. 10 and 13.

[22] In his commentaries on Matt. 16:8; 20:28 and Rom. 2:13. He wrote, 'Now it was the devil who holds us, to whom we had been sold by our sins. He demanded therefore as our price, the blood of Christ.'

[23] McIntyre, p. 31.

[24] The only explicit reference to Christ as the Passover lamb in the New Testament comes in 1 Cor. 5:7.

[25] Cf. Is. 53:11–12.

heaven and earth',[26] they mocked him cruelly, '"He saved others," they said, "but he can't save himself!"' (15:31). The irony is that by refusing to save himself, he did save others. His mission was accomplished.

2. The conquering king

Two competing and ultimately complementary themes vie with each other, like the contrasting major and minor keys of a symphony, throughout Mark's Gospel. On the one hand, there is the minor key of darkness and suffering. On the other, there is the major key of power and victory. It has become fashionable to stress the former at the expense of the latter, because, it is supposed, Mark's readers were facing persecution in Rome and the Gospel was written to encourage them. The way of Christ, as he both taught it to his disciples and exemplified it in his own life, was to be costly. But this supposed purpose of Mark's Gospel can influence our reading of it too much. R. H. Gundry has recently questioned the approach and argued that Mark was written 'not to keep Christians from apostatizing out of the shame of the Cross ... but to convert non-Christians despite the shame of the Cross',[27] Only as we appreciate this, he explains, can all the elements of Mark's Gospel be explained. For, as he points out, the Gospel reports the authority and radicalism of Jesus, his predictive powers, power-packed miracles and exorcisms, popular support from the crowds, supernatural signs at his death and his burial in a rich man's grave, all of which lead him to conclude that 'The Jesus of Mark is overpowering.'[28] Jesus is presented not only as a suffering servant but as a conquering king.

a. An undeniable king

The note of sovereignty sounds out clearly in Mark's account of the crucifixion. Six times Jesus is spoken of as a king. The first occurrence is when Pilate asks Jesus, *'Are you the king of the Jews?'* (15:2). It occurs twice more on the lips of Pilate (9, 12), no doubt quizzically if not sardonically, until it is taken up as a taunt by the mocking soldiers (18). It reaches its zenith as Pilate nails the title of indictment to the cross. *THE KING OF THE JEWS*, it read, starkly unqualified (26). Finally, even the chief priests and teachers of the law take up the insulting chant: *'Let this Christ, this King of Israel, come down from the cross, that we may see and believe'* (32). Here is supreme irony. What they spoke in jest was actually true.

It is evident that the kingship of Jesus is no incidental theme. Mark

---

[26] Spurgeon, p. 36.
[27] Gundry, p. 1026.
[28] Ibid. Mark has a far richer vocabulary of 'astonishment' than all the other Gospels put together.

intends us to see, in P. T. Forsyth's words, that 'He went to death as a King. It was the supreme exercise of his royal self-disposal.'[29]

This should not take us by surprise. All through his ministry Jesus has been demonstrating sovereign power over sickness, nature, hunger, demons and even death. The people had remarked on the authority of his novel teaching as he set out the manifesto of his kingdom (2:27). The spirits had recognized him as 'the Holy One of God' (1:24) and the 'Son of the Most High God' (5:7). The crowds had hailed him as king when he rode into Jerusalem (11:11). It was as a powerful king that he lived, and as a sovereign king that he died. The sovereign power of Jesus reached its summit not by his avoiding the cross but by accepting it.

b. An unrecognized king

For all that, the manner of his kingship could not be measured by any normal criteria, and it was not surprising that many could not see it. He shunned the trappings and status usually associated with royalty. He eschewed the use of force and never subjected his followers to burdensome laws or taxes. When he rode into Jerusalem, it was not on the white horse of a conqueror but on the colt of a peasant. If he was a king, he was a king of a most unexpected sort.

That fact leads to a sharp reversal of the way things should have been as his passion developed. The people in charge, the very people whose job it was to be on the lookout for the coming Messiah, Israel's king, and who should have been skilled in recognizing him, failed to do so. It was the task of the high priest to recognize and then anoint the King of the Jews, and Caiaphas was given every opportunity to fulfil his expected role. As Jesus stood before him, the high priest asked him directly, 'Are you the Christ, the Son of the Blessed One?' (14:61). Jesus affirmed that he was. At last, now that he was in the power of his enemies, he could openly declare what hitherto he had had to veil.[30] He even amplified the claim, calling Psalm 110:1[31] and Daniel 7:13[32] into play to tell Caiaphas of his coming enthronement and the coming vindication of his words about the temple. But the religious leaders dismissed it as blasphemy.[33] They neither saw the truth nor acted upon it.

[29] Forsyth, *Cruciality of the Cross*, p. 37.

[30] Cranfield, *Mark*, p. 444.

[31] 'The LORD says to my Lord, "Sit at my right hand until I make your enemies a footstool for your feet."'

[32] 'In my vision at night I looked, and there before me was one like a son of man, coming with the clouds of heaven.'

[33] Wright explains that the questions put to Jesus by Caiaphas, in 14:53–65, are not *non sequiturs*. The temple was of central, symbolic significance to the Jews, and Jesus' pronouncement of its doom and his promise to rebuild it formed an implicit claim to messiahship. Claiming messiahship was foolish, but threatening the temple was both

The irony is that just a day or so before his arrest a woman (a nobody in the culture of the day – indeed, worse, an embarrassing nobody) had recognized who he was and had anointed his head with expensive perfume (14:1–11). Jesus said that she was preparing him for his burial. But equally she was anointing him as king, for it is through his death and burial, as well as his resurrection, that he is recognized as king of Israel. 'The irony is clear', writes Morna Hooker; 'the very notion that a woman could anoint Israel's King is absurd, for a woman was the very last person to have authority to do such a thing.'[34]

And the irony continued. Pilate showed more recognition of who Jesus really was than the religious leaders. And another Gentile, a hard-bitten Roman centurion who had carried out the execution, also recognized the truth about the king as he hung on the cross. His kingship broke out of the narrow confines of nationalism and is a kingship for all people. He was anointed to rule not only in Israel but over all.

c. An unexpected king

The unexpected nature of Jesus' kingship calls for further comment. It was not a kingship like any they had experienced before, nor did it conform exactly to the expectations people had of the Messiah. True, as N. T. Wright points out, he conformed to their expectations sufficiently to get himself killed.[35] He challenged the existing authorities, and his plans to overthrow them provoked enough concern to get him tried on a passable charge of treason. But 'it was a claim to Messiahship which redefined itself around Jesus' own kingdom-agenda, picking up several strands available within popular messianic expectation but weaving them into a striking new pattern, corresponding to none of the options canvassed by others at the time'.[36]

We have already noted the differences, in terms of status and power, as we explored Christ's death from the perspective of the suffering servant. He differed from others in seeing his mission neither as narrow nationalism nor as a political agenda (for all its political implications). But the greatest difference concerns his death itself. Wright comments:

> We know of about fifteen other messianic movements in Judea in the two centuries surrounding Jesus' day, from about 50 BC to about AD 150. They were all without exception nationalist movements, based on a groundswell of popular expectation and zeal. None of these would-be Messiahs, so far as we have any indication

---

foolish and politically dangerous: *Challenge*, pp. 54–58, 88–89.
[34] Hooker, *Not Ashamed*, p. 60.
[35] Wright, *Jesus and the Victory*, p. 538.
[36] Ibid.

at all, had any thought that their cause would come to fruition through his own death.[37]

Jesus, the Messiah-King, uniquely believed that through his death he would liberate Israel from oppression and forgive their sins. The notion that a crucified king could even be respected, let alone worshipped, was strange indeed. 'A king the world could crucify is no king the world could fear,' writes P. T. Forsyth.[38] But this king, as Forsyth continues, does not find his fate on the cross, but surprisingly judges the world from it, reigns supreme from it and brings his new kingdom into existence through it.

It reminds me of the story Jeremiah Wright tells about a group of tourists who visit a London gallery and view a painting entitled 'Checkmate'. In it, Faust's king is held in checkmate by Mephistopheles. The group continue their tour of the gallery without noticing that they have left one of their number behind. This man paces back and forth in front of the picture. Two corridors later the peace of the gallery is shattered as they hear their forgotten companion cry, 'It's a lie! It's a lie! The king has another move!' The man was a Russian international chess champion and could see the move others had failed to notice. Wright comments, 'And the same thing is true when it comes to the King of kings. The King always has another move.'[39]

That was certainly true when the King of kings died on the cross. His next move, his resurrection, vindicated him; and a further move will follow when one day he comes on the clouds of heaven so that all may see his final vindication.

3. The rejected son

From the major key of sovereignty we must return to the minor key of darkness. To be true to Mark, the former must give way to the latter, not so as to eradicate the major key from the musical score, but so as to give the music its full depth. Not for nothing is Mark's view of the cross often considered to be the grimmest, finding its focus in the cry of dereliction, *'My God, my God, why have you forsaken me?'* (15:34). The cry does not stand alone, for the darkest of all cries is matched by the darkest of all skies.

a. The darkness of the scene
In Richard Burridge's view, 'the whole scene' is one 'of unrelieved

---

[37] Wright, *Crown and Fire*, p. 121.
[38] Forsyth, *Cruciality of the Cross*, p. 38.
[39] Quoted in P. S. Wilson, *The Four Pages of the Sermon: A Guide to Biblical Preaching* (Abingdon, 1999), p. 225.

darkness'.[40] And there is an awfulness, an almost total gloom about the way Mark tells the story, which is unmatched by Matthew or Luke. The darkness descended in the Garden of Gethsemane. There, Jesus was *deeply distressed and troubled*, and *his soul ... overwhelmed with sorrow to the point of death* (14:33–34). He still addressed God as *Abba*. Yet, knowing what was to come, he understandably prayed for the cup of God's wrath to be taken from him (14:36).[41] Still, in obedient submission he expressed his willingness to drink the cup to its dregs. The darkness in his soul deepened as his friends were unable to stay awake and to support him through his vigil (14:37–42). The loneliness of his agony reached its deepest darkness when he was arrested and *everyone deserted him and fled* (14:50). From then on he stood alone, in utter isolation.

With the other Gospel writers, Mark tells us that *darkness came over the whole land* from noon until three in the afternoon (15:33). But in the absence of some of Matthew's more spectacular supernatural signs, there is nothing to relieve it and it hovers more gloomily over the scene. It is analogous to the three-day plague of darkness that covered the earth before the first Passover in Egypt,[42] and speaks of the judgment of God prophesied by Amos.[43]

b. The darkness of separation

The darkness that enveloped him, however, was matched, or rather eclipsed by, the darkness of Christ's dying cry of God-forsakenness: *'My God, my God, why have you forsaken me?'* (15:34). The opening verse of Psalm 22, a psalm of lament, is the only saying from the cross Mark records. So the reader is inevitably drawn to it as of special importance (as Mark intends). This, for Mark, is clearly at the heart of what was happening that afternoon at the place called Golgotha. The depth of Christ's passion was reached in his moment of abandonment by God.

The cry captures the hidden meaning and spiritual reality of the crucifixion. On the cross Jesus experienced profound abandonment by God. Worse than the shame, the nakedness, the torture and the suffering was this: that his Father had deserted him. He who had lived in close harmony with God and proclaimed him to be a God of grace was deserted at the moment of his greatest need. He experienced no grace; only God-forsakenness. At his baptism the heavens had 'been torn open' (1:10) (*schizō* is the word in Greek), but here, though the curtain of the temple may have been triumphantly torn in two (again,

[40] Burridge, p. 60.
[41] Cf. Mark 10:38, and, for the Old Testament background, Ps. 75:8; Is. 51:17–23; Jer. 25:15–28; Lam. 4:21–22; Ezek. 23:31–34; Hab. 2:16; Zech. 12:2.
[42] Exod. 10:21–23.
[43] Amos 8:9.

schizō), the heavens remain firmly closed. On the mount of transfiguration, God had spoken: 'This is my Son, whom I love. Listen to him!' (9:7). On the mount of Calvary, the heavens were silent. God seemed absent from the scene.

Attempts have been made to soften the saying and to reduce its profound despair. It is true that Jesus cried *in a loud voice* (15:34),[44] suggesting a strong, even supernaturally strong, death.[45] It is true that Jesus addressed God as *my God*, which, while not the more intimate term, *Abba*, that he used in the Garden, suggests that his faith in God was still intact. On this basis, some say it is a cry of hope, not of despair.[46] Some, without any supporting evidence, have concluded that Jesus was not forsaken by God; that was just how it appeared to him at that moment. But no attempt to lessen the sheer horror of the cry is convincing. I agree with Jürgen Moltmann that it reveals that, 'just as there was a unique fellowship with God in his life and preaching, so in his death there was a unique abandonment by God ... The torment in his torments was this abandonment by God.'[47]

It is a paradox that 'at the very moment when he was most fully embodying the love of God he found himself totally separated from the love of God, the love which he had known in precious intimacy since childhood'.[48] Why should it be so? Surely it is because in dying in the sinner's place Christ so identifies himself with sin that the close relationship between the Father and the Son is inevitably broken. Is it not true that 'God made him who had no sin to be sin for us, so that in him we might become the righteousness of God'?[49] If so, is it not also true that the God who, in his awesome holiness and moral perfection, is 'too pure to look on evil',[50] must sever the connection at such a time?

How can this be? Some have sought to solve the enigma by saying that it was the human nature of Christ that suffered and died, and was therefore abandoned by God, while his divine nature did not; so in his divinity he remained in fellowship with the Father throughout. But this is 'quite unsatisfactory, because it seems to tear Jesus into two parts with opposite qualities, a humanity that suffered and a divinity that could not suffer'.[51] Christ is one, and either the whole of him suffered or none of him. If we must not tear Christ apart, neither must we tear the Trinity apart (as if we could). There could not have been a vacancy in the Trinity. Jesus died as the incarnate Christ, the divine Son.

---

[44] The loud voice is mentioned again in v. 37.
[45] See Gundry, *Mark*, p. 947.
[46] Senior, *Mark*, p. 123.
[47] Moltmann, p. 149.
[48] Wright, *Crown and Fire*, p. 45.
[49] 2 Cor. 5:21.
[50] Hab. 1:13.
[51] Smail, *Windows*, p. 70.

We are left with a remarkable antinomy that limited human minds will never be able to resolve. The wonder is that the incarnate Christ could die 'the most bitter of all deaths, the death of God-forsakenness that is the lot of sinners',[52] and that, in doing so, God, who abandons his Son, is really present and resolves the problem of our sin. The wonder is, in Luther's terms, that we can *flee from* God, who in his anger justly judges us for our sin, and *flee to* God in the crucified Christ to find mercy.[53] The wonder is that God reveals himself in mystery and in the hiddenness of the cross.

Luther spoke in daring terms about 'the crucified and hidden God'. Alister McGrath, one of his foremost recent interpreters, sums up the Reformer's position and demonstrates its theological and pastoral importance:

> God is revealed and human experience is illuminated through the cross of Jesus Christ. Yet, as the believer contemplates the appalling spectacle of the suffering and dying Christ, he is forced to the recognition that God does not appear to be there at all, and the only human experience that is seen is apparently pointless suffering. If God is to be found in the cross of Christ, then he is hidden in mystery; if human experience is illuminated by that cross, then the experiences which are illuminated are those of suffering abandonment, powerlessness and hopelessness, culminating in death.[54]

The fact that Christ entered into the depth of darkness on the cross means that he is able to identify sympathetically with the darkest of human situations. A God who remained majestically insulated in his heaven, impervious to our suffering, would not be a worthy or credible God in our suffering world. But in the cross of Christ he has entered into our experience of darkness. Therefore we have a theology which, as Moltman has taught us, can address situations like the Holocaust without sham or condescension.[55] It tells us that there are no depths of experience to which men and women can sink to which he has not already plunged. Christ is able to share with us the pain of desertion, the loneliness of suffering, the darkness of depression, the bewilderment of circumstances and the agony of death because he has been there. But, by being there, he did more than tell us he knows how it feels. He did more than tell us that he shares our pain and enters into our

---

[52] Morris, *Cross in the New Testament*, p. 49. See ibid., pp. 42–49, for a discussion of the meaning of separation from God.

[53] A. E. McGrath, *Luther's Theology of the Cross: Martin Luther's Theological Breakthrough* (Basil Blackwell, 1985), pp. 148–175.

[54] McGrath, *Enigma*, p. 102.

[55] Moltmann, p. 1.

suffering. He transforms it by his love, bringing light out of the darkness and life out of death. N. T. Wright sums up the paradox:

> The road ended not only in the bitterness of apparent failure, not only in the physical torment of a cruel and gruesome death, but in the spiritual darkness of separation from God, bearing upon himself the sins of the world. That is how the world was redeemed; not by Elijah and the Messiah coming and ridding Israel of her political foes, calling down fire to burn up all opposition, but by Jesus, commissioned by John in the spirit and power of Elijah ridding Israel and the world of her true enemies. Just as Elijah challenged the powers of darkness to that great contest, in which the god who answers by fire was to be God, so now Jesus takes on the rulers of the world: the might of Rome, the law of Israel, and behind both the usurping and destroying power of Satan. And this time the rules of the contest are: the god who answers by love, let him be God.[56]

4. The exemplary disciple

No account of the death of Jesus in the Gospel of Mark is complete without a consideration of it as a model for believers. It may be that his agenda was driven somewhat by the situation of his initial readers, although, since we can only make tentative suggestions as to who they were, we must be cautious about being too dogmatic in our views and therefore overly influenced in our reading of the Gospel.[57] Even so, many believe that, at least in part, the Gospel was intended to encourage Roman believers to stay faithful to Christ in spite of the persecution they were experiencing. Mark does this by demonstrating to them that what they were experiencing is the norm for disciples of Jesus, and by presenting him in his sufferings as their pattern and example. In this respect Jesus is the exemplary disciple.

a. The experience of the believer

The cross is central to Mark's understanding of what it means to be a disciple. Disciples of Jesus are called to be more than servants. They are called to 'deny themselves and take up their cross' to follow Christ. They are called to lose their lives for Christ and for the gospel if they wish to save them (8:34–35). In Dietrich Bonhoeffer's famous phrase, 'When Christ calls a man, he bids him come and die.'[58] Disciples of Jesus are to be cross-bearers. The cross is not only something he carried for them, but something they carry for him.

---

[56] Wright, *Crown and Fire*, p. 45.
[57] See discussion on p. 142 above, and Gundry, *Mark*, pp. 1022–1026.
[58] D. Bonhoeffer, *The Cost of Discipleship* (1937; ET SCM, 1964), p. 79.

From John the Baptist onwards, Mark leads us to expect that the disciples of Jesus will experience opposition and persecution. A careful analysis of Mark 13 shows remarkable parallels between it and the passion narrative.[59] There is a noticeable coincidence between the suffering Jesus personally endured and the sufferings his disciples will experience. The suffering of the disciples continues the unfolding of the messianic woes that will finally usher in the complete reign of God.

Disciples today are still called to bear the cross. In many parts of our world believers still experience hostility, harassment, imprisonment and even martyrdom. In the tolerant western world, the greatest hostility disciples are likely to reap is misunderstanding or a degree of personal antagonism. But even there, disciples must still bear the cross, for it signifies not only persecution and self-denial 'but on the positive side it is to follow Jesus in the self-giving love for God and for people'.[60] 'True disciples', as Morna Hooker recently claimed, 'will still be found trudging along the road that leads to a cross, following the crucified and risen Lord' as their example.[61]

b. The community of the believer

The cross results not only in the salvation of individuals but in the creation of a new community. It is evident in Jesus' ministry, and particularly in the selection and training of his disciples, that he sought to establish a fellowship of believers who would live his way and spread his message once he had died. A new nation, a new priesthood, a people belonging to God, were being called into existence through him.

But it is a surprising community, not just in that he chose a remarkably unstable and ordinary bunch of men and women to be its members, but because those on the margins of society are found at the community's centre and those on the outside are warmly welcomed in. The passion narrative brings it all to a head. It was *Simon, a man from Cyrene*, a man from the Diaspora, who carried his cross when Jesus stumbled on the way to Golgotha (15:21). According to Mark's note, Simon must have become a disciple, for his family was known within the church. A Roman centurion was the only one to confess the truth without sarcasm or irony when Jesus died (15:39).When all his male disciples deserted him, there at the cross were the women who had cared for Jesus' needs during his lifetime and had followed him from Galilee to Jerusalem. It would have been costly, even dangerous, for

[59] J. B. Green, 'The death of Jesus', in *DJG*, pp. 158–159. He notes the destruction of the temple (13:2; 14:48; 15:38); 'delivered up' (13:9, 11–12; 14:10–11, 18); betrayal (13:12–13; 14:10, 21, 43); darkness (13:24; 15:33); Son of Man, tribulation, parousia (13:26; 14:62); the 'hour' (13:32–22; 14:42–42); and watching (13:5, 9, 23, 33, 35, 37; 14:34, 37–38).
[60] Smail, *Windows*, p. 100.
[61] Hooker, *Not Ashamed*, p. 67.

them to have identified with him (15:40–41). But the cross draws these unlikely people in.

The ripping of the temple curtain in two (15:38) graphically underlines what his selection of disciples exemplifies. The cross has made access to God available to all, irrespective of gender or race. The old 'private access' road of Judaism has been closed. There is only one access route in the new age, and it goes through the cross. And along that way tread men and women, Jews and Gentiles, black and white, rich and poor, all on a level footing, carrying their own crosses, enjoying restored communion with God and forming the new humanity.

In his passion narrative, then, Mark shows Jesus as the suffering servant who bears away the sins of the world; the conquering king who defeats the oppressing powers that threaten our fallen world; the rejected son who enters the darkness of our lives and in a strange and mysterious way brings light to them; and the exemplary disciple who encourages us to go on carrying the cross until his new community is complete and we see him *coming on the clouds of heaven* (14:62). Major keys of a strong and sovereign king mingle with minor keys of suffering and rejection. Yet when the full score is heard, to use Robert Gundry's words, 'the Jesus of Mark is overpowering. Let the weak find in him their champion, the strong their conqueror.'[62]

[62] Gundry, *Mark*, p. 1026.

Luke 22:1 – 23:56
8. Compassionate Saviour

Luke throws open the window, high above the scene of Calvary, and presents us with a third description of the death of Jesus. Choosing new colours, he depicts the events (skilled artist that he is) in a startlingly fresh light, picking out features others have omitted. Gone are both the brooding darkness of Mark and the triumphant supernaturalism of Matthew. Present is a very human Christ who is, above all, both a trusting Son and a compassionate Saviour. That is just as one would expect from Luke, whose theme throughout the Gospel is the good news of a broad and deep salvation; salvation 'in all its fulness to all persons'.[1]

Some say that Luke's understanding of salvation depends more on the resurrection and exaltation of Jesus, after the crucifixion, than on the cross itself; and that he plays down the redemptive significance of Jesus' death.[2] But this view is to be rejected, since a careful analysis of what Luke writes in this regard, in comparison with Matthew and Mark, demonstrates that, although he may omit some significant material (such as the full ransom saying of Mark 10:45),[3] he includes as much as they do but in other ways. If there is less about the death of Jesus in Luke (which is to be doubted), Marshall concludes that 'it is not in any way remarkable'[4] when measured by the standards of the other Gospels. A different perspective on the cross is not to be mistaken for a diminution of the cross's significance in salvation.

As well as ignoring Jesus' saying that he had come 'to give his life as a ransom for many', Luke leaves out a number of other features of the passion story which Matthew and Mark have included. He does not

---

[1] J. B. Green, *The Theology of Luke* (Cambridge University Press, 1995), p. 24. On the scholarly consensus see ibid., *passim*, and I. H. Marshall, *Luke: Historian and Theologian* (1970; Paternoster, 1974), *passim*.

[2] Creed, p. lxxii.

[3] He includes the first half of the saying in 22:27 but omits the crucial phrase about the ransom.

[4] Marshall, *Luke: Historian*, p. 171.

include here the anointing that took place at the home of Simon the Leper in Bethany.[5] The sorrow Jesus expresses in the Garden of Gethsemane is less intense, in spite of earnest prayer and his sweating *drops of blood* (22:44).[6] There are no false witnesses at his trial.[7] The Jewish leaders and temple guards mock Jesus, but neither the Roman soldiers nor the crowds do so. Pilate expresses no frustration or amazement at the silence of Jesus, and is described as *wanting to release Jesus* (23:20). Most remarkable of all, there is no cry of dereliction from the cross.

Yet Luke includes a number of elements of the passion story which Matthew and Mark omit. Only Luke mentions that Jesus was comforted by an angel in Gethsemane (22:43). He alone describes the healing of Malchus' severed ear (22:51). Luke exclusively reports that on three occasions Pilate declared Jesus to be innocent (23:4, 14, 22). None of the other Gospels mentions the trial before Herod (23:6–16), or the weeping women of Jerusalem (23:27–32), or the request of the dying thief (23:39–43). And Luke records three sayings from the cross the others forget to mention (23:34, 43, 46). These additions all put the cross in a different light and contribute to another (complementary, not contradictory) perspective on what happened on Calvary.

Four features of Luke's portrait may be highlighted. He presents the dying Christ as a deliberate victim, a compassionate Saviour, a trusting Son and a coming king.

1. Deliberate victim

Having arrived in Rio de Janeiro one Monday morning, I was struck by a news report that only fifty-six people had died in gun battles that weekend. My hosts told me that such a number was a modest achievement for a city so tragically addicted to violence, and that the previous year some 200 people had died simply by being caught in the cross-fire. They were not the targets of their opponents' bullets; they just happened to be in the wrong place at the wrong time. Luke makes it clear that Jesus was not an unfortunate victim who got caught in the cross-fire, but one whose death occurred because he was the deliberate target of a number of powers, each moving against him for its own motives, which may not have been consistent with those of the others. The combined effect of this alliance was to make his death inevitable.

---

[5] He includes it at 7:36–50.

[6] Perhaps the reference to blood is the sort of detail one might expect a medical doctor to observe.

[7] If part of Luke's intention was to commend the Christian gospel to the Roman authorities, it would be only diplomatic on Luke's part to play down those elements that suggested that the trial was a travesty of justice.

He died as a result of the outworking of divine necessity, satanic manipulation and human engineering.

a. The power of divine necessity

At the very start of Luke's Gospel it is stated that salvation comes about because God has graciously chosen to intervene in history (e.g. 1:46–55, 67–79). It is God's conscious initiative and his calculated action that bring it about, through the life, death and resurrection of Jesus Christ. Luke uses 'a metaphorical arsenal' to communicate that 'the arrival and ministry of Jesus [are] the actualisation of God's redemptive plan in history'.[8]

If that was true of his ministry in general, it was especially true of his death on the cross. It was God's plan that he should die to bring about deliverance and salvation. Jesus understood his death to be an act of divine necessity (9:22). He spoke of it as the outworking of a careful plan (9:51) and as the fulfilment of prophetic Scripture (18:31).

Jesus again recognized the hand of God in it all when, during the last supper, he said to his disciples, *'The Son of Man will go as it has been decreed …'* (22:22). Here is a divine passive. The one who issued the decree was God the Father.[9] Jesus sensed that his destiny is coming to completion in the Garden of Gethsemane, when, quoting Isaiah 53:12, *'And he was numbered with the transgressors'*, he said, *'Yes, what is written about me is reaching its fulfilment'* (22:37). Throughout Luke's account of his trial and death there are several allusions to the way in which the Scriptures were being fulfilled in what was happening (23: 9, 33, 34, 36).[10] And after the resurrection, Jesus tried to make sense of it all to two disciples on the road to Emmaus by saying, 'Did not the Christ have to suffer these things and then enter his glory?' (24:26).

The eternal God had decreed that through this historic event of the sacrifice of his Son, the salvation of the world should be accomplished. We must, of course, be careful when speaking in these terms. We must not drive a wedge between Father and Son, as if an angry Father sadistically meted out punishment to a reluctant Son. There is no discord between them; they work in perfect harmony. As John Stott reminds us, 'We must never make Christ the object of God's punishment or God the object of Christ's persuasion, for both God and Christ were subjects not objects, taking the initiative together to save sinners.'[11] Indeed, the Son is everywhere presented as a willing and obedient Son who voluntarily submits to fulfilling the Father's plan. In Luke's report of the last supper, for example, he seems deliberately to

---

[8] Green, *Luke*, p. 28.
[9] Cf. Is. 53:10.
[10] The allusions are to Is. 53:7, 12; Ps. 22:18 and 69:21 respectively.
[11] Stott, *Cross of Christ*, p. 151.

bring out the willingness of Jesus to suffer in contrast to 'the treachery, rivalry and weakness of the disciples who persist in incomprehension of what is really happening'.[12]

One power that had a hand in the death of Jesus, then, is the power of his own Father, to whom Jesus willingly surrendered in order to effect salvation.

b. The power of satanic manipulation

God was not the only one who had a hand in the crucifixion, even if the other powers that interfered were not the entirely free agents they assumed themselves to be. Satan appears from time to time on the stage of Luke's Gospel, and becomes a key player. We are first introduced to him when he stalks Jesus in the desert of temptation (4:1–13), at the conclusion of which he leaves Jesus 'until an opportune time'. On a number of occasions Jesus encountered hostile, demonic forces in his ministry. But, as Donald Senior notes, 'the definitive battleground was to be the Passion'.[13] The passion was the 'opportune time' for which Satan had been waiting to return.

Behind the scenes, unnoticed but no less sure for that, Satan was at work, enticing even those who were intimate with Jesus to align themselves with those who were hostile to him. He enlisted Judas to his fatal cause (22:3) and even sought to cause Peter to be unfaithful (22:31), as once he did Job. For a brief moment he succeeded with Peter, who proved to lack the steadfastness he had pompously assumed would be his (22:54–66). But the damage of his betrayal was limited and the fall recoverable, because Jesus, a stronger power than Satan, had prayed for his protection.

When Jesus was finally arrested, he submitted to his captors without struggle, commenting, *'this is your hour – when darkness reigns'* (22:53).[14] Although he was addressing his kidnappers, it would seem that behind them Jesus saw Satan at work, since darkness 'is symbolic of the authority of Satan'.[15] This was not the darkness of desertion recorded by Mark, but the darkness of hostility and evil, which reaches the zenith of its opposition to God in seeking to do away with the Lord of glory. Here was a battle of cosmic proportions, far greater than anything that could be explained by the events on earth. Satan, though, was unaware that in playing his dangerous game he was paradoxically fulfilling God's plan and simultaneously overreaching himself and spelling his own defeat. But for the moment, evil seemed to triumph.

[12] Marshall, *Gospel of Luke*, p. 786.
[13] Senior, *Luke*, p. 171.
[14] Cf. John 13:30: 'As soon as Judas had taken the bread, he went out. And it was night.'
[15] Acts 26:18. Green, *Luke*, p. 785.

Putting it this way, Luke, more than any of the other Gospel writers, links the cause of Christ's death with 'ultimate evil'.[16]

c. The powers of human engineering

The events that can be accounted for in terms of the divine plan and of demonic opposition can also be accounted for from a human standpoint. 'Evil's threatening presence weaves its way through the story, masked with a human face,' writes Senior.[17] More exactly, it weaves its way through with a number of human faces. Responsibility for the death of Jesus lies with God, with Satan and, most definitely, with human beings. Any number of people got caught on the web of evil as they plotted, to one degree or another, to be rid of the Christ. Unholy alliances were made and unmade[18] in the cause of disposing of Jesus. Enemies became friends as they combined in the common cause of doing away with the troublesome man from Nazareth. In case the note is missed, Luke bluntly spells it out in the reference to one 'sinister confederacy':[19] *That day Herod and Pilate became friends – before this they had been enemies* (23:12). Even his disciples were implicated. None can escape inclusion in the alliance of guilt that let Jesus die.

i. The disciples: the guilt of self-centredness (22:24–30)

During the last supper, when Jesus was, at least to us, obviously informing the disciples about his impending death and investing the Passover meal with a new meaning, the disciples were preoccupied with their own concerns. *Also a dispute arose among them as to which of them was considered to be greatest* (22:24). Their unreconstructed lust for power and status clouded their perception and prevented them from attending to the needs of their Lord, as they should have done at this moment. Patiently he instructed them once more that in his kingdom true greatness lies in lowly service. Their pride was but one example of their sin, the sin of his friends, which was responsible for his bearing the cross.

ii. Judas: the guilt of greed (22:3–6, 22)

While we cannot be certain of Judas' motives, we can be sure that by his betrayal he bore some responsibility for the death of his master (22:22). It is likely that his motive was greed. Once Satan had inspired him to betray Jesus he went to the Jewish authorities to offer his services. Luke's comment is: *They were delighted and agreed to give him money* (22:5). He portrays him as an opportunist. While he tells us little

---

[16] Senior, *Luke*, p. 172.
[17] Ibid.
[18] Green, *Luke*, p. 745.
[19] Milne, p. 254.

about Judas' character, others describe him as a mercenary individual, capable of stirring up dissent among the disciples. John, who is particularly damning of Judas' character,[20] more than hints that his act of betrayal was triggered by Mary's extravagant anointing of Jesus at Bethany.[21] 'The evangelists, with a sense of high drama,' writes John Stott, 'deliberately contrast Mary and Judas, her uncalculating generosity and his coldly calculated bargain.'[22] The juxtaposition is stark. She poured out her precious ointment. He picked up his useless money.[23] He gave his Lord over into the hands of his executioners for thirty silver coins, the value set on the life of a common slave.[24]

iii. Peter: the guilt of silence (22:31–34, 54–62)

Sin consists not only in betrayal, blasphemy and murder but equally in failure, silence and apathy. Peter, as prophesied, failed to confess his Lord when opportunity arose. His boast that he would go to prison and die for Christ was as worthless as it was grand, as must have been evident not only to Jesus but to the other disciples as well. When the time came, he expressed denial, not discipleship. As soon as the cock crowed he knew his failure and *went outside and wept bitterly* (62). His failure to take a stand for Christ drove yet another nail into the cross.

And yet God specializes in bringing good out of evil, and the failure had a curiously positive result in Peter's life. As Richard Bauckham and Trevor Hart observe, 'since the cross is the place where God's love embraces failure and tragedy, there was no better place to fail than on the way to the cross. Peter's failure was precisely God's opportunity.'[25] It shattered his illusion about himself and the way he would have liked others to think of him – as the cross always does, for it 'forces us to see ourselves as we really are, not as we would like to be seen'.[26] The cross demonstrates that only losers succeed in Christ's kingdom. Consequently, 'Peter's failure qualifies him to begin to be a disciple on the way of the cross.'[27] The future apostle of the church had at last grasped his first vital lesson in leadership. In order to lead, one has to have confidence in Christ and his word, not in oneself and one's own abilities.

iv. The priests: the guilt of religion (22:66–71)

The trial before the Sanhedrin was brief but significant: brief because

---

[20] John 12:4–6.
[21] Matt. 26:6–13; Mark 14:3–9.
[22] Stott, *Cross of Christ*, p. 57.
[23] R. Brown, 'Saving message', p. 65.
[24] According to Exod. 21:32.
[25] Bauckham and Hart, p. 30.
[26] Ibid., p. 35.
[27] Ibid., p. 33.

Luke wants to incorporate in the trial other scenes that Matthew and Mark omit significant because it went to the heart of the matter. Joel Green has said that the battle Jesus fought with the council of the elders was one of hermeneutics. 'Throughout his ministry, Jesus had been involved in a war of interpretation: Who understands and serves the divine aim, really? Who interprets and embodies the divine word, really?'[28] The priests and elders claimed to be the representatives of God, the only legitimate interpreters of his word, the only true custodians of the law and the only qualified directors of worship. Jesus had challenged all that, and had threatened their customs and their temple.

The heart of the issue, therefore, was the identity of Jesus. If he was the Christ, they should have recognized him and should now defer to him. If he was not, he was a blasphemer and deserved death. Jesus' response to their examination indicated that they had had enough time to understand his identity by now – indeed, the crowds had grasped it long ago (19:28–40; 20:41–47) – and at this late moment he was not going to do anything but confirm them in their obtuseness. He would not go through the pointless charade either of answering their questions (since they had already made up their minds and had no desire to learn the truth) or of asking them any questions (since, on the basis of previous experience [20:1–8], they would not reply). He did, however openly declare his messiahship before them. *'From now on,'* he said, *'the Son of Man will be seated at the right hand of the mighty God'* (69). Now that he stood in weakness before them, he announced that the next phase of the salvation drama was about to begin. His disgrace was about to reach its height and, having done so, would bring about a tremendous reversal in his fortunes. The condemned prisoner would become the reigning Lord.

Their religion was getting in the way, as law-bound and respectable religion sometimes still does. They believed that they were serving God by opposing Christ, whereas they were actually serving Satan. Two hundred metres from where the interrogation took place, God was being religiously worshipped in the temple sanctuary. But where they stood, that same religion was leading to the execution of God's Son.

v. Pilate: the guilt of compromise (23:1–5, 13–25)

Luke paints a more favourable picture of Pilate than does any other Gospel writer. The procurator who ruled Palestine somewhat incompetently from AD 26 to 36 was in a difficult position. The charge the Jewish authorities brought against Jesus was that he was seeking to restore the Hasmonean dynasty. Pilate could ill afford to ignore a threat of political insurrection. They all knew, of course, that this man from

[28] Green, *Luke*, pp. 746.

Nazareth was unlike the leaders of any other political revolution they had encountered. Even so, the accusation had to be examined. After the preliminary hearing, Pilate declared Jesus innocent. Then, seeking to shift responsibility, he sent Jesus to Herod, since he discovered that he hailed from Galilee, Herod's territory. In the second hearing before Pilate, twice more he clearly declares Jesus to be innocent: *'I have found in him no grounds for the death penalty'* (22). In spite of all this, he still bent to the wind and surrendered Jesus to be crucified.

True, Pilate did not protest his innocence in the same dramatic way as in Matthew.[29] But he clearly longed to be seen as innocent, and to shift the blame to others. Honest examination compels one to admit, however, that he was far from innocent. In permitting this injustice, Pilate 'not only put cynical power-games before justice (which was normal), but also, on this occasion, put naked self-interest before both'.[30]

The instincts towards self-preservation of this power-hungry politician helped to put Jesus to death.

vi. Herod: the guilt of ridicule (23:8–12)

Pilate next implicated Herod in the web of guilt. Since Herod *had been wanting to see him*, it brought Pilate and Herod into a temporary alliance. Pilate's motive may have been to pass the buck to Herod, or, more likely in view of verse 15, to secure another vote in favour of Jesus' innocence. Herod's motives were less sincere, as Luke's readers should have suspected. Luke has prepared the way for this encounter. Having beheaded John the Baptist, Herod was disturbed at the reports that he seemed to have come to life again in the guise of Jesus from Nazareth. Herod therefore naturally expressed a desire to meet Jesus (9:7–9). But the next time Luke mentions him he tells us that Herod wished to kill Jesus (13:31). So it was unlikely to have been a comfortable interview to which Pilate was subjecting Jesus, and indeed it was not.

Herod was not a dispassionate enquirer after truth. It was not disinterested curiosity that made him want to see Jesus. He wanted to see him only to laugh at him. After the events of the previous night, Jesus must have cut a pitiful figure as he stood before Herod, who tried to entice him to do some sensational trick and harried him with questions, egged on by the Jewish religious leaders. None of this provoked Jesus to reply, which only incensed Herod further. Herod's true motives then became apparent. He unleashed a volley of ridicule on Jesus and permitted his soldiers to do the same. Deriding him as a failed messiah, they dressed him in the mock robes of a king and sent him back to Pilate.

---

[29] Matt. 27:24.
[30] Wright, *Jesus and the Victory*, p. 547.

Far from helping Pilate to establish the innocence of Jesus, Herod's spurious legal hearing only served to knock another nail into Christ's cross and to establish the guilt of all those who, feigning curiosity, really want to ridicule the Christ.

Others, too, were caught up in the web of guilt. The guards who mocked him when he was first arrested (22:63–65), the apathetic crowds who watched him on the cross (23:35) and the soldiers who were just doing their jobs (23:36–37) all bear their responsibility for his death, just as the ordinary men and women who became 'Hitler's willing executioners'[31] shared responsibility for Nazi persecution of the Jews. The picture of guilt built up by Luke suggests that no human escapes some measure of blame for Jesus' execution. It was sin, the sin of religious leaders and of cynical politicians, of outright enemies and of weak friends, of the named and the unnamed – and not only theirs but ours – that nailed him to that tree.

Luke, then, explains the death of Jesus on three levels. It was caused by the Father out of love, by the devil out of hate and by human beings out of sin. Each deliberately targeted him and made him a victim. But only one will prevailed: that of the Father, who willed that the cross would 'give his people the knowledge of salvation through the forgiveness of their sins' (1:77).

2. Compassionate Saviour

The most outstanding feature of Luke's portrait of the death of Jesus is the care and compassion he showed to people as he wended his way to the cross at a time when, surely, he had every right to be preoccupied with his own suffering. Luke seems to have been naturally generous in his estimate of other people. In comparison with Mark, he minimizes the failure of the disciples in the Garden (they seek to defend him rather than desert him, 22:49–50)[32] and the hostility of the crowds (the hostility chiefly comes from the rulers, 23:35),[33] and he alone mentions the sorrow of the women of Jerusalem at his death (23:27) and the remorse of the people as they returned home from the 'spectacle' (23:48, NRSV). What draws our attention, however, is not Luke's generosity but the Saviour's compassion. Four aspects of the story particularly bring his compassion to our notice.

a. The healing of Malchus (22:49–51)

The disciples, still thinking of the ways of human kings, believed that

---

[31] The title of a book by Daniel J. Goldhagan, in which he documents the willing compliance of ordinary people in Hitler's anti-Jewish programmes (Abacus, 1997).
[32] Cf. Mark 14:50.
[33] Cf. Matt. 27:39–40; Mark 15:29–30.

the use of force would deliver their master from his captors and usher in his kingdom. So they took their swords to the Garden of Gethsemane and used them when Judas and his posse made their move. We should credit them with courage and the best of intentions. They were 'not necessarily reckless. Jesus might have been able to escape in the dark while Peter and the others kept the police busy. Jesus might have survived.'[34] Alas, it was not meant to be, and in the mêlée, the unfortunate Malchus,[35] a servant of the high priest, had his ear severed from his head.

Jesus not only commanded his disciples to cease the skirmish immediately, and not only (as so often before) brought peace into an unruly situation, but also *touched the man's ear and healed him*. It was a remarkable act of grace on the part of Jesus. By it he displayed his loving-kindness and saving power towards those who were intent on destroying him. The only one to be hurt in the coming hours was Christ himself.

b. The women of Jerusalem (23:27–28)

It is with some relief that we read that some of the crowd showed sensitivity to the tragedy unfolding around them and that, as he made his tortured way up the Via Dolorosa, the women of Jerusalem *mourned and wailed for him*. They 'grieve over his impending death and play the part of the mourners ahead of time', as was customary for those who followed condemned criminals on their death march.[36] It was a grief that others were later to share (23:48), but which these women anticipated before the final act of crucifixion took place.

Jesus immediately spoke to them, as if still in control. His concern was not for himself but for them. Rather than giving voice to anticipatory grief on his behalf, they should be grieving for themselves. Their future was to be full of suffering, as he already warned them and for the reasons given.[37] The time would shortly come when disaster would strike the city of Jerusalem to the extent that those without children, normally considered unfortunate, would be considered blessed, for there would be no future for children to enjoy. The cause of the impending disaster was the people's long hostility towards God which was, at that moment, reaching its climax as they rejected and crucified his Son.

The Jesus who had wept over Jerusalem (19:41–44) continued to exercise love and compassion towards those caught up in its wickedness, even while he made his way to the cross.

---

[34] Bauckham and Hart, p. 31.
[35] John 18:10 gives us his name and tells us Peter was the aggressor.
[36] Nolland, p. 1139.
[37] Luke 13:34–35; 19:41–44; 21:20–24.

c. The prayer of forgiveness (23:34)

Luke continues to highlight distinctive features of the crucifixion in his report of Jesus' words from the cross. He records three sayings that are not mentioned elsewhere, including Jesus' prayer for forgiveness: *'Father, forgive them, for they do not know what they are doing.'* Some argue that his prayer was limited in its range. He was asking the Father to forgive the soldiers who were carrying out the execution. It was their job to do so, the reasoning goes, and they knew no better. They were acting out of ignorance. They had crucified people before and would do so again. They were not responsible for their actions. The authority for the execution came from elsewhere. It was their task to obey.

It may well be that these infantrymen were the focus of his compassion and pardon as he hung, naked and dying, on the cross. It fits with Luke's account of Jesus' death, with its recurring note that he showed remarkable awareness of those around him and poured out love and kindness on them. John Nolland points out that by immediately describing the soldiers' concern to divide up his possessions, verse 34 draws a deliberate contrast 'between Jesus' concern for his executioners and their disregard of him'.[38] And yet the cry surely cannot be limited to them. It must surely reach out to all those involved in his execution, Jews and Romans, rulers and people, then and now alike. For, although some moved against him in conscious antagonism and could not really claim ignorance as a defence, it is true that all were ignorant of the deeper purposes of God that were being accomplished through his death.

d. The dying criminal (23:40–43)

The compassion of the Saviour certainly extended to a proven and convicted criminal, one guilty of serious crimes rather than a petty thief,[39] who hung on the cross beside him. This man was an undoubted sinner, and yet, in the closing moments of his life, he received from Jesus the assurance that in spite of all the wrong he had done, *today* he would *be with* him *in paradise* (43). He sought 'the Lord's mercy', as Robert Stein says, 'and amazingly found salvation'.[40] Outrageous grace was at work. This man's eternal future had nothing to do with justice. He deserved to die and to face God's judgment. But his eternal future had everything to do with mercy, with the God who 'is kind to the ungrateful and wicked' (6:35) and who, because his Son died for their sin as their substitute, freely forgives. All through Luke's Gospel Jesus

[38] Nolland, p. 1146.
[39] *Kakourgos* in Greek. BAGD defines it as 'one who commits gross misdeeds and serious crimes' (p. 399).
[40] Stein, p. 593.

161

had shown special concern for the poor, the marginalized and the outsider. Now, on the cross, Jesus embraced the greatest outsider of all and promised him a place in paradise. All the suffering criminal had to do was to look to the suffering Christ and ask for mercy. In this regard he is the model for us all. Salvation is by faith in Christ alone, whoever we are.

Two further things are worth noting about this saying. 'Paradise' originally referred to a garden, the garden of the Lord,[41] but eventually came to stand for the home of the righteous. In using the word, Jesus is saying not only that this unrighteous man will live henceforth among the righteous, but that something even grander was happening that day. Jesus not only confirmed the salvation of an individual but hinted at a work of cosmic re-creation in which the Garden of Eden, from which men and women had been expelled, was being restored. The dwelling of men and women would once more be with God.[42]

The second comment should be obvious, but is worth making in view of contemporary theology's emphasis on the cross as the place where Christ identified with our pain and entered into our suffering. What Jesus did for the penitent criminal that day on Calvary was to save him, not just identify with him in his suffering. A theology of the cross that speaks only of identification and not of salvation does not go far enough. Tom Smail makes the point beautifully:

> To meet the penitent thief Jesus had to hang on the other cross beside him, but, when the man turned to him there, he did not say only 'Today I am with you on Calvary', but also 'Today you will be with me in paradise.' The sight of Jesus with us in our pain is the promise of our healing; the sight of Jesus sharing our death is the promise of our life.[43]

The scene leading to and around the cross is a busy, noisy, crowded one. So many different people find a part to play and so many of them are embraced in the love that comes forth from the man who is at the centre of it all. His love particularly embraces the unlikely ones, from a dying thief to a hardened centurion (23:47), from weeping women to a Jewish leader (23:50–54). Richard Burridge suggests that the symbol that most captures Luke's Christ is that of an ox, a bearer of burdens. And here, right at the last (he writes), 'the bearer of burdens is still trying to save women, the ordinary squaddies, and a crucified thief – but then it always was the burden of the ox to carry the weight of

[41] Gen. 2:8; 13:10.
[42] Rev. 21:1–5; 22:1–5.
[43] Smail, *Windows*, p. 73.

others, and to be sacrificed in Jerusalem for sin'.[44] Donald Senior makes the same point. Commenting on 'the magnetic power of the cross', he points out that in each of the unique incidents that Luke records, 'someone burdened with fear or weakness or evil is liberated from their burden by their proximity to the cross'.[45]

Jesus, who had been a compassionate Saviour throughout his life – healing, releasing, forgiving – continued to be a compassionate Saviour in his passion and death. Indeed, it was through his death that he fully entered into his vocation, since it was only by his accepting the weight of sin and death in place of others that he could release them from their debts and free them from the burdens that oppressed them.

3. Trusting Son

Mark presents Jesus as a rejected Son. His haunting memory of Golgotha is of the piercing words of the cry of dereliction. Matthew presents Jesus as a vindicated Son. His memory is not only of the cry of desertion but of the supernatural happenings that accompanied his death. Luke draws something else from the memories of his informants (cf. 1:1–4). If they commented on Jesus' cry of God-forsakenness, Luke chooses not to mention it. What he sees instead in the relationship between the Father and the Son is steady, unwavering, on-going trust.

These pictures need not conflict with one another. Relationships are complex and frequently involve many, even contradictory, emotions simultaneously. The child who is being punished by a parent may well feel that parent to be the enemy, while at the same time knowing and continuing to trust that the parent is a loving friend. So it is with Christ, as Matthew, Mark and Luke view the scene of the cross from their respective vantage points.

Donald Senior insightfully observes that it is when we face crises in life that 'shallow relationships fall away [and] the true values of our deepest soul well up to the surface, and the rare treasures of life and fidelity stand out luminously'.[46] When Jesus faced the crisis of his passion it was towards the Father, not away from him, that he turned – revealing the depth and inseparable nature of their relationship. There was no glimmer of suspicion in Jesus' mind as to his Father's plan. There was no urgent demand for vindication of his sonship. Instead, from the opening scene of the passion narrative in the upper room, he showed a quiet and accepting confidence that he would come through the suffering and enter into his kingdom (22:16, 18).

[44] Burridge, p. 127.
[45] Senior, *Luke*, pp. 163–164.
[46] Ibid., p. 166.

Several moments in Luke's passion narrative reveal the special relationship between Father and Son.

a. In the Garden (22:43)

Only Luke mentions the *angel from heaven* who came to Jesus during his agony in the Garden to strengthen him. For the other Gospel writers, the agony in the Garden was a lonely vigil where his human companions failed him and fell asleep before deserting him altogether. But divine assistance was at hand. His Father arranged for an extraterrestrial visitor to support him through his hour of trial. So, although the power of the gathering darkness was formidable, it could not negate the presence of God, which remained real to the last.

Luke has a special interest in angels, mentioning them often in the story of Jesus' birth. Now those who attended his coming into the world will attend his departure from it. Matthew's passion narrative mentions angels too, but the difference between the Gospels is instructive. Matthew speaks of the legions of angels which Christ could have called to his defence as he was arrested.[47] Luke speaks of a solitary angel who came not to assist Jesus to avoid the cross but to encourage him to go through with it. Again, we see that Matthew thinks in terms of Christ's sonship as being supernaturally vindicated, whereas Luke sees it in terms of trusting obedience.

b. During the trial (22:69)

Each of the synoptic evangelists reports that Jesus, when being interrogated by the Jewish Council, said, *'From now on, the Son of Man will be seated at the right hand of the mighty God.'*[48] But the tone with which Jesus speaks in Luke is again different from the other Gospels. The different context and the shorter statement in Luke make it sound more like the voice of quiet trust than of defiant proclamation. Jesus knew his true identity and was convinced that the cross would be the gateway to his throne. His Father would not let him down.

c. On the cross (23:34, 43, 46)

The most remarkable evidence of Jesus' confidence is found in the words he spoke on the cross. Each of the three sayings exudes confidence. First, enemies were forgiven (34). The fight did not need to go on any longer, for the battle had been won. Jesus was magnanimous in victory. Secondly, to the dying thief there was the promise that *'today you will be with me in paradise'* (43). There was no question or uncertainty about the promise.

---

[47] Matt. 26:53.
[48] Matt. 26:64; Mark 14:62. Matthew and Mark add 'and coming on the clouds of heaven'.

Thirdly, and most astonishing of all, is his dying breath: *'Father, into your hands I commit my spirit'* (46). The cry was spoken not with the hesitancy of doubt but *with a loud voice*, with conviction and with certainty. It did not occur to Jesus that his self-offering would be other than accepted by the Father. His words come from the Psalms, as did the cry of dereliction. They come, though, not from Psalm 22 or any of the other vulnerable formulations found in the Psalms of Lament, but from Psalm 31:5, a psalm that expresses assurance that deliverance will come as one takes refuge in God. So Jesus willingly surrendered his spirit to God and left his fate with God, knowing that his vindication would follow. In his final moment he declared that 'God is trustworthy and [not even] death can discredit God'.[49]

Two days later the resurrection proved that his confidence had not been misplaced. He had suffered death but had not been destroyed by it. He had let Satan do his worst, but had beaten Satan hands down. He had let darkness, lies, betrayal and religion have their way, but, by commending his spirit to God, he had returned from the fight having defeated them all. 'His unbreakable bond of trust with God' meant that, having experienced death, he had now proved himself to be 'the saviour and liberator, God's champion and strong one'.[50]

No doubt Luke's primary reason for this emphasis was to prove Jesus' divine and unbroken sonship. But the picture serves, in a secondary way, to remind Christian disciples that God is present even when the circumstances are grim and he cannot easily be seen. Therefore, he is worth trusting through the most painful and unenviable of situations and when his hand seems heavy on us. For we know that the truth is that he is present with us and never deserts us, and that in the end he will bring us through to a place where we experience the blessing of his full salvation in a more agreeable way.

4. Coming king

The three themes we have examined so far do not exhaust Luke's nuanced account of the death of Christ. One other theme, at least, deserves a brief mention. In an editorial note in 9:51, Luke remarks, 'As the time approached for him to be taken up to heaven, Jesus resolutely set out for Jerusalem.' The word rendered 'taken up' (*analēmpsis*) is a rare word normally used for 'elevation'. It could refer to his death, but the verses following remind one of the ministry of Elijah, and so it is more likely to be a reference to his ascension. However, we do not have to choose. Jerusalem is to be the place where Christ is both lifted up on the cross in shame and taken up to heaven in exaltation. In the final

---

[49] Senior, *Luke*, p. 169.
[50] Ibid., p. 165.

sequence of events, both moves belong together, for the cross inaugurates the coronation of the king.

Then, too, there is the way in which Luke adds future-oriented notes to the words of Jesus at the last supper. The final meal with his disciples takes a form that anticipates the messianic banquet to be held at the end of time, much spoken of in Judaism,[51] and to which they looked forward. The next time he will eat or drink, Jesus says (22:16, 18), is at the banquet 'where the redeemed would sit and feast with the Messiah'[52] and the hungry would be filled and the thirsty satisfied (6:21). It is the cross that grants him final entry to his kingdom and points forward to its consummation. The point of these comments, as Marion Soards has remarked, is that they make the disciples look forward to see in a longer time-frame the significance of the events they are about to witness. The events the disciples were about to see were not just a passing tragedy but were 'of ultimate significance'.[53] The death of Christ was to activate the final phase of the consummation of his kingdom.

Both the saying of 9:51 and the meal of 22:7–38, then, suggest that we must add to the gallery of portraits painted by Luke that of the suffering Christ as the exalted and coming king.

Conclusion

The record of Christ's passion in Luke is totally consistent with the interests displayed in the rest of his Gospel. Luke is interested in people. As a careful observer of people, it is no surprise that he includes more people than his fellow-writers in the story as the events of Calvary develop. Nor should it surprise us that he is interested in the question of where responsibility lay and what motives they had for deliberately selecting him as their victim; nor that he examines the dynamics of relationship between Christ and those around him as he goes to his cross, revealing himself above all to be a compassionate Saviour; nor that he should ponder deeply the relationship between the Father and the Son, leaving us with a model of trust despite the most desperate of all circumstances. But the human dimensions of his story must not eclipse its divine dimensions. The cross was designed by God and carried by his Son so that the Scriptures might be fulfilled, Satan might

---

[51] Is. 25:6–7; 49:10–13; Ps. 107:3–9.

[52] Stein, p. 201.

[53] M. L. Soards, *The Passion According to Luke: The Special Material of Luke 22* (Sheffield Academic Press, 1987), p. 125. Bearing in mind the debate about the kingdom as both present and future, she adds a corrective so as not to be thought to imply that Luke was interested only in the imminent arrival of the kingdom: 'simultaneously Luke clearly implied that human, earthly existence could continue'. On Luke's eschatology, see Marshall, *Luke: Historian*, esp. pp. 128–136.

be drawn into a battle that would spell his defeat, and a kingdom might be set in train towards its consummation, so that salvation in all its fullness might be available to all, even to the most unworthy of people. The one they targeted was the Son who trusted, and he remains still a compassionate Saviour and a coming king.

John 18:1 – 19:42
9. Glorious life-giver

The unique portrait of the death of Jesus that John gives us is 'nothing short of breath-taking'.[1] It reads more like a royal progress tour than the death march of a condemned criminal. It is not so much a passion narrative as a glory narrative, for it is the story of 'how Jesus was glorified and of how God was glorified through his death'.[2]

John brings the Gospel accounts, with their varying and equally valid emphases, to a fitting climax. With him the narratives of the passion end on the highest of all possible notes. Matthew sees Jesus' death as a violent and bloody one that led to his supernatural vindication. Mark sees it as the dark suffering of a servant, through which he became a ransom. Luke sees it as the act of a loving and trusting Son, through which he became the Saviour. These portrayals are complemented by John's meek and majestic king, who brings glory out of shame and life out of death.

It used to be said that in John's understanding salvation owed more to the incarnation than to the crucifixion. The basis for such a judgment is flimsy. John not only devotes as much space to the final weeks of Jesus' life as any of the other Gospel writers, but also stitches prophetic symbols and warning-signs of the cross so tightly into the tapestry of his Gospel that no-one can seriously believe that he thinks the cross is secondary to the incarnation. The kaleidoscopic imagery he uses is dazzling. Jesus is 'the Lamb of God' (1:29) who will destroy the temple (2:19) as he is 'lifted up' from the earth (3:14; 8:28; 12:32–34). The disciples must eat the flesh (6:51–53) of the 'good shepherd' who 'lays down his life for the sheep' (10:11). The high priest thought it expedient (11:49–52) that this grain of wheat should 'fall into the ground and die' (12:24), so fulfilling Isaiah's prophecy (12:38) and producing the greatest demonstration of love it is possible to conceive (15:13). John does not underestimate the importance of the crucifixion.

[1] Carroll and Green, p. 82.
[2] Hooker, *Not Ashamed*, p. 109.

168

It is true that some familiar episodes in the passion narrative are missing in John. There is no last supper with the disciples (cf. 6:25–59; 13:1–17), no agony in the Garden, no trial before the Sanhedrin,[3] no Simon to carry Jesus' cross, no weeping women to mourn his fate, no invective unleashed at the cross and no cry of separation from the Father. The absence of these incidents, the inclusion of different ones and the recasting of familiar ones shows us the cross in an altogether different light.

1. 'Here is your king'

John supremely reveals Jesus to be a meek but majestic king. His majesty is displayed 'at many times and in various ways'[4] during the passion narrative. Not for John the passive Christ of Mark's Gospel. The Christ John presents is in control, as one would expect of a king – the master of ceremonies at his own trial and execution.

a. His command of the timetable

Royal events run like clockwork. No-one is late. Everyone performs exactly as instructed and precisely according to time. I was privileged, one year, to be present at the Cenotaph in London's Whitehall for the Remembrance Day service attended by Her Majesty the Queen. Before the event I was sent a thick pile of briefing papers telling me exactly what to do. They stated that at 10.42am certain members of the Royal Family would arrive. At 10.43, others would come. At 10.45, the Queen Mother would arrive, and at 11.00, 'on the first stroke of Big Ben', all would be in their places and the ceremony would commence. And so it was. The arrivals took place exactly as announced, not a second sooner and not a second later, and the ceremony commenced precisely on the first stroke of Big Ben.

Throughout John's Gospel Jesus has shown himself to be in similarly majestic command of the timetable. When his mother prematurely forced him to reveal his identity at Cana in Galilee, he told her, 'My time[5] has not yet come' (2:4). When the crowds tried to seize him, nothing happened 'because his time had not yet come' (7:30). On a second occasion, despite obvious provocation on his part and ample opportunity, no arrest was made 'because his time had not yet come'

---

[3] There was a trial before Annas, the father-in-law of Caiaphas (18:12–14, 19–24), and Jesus is sent on his way to Caiaphas (18:24), but no details of that trial are recorded. To have included it at this point was unnecessary, for the Sanhedrin's verdict had already been reached and pronounced in 11:47–53.

[4] Heb. 1:1.

[5] The Greek word is *hōra*, 'hour', which NIV usually (and less helpfully) translates by the more general word 'time', except, for some reason, at 12:23. See 2:4; 7:30; 8:20; 12:23, 27; 13:1; 17:1.

(8:20). But when the Greeks came to visit Jesus they served as 'a kind of trigger, a signal that the climactic hour has dawned'.[6] We are never told whether he saw the Gentiles, as requested. What we are told is that 'The hour has come for the Son of Man to be glorified' (12:23). So Jesus set in train the final acts that would lead to his death.

b. His control over events

As the trial and crucifixion unfold, Jesus 'remains in the director's chair throughout'.[7] It was not just that he seemed to anticipate everything (13:1; 18:4), but that he planned everything. His hand was never forced. He never seemed to act under duress. His life was not taken from him, but voluntarily laid down by him (10:17–18), in his own time and in the way he chose. Every detail John includes lends weight to both his regal dignity and his royal authority.

i. The arrest by the mob (18:1–11)

We are made aware of Jesus' authority as soon as the passion commences. He dispatched Judas to begin the process of betrayal (13:27). Later, after Jesus had been engaged in prayer with his disciples (not, note, engaged in an agonized struggle with his Father, unsupported by his disciples), Judas entered the olive grove in the Kidron Valley with a rabble of soldiers and officials intent on arresting him. Immediately, Jesus took command and asked, 'Who is it you want?' (4). Judas, far from coming forward and identifying Jesus, lurked in the background, while Jesus, on hearing that he was the one they sought, revealed himself. He did so with an astonishing choice of words: 'I am he' (5). There can be little doubt that John intends us to hear this not as an innocent marker of identity but as the divine name, 'I am.'[8] His adversaries' reaction proved that, for *they drew back and fell to the ground*, and, in Archbishop William Temple's words, '[yielded] for a moment to the impact of his deity'.[9] Next, showing evidence of the remarkable care for others that would be evident throughout, Jesus negotiated the release of his disciples (8). They tried to resist his arrest, but he restrained their violence and healed Malchus, whose ear had been wounded in the scuffle. The firm impression given is that Jesus was the one in charge.

ii. The hearing before Annas (18:12–14, 19–24)

Annas had been the high priest until deposed by Valerius Gratus, one of Pilate's predecessors, in AD 15; but he was still the power behind the

---

[6] Carson, *John*, p. 437.
[7] Carroll and Green, p. 99.
[8] Exod. 3:13–14. R. E. Brown, *John*, p. 818.
[9] Cited in Milne, p. 252.

throne. Four of his sons had followed him in the office, and his son-in-law Caiaphas currently occupied it. Before him Jesus stood unbowed. He challenged the necessity of the hearing (20–21), since he had taught so openly and everyone knew what he believed. And, when rebuked for impertinence, he still refused to back down (22–23). Either he had done something wrong, in which case they should point it out, or he had not, in which case they were treating him unjustly. The interrogation got nowhere, because Jesus did not allow it to. 'Annas,' as Bruce Milne has written, 'out-manoeuvred by Jesus' implacable integrity, can get no further and sends him to his son-in-law (24) and thereafter to the Sanhedrin.'[10]

No record of the trial before the Sanhedrin is included, since, according to John, the trial had already taken place in Jesus' absence and the verdict had been reached and announced (11:45–53). No doubt, if John had recorded it, we would have encountered the same noble figure on trial, for, when Jesus stood before Pilate (the next scene John describes), he maintained his majestic poise and his sovereign control of affairs.

iii. The conversation with Pilate (18:28 – 19:16)

Jesus now stood, allegedly guilty of the crime of treason, before Pilate, the viceroy of Caesar, the most powerful man on earth. What followed was an extraordinary conversation between them rather than a legal interrogation. Three aspects of it stand out as remarkable. First, Jesus interrogated Pilate as much as Pilate interrogated Jesus. Jesus answered one of Pilate's questions with a question. When Pilate asked, 'Are you the king of the Jews?' (18:33), he received the reply, 'Is that your own idea ... or did others talk to you about me?' (34). Bruce Milne's comment is perceptive: 'Jesus is not in the least degree intimidated by this personal representative of the Roman Emperor and attempts to personalise the conversation, reaching out to Pilate as a man needing to find the grace of God.'[11]

Secondly, Jesus openly declared his kingship, informing Pilate that he was born to reign (37). Yet he was careful to distance himself from the standard ideas of kingship, and explained, 'My kingdom is not of this world. If it were, my servants would fight to prevent my arrest by the Jews. But now my kingdom is from another place' (36). If Pilate was relieved that Jesus' idea of a kingdom was so different from the lies, half-truths, politicking, violence, posturing and deception of the kingdoms he was used to, the relief was not intended, nor was it anything but temporary. In claiming that his kingdom was 'not of this world', Jesus was claiming a higher authority than even that of Caesar. He was saying that a clash

[10] Milne, p. 259.
[11] Ibid., p. 266.

of two worlds was being played out that day in Pilate's judgment hall, and that the world Pilate represented would lose out to the world Jesus represented. It was the kingdom of Jesus that would triumph and last for ever.

Pilate's relief soon passed. When his last-ditch attempt to get Jesus released failed and the crowd finally roared their desire for Jesus to be crucified, we read that Pilate *was even more afraid* (19:8) and went back inside to quiz Jesus further. 'Even though drugged by disbelief, [Pilate] senses that the man he interrogates has a mysterious power and is fearful because of it.'[12] Jesus did nothing to lessen Pilate's torment, and simply repeated his claim to sovereignty (19:11). If Jesus was in control, Pilate wasn't. The conversation made the superstitious Roman determined to release Jesus, but, struggling with forces beyond his control, Pilate was unable to secure his liberty.

Thirdly, Jesus pressed Pilate to make a choice. The surface choice is the one Pilate offered the crowd. Did they want Barabbas or Jesus released, in line with the custom of granting clemency to one prisoner each Passover (18:39–40)?[13] The deeper choice is the one with which Jesus, the prisoner, had just confronted Pilate, the judge, himself. *'Everyone on the side of truth listens to me'* (37). Would Pilate listen to the truth Jesus spoke, or to the lies the Jewish leaders circulated? Would Pilate side with Jesus or with his enemies? Would Pilate submit to the real king or continue to serve the kingdom of this world? The same choice confronts us still today.

c. His coronation on the cross (19:1–37)

Before Pilate capitulated to the will of the crowd, he tried not just one but a number of strategies to secure Jesus' release. He offered them, as just mentioned, the choice of Barabbas or Jesus. They were to determine which one would live and which one would die. They chose to let Barabbas live and Jesus die (18:39–40). Next he attempted a compromise strategy. He would meet the people's desire half-way by having Jesus flogged and made into an object of derision (19:1–5), in the hope that they would see how impotent and harmless he was and provoke their pity. The flogging was probably not that which was administered to prisoners sentenced to death, the *verberatio* (mentioned in Mark 15:15), which was severely dehumanizing and debilitating, but the less severe beating known as the *fustigatio*.[14] The flogging was

---

[12] Senior, *John*, p. 152.

[13] On the historicity of this custom see Carson, *John*, p. 596.

[14] Ibid. p. 597. The less severe flogging was used as a warning, but, on this occasion, it proved insufficient to appease the Jews. This interpretation would fit the sequence of events well, since John records this as happening before the death sentence was pronounced. But it means that Jesus would have received a second flogging after being sentenced (Matt. 27:26; Mark 15:15).

followed by a mock coronation in which the soldiers placed a crown on his head – a crown not of gold but of thorns – dressed him in phoney royal robes, which 'may have been an old shaggy rug',[15] and greeted him in contemptuous homage before slapping him around. Their pantomime made the bruised and bleeding Jesus 'look more like a clown than a king'.[16] How could anyone want such a pathetic figure finished off? What power could he exercise? What harm could he do to the *status quo*? But still they wanted him killed. The mock coronation had been too close to the truth for comfort. The soldiers may have had their sport at his expense, but in doing so they revealed his true status. He really was a king and a threat to the *status quo*.

The pitiful sight of this tortured man failed to move the crowds, and before long they forced Pilate's hand. To let this man go would not be in the interests of Caesar, whom alone (they claimed with obvious insincerity) they recognized as their king. When it was put in these terms, Pilate, whose rule in Palestine was already vulnerable as a result of a series of diplomatic blunders, knew what he had to do. He could not risk losing his favoured status as a *friend of Caesar* (12).[17] So *Finally Pilate handed him over to them to be crucified* (16), still protesting, *'Here is your king'* (14–15).

John makes no mention of a second flogging, the more brutal *verberatio*, but such was likely to have followed.[18] And then the coronation procession set off to Golgotha. The Jesus of John continued to be strong. He carried his own cross (17). The help of Simon from Cyrene is unmentioned. John's focus is on Jesus alone. The two others crucified with him are mentioned only incidentally. He is the central figure in the drama, as John underlines by telling us that Jesus was crucified *in the middle* (18).

John's narration of events continues to stress the royalty of Jesus. What fascinates John is the notice Pilate had fastened to the cross. *It read: JESUS OF NAZARETH, THE KING OF THE JEWS* (19). Naturally the Jews quibbled about its wording. Pilate should have written it, they complained, in such a way as to indicate that that was what Jesus *claimed* to be, not what he *was*. But Pilate was not to be moved on this point. On the question of Jesus' kingship, therefore, he had the final say and came down on the side of affirming that his royal status was authentic. Adding insult to injury, Pilate had the notice prepared in Aramaic (the local language of religion), Latin (the global language of

---

[15] Beasley-Murray, *John*, p. 336.
[16] Ibid., p. 337.
[17] The term may have been a semi-technical one indicating favoured status: Carson, *John*, p. 607.
[18] Ibid., p. 608.

government) and Greek (the language of civilized culture). In doing so, Pilate announced that Jesus was not only king of the Jews but a universal king, a king for all people. And yet it was a notice laden with irony. 'The Jews couldn't believe that a crucified man could possibly be king … the Greeks said that God couldn't possibly die … the Romans couldn't believe it. God – a king, crucified? Why, you couldn't even crucify a Roman citizen. It was illegal to do so. It was the death for a common criminal.'[19] Even in his death, this king who sought to reach out to all was to prove profoundly unsettling to those who had a tunnel-vision picture of what royalty, especially divine royalty, was like.

Even when on the throne of his cross, Jesus remained in control. The care for others that he had showed in the Garden (18:8) continued as he cared for his mother and made provision for her future by entrusting her to the keeping of an unnamed disciple (26–27).[20] As the oldest brother in the family, it would have been his right and duty to ensure she was provided for, but his doing so from the cross demonstrated both his amazing love and his astonishing grip of the situation.

Following that, with the inclusion of only one more incident, John moves his account to a swift and dignified ending. It is the cry of triumph that John remembers as Jesus died. The single word *Tetelestai* rings out from the crucified Christ like a trumpet blast (30): *'It is finished'*, 'It is accomplished.' The work his Father had sent him to do had been completed.[21] The Father's will had been obeyed to the last detail. The Father's love had been revealed in its ultimate form. The Father's grace had been released in the most convincing manner. The Father's forgiveness had been purchased with the costliest payment. The Father's glory had been displayed in the least expected way. The Father's enemies had been definitively defeated, for 'the malevolent ruler of this world is powerless before the one who reigns from the cross'.[22]

Even in his burial we see details that remind us of royalty.[23] Nicodemus buried him, like a king, in a new tomb in a garden (41). He embalmed his body with a huge amount of spices, 34 kg of myrrh and aloes. This was treatment fit for a king. The signs of sovereignty did not desert him even in his grave.

Jesus had often spoken of his being 'lifted up', a term he had

[19] R. Brown, 'Saving message', p. 120.

[20] Cf. 13:23, where an unnamed disciple 'whom Jesus loved' is mentioned.

[21] Note John 4:34: '"My food," said Jesus, "is to do the will of him who sent me and to finish his work."'

[22] Carroll and Green, p. 109.

[23] R. E. Brown, *John*, p. 912, points out that we cannot be certain that John intends us to read them as signs of royalty, but they are 'suggestive' of it and bring the crucifixion scene to 'a fitting conclusion'.

decoded so that his disciples knew that it referred to his death by crucifixion (12:33). His lifting up would bring salvation (as Moses' snake had done in the wilderness; 3:14),[24] prove that his claim about himself was true (8:28), and drive out the evil controller of the world and draw people to himself (12:31–32). But the terminology was ironic. Many saw in it nothing more that a literal statement; his body was lifted on to the cross to die. They would miss the deeper meaning. His lifting up was not only the mounting of his body on a cross but the ascension of a king to his throne. Tom Smail follows the logic of the symbol through to its conclusion: 'Is it going too far', he asks, 'to say that in that phrase John is inviting us to look simultaneously at Jesus lifted up on a cross to die, lifted up from the dead to live and lifted to the right hand of the Father to reign?'[25] Surely not. John has made it abundantly clear, in numerous ways, that Jesus was king and that from his cross he ruled.

2. 'Here is the man!'

Once Pilate presented Jesus to the crowd as a king (19:14). Once also he presented him to the crowd as a *man* (19:5). The marks of Jesus' humanity are not to be missed any more than the marks of his royalty, even if they may be more briefly described. He was tried, mocked, tortured and crucified as a real, fully conscious human being. The fact of his divine and royal nature does not in the slightest degree lessen the reality of the suffering he endured. He experienced the full force of it all. There was nothing counterfeit about his human nature and nothing sham about his sufferings.

a. A real human being[26]

Pilate emphasized Jesus' humanity when he brought Jesus out to display him to the Jews after his soldiers had finished their mock coronation. George Beasley-Murray comments: 'Jesus must have looked a shocking sight, enough to horrify anyone who knew him.'[27] He was a pathetic specimen of humanity, like many a torture victim. And that was precisely Pilate's point. He was an authentic, physical human being, who, Pilate thought, could be crushed by violence just like any other human being. Bruce Milne points out that the suffering he endured was physical (he was flogged), personal (he suffered at the hands of others, not through impersonal circumstances) and emotional (he was derided and to be pitied). The abusive treatment qualifies him

---

[24] Num. 21:4–9.
[25] Smail, *Windows*, p. 80.
[26] I owe these points to Milne, pp. 273–276.
[27] Beasley-Murray, *John*, p. 337.

to be the Saviour of all those who, in the reality of their humanity, have suffered physical or emotional abuse at the hands of others. Jesus entered into our humanity in order to share our sufferings and become the perfect Saviour through them,[28] delivering us from all the totalitarian and oppressing powers we face, up to and including the one 'who holds the power of death – that is the devil'[29] himself.

If his suffering was real, so was his death. It was the real death of a real person. Perhaps it is partly in order to emphasize this point that John omits any reference to Simon's carrying the cross to the site of execution for Jesus (19:1).[30] John's primary reason, no doubt, is to present Christ as strong enough to carry his own cross. Later, teaching circulated that at the last moment Simon took the place of Jesus, so that Jesus himself never actually died on the cross.[31] This is still the belief of Muslims today. While there is no evidence that that belief was circulating in John's day, it may well have already existed in embryonic form. By removing Simon from the story, John was implying that no switch could have taken place. The man who set off from the governor's palace in Jerusalem was the man who was nailed to wood on the hill of Golgotha.

Another of the cameos unique to John serves further to underline the real humanity of Christ. After Jesus had died, *one of the soldiers pierced Jesus' side with a spear, bringing a sudden flow of blood and water* (19:34). The medical explanation of this is complex.[32] Its symbolic meaning is contentious, although there seems a fair agreement that blood, at least, symbolizes sacrificial blood that brings cleansing, and that water, in line with John 7:38–39, symbolizes life.[33] John, therefore, is saying that 'the drama of the cross does not end in death but in a flow of life that comes from death'.[34] But there is a simpler reason for John's inclusion of this episode. All seem to agree that it is included primarily to prove that Jesus died, that he died as a real human being, and that about his death there can be no shadow of doubt.

b. A representative human being

Jesus died not just as a solitary individual but as a representative human

[28] Heb. 2:10.

[29] Heb. 2:14.

[30] The Gospel accounts are easy enough to reconcile at this point. Most likely, John means that Jesus carried his own cross to begin with, whereas the synoptic Gospels record that Simon lifted it off Jesus as they approached the city wall. See Mark 15:21, which says that Simon was 'passing by on his way in from the country'.

[31] This belief is taught by Basilides, a second-century Gnostic heretic, in his commentary on John: Carson, *John*, p. 699.

[32] For details see Beasley-Murray, *John*, p. 356.

[33] R. E. Brown, *John*, p. 913.

[34] Ibid.

being. The charges on which he was tried were those of blasphemy and treason, and, as Bruce Milne points out, it is 'precisely these two perversions [that] are at the heart of all human sinning'.[35] The charges he faced in the judgment halls of the Sanhedrin and of Pilate are the charges we face before the judgment seat of God. Bruce Milne notes that the very question Pilate asked of Jesus, 'What is it you have done?' (18:35), is the very question God asked Adam and Eve in the Garden of Eden.[36] His judgment and death relate, therefore, to the judgment and death sentence under which we stand as sinners before God. By this close association of thought, John is telling us, 'He took our place, he was condemned for us! He is our representative man.'[37]

John introduced his Gospel with the assertion that 'The Word became flesh and made his dwelling among us' (1:14). Now, as the Gospel draws to a close and Jesus prepares to leave his dwelling among men and women, it is still the incarnate Son of God that is John's subject. Incomprehensibly, the eternal Word went to his death as an authentic human being. As a representative human being he stands in our place, bears our judgment, and experiences our death, with the result that we are no longer under condemnation and can experience eternal life.

3. 'Look, the Lamb of God'

No sooner had Jesus begun to emerge from his private years than John the Baptist had pointed to him and said to the bystanders, 'Look, the Lamb of God, who takes away the sin of the world!' (1:29). Ever since, scholars have argued over exactly which lamb it was that John had in mind, because it does not seem to be a ready-made title. Was it the lamb provided for Abraham and Isaac in Genesis 22, the Passover lamb of Exodus 12, the sin offering of Leviticus 4 – 5, the scapegoat of Leviticus 17, the 'lamb to the slaughter' of Isaiah 53, or the 'gentle lamb' of Jeremiah 11?[38] Morna Hooker's verdict on the question is probably right: 'I suspect that had we been able to ask the evangelist himself, he might have found it difficult to choose between them.'[39] No matter. The meaning is fixed even if the metaphor is fluid. Whichever lamb was intended, it was one 'who takes away the sin of the world'. John saw the Lamb sent from God as one who would bring to fulfilment, and therefore to a dramatic end, all the various sacrifices and rituals of Israel and remove the problem of sin in a never-to-be-repeated fashion.

---

[35] Milne, p. 275.
[36] Gen. 3:13.
[37] Milne, p. 276.
[38] For full details of the options see Morris, *John*, p. 144–147.
[39] Hooker, *Not Ashamed*, p. 98.

Several traces of this metaphor are to be seen in John's passion account.

a. The timing of his death

John's Gospel differs from the synoptic Gospels with regard to the timing of the events of Easter Week. The differing accounts are reconcilable, if not easily, as most commentaries explain.[40] Our purpose is not to explain the riddle of the disagreement but to explore the significance of the description John gives. He tells us that the trial came to an end on *the day of Preparation of Passover Week, about the sixth hour* (19:14). Beasley-Murray draws out the significance of the remark:

> The place, the day, and the hour are all mentioned, for the Evangelist is conscious of the momentous nature of the event now taking place ... It is the sixth hour (noon) of Preparation day; at this hour three things take place: Jews cease their work, leaven is gathered out of their houses and burned, and the slaughtering of Passover lambs commences.[41]

There can be no surer way to indicate the meaning of what was happening to Jesus. He was handed over to be crucified at the exact moment that the Passover lambs were being slaughtered. The first Passover was reaching its sell-by date and was being superseded by the offering of a greater Passover lamb who would work an exodus that will eclipse the deliverance from Egypt once and for all, and be the instrument of a universal deliverance.

Those with eyes to see might have observed a hint of such matters earlier in John's account. When the Jews delivered Jesus to Pilate they refused to enter his palace *to avoid ceremonial uncleanness* (18:28). If they had contaminated themselves by entering the property of a Gentile, they would have been unable to eat the Passover meal. How ironic!

> They hold fast to the ceremonial law while they seek the execution of the promised Deliverer of Israel, the Son of God and Saviour; and in their zeal to eat the Passover lamb they unwittingly help to fulfil its significance through demanding the death of the Lamb of God, at the same time shutting themselves out of its saving efficacy.[42]

---

[40] See also Blomberg, *Historical Reliability*, pp. 175–180.
[41] Beasley-Murray, *John*, p. 341.
[42] Ibid., pp. 327–328.

b The details of his death (19:28–34)

Two details of the crucifixion scene, mentioned only by John, further emphasize the sacrificial nature of Jesus' death. First, as the final moments approached, Jesus said that he was thirsty (28), and they gave him some cheap wine to drink.[43] John noticed the stick on which they had impaled the sponge so that they could lift it to Jesus' lips. It was *a stalk of a hyssop plant* (29). It would not have escaped John's notice that it was the hyssop plant that, according to Exodus 12:22, was to be used to paint the blood of the Passover lamb around the door-frames of the Israelite homes to prevent the angel of death from doing his terrible work of killing their firstborn. Once again, there is an intimate connection between the lamb sacrificed in Egypt and the man sacrificed on Calvary.

Secondly, as the executioners moved to hasten the deaths of their victims by breaking their legs (31),[44] they discovered that Jesus was already dead and so *they did not break his legs* (33). His rapid death, resulting perhaps from his double flogging and prolonged trial, is not John's chief concern. That his legs were not broken is. Exodus 12:46 and Numbers 9:12 stipulate that the bones of the Passover lamb must not be broken. John's note is yet another way of making the connection between the Passover lamb and Jesus as the Lamb of God.

c. The meaning of his death

Without realizing the full import of his words, Caiaphas had once said, *'You do not realise that it is better for you that one person die for the people than that the whole nation perish'* (11:50). To him, the words were simply a cynical expression of expediency. His was the world of realistic politics in which life was cheap and a preacher from Nazareth was dispensable if his death would save the nation from disaster. But, unwittingly, he was expressing a more profound truth. In saying that Jesus should *die for [hyper] the people*, he was using the vocabulary of sacrifice. John always uses *hyper* to speak of sacrifice and substitution.[45] It was the word used when an animal took the place of a sinner and died to make atonement for the one who was penitent. A substitute acts in the place of someone so as to render that person's action unnecessary. 'Just so,' writes John Stott, 'as our substitute Christ did what we could never do ourselves: he bore our sin and judgment.'[46]

---

[43] This is different from the sedative of wine and myrrh offered to him to dull the pain, which he refused (Mark 15:23).

[44] To break their legs would be an added shock to their physical systems and prevent them from pushing themselves up to assist with their breathing. Asphyxiation would soon hasten their deaths.

[45] Carson, *John*, p. 386.

[46] Stott, *Cross of Christ*, p. 276.

It is a mystery how one man could die for the people. How can a solitary figure bear the sins of many? Is it possible? Yes. The sacrificial system of the Old Testament had long established the principle of an innocent substitute's bearing the sins of the guilty, while the Day of Atonement demonstrated that a single victim could bear the sins of all. Tom Smail answers further: 'Yes,' especially 'if that man is the incarnate Creator come to re-create his people by fulfilling the covenant that they broke and could not fulfil, by taking the old humanity down to death and in the doing of it raising a new humanity to life in which by his Spirit we might all share.'[47]

If the sacrificial framework is not John's dominant perspective on the work of Christ, its traces are none the less unmistakable and the interpretation is none the less valid. As Jesus surrendered to death, he became the full and perfect sacrifice for sins and in him 'all the sacrifices of the ages are gathered up and rendered obsolete for ever'.[48]

In his deceptively little book, *Windows on the Cross*, Tom Smail writes of a visit he made to Jerusalem. One night he was unable to sleep because of the heat.

Towards dawn I wandered to the edge of the balconied roof and looked at the nearly empty street below. It was not entirely empty because half-way along it was a donkey pulling a dustbin into which was being loaded all the refuse from the previous day. The street where the donkey had not yet reached was full of the rubbish of yesterday but, where the donkey with the dustbin had passed, everything was clean and clear ready for the new day. A donkey with a dustbin: it makes you think of the foolishness of the cross and the abasement of the one who walked that same road on the same kind of enterprise. 'Behold the lamb of God who takes away the rubbish of the world.'[49]

4. 'We have seen his glory'

It is hard to imagine a more perverse way of describing crucifixion than as a display of bright splendour, and yet that is how Jesus spoke of his cross on more than one occasion, according to John (12:23, 27–28; 13:31–32; 17:1).[50] Twice John refers to the cross in the same way (7:39; 12:16). The cross was to reveal God's glory and concurrently be the means by which God would confer honour on his Son.

---

[47] T. Smail, 'Can one man die for the people?' in Goldingay (ed)., p. 91.

[48] Milne, p. 283.

[49] Smail, *Windows*, pp. 110–111.

[50] Eugene Peterson paraphrases John 17:1: 'Father, it's time. Display the bright splendor of your Son.' *The Message* (NavPress, 1993), p. 264.

a. Glory glimpsed

As the elect people of God, the Jews had more than once glimpsed the glory of God: that is, the manifestation of his divine splendour and the revelation of his divine qualities. To them glory was the awe-inspiring disclosure of his holiness in dazzling, transcendental power. They had seen it in the spectacular events of the exodus,[51] observed it in the fire, cloud and darkness at Sinai[52] and drawn back from it in tabernacle and temple alike as the Shekinah presence of God saturated their sanctuaries.[53] They knew they could not face the full force of it and live.[54]

John's claim is that the glory of God became visible in the life of Christ (1:14). Archbishop George Carey likens it to a schoolboy concentrating the sun's rays through a magnifying glass: 'John sees God's glory centring in Jesus.'[55] People caught a glimpse of it more than once as he performed his miraculous signs[56] and rode triumphantly into Jerusalem to be hailed as 'King of Israel' (12:12–16). Here were the whispers of glory which they expected to build into a loud crescendo of splendour as Jesus reached the zenith of his ministry.

b. Glory veiled

None of this had prepared them to detect God's glory in as repugnant, humiliating and impotent an act as crucifixion. Their expectation was that God would show himself in spectacular events, in sensational miracles, in marching armies, in the subjugation of enemies and in the magnificent display of majesty. But they could not see it in a crucifixion. Dazzling light, righteous judgment and victorious power, the signs of glory, all seemed absent there. Instead, the very reverse of the expected indications was only too present.

Darkness, rather than light, hung over the whole sequence of the events of crucifixion. John does not tell us that the sun ceased to shine for three hours when Jesus hung on the cross. But he has already made the point in his own graphic way. Jesus warned his disciples that darkness would overtake them, and now it had (12:35). When Judas left the other disciples to betray Jesus, John tellingly comments, '... he went out. And it was night' (13:30). The darkness was palpable. Evil, rather than righteousness, seemed to have the upper hand. The cosmic battle between good and evil seemed to be going the wrong way. Satan successfully inspired Judas to betray Jesus (13:2, 27). And Jesus acknowledged Satan's fingerprints are all over the events of his passion

[51] Exod. 15:19–21.
[52] Deut. 5:22.
[53] Lev. 9:23–24; 2 Chr. 7:1–3.
[54] Exod. 33:22.
[55] G. Carey, *The Gate of Glory* (1986; Hodder and Stoughton, 1992), p. 90.
[56] John 2:1–11; 4:46–54; 5:1–9; 6:5–13, 19–21; 11:1–44; 21:1–11.

(14:30). The trials, far from establishing the truth and vindicating the one who was in the right, denied justice and let wickedness go on its way unchecked. The just one stood condemned while the unjust one went free.

Far from a demonstration of power, the crucifixion was the epitome of weakness. Jesus was denied liberty, hounded relentlessly, stripped shamefully, flogged mercilessly, mocked ruthlessly, degraded utterly, until nailed excruciatingly and lifted high on a cross. Where is the glory in that?

c. Glory revealed

And yet, in the reverse economy of God, Jesus' death was the supreme manifestation of his glory and would prove to be the gateway to the further glory of his resurrection and exaltation. The idea that the glory of God would be realized in an act of absolute self-sacrifice was revolutionary. For sure, it proved that God's folly was wiser than our combined wisdom, his weakness stronger than our united strength, and his shame more exalted than our feigned glory.[57] It showed, beyond question, that there was more honour in his humiliation than in all our grandiose attempts at dignified magnificence put together.

The cross was God's chosen path to glory, the fulfilment of a long-held divine plan, as John mentions on four occasions in his record of the passion (19:24, 28, 36, 37).

The cross demonstrated that Satan really did have 'no hold' on Jesus (14:30). For by submitting to the prince of this world and allowing him to do his work, and then rising from the dead, Jesus proved that the power of which Satan boasted was hollow.

The cross confirmed that Christ spoke the truth in saying that 'unless a grain of wheat falls to the ground and dies, it remains only a single seed. But if it dies, it produces many seeds' (12:24). With dramatic force it demonstrates the mysterious paradox that 'death leads to life – an assertion that overturns the power of darkness'.[58] 'Those who hate their lives in this world', as Jesus himself said, obviously do 'keep them for eternal life' (12:25).

The cross transformed suffering and humiliation. Through it 'an instrument of grisly death' was converted into 'a sign of overwhelming love'. It testified, as nothing had done so convincingly before, to the 'endless mystery of God's love for the world'.[59]

The cross founded a new humanity. From the death of this one solitary man, abundant new life would come. In being 'lifted up', he drew many to himself (3:14) from every nation, tribe and tongue, to

---

[57] 1 Cor. 1:18–31.
[58] Senior, *John*, p. 152.
[59] Ibid., p. 147.

create a new people for God and to set in motion the re-creation of all things.[60] When lifted up, he drew people to him (as Spurgeon said) like a trumpet, alerting people to hear good news; like a net, enfolding people in the gospel; like the cords of love, tugging back those who stray; like a standard, rallying believers around him in unity; and like a chariot, drawing people onwards and upwards into heaven.[61]

The cross fulfilled Zechariah's prophecy that one day people would *look on the one they have pierced* (19:37) in grief, mourning and repentance,[62] and that 'a fountain' would be 'opened to the house of David and the inhabitants of Jerusalem, to cleanse them from sin and impurity'.[63]

The cross was the vehicle of God's glory, for, as John Calvin wrote,

... in the cross of Christ, as in a splendid theatre, the incomparable goodness of God is set before the whole world. The glory of God shines, indeed in all creatures high and below, but never more brightly than in the cross, in which there is a wonderful change in things – the condemnation of all men was manifested, sin blotted out, salvation restored to men; in short, the whole world was renewed and all things restored to order.[64]

'In that death we see a boundless glory',[65] for in that death we see that 'Love and faithfulness meet together; righteousness and peace kiss each other.'[66]

Jesus died as a sovereign king, a real man, a sacrificial lamb and a glorious life-giver. Not for nothing does Richard Burridge liken Christ, as John pictures him, to a high-flying eagle. 'The sight of an eagle climbing into the sky is glorious,' he writes. 'So, too, for John the death of Jesus sets him free of the earth to return to his Father on high; the hour of his passion is the hour of his glory. This is the supreme irony.'[67] Thank God that it is so. *Tetelestai*: it is accomplished.

[60] Col. 1:20.
[61] Spurgeon, pp. 161–166.
[62] Zech. 12:10.
[63] Zech. 13:1.
[64] Calvin, *John* 2, p. 68. Cited in Stott, *Cross of Christ*, p. 206.
[65] Calvin, *John* 2, p. 135.
[66] Ps. 85:10.
[67] Burridge, p. 156.

PART 3
THE CROSS EXPLAINED

Romans 3:21–26
10. The cross as undeserved righteousness

'The message of the cross'[1] is central to the apostle Paul's theology. It is the defining reference point from which all else takes its cue. He could summarize the substance of his preaching in two words: 'Christ crucified'.[2] He confessed that he had no other ambition than to know and preach 'Jesus Christ and him crucified'.[3] The only thing about which he ever sought to boast was 'the cross of our Lord Jesus Christ'.[4]

With the apostle Paul, the meaning of the events the Gospel writers had described concerning the death of Jesus of Nazareth comes to be more fully explored and explained. Neither Paul nor the other writers of the New Testament letters can be accused of projecting foreign interpretations on to the events of Good Friday. Their reflections are 'a development of, not an evolution away from',[5] what Jesus himself understood and intended. They all saw that in the cross God had done something extraordinarily decisive, not just for the Jews but for the whole world, and they sought to unlock the meaning within it. His death was not only a historical fact but an event of momentous significance for all humankind.

Underneath all the layers of theology there lies the simple confession 'that Christ died for our sins according to the Scriptures'.[6] Christians came to see in that act of dying an incredible expression of God's love[7] and a substitutionary and redemptive significance which Paul could capture only by using a 'dazzling array of colours' for his portrait of the cross. He employs several dozen metaphors to describe the benefits of

---

[1] 1 Cor. 1:18.
[2] 1 Cor. 1:23.
[3] 1 Cor. 2:2.
[4] Gal. 6:14.
[5] Wright and Borg, p. 104.
[6] 1 Cor. 15:3.
[7] Gal. 2:20.

the cross.[8] How sad that, in our desire for systematic neatness, we have frequently reduced his brilliantly varied portrait to a two-dimensional, monochrome picture!

Our sampling of Paul's teaching begins with Romans 3:21–26. Few doubt the importance of this short, concentrated paragraph in his writing. Martin Luther scribbled in the margin of his Bible that this was 'the chief point, and the very central place of the Epistle, and of the whole Bible'.[9] More recently, Charles Cranfield has written that it is 'the centre and heart of the whole of Romans'[10] and that it stands out because it is impressive in style, in its use of language and repetitions and, above all, in content. 'It reads', he says, 'like a solemn proclamation.'[11] Similarly, Martyn Lloyd-Jones said of verse 25, 'We are looking here at one of the most important verses in the whole of Scripture; there is no doubt about that.'[12]

Its importance lies in the concise way in which Paul speaks of the wonder of our salvation as it relates to the righteousness and grace of God; the need and impotence of humanity; and the cross and achievements of Christ. It tells us that as a result of Christ's death we sinful human beings *are justified freely by* God's *grace* (24).

1. The source of justification (3:21)

The gospel begins not where we so often start to explain it, with the needs of people, but with the righteousness of God. It tells us that a decisive shift has occurred in God's dealings with his creation. This has come about by his gracious initiative, not ours, and is designed to bring people into a right relationship with him.

a. A decisive shift

Paul's phrase *But now* marks a decisive shift not just in Paul's argument but in God's economy. 'There are no more wonderful words in the whole of Scripture', claims Martyn Lloyd-Jones, 'than these two words "But now". What vital words they are.'[13]

Up to this point in his letter to the Romans, Paul has been dis-

---

[8] Green, 'Death of Christ', p. 204. He writes: 'Just as Jesus' death lies at the foundation of Pauline theology, so Paul seems never to tire of adding new images to his interpretive vocabulary by way of explicating its significance' (p. 203). This, he says, should make us cautious of 'positing for Paul a single (or any one as *the* central) theory of the atonement' (p. 205).

[9] Quoted in Moo, p. 218.

[10] Cranfield, *Romans*, p. 199.

[11] Ibid.

[12] Lloyd-Jones, p. 65. Leon Morris comments that it 'is possibly the most important single paragraph ever written': *Romans*, p. 173.

[13] Lloyd-Jones, p. 25.

coursing on the sinfulness of humanity, Jew and Gentile alike, which has earned the wrath of God (1:18). The Gentiles have failed to live up to their knowledge of God, inherent in creation (1:21–23), while the Jews have failed to live up to their covenant relationship with God, in spite of their protestations to the contrary (2:17–29). All are indicted, therefore, and are without excuse as they stand accountable before a holy God (3:19). Our failure, far from provoking us to justify or excuse ourselves before God, should lead us to stand in penitent silence before him. But what is to be done? How can we, the unrighteous, be enabled to relate to him, the righteous one? From the negative diagnosis of our condition, Paul turns to the positive proclamation of God's solution.

The solutions available before Christ's coming had failed to deal with the problem effectively. They were sticking-plasters, when radical surgery was required. *But now* a new chapter has opened, and a clear-cut, fresh start has taken place in God's programme of salvation. What was foreshadowed by the law and provisions of the old covenant, but could not be achieved by them, has become possible through Christ. Something that *has been made known* means that a new era has been inaugurated, a new time reached, a new epoch begun.

b. A gracious initiative

What is it that marks the beginning of this new time? What distinguishes it from all previous eras is that *a righteousness from God, apart from law, has been made known.* John Stott highlights the difference thus: 'over against the unrighteousness of some and the self-righteousness of others, Paul sets the righteousness of God.'[14]

How is it that his *righteousness* can come to help us in our predicament? It would be more intelligible, surely, for God's righteousness to lead to our conviction and condemnation rather than to our salvation – if, that is, 'righteousness' means his justice in judging sin. So the key question is: what does Paul mean by the phrase *righteousness of God*? He means the same here as he did in Romans 1:17, where it refers to the action God took to bring an unrighteous people into a right relationship with himself and to bestow on them the status of right standing before him.

Recent discussion of the *righteousness of God* has stressed that it is a relational term. James Dunn reminds us that 'People are righteous when they meet the claims which others have on them by virtue of their relationship.'[15] So here, God acts to restore and sustain his people in a

---

[14] Stott, *Romans*, p. 108.
[15] Dunn, *Romans*, p. 41. N. T. Wright develops the argument in a different way, and argues that 'the righteousness of God' here is not a moral quality of God, but his covenant faithfulness because of which he will vindicate his people: *Paul*, pp. 95–103, 105–107.

new-covenant relationship with himself. Just how God has done this becomes clear in verses 24 – 25. For the moment, Paul's concern is to stress the fact that it was God who took the lead in bringing about this new situation and making the restoration possible. He is the source of our justification.

c. A consistent development

Although this saving act of God has brought about an entirely new situation, it was not unanticipated in *the Law and the Prophets*, a way of speaking about the whole Old Testament. If Paul had particular Old Testament scriptures in mind, he does not specify them.[16] But it is likely that he simply means that in many ways and in different places the Old Testament anticipated this new revelation of God's righteousness in Christ and paved the way for it. His point is that this fresh way by which God will bring his people back into a right standing with himself is not a change of mind on God's part. Still less does it indicate a previous failure on God's part (as we shall see). It is all of a piece with God's previous revelation of himself, and in harmony with his character, which is always consistent in its blend of holiness and grace. It is not that a God of wrath in the Old Testament is now replaced by a God of grace in the New. Rather, God's plan of salvation was gradually unfolding until the coming of Christ, when it reached its fullness.

Paul's phrase *apart from law*, which comes earlier in this verse, seems to stand in tension with this stress on the continuity of God's plan. Is Paul in danger of contradicting himself? Various interpretations of this phrase have been given. First, it might mean that since salvation was never going to be achieved by the works of the law, God offers a new way of obtaining it: namely, faith in Christ.[17] This would still not mean that God had changed his mind, because, as Romans 4 will prove, even in the era of law the key requirement in relating to God was belief in his promises.

Secondly, it might mean that God chooses a way to make his righteousness known other than through the law.[18] The emphasis is not on our keeping the law (or on our failing to keep it), but on God's new revelation of himself. That would be consistent with the Old Testament's anticipation of this new era, and it would recognize the law as a revelation of God.

Or, thirdly, Paul could be using the law as a way of speaking about the whole Jewish covenant, as he does elsewhere. If so, he is saying that

[16] Is. 11:5; 42:6; 46:13; 51:5, 6, 9; 61:3, and many others are suggested by the commentators.
[17] Morris, *Romans*, p. 174.
[18] Moo, p. 223.

God is no longer confined to working within the boundaries of nationality and religion which the law defines.[19] He is free now to work outside those boundaries and to include the Gentiles in his plan of salvation.

Any of these might be right, but the first does not quite do justice to the meaning of the phrase in this setting. The second seems to have much to commend it as to clarity and context. But the third best fits the total sweep of Paul's argument in Romans.

The twofold reference to the law in this verse should be held in tension but not in contradiction. What God has now done for us in Christ stands in both continuity and discontinuity with his previous saving dealings with people.

2. The need for justification (3:22–23)

Before revealing what it is that God has done to bring about this new era of salvation, Paul briefly restates the conclusion reached in his first three chapters. Why is it that people are not in a right standing, or a right relationship, with God?

a. A tragic shortfall

Paul's emphasis is on the human factor in the equation of sin: *All have sinned and fall short of the glory of God*. Men and women were meant to be the summit of God's creation. 'A man', according to 1 Corinthians 11:7, '… is the image and glory of God.' But something has gone drastically wrong to mar the image and to cause human beings to be deficient in glory. The cause is sin. Paul writes of sinning in the aorist tense, as something that is accumulated and past. It may be that he is 'gathering up the sins of the people through the past into a single moment',[20] but he is more likely to be referring to the fact that we are all caught up in the sin of Adam and suffer from the consequences of the original fall. Romans 5:12 would suggest that this was in Paul's mind. Adam, trying to escape the limitations of his creatureliness, lost that which most distinguished him from the rest of creation and raised him above it.[21] He fell short of the honour God intended him to have, and failed to reach the goal of God's continuing approval. But Paul's thoughts are not trapped in history. If *have sinned* is in the aorist tense, *fall short* is in the continuous tense. In this way he emphasizes not only the historical root of our trouble but the continuing blight we all suffer as a consequence of that original fall.

The blight of sin is universal. Everyone is affected. No-one escapes.

---

[19] Dunn, *Romans*, p. 165.
[20] Moo, p. 226.
[21] Dunn, *Romans*, p. 178.

Several commentaries understandably quote Bishop Handley Moule's comments on this, 'The harlot, the liar, the murderer are short of it; but so are you. Perhaps they stand at the bottom of a mine, and you are on the crest of an Alp; but you are as little able to touch the stars as they.'[22] And that is true. But Paul's point, of course, is not so much to prove that every individual person is a sinner before God as to demonstrate that it makes no difference whether we have the privileges of Jewish covenant blood in us or come from pagan Gentile stock. Jew and Gentile alike lack the glory of God in their lives. *There is no difference* at all on the basis of race. All stand in need of God's intervening grace. There is no other effective solution to sin.

b. Divine wrath

Unspoken here, but clearly assumed,[23] is the other factor in the equation that needs resolving. Sin is a problem in itself, since it destroys both those who commit it and the social and physical environment in which they live. But the primary problem of sin is what it does to a just and holy God. It offends him and provokes his anger.

Many today are hesitant to speak of the wrath of God, at least as traditionally understood: as personal anger that implies God's meting out retributive punishment on his sinful creatures. They think the idea unworthy of the loving and merciful Father of our Lord Jesus Christ. Opposition comes in many forms. Some reject the concept of God's anger altogether and dismiss it as primitive, attributable to people who did not know better. It comes, they say, from ancient religious practices such as animism, where spirits and ancestors had to be placated to ward off evil. But these unworthy notions, associated with vengeful, unpredictable and capricious gods, should not be confused with the righteous wrath of the holy God revealed in Scripture. As Leon Morris explains, God's wrath is spoken of over 580 times in the Old Testament, and over twenty words are used to describe it.[24] The theme continues into the New Testament. So it is hardly a secondary issue that can be easily dismissed.

C. H. Dodd advocated the view that the wrath of God was not a personal attitude of anger towards us but 'some process or effect in the realm of objective facts'.[25] In other words, the wrath of which Paul speaks in Romans 1:18 is the inevitable and impersonal outworking of the consequences of our sin, rather than the personal and judicious anger of God. Dodd supports his argument by saying that Paul never makes God the direct subject of the anger, in the way in which he

---

[22] Moule, p. 97.
[23] It is developed in 1:18 – 2:29.
[24] Morris, *Atonement*, p. 153.
[25] Dodd, p. 49. The position is more fully explored and advocated in A. T. Hanson.

happily speaks of God's loving us. And although Dodd recognizes that Paul uses the expression 'the wrath of God' three times,[26] he contends that Paul's more usual way of referring to wrath is impersonal and absolute: just 'wrath'.

Dodd's observations are accurate, but his conclusions do not necessarily follow from them. Paul may wish to speak cautiously about the relationship between anger and God, not because he is doubtful about it, but precisely so as not to encourage the projection of pagan ideas about vengeful gods on to the God and Father of Jesus Christ. John Stott points out that, similarly, Paul sometimes speaks of grace without referring to God. On occasions it too can sound like an impersonal force (e.g. 5:20–21). 'Yet we do not on that account depersonalize grace and convert it into an influence or process.'[27]

The real basis of Dodd's view is ideological rather than exegetical. But why object to the statement that God is angry against sin and, therefore, inevitably against those who perpetrate it? What sort of a God would he be if he failed to react negatively to wrong, showing repulsion at what harms his creation and repugnance towards evil? Surely he would not be a God we could trust or find worthy of worship![28]

More recently, a number of evangelical scholars have sought to revise the concept of God's anger. Their concern is not so much with the concept of anger itself, or even with its personal character – both of which they affirm – but with the retributive nature of the anger we attribute to God. Stephen Travis, who has researched much in this area, summarizes his position like this:

> ... in Paul's understanding of divine judgement ideas of 'punishment' or 'retribution' lie on the periphery of his thought. He thinks not so much of God imposing a retributive penalty for human sins, but of people experiencing the God-given consequences of their choices and actions. He understands both salvation and condemnation primarily in relational terms: people's destinies will be a confirmation and intensification of the relationship with God or alienation from him which has been their experience in this life.[29]

He questions the penal view of atonement and proposes a covenant perspective instead. God's wrath then becomes real and personal but

---

[26] Rom. 1:18; Col. 3:6 and Eph 5:6. Note also Rom. 9:22.

[27] Stott, *Cross of Christ*, p. 105.

[28] See ibid, pp. 102–111, for a full and excellent discussion of the issues involved.

[29] S. Travis, 'Christ as the bearer of divine judgment in Paul's thought about the atonement', in Goldingay (ed.), p. 21. See also Fiddes, ch. 5.

not retributive, 'since there cannot be genuine retribution in the context of personal relationship'.[30] His wrath consists in the intrinsic consequences of sin. So it is unnecessary to view Christ's death as propitiating an angry God. Instead, it becomes 'the supreme demonstration of God's commitment to bring human beings into relationship with himself'.[31] While he wants to hold firmly to the absolute seriousness of sin and to the fact that Christ experienced divine judgment on the cross on our behalf, to speak in terms of punishment or retributive penalty is, Travis claims, 'to go further than Paul himself goes'.[32] The supreme punishment is, he believes, 'the withdrawal of God's presence from the people'.[33] The concept of retribution is inadequate because it means the external imposition of punishment, whereas this covenant view of punishment emphasizes its intrinsic and relational nature.

There are, however, some serious problems with this desire to eradicate the idea of God's punitive anger from our doctrine of the atonement. First, and most importantly, as Travis himself agrees, 'retributive punishment is a familiar concept in the Old Testament'.[34] The *lex talionis*[35] is a well-enshrined and accepted principle which establishes a calm and measured approach to justice from the stand-point of retribution. It not only outlaws the uncontrolled vengeance of human spite and personal animosity, but sets limits on the actions of judges too.[36] The thinking of Paul and other New Testament writers was very much governed by the Old Testament.

Secondly, even if one concedes that such an idea is not found in Paul's writing as frequently as often implied, this does not mean that it is absent altogether.

Thirdly, the Pauline passages Travis examines are certainly capable of being interpreted as speaking of God's penal wrath against sin, as many scholars (whom he acknowledges) do.[37] Whether or not we do so, therefore, depends more on our wider philosophical approach than on the specific texts themselves.

Fourthly, cannot retributive justice also be personal?

There seems no convincing reason why we should not understand the wrath of God against sin as expressing his personal anger at evil

---

[30] S. Travis, *Christ and the Judgment of God: Divine Retribution in the New Testament* (Marshall Pickering, 1986), p. 44.

[31] Travis, 'Christ as the bearer', p. 32.

[32] Ibid., p. 33.

[33] Travis, *Christ and the Judgment*, p. 11.

[34] Ibid., p. 13.

[35] Exod. 21:23–25; Lev. 24:19–20; Deut. 19:21.

[36] Jesus' comments in Matt. 5:38–39 were directed to a misapplication of the *lex talionis*.

[37] Travis, 'Christ as the bearer', p. 31.

leading to his punishment of those who commit it – and several reasons why we should, even if the concept of his wrath is fuller than that alone. Such wrath, P. T. Forsyth argued, was 'the necessary reaction to sin in a holy God. There alone you have the *divine* necessity of the cross in a sinful world – the moral necessity of judgment.'[38]

The need for justification, therefore, is twofold. Human sin has to be overcome, and divine anger has to be appeased, if God is to be reconciled to his people and live in harmony with them. But how is that lethal equation to be resolved? The Law and the Prophets could prefigure the solution, but they could not provide it. The real solution lay in *the redemption that came by Jesus Christ* (24).

3. The nature of justification (3:24–25)[39]

To help us understand the mysterious wonder of God's grace to us through the cross of Christ, Paul uses three metaphors. The sinner is *justified freely, through ... redemption* and by the offering of *a sacrifice* of atonement. The pictures come from the lawcourts, the slave market and the temple.

a. The picture of justification

The picture of justification can be used in a trite way, and it would be foolish to pretend that evangelical preachers have never done so. We should disabuse ourselves of any notion of impersonal forces of justice at work without engaging with and affecting the persons involved; of mathematical formulae whereby justice is satisfied; and of superficial ideas of judges coming off the bench and *effortlessly* substituting themselves for the prisoners in the dock. To present justification in this manner is to make it into a legal fiction.

Justice in Israel was a profoundly personal process. It was much more akin to the process of justice in our civil courts than in our criminal courts. There was no Crown Prosecution Service accusing the defendant on behalf of some abstract 'law' or 'state'. The accused and the accuser argued it out before the judge, and the judge put the defendant either in the right (that is, he justified him or her) or in the wrong (and so condemned him or her). When justified, the accused was received back into the community and relationships were restored. When condemned, relationships continued broken to some degree. Condemnation for serious offences might lead to banishment, or to the death sentence, either of which heralded a final separation between the

---

[38] Forsyth, *Cruciality of the Cross*, p. 29.
[39] For an exposition of justification from the standpoint of 'the new perspective on Paul', see Wright, *Paul*, pp. 113–133, and J. D. G. Dunn, 'Romans, Letter to the', in *DPL*, pp. 838–850.

transgressor and the community, an ultimate and irreversible severance of relationships. Paul Fiddes rightly asserts that 'this Hebrew setting means that "justification", while a legal term, is at root a matter of relationship'.[40]

God is both accuser and judge. The marvel of it is that he has devised a way to ensure that we who are rightly accused and un-questionably guilty of wrongdoing can be restored to a right relation-ship with him and declared free from all accusations without cost to ourselves. This 'act of sheer generosity which depends on no payment man can make'[41] is not a legal fiction 'but a legal reality of the utmost significance'.[42] It is no arbitrary act on God's part. The demands of his just and holy character have to be satisfied, but he himself supplies the means to do so.

'Justification' is a marvellously positive word. It exceeds the idea of pardon and forgiveness. Pardon says that although we are wrong, God reprieves us, and punishment, though deserved, is remitted. Justification says that the accusations have been altogether dismissed; that there is no reason for the verdict of guilt or the infliction of punishment. To paraphrase Marcus Loane's words, pardon says, 'You may go; you have been let off the penalty which your sin deserves.' Justification says, 'You may come; you are welcome to all my love and my presence.'[43]

Contemporary acts of grace illustrate how extraordinary the love of God is towards us. When Jimmy Carter became President of the United States of America, one of his first acts was to ask the Georgia Pardon and Parole Board if they would agree to release Mary Fitzpatrick into his custody so that she could take care of his daughter Amy. Mary Fitzpatrick was a poor black woman who, without the benefit of proper legal representation, had been convicted of murder and was serving a life sentence. She lived in the White House, 'performed her duties in an exemplary manner' and became very close to Amy. Later, she was granted a full pardon by the State of Georgia. It was an act of extraordinary grace on the Carters' part, not only to seek pardon for one who had been declared legally guilty of murder, but to invite her into their home and entrust their precious daughter into her care. The Carters, of course, received some ugly letters for doing such a thing. It was an act of daring grace.[44] But it still falls short of the amazing grace of God, who freely justifies us.

[40] Fiddes, p. 87.
[41] Dunn, Romans, p. 179.
[42] Moo, p. 228.
[43] Quoted in Stott, Romans, p. 110.
[44] Jimmy Carter, Keeping Faith: Memoirs of a President (Collins, 1982), p. 30.

b. The picture of redemption[45]

Our acquittal can take place only because someone has stood in our place and met the demands of righteousness. Jesus offered his perfect life of obedience in exchange for our lives of sin. The means by which God justifies us without 'winking at sin' and without detriment to the interests of justice is illustrated by the second picture Paul introduces: the picture of redemption. It would have been all too familiar to his readers. Slaves purchased in the slave markets of Rome thereby became the property of their new owners. Their freedom could be obtained, but only on payment of a ransom price, by which they would be redeemed.

Redemption becomes one of the favourite metaphors of salvation in Scripture. It reaches back to the great act of redemption in the exodus and stretches forward to the song of the 144,000 redeemed in heaven.[46] All other uses recede into the background, however, when compared with *the redemption that came by Christ Jesus*. For he himself became the ransom price that secured our freedom.

c. The picture of atonement

From the simplicity of the picture of redemption we turn to the complexity of what the NIV translates as *a sacrifice of atonement*. It is clear that Paul's mind travels away from the lawcourts and the slave market into the temple. But precisely what he had in mind when he spoke of Christ's work as a *hilastērion* is much debated.[47] Three major ideas may lie behind it.

In recent times many have revived the view of the Reformers, that it referred to the 'mercy seat', the lid on the ark of the covenant, where God appeared and blood was sprinkled on the Day of Atonement.[48] When the word is used in Hebrews 9:5 (its only other occurrence in the New Testament), it plainly refers to the mercy seat. Furthermore, twenty-one of the twenty-seven occurrences of the word in the Septuagint use it this way. But this is not the only translation, nor is it without problems. It is unlikely that Paul would speak of the work of Christ as if it were an object, a place. If he had done so, he would probably have used the definite article, which he does not. And Paul, unlike the author of Hebrews, makes little use of Levitical symbolism. Such a technical allusion would almost certainly have escaped his Roman readers. Even where it is used like this in the Septuagint, it

---

[45] The concept of redemption will be explored more fully in ch. 16, below.

[46] Rev. 14:3.

[47] See J. M. Gundry-Volf, 'Expiation', in *DPL*, pp. 279–284, for a recent helpful discussion.

[48] Lev. 16:2, 14.

speaks of the function of the mercy seat – what was achieved there – rather than of the place itself. This interpretation is almost certainly wrong.[49]

Many prefer to translate it as a reference to expiation. 'To expiate' means to perform an act that deals with sin by covering it, removing its defilement and doing away with its guilt. The primary reason for this interpretation (which was advocated by C. H. Dodd and is widely supported) is that this is its usual meaning in the Septuagint. Using the word to refer to propitiating God (as in secular Greek), says Dodd, 'is practically unknown'[50] there. He supports his argument by saying that 'the idea underlying it [the meaning 'expiation'] is characteristic of primitive religion' where acts of ritual cleansing were regularly practised to disinfect some religious person, property or place that had become defiled. The NIV fudges the issue by translating it *a sacrifice of atonement* (as does NRSV), but the NIV shows itself in favour of the interpretation 'expiation' by relegating the third interpretation of the word, 'propitiation', to the margin.

Leon Morris's careful examination of the word *hilastērion*[51] has, however, called into question Dodd's conclusions about its usage and, therefore, whether 'expiation' is a sufficiently accurate translation. The primary motivation for arriving at the meaning 'expiation' seems to be more theological than linguistic. If we deny that God expresses personal and judicial anger towards evil, 'propitiation' is certainly an inappropriate translation. But if we accept that view of God's wrath, 'propitiation' becomes entirely appropriate, and 'expiation' alone is insufficient.

The third interpretation of the word, 'propitiation', 'has an inner consistency (if one grants the possibility of retributive justice) and a long pedigree of interpretation in its favour'.[52] It is a fuller concept than expiation, which, while included within propitiation, simply refers to making amends for sin. *Hilastērion* was used to mean 'propitiation' on many occasions in the Septuagint, not just in secular Greek. Douglas Moo concludes: 'When to the linguistic evidence we add the evidence of the context of Romans 1 – 3, where the wrath of God is an over-arching theme (1:18; cf. 2:5), the conclusion that *hilastērion* includes references to the turning away of God's wrath is inescapable.'[53]

To propitiate the God of the Bible is, of course, altogether different from propitiating the gods whom others seek to appease. Three things

---

[49] See Moo, pp. 233–235, for a more detailed justification of this conclusion.

[50] Dodd, p. 78.

[51] Morris, *Apostolic Preaching*, pp. 144–178. A less technical version of his argument is found in *Atonement*, pp., 151–163.

[52] Travis, 'Christ as the bearer', p. 31.

[53] Moo, p. 237. See also Cranfield, *Romans*, pp. 214–218; Morris, *Romans*, pp. 180–182; and Stott, *Romans*, pp. 113–116. For a contrary and, to me, persuasive but ultimately unconvincing evangelical viewpoint, see Smail, *Once and for All*, pp. 90.

make it so.[54] First, God's anger is unlike either theirs or ours. It is not the unpredictable and irrational anger that other gods demonstrate. It is stirred into action only by evil. And 'unlike human wrath, [it] is perfectly righteous, and therefore free from every trace of irrationality, caprice and vindictiveness'.[55] Secondly, in contrast to pagan religions, it is not we who placate God, but God who propitiates himself in an act of grace. God both takes the initiative and provides the sacrifice to die in our place. Thirdly, the nature of Christian propitiation is different. We do not 'bribe the gods with sweets, vegetable offerings, animals and even human sacrifices'.[56] We offer what we have first received. We do not have to offer a sacrifice to change God's attitude towards us, as if he were persuaded to forgive us only reluctantly on seeing his Son's blood flowing down from the cross. As P. T. Forsyth reminds us, 'The atonement did not procure grace, it flowed from grace.'[57] For God so loved us that he gave us his Son to be our propitiating sacrifice. So now it is Christ who has become the focal point of the whole sacrificial system through which people made atonement earlier. He is the means of our propitiation.

James Dunn finds the debate between expiation and propitiation 'an unnecessary polarizing of alternatives'.[58] And so it can be, if the former is swept up in the latter; for, as he himself says, 'the logic of Paul's position is that the wrath of God (expounded in 1:18 – 3:20) is somehow averted by Jesus' death', adding that 'the passage also portrays God as offerer of the sacrifice rather than its object'.[59] But mysteriously both must be true. He is both the offerer and the object of the sacrifice. It is, in the end, only this third interpretation of *hilastērion* that does justice to the word, to the context and to the problem. Only propitiation deals adequately with the wrath of God, which has been justly provoked by our sin.

4. The receiving of justification (3:22, 25–26)

Three times Paul tells us that the benefits of God's grace become applicable to us *through faith*. It has become fashionable recently to regard this *faith* as 'the faithfulness of Jesus' rather than as our faith in Jesus. But this is not how Paul uses the term elsewhere, and it seems ill-fitted to the several uses of the word here.[60] It is almost self-evident that it is our trust in Christ that Paul has in view.

---

[54] The points are developed in Stott, *Romans*, p. 115.
[55] Cranfield, *Romans*, p. 216.
[56] Stott, *Romans*, p. 115.
[57] Forsyth, *Cruciality of the Cross*, p. 41.
[58] Dunn, *Romans*, p. 171.
[59] Ibid.
[60] Ibid., p. 166.

Our righteous status, he says, *comes through faith in Jesus Christ* (22). Our atonement comes *through faith in his blood* (25). And our justification depends on having *faith in Jesus* (26). The second of these phrases is unusual. Nowhere else does Paul speak about having faith 'in his blood'. It is better to understand Paul as saying that propitiation is brought about through faith and in Christ's blood.[61] Our faith must be in the person of Christ, not in any object. And that is Paul's chief point. It is not 'faith' of any kind or in anything that counts – as when people tell the hospital chaplain, 'It's my faith that got me through my illness', and mean that they found some inner strength in themselves which sustained them. The object of our faith makes all the difference. Only faith in Christ enables us to appropriate justification personally. To have faith in him requires us to relinquish faith in anything else or anyone else as the hope of our salvation. It is to trust in him entirely and exclusively.

John Stott describes it beautifully:

> Faith is the eye that looks to Christ, the hand that lays hold of him, the mouth that drinks the water of life. And the more clearly we see the absolute adequacy of Jesus Christ's divine-human person and sin-bearing death, the more incongruous does it appear that anybody could suppose that we have anything to offer. That is why justification by faith alone, to quote Cranmer again, 'advances the true glory of Christ and beats down the vain glory of man'.[62]

5. The glory of justification (3:25–26)

Men and women have an acute sense of justice and, in their sinful state, are all too ready to accuse God of injustice. In the orderly, bureaucratic world in which we live, we want things, above all, to be fair and to work according to the rules. If they do not do so, we quickly speak up for our rights and demand our deserts. Of course, we are not so keen to do so when we are the offenders, rather than the offended party. But although we are the ones who have fallen short of God's glory, we easily adopt a quite unwarranted role reversal. We see ourselves as the offended party, and demand justice; whereas the truth is that it is God who is offended, and we are the offenders.

Something of that debate is voiced by Paul's Jewish interrogators in the opening chapters of Romans. The justice of God stands in the dock of humankind. Surely, the Jews argued, their relationship with God was secure because they were the people of the covenant and the guardians of the law. But Paul has to disillusion them and show them that,

---

[61] Morris, *Romans*, p. 182.
[62] Stott, *Cross of Christ*, p. 187.

although there are advantages in being Jewish (not least in that 'they have been entrusted with the very words of God', 3:2), they stand in need of justification by grace as much as Gentiles do. So where is the justice in that?

a. God's primary purpose

God demonstrates his justice, Paul says, not primarily in the law but in the cross. God shows his absolute integrity in the way he handles Jew and Gentile alike, deals with the law and sin, and provides for sacrifice and atonement. And it all comes into the sharpest focus at the cross.

To be true to himself, God could not condone sin carelessly, pass over it lightly or forgive it cheaply. There would be no justice if he had done so. But that left God with a dilemma. How could his holiness be satisfied without compromising its judgment on sin, while at the same time he released his love without limit in reconciling sinners to himself? Majestic holiness and gracious mercy vie with each other in the very heart of God.

The cross demonstrates God's answer. 'The cross shows us that God's inflexible righteousness is the very means whereby sin is forgiven.'[63] For God maintains the integrity of his holiness and makes available the pardon of his grace by the cross of Christ. The answer lies in Christ, the perfect one, the unblemished sacrifice, offering himself as the propitiatory sacrifice for sin in place of sinful men and women. Charles Cranfield puts it thus: 'in His mercy [God] willed to forgive sinful men and, being truly merciful, willed to forgive them righteously, that is, without in any way condoning their sin. [He] purposed to direct against His own very Self in the person of His Son the full weight of that righteous wrath that they deserve.'[64]

So Paul is able to reach the triumphant conclusion that God is both *just and the one who justifies those who have faith in Jesus.*

b. One possible objection

All this, Paul says, publicly demonstrated God's justice in their own time. But that raises one possible objection. God is not to be released from the dock too readily. What about the sins committed earlier? Why had God delayed? Was his justice not compromised by overlooking sin in the past? If he did not care about sin then, why has he taken steps to do something about it now?

Paul's answer is that we need to understand what God was doing in previous generations before reaching the conclusion that he is, after all, an unjust God. Previously, it was God's forbearance, not his in-

[63] Morris, *Romans*, p. 183.
[64] Cranfield, *Romans*, p. 217.

difference or lack of justice, that *left the sins committed beforehand unpunished* (25). He postponed punishment and restrained his hand of justice from earlier generations, not because their sins did not matter, but because 'his intention has all along been to deal with them once and for all, decisively and finally, through the cross'.[65]

The cross functions retrospectively as well as prospectively. It demonstrates the justice of God for the past and in the present, as well as for the future. And it secures redemption for those who lived before the event, those alive at the time, and those who have followed since. We must be careful when we read Charles Dinsmore's words, 'There was a cross in the heart of God before there was one planted on the green hill outside Jerusalem', lest they reduce the cross to a mere symbol of God's redeeming love.[66] It was more than a symbol. It was the actuality of God's atonement for sin, an actuality that was realized and manifest at one point in history in the crucifixion. But the achievement of 'the Lamb that was slain from the creation of the world'[67] benefits all who have faith, whenever they live.

Packed within these closely argued verses, then, lies the heart of Paul's gospel.[68] It speaks of the righteousness of God, which has revealed his justice; the sacrifice of Christ, which has secured our redemption; and the justification freely bestowed on all who have faith. They are words to bring sweet release. When John Bunyan was in despair and about to give up all as lost, he testified:

> ... just then as I was walking up and down in the house in the most dreadful state of mind, this word of God took hold upon my heart: Ye are 'justified freely by His grace through the redemption that is in Christ Jesus' (Romans 3:24). Oh, what a turn this made upon me! Oh what a sudden change it made!
>
> It was as though I had awakened out of a nightmare. Now God seemed to be saying to me: 'Sinner, you think that I cannot save your soul because of your sins; behold my Son is here and I look upon Him not on you, and I shall deal with you according as I am pleased with Him.' By this I was made to understand that God can justify a sinner at any time by looking upon Christ and imputing His benefits to him.[69]

Paul would say 'Amen!' to that.

[65] Ibid., p. 212.
[66] Quoted by Baillie, p. 194. Baillie does not perhaps altogether escape the problem of reducing the cross to a symbol.
[67] Rev. 13:8.
[68] In Rom. 2:16, Paul refers to the gospel as 'my gospel'.
[69] John Bunyan, *Grace Abounding to the Chief of Sinners* (Moody, 1959), p. 89.

1 Corinthians 1:18 – 2:5
11. The cross as wise folly

When Patricia Gearing's daughter died of Batten's disease in 1998, her grave in a cemetery in the small Lincolnshire seaside town of Mablethorpe was marked by a simple cross. Before long Mrs Gearing was instructed by the local authority to remove it. Their rules said: 'Crosses are discouraged, as excessive use of the supreme Christian symbol is undesirable.' The family was given permission to erect a headstone featuring Mickey Mouse instead.[1]

The incident revealed where the true values of our society lie. The Disney interpretation of the world has supplanted the Christian one, even in a place as far removed as Mablethorpe from the mega-conurbations which are normally considered the centres of sophistication.

The scandal of the cross continues. From Paul's day to our own, it has never been anything other than a scandal, a cause of offence.[2] People respond to its offensiveness in different ways. Some ridicule it. Others try to ignore it. Christians, no less than others, have their techniques for reducing its shame. Long familiarity with it has lessened its absurdity and repugnance and led us to turn it into an item of beauty. We are more used to the cross as a highly polished brass adornment in our sanctuaries, or as an object of art that tops off our buildings, than as an instrument of torture and a device for executing the death penalty by the most excruciating method possible. Morna Hooker points out that we have a problem with the cross. She comments:

> Our problem is simply that we are too used to the Christian story; it is difficult for us to grasp the absurdity – indeed, the sheer madness – of the gospel about a crucified saviour which was proclaimed by the first Christians in a world where the cross was the most barbaric form of punishment which men could devise.[3]

[1] *The Times*, 6 September 1998.
[2] *Skandalon* is better translated 'offence' rather than 'stumbling-block' in 1 Cor. 1:23. See Witherington, p. 109.
[3] Hooker, *Not Ashamed*, p. 8.

They were under no such illusion in Corinth, as Paul's first letter to the Christians there reveals.

1. The folly of the cross (1:22–25)

The sum and substance of Paul's preaching was *the message of the cross* (18). But immediately he recognizes how stupid a message that would appear to be to the citizens of Corinth, whether their background was Jewish or Gentile. The cross ran counter to all expectations of how God would make himself known, whatever the religious or cultural upbringing one had. So absurd was it that no-one would have invented it with any hope that people would believe it to be true. This provides us, ironically, with a good reason for believing that it did happen and that it was God's doing. For 'no mere human, in his right mind or otherwise, would have ever dreamed up God's scheme of redemption – through a crucified Messiah. It is too preposterous, too humiliating.'[4] Why should this be so?

a. A scandal to the Jews

While Jews and Greeks were united in their verdict that the cross was absurd, each community had its own reasons for coming to that conclusion, as Paul explains. *Jews demand miraculous signs and Greeks look for wisdom* (22). And neither found what they were looking for in the cross.

During the course of his ministry Jesus was regularly asked to produce signs as a way of persuading people to believe in him.[5] They did not seek signs out of a genuine desire to see God display his grace and power, or to authenticate the messianic status of Jesus. People solicited these spectacular happenings so that they could evaluate Jesus and test him out, using themselves and their own puny and sin-infected minds as their yardstick. Their attitude, though often dressed up as religion, was 'fundamentally sceptical, and essentially egotistical'.[6]

What fed their appetite for the sensational and miraculous was a wrong understanding of God. The Jews believed that if God were to visit his world with salvation, it would be in power. As they waited for the coming Messiah, they had every expectation that he would be like a military commander, such as General Schwarzkopf of Gulf War fame. He would come to evict the Roman armies from their land and give them back their freedom.

The word of the cross did not come within a million miles of

[4] Fee, *1 Corinthians*, p. 68.
[5] Matt. 12:38–39; 16:1; Mark 8:11–12; John 2:18; 4:48.
[6] Barrett, *1 Corinthians*, p. 54.

conforming to such expectations. It spoke of weakness, not power; of defeat, not victory; of humiliation, not conquest. To speak of a crucified Messiah 'must have sounded like a contradiction in terms, like frozen steam or hateful love or upward decline or a godly rapist – only far more shocking'.[7]

N. T. Wright sums up the position. 'Whoever heard of a *crucified* Messiah? It's failed Messiahs who end up on crosses: crucifixion is what Roman soldiers usually do to poor deluded fanatics who think they're God's chosen hero and find out, too late, they're not after all.'[8] While the Jews, particularly since the Maccabean period, had an appreciation of the suffering of the righteous, they could not stretch their imaginations far enough to accommodate a Messiah who was martyred. No such category of thinking existed.

The fact that crucifixion was the method of execution aggravated matters. This form of execution was particularly humiliating (a point to which we shall return). Jewish eyes often had to be shielded from the nakedness of bodies hanging on wooden stakes as men suffered their slow, lingering deaths as slaves or as enemies of the Roman state. But it was not the form so much as the symbolic meaning of crucifixion that proved to them that Jesus could not be the Messiah. The law, in Deuteronomy 21:23, had declared that 'anyone who is hung on a tree is under God's curse'. And although originally that statement almost certainly referred to displaying a previously executed corpse on a tree, the thinking was easily transferred to those who died by crucifixion. How could one who was so evidently cursed by God be the agent of their salvation?

Crucifixion had been widely used by the Romans to pacify Judea. So the Jews came to see the cross as an instrument of oppression. A Jewish friend of mine from Hitler's Germany, where many of his family had died in Auschwitz, once told me that asking a Jew to boast about a cross was like asking him to boast about a gas chamber. How absurd!

b. An embarrassment to the Romans

What was foolish to the Jews was embarrassing to the Romans, and, although Paul does not directly mention them in this passage, a brief digression will help us understand something more of the Greeks' reaction to the crucified Christ.

If Greece shaped the culture of the ancient world, Rome shaped its social and political environment. Rome had not devised the punishment of crucifixion. That honour probably belongs to the Persians. But it made good use of it to ensure that all opposition to its will was eradicated. Crucifixion combined pain with indignity, and torture with

[7] Carson, *The Cross*, pp. 21–22.
[8] Wright, *Crown and Fire*, p. 5.

humiliation, to maximum effect. It reminds one of Ivan Karamazov's comment, after witnessing the Bulgarian atrocities of the nineteenth century, that 'no animal could be so artfully, so artistically cruel'.[9] But where animals failed, the Romans succeeded. The victim was stripped naked, flogged to within an inch of his life and made to parade through the streets carrying the crossbeam to which his deformed and already mutilated body would be nailed when he reached his place of execution. There he would be held up to public view while enduring a long-drawn-out agony until death arrived. Martin Hengel, to whose research we owe much in this area, writes that 'crucifixion was a punishment in which the caprice and sadism of the executioners was [sic] given full rein'.[10]

Rome was practised in the art of crucifixion. Its deterrent value was great. It was considered the most severe of all forms of execution, and was reserved only for the lower classes. Roman citizens were very rarely put to death this way.[11] So embarrassing was it that polite Roman company avoided speaking of it, finding circumlocutions such as 'the unlucky tree' when they had to do so. Cicero, in defending C. Rabirius, said that 'the very word "cross" should be far removed not only from the person of a Roman citizen but from his thoughts, his eyes and his ears'.[12] Not for nothing did Josephus refer to it as 'the most wretched of deaths'.[13]

If the powerful gods of Greece and Rome died, as some of them did, they died heroic deaths which added to their mystique and majesty. They would never have succumbed to such a humiliating form of death as this. To claim, as Christians did and do, that one who died like a slave was now not only Saviour, but exalted to be the Lord of the whole creation, was patent nonsense.

c. An absurdity to the Greeks

If the cross is a scandal to the Jewish religion and an embarrassment to polite Roman society, it was an absurdity to Greek culture. The wisdom of the Greeks was not the practical wisdom of the Old Testament but the philosophic wisdom of reason. They sought to know God by argument, and 'asserted that reasoning from first principles was the proper manner to attain knowledge of God'.[14] While only a minority studied philosophy in depth and became professional philosophers, searching for wisdom was the mindset of the whole of

[9] J. Glover, *Humanity: A Moral History of the Twentieth Century* (Jonathan Cape, 1999), p. 31.
[10] M. Hengel, *Crucifixion* (1976; ET SCM, 1977), p. 25.
[11] Ibid., p. 39.
[12] Quoted in ibid., p 42.
[13] Quoted in Hooker, *Not Ashamed*, p. 9.
[14] T. Page, 'Philosophy', in *DPL*, p. 716.

Greek culture. Public philosophers were trained in rhetorical arts and put forward their worldviews, claiming to offer a coherent explanation for life, death and the universe. Whole value systems, such as those of the Stoics or the Epicureans, were built on these speculative and competing, even contradictory, philosophies.

Underneath them all lay the sin of egotism. If the Jews reserved judgment about Christ until he matched the criteria of power they had chosen, no less did the Greeks reserve judgment about him until he matched the intellectual criteria they had chosen. 'Their idolatry, writes Gordon Fee, 'was to conceive of God as ultimate Reason, meaning of course what *we* deem reasonable.'[15]

By their standards, *the message of the cross* seemed extremely foolish. The notion that God would manifest himself in human flesh and claim to save the world in such a savage and naïve way was clearly nonsense. F. F. Bruce draws attention to the bottom line, as it were, of their argument. 'Over and above the disgrace of crucifixion, how could anyone accept as lord and deliverer a man who had not sufficient wit to save himself from so ghastly a death, or look to such a man as an exponent of wisdom?'[16] They could not.

So the wise people of Greece, the religious teachers of Judea and the sophisticated public commentators of the age (20) all rejected the possibility that God had done anything of revealing and saving significance in the cross of Christ. It so contradicted their expectations, formed according to their conventional canons of wisdom and power, that they failed entirely to see the true situation.

2. The reality of the cross (1:23–25)

The truth was that the reality of the cross was entirely different from how they saw it. It manifested *the power ... and the wisdom of God* (24). The 'scandal' was the greatest good news the Jews would ever hear. The 'embarrassment' unveiled the majesty of God. The 'foolishness' was the greatest wisdom the Greeks would ever encounter. When all human systems of religion and thought failed to relate people to God, *God was pleased through the foolishness of what was preached to save those who believe* (21).

How could this be? Simply because *the foolishness of God is wiser than human wisdom, and the weakness of God is stronger than human strength* (25). They were judging God by entirely the wrong criteria. He operated on a plane different from theirs and, as the majestic, all-powerful Creator, summoned up dimensions of wisdom and power they never knew existed. There was, to use a colloquialism, more power

---

[15] Fee, *1 Corinthians*, p. 75.
[16] Bruce, *Corinthians*, p. 35.

in God's little finger than in all the might of the Jews and the Greeks put together.

In that cross God was outsmarting the world and accomplishing something to our advantage by overpowering our enemies and releasing us from their grip.[17] His power may have appeared as weakness, and his shrewd wisdom may have appeared as folly, but his plan was deliberate. While the world functions on the basis of self-centredness, God functions on the alternative basis of self-denial. He surrenders himself to folly and weakness, and in so doing establishes his real wisdom and demonstrates his mighty authority.

The power of 'the message of the cross' is primarily the power to deal with sin and to restore people to a right relationship with God. It is power to effect atonement. It is power to transform and make new. John Stott reminds us:

> There is wonderful power in the cross of Christ. It has power to wake the dullest conscience and melt the hardest heart; to cleanse the unclean; to reconcile him who is far off and restore him; to redeem the prisoner from his bondage and lift the pauper from the dung hill; to break down the barriers which divide people from one another; to transform our wayward characters into the image of Christ and finally make us fit to stand in white robes before God.[18]

How did Paul work that out? The resurrection was the clue that enabled him to solve the riddle. If Jesus really had been cursed on the tree, as the Jews supposed, and if he really had been extremely foolish and unable to save himself from death, as the Greeks supposed, then he would certainly not have been raised from the dead three days later. But the resurrection means that while Christ did bear the curse of God on the cross, he did not do so on his own account, or death would have consumed him. Rather, he bore the curse for us. The resurrection declares that God accepted his sacrificial offering as a sufficient answer to the curse, and so Christ was released from any further suffering and raised from the dead. The resurrection declares that no power can hold him. Satan had done his worst and death had dealt its last card, and yet, even when Christ was reduced to the severest weakness, he was able to defeat them. Here, again, we are compelled to acknowledge the delicious irony of God at work.

What the religious and intellectual leaders of Paul's day wrote off as an unconvincing absurdity, much like many of the intelligentsia in our own day, was, in reality, God's brilliant strategy for providing salvation. Human wisdom would never reach such a conclusion. It came at the

[17] Fee, *1 Corinthians*, p. 77.
[18] Stott, *Cross of Christ*, p. 225.

question from entirely the wrong angle. Here was truth that could not be argued from first principles. It had to be revealed. It was only as the gospel was announced and as the Holy Spirit gave insight[19] that people would perceive the truth, discerning in the cross the authentic wisdom and genuine power that save.

3. The impact of the cross

The impact of the cross is manifold. In providing salvation for some, it simultaneously has other consequences that Paul weaves into this passage.

a. The cross creates division

D. A. Carson points out that the ancient world was fond of using polarities to describe humanity. They spoke of Romans and barbarians, Jews and Greeks, slaves and free.[20] Here Paul puts forward another polarity: *those who are perishing* and *us who are being saved* (18). It is the most significant division of all, for it relates to people's eternal destiny. The dividing-line between the two is drawn by the cross, which not only splits humanity asunder but cuts history in two. The cross inaugurates a new age and brings the old world under judgment. Those who reject the message of the cross line up with *the philosophers of this age* (20) and demonstrate their unreadiness to enter the new era – an era begun at Calvary but yet to be brought to its fulfilment when Christ returns, no longer in weakness and folly, but in power and glory.

Those who write off the cross as patent nonsense, Paul claims, are in the process of perishing. The old era is passing away and they are passing away with it. By contrast, those who see in it God's power at work and avail themselves of its benefits are children of the new age and reveal that they are in the process of being saved. Paul further defines these people of the new age as *those who believe* (21). It is those who cling to the cross as their only hope who experience God's salvation. In both cases Paul uses a continuous tense to describe what is happening in the lives of the two groups. Those who reject the cross are on the way to destruction. But those who trust in the Christ of the cross are in the process of being saved. They have begun their journey and already experience many of its delights, but they have not yet reached its destination and have many more delights yet in store.

How enduring is the desire to divide the world into two! In our day we are concerned about North and South, rich and poor, haves and have-nots, men and women, private and public education, rented or owner-occupied housing and so on. But the greatest division of all

---

[19] 1 Cor. 2:7–12; 2 Cor. 4:3–6.
[20] Carson, *The Cross*, p. 14.

remains that between those who see the cross as nonsense and those who see it as the power of God. In our tolerant age, when the church has lost its edge, perhaps we need to rediscover something of the awfulness of that division. In our materialistic age when Christians, no less than others, seem preoccupied with the affairs of this world, we need to refocus on the division that will be fully revealed in the world yet to come. In an age of 'user-friendly' evangelism, perhaps we should be more prepared to accept that the cross will cause offence to some, and that many, even among our family and friends, will reject its message. Not everyone can be won to Christ by affable evangelism and genial friendship.

b. The cross unmasks folly

The cross not only proclaims the wisdom of God; it simultaneously unmasks the folly of the world and reveals it for the pretentious nonsense that it really is. Three times in these verses Paul returns to that aspect of the cross's work. In verse 20 he summons the teachers of wisdom, the Jewish rabbis (*scholars*)[21] and the world's *philosophers*. He may be doing so in order to debate with them. But since his questions follow the condemnatory quotation from Isaiah 29:14 in the previous verse, it is more likely that he is being sarcastic:[22] 'Where have they fled to now? In the light of what God has done on the cross, how does their logic stand up? Where are they hiding themselves?'

In the next verse he exposes the total spiritual bankruptcy of their positions. They claim to be able to know God through their law and rituals or their reason and philosophies, but Paul's damning verdict is that by those means they *did not know him* (21). They were still enquiring, still searching, but they had not arrived. God can be known only through the cross, a route that human pride finds difficult to accept and constantly tries to circumvent by devising its own worldviews. But these all prove to be dead ends. There is only one place where God has chosen to make himself fully known in order to save men and women, and that is the cross of Christ.

Paul's third sortie into this area is even more devastating. In verse 28 he speaks of the people of the cross, totally unimpressive as they are by any worldly standards, as being chosen by God to negate the misplaced arrogance of the world. Through them, and more particularly through what they believe in, says F. F. Bruce, 'he annuls the conventional

---

[21] 'The rendering *scholar* is misleading. *Scholar* suggests an academic, perhaps a very gifted one. The Greek word *grammateus* used here was not used in Greek culture to denote any kind of advanced scholar. What Paul has in mind is the use of the term among Greek-speaking Jews: the *grammateus* was the "scribe," the expert in the law of God, the person knowledgeable in biblical heritage and in all the tradition that flowed from it.' Carson, *The Cross*, p. 17.

[22] Fee, *1 Corinthians*, p. 70.

canons of wisdom, power, reputation and value. Nothing could be more subversive of these canons in the first-century Graeco-Roman world than the proclamation of a crucified man exalted as Lord over the universe.'[23] The cross nullifies them by exposing them for the self-centred, prideful and hubristic systems that they are. It demonstrates that they understand neither the nature of the God they claim to know nor his ways. These are not matters of debate, as if God takes his seat alongside others in some seminar group to grope with them towards solutions for the world's problems. These are matters where God, the sovereign Lord, has spoken and acted in 'the message of the cross', a message contrary to those the wise of the world are used to uttering. In the cross God not only exposed their emptiness but judged their pride. He negated them.

The cross still negates the illusory 'wisdom' of our age, standing in the crowd like the little boy who dared to voice the truth and cry out that the emperor had no clothes. So today, because it shows Christ denying himself the choice of walking away, but rather as dying to create a new humanity, the cross unmasks our secular individualism. Because it demonstrates Christ's acceptance of our guilt and his taking on himself the judgment of God for the moral laws we have transgressed, the cross unmasks our therapeutic attempts to heal our own hurts by denying any guilt and questioning moral boundaries. Because it portrays a Christ who never possessed a home and had nowhere to lay his head, stripped even of his clothes as he hangs on a tree, it lays bare our trust in money and power as the solution to our ills. Because in Christ God provides a very personal, incalculable and 'unscientific' answer to our problems, the cross shatters our confidence in science as the way to alleviate our ills and improve our world. Because a sinless Christ took upon himself the world's hurt and hatred, dying unjustly and yet without protest, and in doing so brought mercy and grace to the oppressed, the cross breaks down our desire to retaliate and to get even with those who have abused us as a means of resolving our conflicts and securing our rights. Because Christ demonstrates love that goes beyond reason and willingness to die out of sheer unreasonable grace, the cross destroys our faith in reason as the unshakeable foundation of knowledge. The cross still unmasks our folly and deflates our pretentious worldviews.

c. The cross engenders humility

If the cross has an impact on the world by creating a division, and has an impact on unbelievers by nullifying their worldviews, it also has an impact on believers by engendering humility. It does so because it tells us that by ourselves we are unable to find God or to live righteously

[23] Bruce, p. 36.

before him. It exposes our own thoughts and systems as an illusion. It shows our wisdom to be folly, our power to be feeble and our goodness to be inadequate. It reveals our dependence on the wonderful mercy of God to seek us, to initiate the relationship with us, and to provide the means of our salvation. It shows our unworthiness and his marvellous grace. It reveals too that not one of us has any advantage as we come to the cross. Gordon Fee writes:

> The ground is level at the foot of the cross; not a single thing that any of us possesses will advantage him/her before the living God – not brilliance, 'clout,' achievement, money, or prestige. By choosing the lowly Corinthians God declared that he has forever ruled out every imaginable human system of gaining his favor. It is all – trust him completely (v. 31) – or nothing.[24]

Paul makes his point negatively to begin with. The cross means that *no-one may boast before him* (29). No human being has any ground for pride before such a righteous and gracious God. We must approach him with reverent and thankful humility. He then makes the same point positively. Quoting Jeremiah 9:24, he says there is a kind of boasting that is to be encouraged. *'Let those who boast boast in the Lord'* (31).What we are to take pride in is the redemptive work of Christ on the cross. The word Paul uses for *boast* (*kauchaomai*) is one of which he is particularly fond.[25] It is capable of a wide spectrum of meaning, from 'exulting in' something to 'trusting wholly in' something. Here, Paul surely incorporates both ends of the spectrum of meaning. The Corinthians are to trust completely and only in the cross of Christ, and also brag about it in a world that may despise it but where wise people, truth be told, brag about much sillier things.

In Galatians 6:14 Paul returns to the theme of boasting in the cross as a matter of personal testimony. There he writes, 'May I never boast except in the cross of our Lord Jesus Christ, through which the world has been crucified to me, and I to the world.'[26] John Stott's comment on this verse is worth recalling. Speaking of the difficulty of translating the Greek word, he writes, 'It means to boast in, glory in, trust in, rejoice in, revel in, live for. The object of our boast or "glory" fills our horizons, engrosses our attention, and absorbs our time and energy. In a word, our glory is our obsession.'[27] It is to such boasting in the cross, absurdly counter-cultural as it is, that Paul was calling the Corinthian believers.

[24] Fee, *1 Corinthians*, p. 84.
[25] Fifty-five out of the fifty-nine New Testament references occur in Paul: ibid.
[26] 'May I never boast ...' (NIV and NRSV) seems a lame translation of *mē genoito kauchasthai* in comparison with the AV's 'God forbid that I should glory ...'
[27] Stott, *Cross of Christ*, p. 349.

3. The achievement of the cross (1:30)

Before applying his teaching to the way the church must proclaim its message as the community of the cross, using himself as an example, Paul summarizes the achievements of Christ for us. In contrast to those outside the church, whose ways of life have been nullified by God, believers, who have been called by God, owe their very existence to being *in Christ Jesus*. In sharp contrast to the wisdom available in the world, *Christ has become for us wisdom from God*. Paul then spells out what this gift of wisdom means in the three expressions that follow. They come from the lawcourts, the temple and the slave market respectively. Christ is *our righteousness, holiness and redemption.*[28] *Righteousness* means that we have been brought into a right standing before God and a right relationship with him. *Holiness* means that we have been set apart for him and are now under his exclusive ownership. *Redemption* means we have been set free by him from the power and consequences of sin. Christ's work brings us, then, into a relationship *with* him so that we might live *for* him, all of which depends on what God achieved *through* him. Paul's phrase encapsulates the who, how and why of the Christian life. Who are we? Righteous ones. How do we live? As holy people. Why is this so? Because of redemption.

4. The community of the cross (1:26 – 2:5)

Paul has had a particular purpose in reflecting on the cross. He has not done so to comment on the state of society, or even to lead into preaching the gospel, although he does both of those. His purpose is pastoral. He is seeking to instruct the church about their true identity, so that their lives may conform more than they are currently doing to God's will and purposes for them. Through the cross God saves individuals. But he does much more than that. It is also the means by which God creates a new community, the community of the new age, where the cross is of central, symbolic significance and where it should still be found modelled among its members.

a. A community formed by the cross

The crucified Christ is the foundation of this community. Nothing else distinguishes its members; from the standpoint of the conventional world, they are nonentities. Although some of the Corinthian Christians were people of standing – such as Crispus, who had been the

---

[28] Paul is not saying that in Christ we receive four gifts, namely wisdom, righteousness, holiness and redemption, but one gift: the gift of wisdom, which is defined by righteousness, holiness and redemption. *Contra* AV. See Fee, *1 Corinthians*, pp. 85–86.

ruler of the synagogue,[29] Gaius, who, as Paul's personal host, would probably have been relatively wealthy,[30] Stephanas, who was able to support mission work (16:15), and Erastus, the city treasurer[31] – the majority were neither wise nor influential (1:26). Almost certainly most of them would have been slaves. Insignificant though they may have been in the world, however, they were not insignificant to God, who had called them to be his own special people. That he should have chosen them was entirely consistent with the message of the cross. If the cross was considered weak and foolish, it was appropriate that powerless people and those deficient in the world's wisdom should be drawn to it. How foolish of God to think that he could do anything through the likes of them![32] The composition of the church in Corinth mirrored the message of the cross itself.

b. A community marked by the cross

The community also needed to mirror this message in its on-going life. And this its members were not doing. Paul had begun his letter by expressing concern about the divisions in the church, as one faction competed with others for position and recognition (1:10–17). By living such argumentative and self-promoting lives, they were proving that they had not grasped the meaning of the cross sufficiently, nor worked through its values as extensively as they ought. The critical function of the cross in this context was that it denounced the values of the world, which were based on egotism, pride and self-assertion.[33] How could they say they were followers of a crucified Christ and live such uncrucified lives?

This issue runs right through 1 Corinthians, which is why it was important for Paul to lay such an uncompromising theological foundation at the start. When, for example, they boasted about human leaders, or about their own wisdom, strength and honour (3:18 – 4:21), they were still thinking just like those outside of Christ. Or, when the 'strong' members of the congregation belittled the 'weak' members by their behaviour at the Lord's table (11:17–34), they were demonstrating that they had not adequately adopted the lifestyle defined by the cross but were still thinking along conventional worldly lines. And when, to give a third illustration, they were so concerned about the exercise of powerful spiritual gifts in worship that they moved out of love into self-assertiveness, again they were displaying their failure to

[29] 1 Cor. 1:14; Acts 18:8.
[30] Rom. 16:23.
[31] Rom. 16:23.
[32] Fee, *1 Corinthians*, p. 84.
[33] Pickett, p. 69. Also Tomlin, esp. ch. 5. He writes of the cross becoming for Paul 'the central polemical focus' and a 'counter ideology to the uses of power current within the church' (p. 101).

allow the message of the cross to affect them as deeply as it should have done (chs. 12 – 14, esp. 14:26–28).

Peter Lampe has expressed their problem in stark terms:

> The Christian theology of the Corinthians, being so enthusiastic and so proud of possessing wisdom about God, stands on the same level as the wisdom of the rest of the world. Both are driven *ad absurdum* by the word of the cross. Both are equally godless. The wisdom of the theologians in Corinth is in no way superior to that of the rest of the world.[34]

Throughout much of the letter, then, Paul is concerned to encourage the church to be a community not only called out by the cross but also characterized in its day-to-day life by the same cross. To use Raymond Pickett's words, 'He reminds the Corinthians that the community has been shaped by the "word of the cross" and hence that its social structure reflects (or should do) God's displacement of worldly wisdom and power.'[35] How dare the richer members of the community still behave towards and judge their fellow-members according to worldly standards (3:1–4)! There could no longer be room for arrogance or any form of superiority. The message of the cross led not only to personal salvation but also to social transformation.

This explains why Paul starts negatively (as we saw) when he encourages his readers to humility. To invite them to boast in the Lord would not register sufficiently with them. He has to emphasize what that does *not* mean before he can tell them what it does mean. What it does not mean is that they have grounds for boasting in themselves and their own wisdom. They must feel pride in the Lord, and the Lord alone. Only then will they stop thinking like people in the world, who are on the way to destruction.

c. A community that proclaims the cross

From the shape of the community Paul turns to the proclamation of its message (2:1–5). Although it looks as if he is addressing a new subject, he is in fact developing the same one in a different way. Paul reminds them that his preaching of the gospel did not adopt the rhetorical techniques common among peddlers of philosophy in the ancient world. He told the truth plainly, trusting in God alone to persuade them of the truth of what he said.

By contrast, the philosophers of the ancient world were devoted to the study and performance of rhetoric. They would search for persuasive and eloquent ways to present their materials, and use a whole

---

[34] P. Lampe, '1 Corinthians 1 – 4', *Int* 44 (1990), p. 125.
[35] Pickett, p. 73.

armoury of techniques to convince their hearers of their message. They did everything they could to make their messages popular, palatable and powerful. They would package them like clever salesmen who make their products irresistible, even if it means concealing the small print on occasions.

Paul renounced such an approach in an act of conscious resolution (2). Instead, his approach is 'determinedly straightforward and open'.[36] His favourite terms for 'preaching' demonstrate as much: he announces the message like a herald, tells good news as if chatting to a neighbour about a wedding or the birth of a baby, and witnesses to the truth as if giving evidence in a court of law. According to Duane Litfin, none of the Greek words that lay behind these images were words that self-respecting orators would use in the wider world. Yet Paul loves them.[37] He rejects the more powerful words of persuasion he could have chosen and opts for plainer, less manipulative vocabulary. Again, this is a matter not of human strategy but of deep theology. The form of his preaching is collapsed into the content of his preaching. His method is consistent with his message, and that was one of weakness and folly.

This does not mean to say that Paul cultivated incompetence as a speaker, or that he is advocating a poor proclamation of the gospel. Acts 14:12 would suggest otherwise. Nor does it mean he was sloppy in his thinking. Any study of his preaching as reported in Acts should disabuse us of that idea. He clearly thought carefully about how to proclaim Christ in ways suitable for the cultural contexts in which he spoke. What it does mean is that he avoided 'artificial communication that won plaudits for the speaker but distracted from the message'.[38] The cross, in all its folly and weakness, had to be up front – not the preacher!

D. A. Carson asks about the implications of this for our patterns of evangelism today.

> Why is it that we constantly parade Christian athletes, media personalities, and pop singers? Why should we think their opinions or their experiences of grace are of any more significance than those of any other believer? When we tell outsiders about people in our church, do we instantly think of the despised and the lowly who have become Christians, or do we love to impress people with the importance of men and women who have become Christians? Modern Western evangelicalism is deeply infected with the virus of

[36] D. Litfin, *St Paul's Theology of Proclamation: 1 Corinthians 1 – 4 and Graeco-Roman Rhetoric* (Cambridge University Press, 1994), p. 194. Litfin's is a fine study of the ancient art of rhetoric and Paul's contrasting theology' of proclamation.
[37] Ibid., p. 195.
[38] Carson, *The Cross*, p. 35.

triumphalism, and the resulting illness destroys humility, minimizes grace, and offers far too much homage to money and influence and 'wisdom' of our day.'[39]

'The message of the cross' must not only shape our community living but determine our evangelistic method. It is not possible to proclaim the message of a Christ who was 'crucified in weakness'[40] in a triumphalist or overpowering manner. To do so would be to sell out to the ways of the world and build in a contradiction between the form and substance of the gospel.

Throughout this passage the apostle is not only contrasting the ways of God with the ways of the world, but also the ways of God with the ways of the church. The Corinthian church had been called into being by the cross as a sign of the age to come, but was still too affected by the conventional thinking of the world. Whatever the cross had nullified, they still behaved as if power and wisdom continued to matter. They had not grasped that the cross was not just the means of their salvation but the foundation on which their worldview had to be reconstructed and the cue from which all their behaviour should flow. Their reorientation to this new way of thinking and living was far from complete. They were still in process, and it was a process Paul wrote with some urgency to encourage. They still had to hear and appreciate the message of the cross in all its fullness.

In the second of Paul's portraits of the cross, then, we capture a very different image of it from that portrayed in Romans. Here, the weakness of God clashes with the power of the world, and the folly of God runs headlong into the wisdom of the world. But in both cases it is surprisingly the weakness and the folly that gain the upper hand.

On the morning of Monday 12 September 1994, a small biplane crash-landed in the garden of the White House, causing considerable damage to President Clinton's bedroom and havoc to the functioning of the President's office. It had been flown there by a patient who had escaped from the psychiatric unit where he normally resided. It was a beautifully ironic scene. A tiny, insignificant plane, piloted by someone whom normal society would reject as mentally challenged and write off as contributing nothing useful to society, had eluded the most sophisticated security systems in the world, designed to protect the most powerful man in the world. That silly little plane exposed the real weaknesses of all the advanced technological paraphernalia that surrounds the White House, and proved itself to be 'wiser' than all of it.

It is not an exact parallel to the cross, for no useful purpose was

[39] Ibid., p. 29.
[40] 2 Cor. 13:4.

served by this escapade. Nevertheless, it serves as a contemporary reminder that weakness sometimes masks real strength and folly sometimes hides genuine wisdom. And the strength and wisdom of the world are sometimes easily fooled and defeated. They were certainly so in the cross.

2 Corinthians 5:16–21; Ephesians 2:11–22; Colossians 1:19–20
12. The cross as fatal reconciliation

One of the most popular parables Jesus ever told was that of the prodigal son.[1] A young man alienated from his father left home to squander his inheritance years before he should have received it. Having sunk to the lowest depths imaginable, the son came to his senses and returned home, not expecting to receive a warm welcome. His father, however, had been on the lookout for him, and as soon as he saw him he ran to bid his son welcome. The father was reconciled to his rebellious son, embraced him with lavish and undeserved generosity, and restored him to his place within the family. The parable is popular, not only because it is beautifully crafted and elegantly told, but because the situation it describes is all too human and its truth is timeless. Many can identify with a story of broken relationships, and many long for such a wonderful reconciliation. If it does not tell us all there is to know about reconciliation,[2] it tells us the most important thing: God, the Father, longs for it, and, although he has good reason to do otherwise, he makes it possible.

The parable gives us in story form what Paul states and explains in his letters. In exploring the idea of the cross as the means of reconciliation, Paul fills in the parable's gaps and expands its horizons, so that what was already evident as an act of amazing grace is seen to be more extraordinary still.

1. The centrality of reconciliation

a. In Paul

Several factors make us aware of how significant the concept of reconciliation is to Paul. He resorts to it on five occasions as a way of

[1] Luke 15:11–24.
[2] It does not, for example, do more than hint at the cost of reconciliation. But stories are not designed to express truth systematically, and therefore will not always be comprehensive in their treatment.

216

describing the work of Christ on the cross.[3] There is the 'mildly surprising' fact[4] that Paul, alone among New Testament writers, describes the cross as a work of reconciliation, even though that seems such an obvious effect of Christ's death. He seems to use language in an unprecedented way to speak of God's reconciling himself to us.[5] Finally, there is the value, not just the appeal, of the explanation of the cross as reconciliation itself. It is the least metaphorical and most concrete way of speaking of the new relationship between God and human beings that arises from the death of Christ.[6]

The idea takes us in two directions at once. It leads into the heart of the gospel, giving us more precise information on how it was effected; but it also extends out to the circumference of the gospel, telling us more than any other metaphor of salvation about how it is to be applied. The way Paul develops it indicates that it was important to him, not just in terms of salvation, but more widely in relation to a range of experiences and duties in the Christian life. In the light of this, Ralph Martin has gone so far as to claim that reconciliation 'can be presented as an interpretive key to Paul's theology; and if we are pressed to suggest a simple term that summarizes his message, the word reconciliation will be the "chief theme" or "centre" of his missionary and pastoral thought and practice'.[7]

Paul does not unfold the theme of reconciliation in isolation from other perspectives on the cross. In 2 Corinthians 5, where he expounds it most fully, it shares the stage with other ideas.[8] The work of Christ leads to a new creation (16–17). It is a vicarious substitution; he 'died *for* all' (14–15). He died as our 'representative' (14, 21), conveying what Morna Hooker contends is Paul's key concept of the atonement, our interchange in Christ.[9] His death was a sacrifice, namely, a sin offering (12). It leads to our forgiveness (19) and justification (19, 21).

---

[3] Rom. 5:9–11; 11:15; 2 Cor. 5:16–21; Eph. 2:11–22; Col. 1:20–23.

[4] I. H. Marshall, 'The meaning of "reconciliation"', in R. A. Guelich (ed.), *Unity and Diversity in New Testament Theology* (Eerdmans, 1978), p. 117.

[5] Ibid., pp. 127–128.

[6] Ibid., p. 117.

[7] Martin, *Reconciliation*, p. 5.

[8] Green, 'Death of Christ', in *DPL*, p. 204.

[9] M. D. Hooker, *From Adam to Christ: Essays on Paul* (Cambridge University Press, 1990), pp. 13–41. She writes of Christ's solidarity with humanity and his sharing of the human situation even to the point of death as the vitally important factor in Paul's thought. As a result, the Christian, through identifying with him and dying to sin, is able to share in his resurrection. She concludes: 'The idea of interchange of experience in Christ is a vital clue to Paul's understanding of atonement.' The perspective is obviously true and valid, but not, in itself, the sole one or a sufficient one. Christ is not only our representative but our substitute. Stott explains: 'A "substitute" is one who acts on behalf of another in such a way as to render the other's action's unnecessary. A "representative" is one who acts on behalf of another in such a way as to involve the other in his action.' *Cross of Christ*, p. 276.

All these are referred to in Paul's immediate argument. But the idea of reconciliation is clearly centre stage, with the others playing only supporting roles.

b. For us

Although not widely mentioned in the New Testament, or taken up by others in the immediate post-apostolic period, the interpretation of the cross as reconciliation is one of the most dominant today. There is probably a simple explanation for its popularity. 'It is probably the most popular', John Stott writes, '... because it is the most personal.'[10] Unlike other images, which have to do with the bygone era of the Israelite judicial system, the temple or the slave market, this one belongs to the contemporary world. In a postmodern culture, where people are searching for authentic relationships and struggling so much with the effects of unsatisfactory ones, understanding the cross from the vantage point of reconciliation becomes even more urgent.

The painful problem of broken relationships is all too real for most. It affects every kind and level of relationship. In the family, the incidence of broken relationships between husbands and wives, and parents and children, has never been higher. In schools, never have so many children been excluded, a symptom of relationships having finally broken down. Whether it be the gender divide between men and women, the industrial divide between managers and employees, the social divide between rich and poor, the political divide in Northern Ireland between unionist Protestants and republican Catholics, or the racial divide between black and white, everywhere there is a need for reconciliation. On the international front, the need for reconciliation is just as evident: between Israeli and Palestinian in the Middle East; Tutsi and Hutu in Rwanda; Bosnian and Serb in the former Yugoslavia; Kurd and Turk in Turkey; Russian and Chechen in Grozny; Muslim and Christian in Indonesia, Pakistan and Northern Nigeria ... The list could go on. The need for reconciliation is high on the world's agenda.

Even what seem like good relations on the surface can disguise a state of non-relationship underneath. Real engagement and acceptance between people are rare. There is often a need, at work, at home and even at church, as much as in wider society, to penetrate the uneasy ceasefire or to go beyond the unspoken peace treaty and to work for a genuine, deep reconciliation that leads to a real bonding of people with one another.

[10] Stott, *Cross of Christ*, p. 192.

2. The nature of reconciliation

'To reconcile' is to bring enemies into a state of friendship, to overcome alienation and to create affinity. It is to heal broken relationships, so that those who have suffered them can put away the cause of their hostility and live in close harmony with one another from then on.

The word 'reconciliation' is, of course, used in all sorts of ways and often suffers from being given a romantic and sentimental tinge. It is not just a reuniting of people who have merely been separated from one another without experiencing any other break in their relational bond. That may be a restoration of relationships, but it is not a reconciliation. To be reconciled is not to paper over the cracks and pretend that the cause of the disruption never occurred. Reconciliation is to face up to and resolve the cause of the disruption, realizing that only when the cause has been dealt with can true friendship be restored. Many people want reconciliation without understanding that it is no easy goal to achieve, and without confronting the issues and paying the cost involved.

It is this insight that motivated Archbishop Desmond Tutu regarding the situation in South Africa following the end of apartheid. Injustice had taken place; offence had been caused; evil had taken its harmful and fatal toll. Following the election of Nelson Mandela to the Presidency and of the ANC into government, it was not sufficient to act as though the wrongs of the apartheid years had never taken place. Hence the Truth and Reconciliation Commission was set up so that people on all sides could openly confess their wrongdoing, and receive forgiveness once the truth had been brought out into the open.

Speaking at the Rustenberg Church Conference in 1990, which, for the first time, brought together the leadership of the white Dutch Reformed Church and that of the 'anti-apartheid' church, Desmond Tutu had said:

If there is to be reconciliation, we who are ambassadors of Christ, we to whom the gospel of reconciliation has been entrusted, surely we must be Christ's instruments of peace. We must ourselves be reconciled. The victims of injustice and oppression must be ever ready to forgive. That is a gospel imperative. But those who have done wrong must be ready to say, 'We have hurt you by our injustice, by uprooting you from your homes, by dumping you in poverty-stricken resettlement camps. By giving your children inferior education. By denying your humanity and trampling down your fundamental rights. We are sorry, forgive us.' And the wronged must forgive.[11]

[11] D. Tutu, *The Rainbow People of God* (Transworld, 1994), p. 215.

As Paul expounds the reconciliation of God and sinful humanity, which is made possible through the cross, it is the full and exact meaning of reconciliation, as opposed to superficial ones, that he has in mind. It is a reconciliation that deals effectively with sin and does not side-step the issue of offence. Paul's explanation of *the message of reconciliation* (19) divests it of triviality and saves it from sentimentality.[12]

a. Sin is the problem

The cause of our broken relationship with God is sin. In 2 Corinthians 5, Paul alludes to the problem only once (in saying that *in Christ ... people's sins* are not counted *against them*, 19), since his real purpose in mentioning reconciliation here, as we shall see, is pastoral. But even here he is careful not to omit the cause of the breach of our relationship. Elsewhere he writes about it more directly.

In Romans 5:6–11 Paul gives a damning appraisal of our condition before God. In verse 6, he speaks of our being 'ungodly', that is, alienated from him and without a true and living relationship to him. The reason for that (7–8) is that, far from being righteous, we are active sinners. The result of our sin and alienation is not that we stand in a neutral position before God (for there can be no neutrality in relation to our holy Creator) but that we have become his enemies. This antipathy to God cannot be ignored or discounted. It must be dealt with. Our aversion to God must be overcome if we are to be reconciled, and our hostility to him must be transformed by forgiveness.

In Colossians 1:21, in the context of the theme of reconciliation, Paul again connects our alienation from God to sin, which he defines as not just our superficial actions but something that affects our total mindset. It is the way we think *and* behave that distances us from God and severs the friendship that should be a joy to us both.

If reconciliation is to be achieved the obstacle of sin has to be overcome.

b. God is the reconciler

Paul's diagnosis of our condition makes it clear that we are incapable of doing anything to resolve the situation ourselves, even if we wished to do so. Sin has rendered us powerless,[13] as well as reducing our desire for reconciliation with God. Absence does not always make the heart grow fonder, and although, in our sinful state, we often yearn for something more than we are yet experiencing and realize that something is lacking, our thinking has been so impaired that often we do not know that our relationship with God is what is fundamentally missing. Even if we

---

[12] Gunton, p. 177.
[13] Rom. 5:8.

were motivated to seek peace with God, what could we offer him as a sufficient sacrifice for our past wrongdoings and to gain his favour?

> Not the labours of my hands
> Can fulfil Thy law's demands;
> Could my zeal no respite know,
> Could my tears for ever flow,
> All for sin could not atone:
> Thou must save, and Thou alone.[14]

But Paul is emphatic: while we are helpless, God takes the initiative in reconciling himself to us. Three times he stresses the point in 2 Corinthians 5. *All this is from God* (18). God was reconciling *the world to himself* (19). And *God made him who had no sin to be sin for us, so that in him we might become the righteousness of God* (21). The same stress on God's initiative is found in Romans 5.

In examining the precise way in which Paul writes about reconciliation, Howard Marshall points out that God is never the implied subject of a passive verb or the object of an active one. We never read that 'God is reconciled by us', or that 'we reconcile God'. God always does the reconciling. 'Further,' Marshall explains, 'it is generally accepted that God's act of reconciliation takes place prior to, and independently of, any human action: it was while we were still sinners that we were reconciled to God.' Reconciliation is something we receive from him.[15] 'All this', he concludes, 'suggests that the act of reconciliation is primarily something done by God.'[16]

Why should this be so? For the simple reason that God is the offended party. The problem of sin is 'incomparably more serious on God's side'[17] than on ours, for sin is primarily an offence to him. He, therefore, must take the steps to forgive and set aside the offence. Since we have done the wrong, we may wish to apologize to him (although in our proud and sinful nature we are usually most reluctant to do so), but we are not in a position to undo what we have done and remove the hurt caused to God or appease the just anger we have provoked in him. Only he can do that. And in an unprecedented way, Paul claims, God removed the cause of his own anger against us. He did so both as an injured party seeking justice and as an injured partner, like a husband or wife, seeking reconciliation.[18]

[14] Hymn, 'Rock of ages, cleft for me', by Augustus Montague Toplady.
[15] Cf. Rom. 5:11, 'through whom we have now received reconciliation'.
[16] Marshall, 'Reconciliation', p. 122.
[17] Martin, *2 Corinthians*, p. 154.
[18] *Contra* J. D. G. Dunn, who wishes to jettison the first of these images in favour of retaining only the second: *The Theology of Paul the Apostle* (T. and T. Clark, 1998), p. 229.

How, then, was reconciliation to be accomplished? He could not simply decree reconciliation by fiat, for he would then have been untrue to his holy, righteous character and would have made light of sin. He did not reconcile himself to the world by changing his mind about sin, compromising his holiness or giving up on making people righteous. He did not 'reconcile himself to the situation' in the way we sometimes recommend people to do: 'You can't change it, so just accept it as it is. Be reconciled to it.' His reconciliation was far more fundamental and therefore far more satisfying. In his mercy and grace he devised a way of dealing with the offence and satisfying his righteousness[19] while being reconciled to the offenders, through the offering of his own Son on the cross.

c. Christ is the agent

God reconciles the world to himself in Christ. Christ is to be viewed by the Corinthians no longer as a national or political leader but as the agent of God introducing the new era of reconciliation (16–17). What is taken for granted here is made explicit in the other places where Paul writes about reconciliation. It was particularly the cross of Christ that brought about this situation. The life of Christ alone would have been insufficient to reconcile us. His death was essential. So, for example, in Romans 5:10 Paul says that 'we were reconciled to him through the death of his Son'. In Ephesians 2:13–16, those who were alienated from God are 'brought near through the blood of Christ', adding that the reconciliation of Jews and Gentiles into one family of God took place 'through the cross'. In Colossians 1:22 the message is the same: 'But now he has reconciled you by Christ's physical body through death to present you holy in his sight, without blemish and free from accusation.'

Paul gives us an idea of how the cross alters the situation and brings about reconciliation. He presses two idioms into use to explain it. First, in verse 19, there is a forensic/accounting idiom: *not counting people's sins against them.* Secondly, in verse 21, there is a sacrificial/cultic idiom: *God made him who had no sin to be sin for us, so that in him we might become the righteousness of God.* In both cases, it happens by way of transference and substitution.

In the first place, as far as sinful people are concerned, the cross means that 'God does not post to their accounts debts that are rightfully theirs',[20] but instead charges the liability for them to the account of Jesus Christ. This does not mean that God just ignores sin. For, in Philip Hughes' words, 'there is a reckoning of sins; they are reckoned,

---

[19] Forsyth, *Cruciality of the Cross*, p. viii.
[20] Barnett, p. 307.

however, not to the sinner but to Christ, the sinner's substitute',[21]

In the second place, Christ became a sacrifice for sin as prefigured in Isaiah 53.[22] In any of the sacrifices of the ancient cult, an interchange took place between the worshipper and the offering. So here too there is an interchange. The sin of unrighteous people was laid upon Christ and the righteousness of Christ was transferred to us.[23] In his obedience to the Father, Christ identified himself so perfectly with sinners that he took upon himself the burden and penalty of their sin. Paul is careful not to say that Christ became a sinner, but rather that he was made to be sin. What Christ gives in exchange for sin to those whom he relieves of it is the right standing before God which he alone deserved, through his perfect obedience. In this way reconciliation with God is effected.

It can readily be seen that though this portrait of atonement may be new, the explanation of it is the same. Whether the picture is justification, redemption, liberation, or another of the many metaphors Paul uses, the explanation is one. James Denney sums it up like this:

> He became sin, became a curse for us. It is this which gives his death a propitiatory character and power, which makes it possible, in other words, for God to be at once righteous and a God who accepts as righteous those who believe in Jesus. He is righteous, for in the death of Christ, his law is honoured by the Son who takes the sin of the world to himself as all that it is to God; and he can accept as righteous those who believe in Jesus, for in so believing sin becomes to them what it is to Him. I do not know any word which conveys the truth of this if 'vicarious' or 'substitutionary' does not. Nor do I know any interpretation of Christ's death which enables us to regard it as a demonstration of love to sinners if this vicarious or substitutionary character is denied.[24]

One misunderstanding of this doctrine must be faced before proceeding. It easily leads to the view that God had to be reconciled to us by being persuaded to change his attitude towards us by the gruesome sacrifice of his Son on the cross. Only when an angry God saw the blood dripping from his wounds was he pacified and won over to be conciliatory towards sinful men and women. But such a position is flawed for several reasons. It is God who takes the initiative in reconciling us to him, not Christ who takes the initiative in persuading his reluctant Father to relent. The cross occurred because God *is* a God of grace, not to *make* him a God of grace. In sacrificing Christ, God

---

[21] Hughes, *2 Corinthians*, p. 209.
[22] Martin, *2 Corinthians*, pp. 140, 157.
[23] A parallel (although not exact) idea is found in Rom. 5:19.
[24] Denney, p. 103.

was sacrificing nothing other than himself, for *God was ... in Christ*.[25] Father and Son are not to be set in opposition to each other. The cross did not change God's attitude towards us from hostility to love. His attitude was always love towards his creatures but hatred towards our sin. It remains so still. For once our sin has been removed from us, the obstacle to his uninhibited love is removed. What the cross changed was not his attitude but our standing before him. It is we who have been reconciled to him, by receiving the righteousness of Christ, not he who has been reconciled to us by any change of character on his part.

d. Peace is the result

Although some of Paul's statements seem to suggest that God was engaged in a process of universal reconciliation which takes place automatically in the lives of all, it is evident that that was not the apostle's intention. The benefits of reconciliation belong to those who are *in Christ* (17), not to all, irrespective of their relationship with him. Being 'in Christ' does not carry the mystical overtones of union with him that are to be found elsewhere.[26] Rather, it involves exercising faith in him and so entering into the new order of things which he has brought into existence and will bring to completion on his return. To many, this new creation is not an observable reality. But *anyone* who trusts in him, exchanging his or her sin for Christ's righteousness, may enter the new creation now and start experiencing it right here. Paul later nominates himself as the worst of sinners because of his history of persecuting the church.[27] But he is confident that *anyone* includes him, and, if this is so, no-one is excluded.[28] None are too good to need faith in Christ and none are too bad to have faith in Christ. All who trust him may benefit from his gift of reconciliation and the fruits that follow it.

Reconciliation brings us into a state of peace with God.[29] We do not understand the biblical concept of peace if we think it simply means that our war with God is declared over. The concept is far richer and deeper than that.[30] It means not so much the absence of hostility as the presence of positive harmony. It speaks not of the absence of wrong relationships but of the presence of right relationships. It is the soil in which our well-being can grow. It leads to our wholeness. It stands for all the benefits of salvation that we find in Christ.

Our initial focus on Christ's death, our reconciliation with God and

---

[25] See Stott, *Cross of Christ*, ch. 6.
[26] Barrett, *2 Corinthians*, p. 173.
[27] 1 Tim. 1:15.
[28] Barnett, p. 298.
[29] Rom. 5:1.
[30] See W. Foerster, '*eirēnē*', *TDNT* 2, pp. 400–420.

our entry into the new creation order need to develop into a concern with the life of Christ, with the on-going outworking of our reconciliation with God and with what it means to live in this new creation order. Paul expresses it like this: 'If, when we were God's enemies, we were reconciled to him through the death of his Son, how much more, having been reconciled, shall we be saved through his life!'[31] All the benefits of access to God – joy in suffering, perseverance in difficulties, transformation of character and a firm, unshakeable hope – are ours. Life starts all over again, and has a richness, even in the most adverse of circumstances, that we have never known before.

3. The messengers of reconciliation

Paul's primary motive for writing about reconciliation in 2 Corinthians 5 is pastoral, not soteriological. It relates to the particular situation in Corinth and the broken relationships between the apostle and the church.

a. The apostle as a preacher of reconciliation

The good news of the reconciliation accomplished by Christ now needs to be announced so that others may share in its harvest: ... *he has committed to us the message of reconciliation. We are therefore Christ's ambassadors, as though Christ were making his appeal through us* (19–20). The apostle leads the way, but he is not alone in his proclamation. An unbroken chain down the centuries links many, old and young, women and men, professional and blue-collar, in being his ambassadors.

We are accustomed to think of ambassadors as figures of authority and dignity. They speak their sovereign's word confidently and without apology. They command as much as negotiate, for they have the backing of the country they represent, with all its diplomatic and military resources. Yet this is not how Paul fulfils his ambassadorial role here. He does not command so much as *appeal* (20). He does not decree so much as *implore* (20). Rather than standing in a position of authority, he seems to announce his message on bended knee from a position of weakness.

Recent research has shown that this is much more in keeping with the role of the ancient ambassador than are the grandiose ideas which have sometimes been put forward. Antony Bash[32] has shown that in Roman times ambassadors would rarely be figures of commanding

[31] Rom. 5:10.
[32] A. Bash, *Ambassadors for Christ: An Examination of Ambassadorial Language in the New Testament* (Mohr, 1997), *passim*. For the application of the metaphor to Christian leadership see D. J. Tidball, *Builders and Fools: Leadership the Bible Way* (IVP, 1999), pp. 17–33.

authority who negotiated peace deals on equal terms with their opponents (still less as their superiors). They would undertake their embassies as representatives of a weaker party pleading for peace with a stronger one. That is certainly consistent with the tone of Paul's writing to the Corinthians. It is also consistent with the message of the cross, for Christ, who was 'crucified in weakness' (13:4), is the one who effects the reconciliation.

As Paul's successors as ambassadors of Christ, our message could not be more apt for our time – the message of reconciliation. But we must be careful to imitate Paul's method as well as to proclaim his message. We must never preach at people from a position of superiority, but must come to bear the pain of their unreconciled state and, from a position of lowliness, entreat them with gentleness to look to Christ for salvation.

b. The church as a community of reconciliation

The sad fact was that Corinth was not the community of reconciliation it should have been. 1 Corinthians presents its members as divided among themselves and splintered into factions. 2 Corinthians indicates that they were estranged from the apostle Paul, who had founded their church.[33] The alienation had been caused by a complex series of issues ranging from misunderstandings about his travel plans, through suspicions regarding his handling of money and his refusal to receive patronage from them, to the interference of 'super-apostles' who denigrated his missionary accomplishments.[34]

All this demonstrated that they had not really grasped the meaning of reconciliation. It was impossible to be reconciled to God while remaining unreconciled to one another, and even less while remaining unreconciled to God's messenger. So, using 'language more germane to a call to unbelievers',[35] he takes them right back to basics and reminds them of the 'simple' gospel all over again. He pleads with them to *Be reconciled to God* (20). Note that he implores them to be reconciled to *God* rather than to one another or to himself. To live in a state of estrangement from fellow-believers is to alienate oneself not just from them but from God himself. And to reject his divinely commissioned messenger in the person of the apostle Paul was tantamount to rejecting God himself. Authentic reconciliation on the vertical dimension, with God, will result in genuine reconciliation on the horizontal dimension, with one another. The church must not only preach the message of reconciliation, but also model it in its relationships.

---

[33] 1 Cor. 4:15.
[34] 2 Cor. 10 – 13 offers the fullest insight into his difficulties with Corinth.
[35] Martin, *Reconciliation*, p. 109.

4. The scope of reconciliation

The repercussions of this interpretation stretch far and wide. In his later letters, Paul develops the idea in two wonderfully new ways. God, who in Christ was reconciling us to himself, was also making possible the reconciliation of Jews and Gentiles and setting in train the reconciliation of the cosmos.

a. Ethnic reconciliation (Ephesians 2:11–22)

The cross brought an end to the animosity between Jews and Gentiles by putting it to death (16), creating one new humanity and bringing about a state of peace where previously there was only hostility. Again, sadly, the early Christian believers had failed to understand fully the implications of this aspect of the work of the cross. In Ephesians Paul is addressing Gentile believers (11)[36] who were evidently assuming superior attitudes towards the Jews in the church and needed to be reminded of their true position. The Jews were the ones who had a long heritage of covenant relationship with God and from whom the Messiah had come. By contrast, listing five disadvantages from which they had suffered until the cross, Paul says the Gentiles had been *separate ... excluded from citizenship ... foreigners to the covenants ... without hope and without God* (12). They were removed from him by an immense distance and lived alienated lives in his world.

In Christ, however, the situation has dramatically changed. Those who were excluded are now *fellow-citizens* (19). Those who were *foreigners* are now *members of God's household* (19). Those who *were far away have been brought near* (13). And two ethnic groups who had been in continuous conflict are now united in one peaceful new humanity (12–15). Gentile Christians dare not consider themselves superior, then, to Jewish Christians. They were the ones who had the most ground to make up. The fact that they have done so owes nothing to them and everything to Christ. Through his cross he cancelled all their disadvantages and made over to them all the fruit of the peace he secured there. Now, together with Jews, they stand on a level playing-field before God – the field of his grace. So there can be no possible room for any sense of superiority or inferiority in the church on the basis of ethnic background, or indeed on the ground of any other dividing-line that the world loves to draw.

But just how did Christ bring about this equalization of Jew and Gentile? He did it by destroying *the barrier, the dividing wall of hostility* and *by abolishing in his flesh the law with its commandments and*

---

[36] Martin believes we are 'to catch some undertones of controversy' here: *Reconciliation*, p. 166. Others are less convinced, arguing that, as a circular letter, it would not address an issue from one particular context. See O'Brien, *Ephesians*, p. 183.

regulations (14–15). The 'barrier' or 'dividing wall' might allude to the wall that separated the court of the Gentiles from the inner courts of the temple, which were to be entered only by Jews. It prevented Gentiles from going further and warned them that they took their lives into their own hands if they did so. Many, however, feel that such an allusion may not have made much sense to those living in Ephesus and that, in any case, the actual wall was only symbolic of the dividing wall in their minds. Peter O'Brien and others argue, therefore, that Paul meant the barrier of separation created by the Mosaic law mentioned in the next clause.[37] These Jewish laws were both ceremonial and moral. They included the great commands such as 'You shall not murder', and petty dietary and other regulations that were designed to mark out a real distinction between Jew and Gentile and to maintain a safe distance between them. On either count, Gentiles would have been excluded.

Christ did not abolish the moral law by rendering it no longer relevant. If Paul were claiming that, he would be contradicting Christ's own teaching.[38] But on the cross Christ did nullify the condemnation this law brings us under when we break it, by removing the penalty of our disobedience from us and bearing it himself. He nullified the ceremonial law, abolishing its regulations through fulfilling it in himself, thus making them an anachronism. Because he did so, these laws can no longer exercise their divisive powers. The two great ethnic elements of the ancient world need no longer be kept apart. The cross brought them together to create one new humanity.

No interpretation of the cross can be more applicable to our divided world today than this one. We have already seen its relevance to the South African situation. How many more trouble-spots in the world would find the belligerent attitudes of combatants changed, their hostilities ended and their ethnic-cleansing policies done away with, if only they appreciated that the wooden stake erected centuries ago on a hill opposite Jerusalem was set up not merely for the salvation of individuals but for the transformation of ethnic relations too?

b. Cosmic reconciliation (Colossians 1:19–20)

The final reference to reconciliation in Paul's writings comes in his letter to the Colossians. In it he goes over familiar ground, asserting that reconciliation with God is available through the death of Christ to anyone who has faith (2:21–23). The same stresses on the alienation of humanity from God, the initiative of God in reconciliation, the agency of the Son and our need to receive reconciliation through faith are as apparent here as in the earlier texts we have examined.

---

[37] O'Brien, *Ephesians*, pp. 195–196.
[38] Matt. 5:17–20.

But new aspects of the work of reconciliation are also included. Paul has not previously mentioned that God is pleased *through* Christ *to reconcile all things, whether things on earth or things in heaven, by making peace through his blood, shed on the cross* (20). Two developments in his thinking take place in this verse. First, he uses the compound verb *apokatallasō* here for 'reconcile', instead of the usual *katallassō*. The word is possibly his own creation. He uses it to intensify our focus on God's work of reconciliation.

Secondly, only here does Paul talk about the cross reconciling *all things* as distinct from reconciling repentant and believing sinners. True, he had written in 2 Corinthians 5:19 about God reconciling 'the world' (*kosmos*) in Christ. But it is clear that there he means the world of sinful humanity, and does not have a broader category in mind. Yet here he speaks in a non-personal way of 'all things'. What does he mean?

Some scholars[39] attach the phrase strongly to the verses that follow and say that the emphasis of the verse is on reconciliation, not on 'all things'; a reconciliation that has been provided for the world but which is realized only by those who have faith and believe the message Paul preached. If this is so, Paul is saying nothing different here from what he has said several times before. It has the value of consistency with Paul's wider teaching and with the use of 'reconcile' as properly belonging to the world of persons rather than to anything inanimate. But this does not seem to do justice to the positioning of the claim that comes as the climax to his hymn of praise to Christ (15–20), in which Christ's work is viewed from the perspective of the creation and the new creation.

Others broaden the scope of reconciliation but interpret the 'all things' to refer to the world of angels, rulers, powers and authorities with which Colossians is much preoccupied and which are mentioned specifically in 2:16. But, although they are almost certainly included, there seems no reason to limit Paul's claim in this way.

The most natural interpretation, given the choice of words and the context in which they are found, is that 'all things' speaks of the whole universe. The term presupposes that the total world has experienced a considerable disruption in its relationship with God and is now functioning, in all its aspects and in every dimension, in a state of alienation from him.[40] The death of Christ has changed all that, and has made it possible for the universe to be restored to peace with God and to be brought once again to a state of order under his control. The explanation of how Christ's death accomplished such a reconciliation is

---

[39] Marshall, 'Reconciliation', pp. 126–127. For a good guide to the various interpretations, see O'Brien, *Colossians*, pp. 53–56.

[40] Gen. 3:17–19.

postponed until 2:15. But the important point, established here, is this: 'Paul affirms that this universal reconciliation has been brought about, not in some other-worldly drama, but through something done in history, the death of Jesus on the cross.'[41] His claim here is akin to, but not exactly the same as, his vision of the future liberation of creation to be brought about when the children of God are finally revealed, which he mentions in Romans 8:19–21.

As James Dunn comments, 'The vision is vast. The claim is mind-blowing.' It is about the restoration of the original creation, about overcoming the fractures and brokenness of the present universe, and about restoring it to wholeness. The early Christians had amazing faith to connect such a cosmic restoration with the death and resurrection of Jesus and to see in it 'quite literally the key to resolving the disharmonies of nature and the inhumanities of humankind, [and to consider] that the character of God's creation and God's concern for the universe in its fullest expression could be so caught and encapsulated for them in the cross of Christ'.[42] But that is precisely the claim.

Inevitably, such a bold claim raises questions. Is Paul teaching here that a universal salvation will take place and that all will be reconciled to God in the end, regardless of faith? How does Paul envisage that such a reconciliation of all things will occur? We must disabuse ourselves of any thoughts of universalism, if by it we mean that in the end all will be saved, irrespective of their desire to believe in and follow Christ. Such a view would be contrary to Paul's wider theology[43] and would jar with the verses that immediately follow, where faith is specified as essential on our part to obtain salvation. 'Reconciliation' must take place in some other way – as is entirely possible, for there is more than one way in which reconciliation can be implemented.

Although Paul does not spell out what total reconciliation with God will mean, it is possible that he thought it would take place in a number of different ways. First, those who exercise faith in Christ enter now into a reconciled state with God and have already begun to experience the benefits of Christ's saving work on Calvary. This is where the main thrust of Paul's teaching has been. Secondly, powers, rulers, authorities or angels who resist God's will and continue to oppose him will be reconciled through pacification, a concept the ancient Roman colonies would have readily understood. They will be subjugated, and peace will be imposed on them, for 'the peace effected by the death of Christ may be freely accepted or compulsorily imposed'.[44] Thirdly, the universe

[41] O'Brien, *Colossians*, p. 56.
[42] Dunn, *Colossians*, p. 104.
[43] J. M. Gundry-Volf, 'Universalism', in *DPL*, pp. 956–961.
[44] Bruce, *Colossians*, p. 210.

itself will brought back under God's control and re-created. Its fractures will be mended and its disjointedness healed, and the peace of God will be all and in all.

The cross of Christ, then, effects reconciliation with God not just for those who come to believe in him but for the whole cosmos. It is breathtaking in its scope. But anything less would surely be incomplete. If the cross effected only the reconciliation of believers, God would need to find another means of restoring the creation and overcoming those who persisted in evil. But the fullness of God dwelt in Christ (2:9), and the fullness of his pleasure was accomplished on his cross. The cross brings about personal, ethnic and cosmic reconciliation. It is the one means by which God brings the total creation into harmony with himself.

Reconciliation defines the heart and the circumference of atonement. The heart of it lies in the restoration of sinful human beings to a relationship of friendship with God. The circumference is found to encompass the universe itself, which, by the same act of crucifixion, is in the process of being restored to its right relationship with God. Both are effected by a gracious plan and act of God to reconcile the offending parties to himself, the offended one. He never reconciles himself to us. We are always reconciled to him and by him. But this marvellous act is a fatal reconciliation, for it is brought about only through the death of his beloved Son.

Galatians 2:20; 5:24; 6:14;
Philippians 3:10–11
13. The cross as present history

The cross is not only the most decisive event in history. It is to be a present experience as well – the most transforming power in the lives of believers. Using language that is nothing short of astonishing, disciples of Christ are called upon not only to derive the benefits from his historic crucifixion but to crucify themselves with him daily. The Christian life paradoxically means dying with Christ. The believer's lot is to live a cruciform way of life.

Recent evangelical preaching and teaching have tended to neglect this biblical truth and to emphasize instead a theology of glory and the transforming power of the Holy Spirit. It has moved its focus from Calvary to the empty tomb and the day of Pentecost as it has sought to overcome the gloomy defeatism of some forms of Christianity and replace it with a more positive and joyful expression of the faith.[1] Or it has succumbed to a more technique-oriented approach to Christian living that stresses the importance of practising the spiritual disciplines – prayer, Bible-reading, fasting, witnessing and so on – in order to reach maturity and enjoy Christ. But few make mention of our need to die with Christ.

These perspectives are not to be discounted, as earlier generations sometimes did. However, to speak of resurrection life, Spirit-empowered life or a spiritually disciplined life, without laying a thorough foundation of teaching about our need to die with Christ before we can live and reign with him, is to build on sand. The charismatic theologian Tom Smail has wisely reminded us that 'The way to Pentecost is Calvary; the Spirit comes from the Cross.'[2] Yet too often we want Pentecost without Calvary, victory without pain, transformation without cost and resurrection without dying first. Hugh Evan Hopkins, an early voice at the Keswick Convention, in describing the vital connection between the death of Christ and practical holiness,

---

[1] See Introduction, above, p. 27.
[2] Smail, 'Cross and Spirit', p. 55.

put it thus: 'The condition of all real progress will consist therefore in the being made conformable to that death. Willingness to die to sin with Christ is a truer evidence of the soul's advance than anxiety to be filled with His life.'[3] Holiness is impossible unless the death of Christ becomes a present experience as well as a past event.

While Paul does not give us any extended exposition of what it means to die with Christ, it is a theme he frequently raises and advances briefly in a number of ways. So important is it to him that when Professor Richard Hays, of Yale, recently sought to capture the contours and concerns of Paul's thinking in his earliest five letters, he entitled his paper, 'Crucified with Christ'. He examined the place of the church in response to God's action in Christ and looked at its role in the new age of the gospel, and concluded: 'One of Paul's most characteristic theological emphases is his steadfast insistence on the *cruciform* character of that role.'[4] Paul assumes (Hays continues) that the cruciform way of life will be a fact of the church's experience in this in-between time; by the phrase 'I have been crucified with Christ'[5] or similar phrases, Paul meant a rich diversity of things. His teaching falls into two basic groups, described by Richard Tannehill as 'those which refer to dying with Christ as a decisive, past event, and those which refer to dying with Christ as a present experience'.[6] Another way of looking at this basic division is to say that some texts speak of dying with Christ in the indicative mood, such as the statement 'I have been crucified with Christ';[7] while others speak of it in the imperative, such as the command, 'Put to death ... whatever belongs to your earthly nature.'[8]

In Paul's thinking, from the one crucifixion of Christ several other crucifixions in the lives of his followers will inevitably flow. Their *justification* involves their being crucified with Christ. Their *sanctification* requires them daily to crucify their sinful way of life as well as the sinful mindset and lifestyle of the world. Their *vindication* depends on their bearing the shame of the cross and suffering for their faith now on earth. Their *identification* with Christ necessitates their being conformed to him in his death. All this is encapsulated in Paul's brief references to dying with Christ.

[3] H. E. Hopkins, *The Law of Liberty in the Spiritual Life* (Marshall, Morgan and Scott, 1952), p. 82.

[4] R. B. Hays, 'Crucified with Christ: a synthesis of the theology of 1 and 2 Thessalonians, Philemon, Philippians and Galatians', in J. Bassler (ed.), *Pauline Theology* 1 (Fortress, 1991), p. 240.

[5] Gal. 2:20.

[6] R. C. Tannehill, *Dying and Rising with Christ* (Topelmann, 1966), p. 6.

[7] Gal. 2:20.

[8] Col. 3:5.

1. Our justification by Christ: realizing the benefit of the cross (Gal. 2:20)

Our first reference is to the indicative statement: to our being joined in a faith-union with the crucified Christ as the means by which we appropriate the benefits of his cross. *I have been crucified with Christ and I no longer live, but Christ lives in me. The life I live in the body, I live by faith in the Son of God, who loved me and gave himself for me.*

It is easy to see why many Christians have extracted this wonderful 'sound-bite' from the wider text of Galatians and used it as a platform for all sorts of teaching about the Christian life. But we must resist the tendency, for we must read and interpret the text first of all within its own context. Having set out the reason for his letter and the personal circumstances which led him to write it, Paul has reached the point of stating, in a highly condensed form, the basic argument he is going to elaborate in the rest of his letter.[9]

The nub of his argument, expressed in verses 15–16, is that in order to be restored to a right relationship with God (that is, 'justified'), we need to put our faith in Christ alone and not in our ability to keep the law. If we relied on the latter, it would soon become evident that we were going down a blind alley, since we would never be able to keep the law perfectly and thus merit justification by God. The path of legalism is a dead end.

Most Jewish Christians would have agreed with Paul about that. They would readily concede that keeping the law was not merit-earning or favour-inducing. Recent research[10] has demonstrated that the Jews were not legalists in the sense in which we have often thought of them. Even so, they still valued the law and saw it as an indispensable response to God's grace in saving them. Those within the covenant were required to keep it, even though it did not gain them entry into the covenant to start with. But what place was there for the law in Paul's radical gospel of faith? Does the law have a place in our Christian lives? If one threw it over in the way Paul's radical preaching of the gospel seemed to imply, would it not lead to antinomianism – that is, to an absence of constraints, in which anything would be permitted? While the Galatian Christians may not have seen the law as a means of gaining God's favour in the first place, they apparently still felt that it was crucial for Christians to keep the law and avoid antinomianism. Paul, of course, refutes the idea that grace leads to antinomianism, both here and in Romans 6.

[9] For a superb exposition of the whole passage, 2:15–21, see Longenecker, pp. 82–96.
[10] For a succinct summary of recent understanding of Paul since E. P. Sanders, see S. J. Hafemann, 'Paul and his interpreters', in *DPL*, pp. 666–679, esp. pp. 672ff.

The law in question, as becomes clear, is not the moral law, or what James called the 'royal law' of love,[11] but the Jewish customs and secondary regulations that defined their covenant and provided the boundary markers that distinguished them from other races, such as the practice of circumcision, their dietary regulations and the rules concerning who one should and should not eat with (2:11–14). Some Jewish believers taught that, even after trusting in Christ, it was important to continue to observe these things. They therefore sought to impose them on Gentile converts, teaching that they were an essential, indispensable response to God's grace in Christ. Paul argues that this cannot be so. If we seek to put such laws back in place after coming to faith in Christ, and preach that we can continue to please God only by obeying such customs, all we are doing (he says in verse 18), is establishing all over again that we are sinners. Our attitude to these laws and covenant customs, he argues, has to be much more drastic. Living for God means trusting in Christ alone, and that means dying to the law.

It is while Paul is in mid-flow, developing this proposition, that he first talks about having been *crucified with Christ*. In the context, then, he is not writing of some mystical experience in which the self is exterminated, the personality negated and the world avoided, so that the life of Christ might express itself metaphysically in us (as some have suggested). Indeed, his mention of *the life I live in the body* should be sufficient to rule out that interpretation, for it keeps our feet firmly on the ground and tells us that experiencing the living Christ within is not about being caught up in the Spirit but about living in the ordinary, everyday, workaday world. Rather, he is saying that being crucified with Christ brings an end to the jurisdiction of the law, and indeed of the self ('*I* have been crucified ...'), with their attempts to merit and maintain God's favour. It brings an end to their rule even as a supplementary aid to faith. Faith means that they are dead.

The first phrase of verse 20 rightly belongs to verse 19.[12] Paul is completing the thought of that verse, not starting a new one; he is saying that to be 'crucified with Christ' means to be dead to the law. Since the law 'clamours for my death as a law-breaker, how can I possibly be justified?' asks John Stott. 'Only by meeting the law's requirements and dying the death it demands.'[13] But if I were to do that myself I would die. God, knowing this, in his mercy, has provided another way to satisfy the law and simultaneously release me from its grip. The perfect Son of God took my place, died my death and released me from the tyranny of the law's demands. The law, then, no

---

[11] Jas. 2:8; cf. Gal. 5:13–14.
[12] Longenecker, p. 92, and George, p. 199.
[13] Stott, *Cross of Christ*, p. 341.

longer has any authority over me, or over anyone who believes. We are entirely free from it, for its authority was destroyed on the cross when Christ took on to himself all the consequences of our failure to observe it, and so released us from its authority once and for all. Here Paul is content simply to assert the truth. Later on he explains it more fully. 'Christ redeemed us from the curse of the law by becoming a curse for us' (3:13). From the time of the cross onwards, the law has had no hold over us and is the means neither of earning our way into God's favour nor of maintaining ourselves in God's favour. The ego, no less than the law, was also put to death and done away with by the cross of Christ. We have nothing of ourselves to bring to enable us to enjoy a relationship with God. All that we need is faith in the crucified one; that and that alone is sufficient.

What does it mean to be 'crucified with Christ'? It does not mean to mount our bodies physically on the wooden stake on which he died and nail ourselves there as he did. It means to identify with him by faith and to unite ourselves to him by trusting that he died for us. Paul, note, writes of it here in the perfect tense. It is something that has happened to us who believe. It 'signals the believer's once-and-for-all act of commitment'.[14] The tense indicates that it is an act which, though completed, nevertheless has implications for the present. For to die with Christ means not only that we have done away with the old means of justifying ourselves before God, but also that we have been raised with him to live in the power of his new life. Hence Paul speaks not only of being 'crucified with Christ' and no longer living for self, but of Christ living within us. Just as it is impossible to separate the dying and the rising of Christ, so it is impossible to separate the crucifixion of believers from the resurrection life of Christ that they come to live. The one leads to the other. The one is impossible without the other.

Paul's phrase *Christ lives in me*, then, is not about mysticism or perfectionism, but about the transformation that takes place when we trust in his cross. When we join in faith-union with the crucified Christ, the indwelling Christ, in the person of the Holy Spirit, takes up residence and transforms us from within. 'Christ in me' means that I become a new person from the inside out, not from the outside in, and that I orient my life around a completely different set of goals and desires than was the case before I trusted him.

In the last part of the letter, Paul goes on to explain what this means. It will have a transforming effect on our network of relationships: with God, with the law, with our own character, with our neighbours and with the church. It means that we shall be able to enjoy the full benefits of being God's children, rather than living fearfully as his slaves (3:26 –

[14] Longenecker, p. 92.

236

4:7). It means that we shall enjoy the full liberty of the redeemed, rather than still seeking to please the law (5:1). It means that we shall love our neighbours with practical, serving love (5:13–15). It means that we shall walk in harmony with the Holy Spirit and give him free rein to reconstruct our characters and change us (5:16–25). It means that we shall humbly play our part in the church of God (5:16 – 6:6). All this fully answers the charge that Paul's attitude to the law might lead to antinomianism. How could it? To exercise faith means to die with Christ, and equally to rise with him too, and to let his risen life dwell within.

So, in speaking of our dying with Christ, Paul means first that we identify through faith with the death of Christ and take ourselves out from under the rule of the law and of our egos as means of justifying ourselves before God. To die with Christ is what all believers do as they commit themselves to Christ and are justified.

2. Our sanctification through Christ: dying the death of the cross (Gal. 5:24; 6:14)

We now move from the indicative to the imperative mood. The imperative is firmly based on the indicative. It would be useless to exhort believers to put sin to death unless they had first died to the law and to the self with Christ. But in the light of what has taken place, Paul now uses the metaphor to teach what needs to happen continuously in the daily experience of believers. Both the sinful nature and the world are to be consciously, purposefully, crucified. If Paul's first use of the metaphor stressed our freedom from the law's condemnation, his second stresses our freedom from sin's domination. Sin need no longer exercise power over us, because its stranglehold has been broken by the cross.

a. Death to the sinful nature (Gal. 5:24)

Those who belong to Christ Jesus have crucified the sinful nature with its passions and desires. The point Paul makes here is quite different from that in 2:20. There he wrote in the passive voice about having been crucified with Christ; that is, something was done to us as Christ died in our place. Here he writes in the active voice about crucifying the flesh. He summons us to do something to ourselves, as he also does in Romans 8:13 ('... if by the Spirit you put to death the misdeeds of the body ...') and in Colossians 3:5 ('Put to death, therefore, whatever belongs to your earthly nature'). The former is a completed act, speaking of the once-for-allness of the event that leads to a change in our status before God. The latter is a continuous act, speaking of the process that changes our characters until we become like Christ. Dying with Christ is the means both of our immediate justification and of our

237

progressive sanctification. Two images of death arise from the cross. First, crucifixion produces death from which, ordinarily, there is no way back. It is a decisive and irreversible act. Secondly, crucifixion produces death not instantly, as death by hanging or a firing squad would do, but in a slow, lingering way. Dying by crucifixion took time. It is perfectly legitimate, therefore, for Paul to say both that we have died with Christ and that we need to crucify the flesh daily.

Again, the context is important. Verses 19–21 describe what it is to live according to the sinful nature. They provide a comprehensive catalogue of sin, covering sexual immorality ('sexual immorality, impurity and debauchery'), religious adultery ('idolatry and witchcraft'), self-centred living ('hatred, discord, jealousy, fits of rage, selfish ambition') and socially destructive behaviour ('dissensions, factions and envy, drunkenness, orgies, and the like'). By contrast, those who live under the reign of the Spirit will see the fruit of 'love, joy, peace, patience, kindness, goodness, faithfulness, gentleness and self-control' developing in their lives (22–23). The fact that this fruit is produced by the Spirit does not permit believers to sit back and do nothing, waiting for him to produce it without any help. Rather, they must engage in willing co-operation with him to enable the fruit to grow. His part is to produce the life. Theirs is particularly to engage in the pruning, the cutting out of the old life, and to show the commitment without which the harvest could not come to fruition.

How do we crucify our sinful passions? It is a graphic and brutal image, which calls us to renounce our sinful nature decisively. We are called to give it no comfort or quarter, no encouragement or room, but to cut it off.[15] A. W. Tozer spelled out the symbolism of crucifixion in his usual blunt manner. 'The cross in old Roman times knew no compromise; it never made concessions. It won all its arguments by killing its opponent and silencing him for good ... It wins by defeating its opponent and imposing its will upon him. It always dominates.'[16] As Timothy George explains, 'Paul was here describing the process of mortification, the daily putting to death of the flesh through the disciplines of prayer, fasting, repentance, and self-control.' He rightly reminds us that this teaches us that there are no short-cuts to holiness, no quick-fix solutions that will lead to perfection, but only 'the consistent, obedient vigilant renunciation of the world and mortification of the flesh'.[17]

Such teaching is hardly popular today, and even the language of it smacks of a bygone era. Why do few of the manuals of spiritual discipline mention mortification? Most of us would like to go for easier

[15] Stott, *Cross of Christ*, p. 348–349.
[16] W. W. Wiersbe, *The Best of A. W. Tozer* (1978; Crossway, 1991), pp. 134–135.
[17] George, p. 405.

options and long for God to zap us instantly with holiness, or to take out the chip of our sinful desires and replace it with the chip of godly desires, so that we are instantaneously reprogrammed for holiness. But daily self-mortification is an indispensable requirement if we are to pursue holiness. We must progressively kill off the habits of sin and redirect the desires to God, if we are to grow spiritually. Steady commitment, effort and perseverance are required of us if we are to prevent sin from usurping control in our lives. For although sin's power has been broken by the cross, it still pretends that it has a claim over us. Therefore, as Paul tells the Romans:

> ... count yourselves dead to sin but alive to God in Christ Jesus. Therefore do not let sin reign in your mortal body so that you obey its evil desires. Do not offer the parts of your body to sin, as instruments of wickedness, but rather offer yourselves to God, as those who have been brought from death to life; and offer the parts of your body to him as instruments of righteousness.[18]

We are consciously, daily, to repudiate sin and yield to God.

The Puritans have much to teach us in this regard, and if we turn a deaf ear to their teaching because it is no longer fashionable, we do so at our peril. A passage from J. I. Packer's writings is worth quoting at length:

> Puritan teaching on mortifying the lusts that tempt us is businesslike and thorough. It includes the disciplines of self-humbling, self-examination, setting oneself against all sins in one's spiritual system as a preliminary to muscling in on any one of them, avoiding situations that stoke sin's boiler, watching lest you become sin's victim before you are aware of its approach, and praying to the Lord Jesus Christ specifically to apply the killing power of his cross to the particular vicious craving on which one is making one's counterattack. 'Set faith at work on Christ for the *killing* of thy sin,' wrote the greatest Puritan teacher, John Owen. 'His blood is the great sovereign remedy for sin-sick souls. Live in this, and thou wilt die a conqueror; yea, thou wilt, through the good providence of God, live to see thy lust dead at thy feet.'[19]

In teaching this, Paul only repeats what Christ himself taught his disciples when he said, 'Those who would come after me must deny

---

[18] Rom. 6:11–13.
[19] Packer, *Holiness*, p. 108. The quotation is from John Owen's *Of the Mortification of Sin in Believers*.

themselves and take up their cross daily and follow me'.[20] The regular habit of following Christ to the place of his crucifixion through the daily practice of self-denial is not offered as an optional choice for those who wish to be exceptional Christians, but is stated as the basic prerequisite for all disciples. The metaphor is stark, even shocking, and we must be cautious about attempts to soften it. If all that Christ had in mind in using this daring imagery was our occasional denial of a luxury, like chocolate in Lent, or bearing suffering or a problem grudgingly, like having an elderly relative to live with us, Christ could be justly accused of overstating the case. But he is asking more of us that that. He is saying that as his disciples we must 'fasten our slippery fallen nature to the cross and thus do it to death'.[21] Nothing less is called for than a denial of self and a renouncing of our own right to choose and govern our lives according to old sinful ways.

So far, we have stressed only the negative side of the process. Mortification is vital but so, too, is 'vivification'; the making alive of the believer by the Holy Spirit and his strengthening of Christ-like habits within.[22] Paul mentions both. He tells us that we are to crucify the sinful nature. But he also writes, 'Since we live by the Spirit, let us keep in step with the Spirit' (5:25). As we do our work, he does his, and gives us the spiritual vitality and the wholesome desires we lack ourselves. The essence of holiness is to have a passion for God and to have crucified any other passion for less worthy things.[23] But perhaps we are justified in emphasizing the negative, for today's church hardly mentions it at all. In an apt description of the contemporary church, A. W. Tozer warned that 'Shallow leadership would modify the cross to please the entertainment-mad saintlings who will have their fun even within the very sanctuary.'[24] But to engage in such a modification of the gospel is to court spiritual disaster.

Why is there such an uneasy silence about crucifying the sinful nature with its passions when it is clearly so crucial to the Bible's teaching about holiness? For all our excuses, the truth is perhaps that such teaching does not fit easily into a comfortable world where self-indulgence and self-satisfaction reign supreme. Our silence betrays how deeply the atmosphere of the world has infected the church, and how we fear the opinion of the world more than the opinion of the Lord. The cross, however, cannot easily be shunted to the sidelines. It stands high on the hill of Calvary and calls individual believers to stand apart from the cultural values of the world. It equally calls the church as a

---

[20] Luke 9:23.
[21] Stott, *Cross of Christ*, p. 279.
[22] Packer, *Holiness*, p. 106.
[23] Ibid., p. 101.
[24] Quoted in Wiersbe, p. 135.

whole to a deep repentance for its compromise with the world, to take radical action in ejecting sin from its midst and to demonstrate a new seriousness about holiness.

b. Death to the world system (Gal. 6:14)

It is to the mindset of the world that Paul turns as he mentions the cross and its effect on the life of the believer one final time at the end of Galatians. The cross, he claims, is the sole cause of his boasting. Then he adds, as if by way of explanation, that through it *the world has been crucified to me, and I to the world.*

Once more the context is important. Signing off in his own hand (6:11), he succinctly summarizes the message of the letter. Some people, he reminds his readers, go in for a religion that is literally only cosmetic, or skin-deep.[25] What matters to them is the number of circumcisions they can notch up, for religion is all about external conformity to the old-covenant customs and regulations. The way of circumcision is more comfortable than the way of the cross, not because circumcision of the foreskin is not fatal like crucifixion, but because the social conventions of the world have defined it as honourable while they have defined death on a cross as shameful, despicable and contemptible. But, Paul continues, fulfilling the outward regulations does nothing to transform a person inwardly. It does not help one to keep the real law of God (5:13). By contrast, he is not ashamed of the cross. Rather, he glories in it because it deals with the heart of the problem and brings about an inner transformation – from sinful practices to holy living – in all who identify with it.

'The cross', Luther said, 'puts everything to the test.'[26] And when it tests the mindsets of the world, including the mindset of these nice Jewish religious people who are keen to keep up standards and observe the old religious rituals, they fail the test abysmally. For the cross turns everything upside down and establishes an entirely new set of criteria by which to judge truth and values. Their worldviews and philosophies (which is what Paul means by *the world*) neither deal with the problem of sin, nor lead to a secure relationship with God, nor provide any power to enable people to change. Only the cross can achieve that. So, from his perspective, the world has nothing to offer. It no longer has any appeal or attraction. It is dead territory offering ineffective, defunct and lifeless solutions. It is as if, on the cross, *the world had been crucified to me, and I to the world.*

In a devastating critique of some of the theories that lie behind postmodernism, Brian Ingraffia has recently shown how relevant Paul's

---

[25] 'Those who want to make a good impression outwardly' (6:12) could be literally translated, 'those who want to put on a fair face ...'
[26] Quoted in McGrath, *Enigma*, p. 12.

comments are to our contemporary world. The choice before us, he argues, is either to follow a postmodern 'ontotheology' based on 'human imaginings about God', in which we attempt to formulate an understanding of God for ourselves, or to follow God's own revelation of himself. The former leads us to a quite wrong relationship with God where we are the subject and God is the object. The truth is that God is the subject who creates us. It is in him that 'we live and move and have our being'.[27] How then dare we seek to create God in our image, 'an image made by human design and skill'?[28] Ingraffia concludes that Christian theology 'which remains faithful to biblical revelation "completely reverses the direction of [contemporary ontotheology]: it is not the ascent of man to God but the revelation of God in his self-emptying in the crucified Christ" which is the "essence of Christianity"'.[29] The cross calls the postmodern theological enterprise into question and 'pronounces an either/or: either biblical revelation or philosophic speculation.'[30] It is only a theology of the cross, he says, that will enable Christianity to recover its lost prophetic voice. In writing these disturbing and challenging words, Ingraffia has picked up what Paul meant by his phrase *the world has been crucified to me, and I to the world*, and applied them pungently to our own day.

So the daily dying in which Christians must engage, as a result of the one-off crucifixion of Christ, relates to the totality of our beings and our lives. It affects us at the core of our being. Our wills and our emotions, our actions and our desires, and equally our minds and our thought systems, need to be crucified daily lest we still give way to our fallen and sinful natures. Our philosophies and our worldviews need to be crucified daily in so far as they are still functioning along worldly lines. In our willing, feeling and thinking, we need to die daily to sinful patterns in order to become fully alive to God. The road to resurrection cannot be rerouted. The only way to experience life is to experience death first.

3. Our vindication: walking the way of the cross (Phil. 3:10–11)

The third sense in which Paul speaks of the Christian's experience of the cross is in the sense of suffering for Christ. In this respect, it is not an ideal to be courted but a fact of life to be experienced.[31] Christians will suffer for Christ. Paul again mentions this theme several times,

---

[27] Acts 17:28.
[28] Acts 17:29.
[29] B. Ingraffia, *Postmodern Theory and Biblical Theology* (Cambridge University Press, 1995), p. 241.
[30] Ibid.
[31] Hays, 'Crucified with Christ', p. 241.

each time connecting the suffering he endures with the suffering of Christ;[32] but nowhere is the theme more prominent than in the letter to the Philippians. Writing against a background of suffering, Paul begins by speaking about his own suffering for the gospel (1:12–14), before informing them that their own suffering is a privilege to welcome rather than a path to avoid, since it proves the genuineness of their faith (1:29). It was all part of the ongoing story of Christ, who 'humbled himself and became obedient to death – even death on a cross!' (2:8). He calls on the Philippians to rejoice even if he himself is sacrificed in the course of serving them (2:17–18). The ground is therefore well prepared when Paul comes to what is arguably the pivotal point of his letter, and writes: *I want to know Christ and the power of his resurrection and the fellowship of sharing in his sufferings, becoming like him in his death, and so, somehow, to attain to the resurrection from the dead.*

It is a complex saying. Gordon Fee[33] helpfully comments that we will understand it better if we bear two things in mind. First, Paul is not suggesting that we should know three things: Christ, the power of the resurrection, and participation in his sufferings; but only one: namely, Christ. Paul's great desire is to know Christ more fully than he does already, 'not as a theological topic to be discussed … but as a person to be enjoyed'.[34] Both *the power of his resurrection* and *the fellowship of sharing in his sufferings* explain what it means to know Christ. One cannot know Christ apart from entering with him into the experience of his death and resurrection. Secondly, these two comments are mirrored by a further two, which say the same thing but in reverse order. Hence Paul continues: *becoming like him in his death, and so, somehow, to attain to the resurrection from the dead.*

The fact that Paul begins with the resurrection and then goes back to the crucifixion is obviously designed to make us sit up and take notice. Logically, it should be the other way around. But Paul knows what he is doing. The resurrection is what makes all the difference when struggling with suffering. It puts everything into a different light. Without it, suffering might well be pointless, an endless struggle towards ultimate defeat and futility. But the resurrection tells us ahead of time that it is not. The same power that raised Jesus from the dead will one day raise us to eternal life too. This is no cheap triumphalism. Paul knows all too well that suffering was both rough and real. He had the scars to prove it.[35] He does not pretend that it is insignificant. He is soberly realistic about it. But there is a greater reality that governs his

[32] 1 Cor. 15:30–31; 2 Cor. 4:9–10; 13:4; Gal. 6:17; Col. 1:24.
[33] Fee, *Philippians*, NTCS, pp. 147–148. For more detailed comments, see the appropriate pages in his NICNT commentary.
[34] Hawthorne, p. 147.
[35] 2 Cor. 12:23–29.

thinking, and that is the reality of the resurrection. So, as Fee says, he knows nothing 'of the rather gloomy stoicism that is often exhibited in historic Christianity, where the lot of the believer is basically to "slug it out in the trenches" with little or no sense of Christ's presence and power'.[36] Instead, the 'stiff upper lip' approach is replaced by a joyful embracing of suffering, since it heralds the certainty of the resurrection to come and sets believers on the path to vindication.

Having set out the reason for his hope, he does not then slip over the reality of suffering as if there was nothing to say about it. There is more, not less, to say about it in the light of the resurrection. There would have been no resurrection had there not first been a crucifixion. Death precedes life, and resurrection life, by definition, is impossible without it. So suffering is likely to be the paradigmatic experience of every Christian.[37] We must neither court it, nor provoke it by being awkward neighbours or unreasonable people, as some Christians seem to rejoice in being. The cause of our suffering ought only ever to be our proclamation of the cross. But we should never be surprised when suffering comes as a result of our standing for the gospel, for we live in the midst of a 'crooked and depraved generation' (2:15), and are surrounded by people who 'live as enemies of the cross of Christ' (3:18). Why should we expect them to make life comfortable for us?

But there is a deeper reason why Christian believers should anticipate suffering. To endure suffering is to be brought into close communion with Christ himself. It is *his* sufferings that we share when we suffer. And that, in Gordon Fee's words, 'is the clue to everything'.[38] Our sufferings will never be redemptive in the way in which Christ's were. Nevertheless, they are 'intimately related to his'.[39] To be put in touch with our Lord like this can surely never be a cause of regret. It will surely always be a cause of rejoicing. What a privilege it is to share the lot that was his!

While Paul is essentially talking of himself and his experiences as an apostle, it is obvious from the wider references to Christians' suffering that he sees himself as a pattern for all believers. In Philippians, he often uses his own experience, notably in this very section that includes his testimony (3:4–14), as an example by which to teach believers truth that applies to them all. He would say about his understanding of suffering, as he says about the goal that lies before him, that 'all of us who are mature should take such a view of things' (3:15). We have the immense privilege of bearing the shame of the cross and walking the way of the cross to Calvary, in the footsteps of Jesus himself.

[36] Fee, *Philippians*, NTCS, p. 148.
[37] Cf. Acts 14:22; 1 Thess. 3:3; 2 Tim. 3:12.
[38] Fee, *Philippians*, NTCS, p. 149.
[39] Ibid.

Thoughts like these can often provoke guilt feelings in the consciences of some Christians whose circumstances do not seem to lend themselves to persecution. Are they disqualified from dying with Christ, in this sense? Are they missing out? Richard Bauckham's exposition of 2 Corinthians 4, one of the passages parallel to the one we are considering, might be helpful here. He points out that Paul does not apply the thought of dying and rising with Christ only to the dramatic persecutions or extraordinary miracles in his life, but to the ordinary weakness he encountered in the face of the demands of ministry and the victories he gained, which often included things that appear outwardly unremarkable. 'Dying and rising' was the perspective from which Paul saw his total ministry. 'All the ups and downs of his ministry were for Paul experiences *of God*, events in which he experiences an identification with Jesus in his dying and rising.'[40] Bauckham goes on:

> To identify with Paul's experience we do not need to be shipwrecked or imprisoned or lowered in a basket from a city wall. Even without the physical dangers of Paul's career, anyone who throws himself into the work of Christian ministry with half the dedication of Paul will experience the weakness of which Paul speaks: the times when problems seem insoluble, the times of weariness from sheer overwork, the times of depression when there seem to be no results, the emotional exhaustion which pastoral concerns can bring on – in short, all the times when the Christian minister or worker knows he is stretched to the limits of his capacities for a task which is very nearly, but by God's grace, not quite, too much for him.[41]

This, too, is a dying with Christ. So any authentic Christian life, though lived in the power of the resurrection Christ, will lead us to identify with the Christ who was crucified in weakness and will be 'forever marked by the cross.'[42]

4. Our identification with Christ: imitating the Lord of the cross (Phil. 3:10)

Paul takes the argument a step further. To suffer like this means that we become *like him in his death*. It is how we come to be refashioned to be like Christ. Typically, Paul invents the word for 'being conformed to' or 'being made like'. The word he uses is *symmorphizomenos*, and is

---

[40] Bauckham, 'Weakness – Paul's and ours', *Themelios* 7.3 (1982), p. 5.
[41] Ibid., pp. 5–6.
[42] Fee, *Philippians*, NTCS, p. 150.

used only here in the New Testament. The prefix *sym-* is a special favourite of Paul's because he is always trying to unite the believer to Christ and believers to one another. Paul is not primarily thinking here of martyrdom, or even just of physical suffering, but of a more general dying with Christ and so being incorporated with him.[43] Here the closest identification between Paul and his Lord is intended. He has in mind a 'growing together' of the sort one often sees in the lives of a couple who have been happily married for many years. They often think alike, react alike, enjoy the same things, share the same values, and copy each other's mannerisms. Sometimes they have even grown to look alike! To become like Christ is an idea rich in its implications. We, too, come to think and act, judge and react, love and serve, trust and obey, pray and abide, submit and give, just as he did.

Such identification with Christ will be fully achieved only once we see him,[44] but progress towards that goal can be made now, as we 'are being transformed into his likeness with ever-increasing glory' by the Spirit.[45] Such conformity to Christ, though ultimately the work of the Spirit, is possible only if we conform to Christ now at the most demanding point of his life, that is in his death. We shall never be like him unless we renounce self, give up any ambitions to run our own lives in our own way, and let them die. If we want to be like the Lord of the cross, we must imitate him not only in his living but in his self-giving and his dying.

'We must do something about the cross,' wrote A. W. Tozer, 'and one of two things only can we do – flee it or die upon it.'[46] The cross is meant to be the place where Christians die daily. It is both indicative of our position in Christ and imperative for our likeness to Christ. We can never escape the tension of continually dying with him while simultaneously living in the power of his resurrection. By uniting with the cross of Jesus, believers appropriate its benefits and are granted justification; they realize its power and make progress in sanctification; they walk its way, bearing its shame, towards their final vindication, and imitate its Lord until they reach complete identification with him. While some, today, point to life with the risen Christ as the secret of 'victorious Christian living', and others point to the power of the Spirit, we cannot experience either of those without going via the cross. Without Good Friday, there would have been no Easter Sunday and no Pentecost. We are called not only to rise and to reign with Christ, but to die with him. The cross is not only past history but present reality too, in the life of every follower of Jesus.

[43] O'Brien, *Philippians*, pp. 408–410.
[44] 1 John 3:2.
[45] 2 Cor. 3:18.
[46] In Wiersbe, p. 135.

Colossians 2:8–15
14. The cross as tragic victory

According to Gustav Aulén in his celebrated book *Christus Victor*, the 'classic' idea of the atonement is that of Christ's gaining the victory over evil. It views the cross as a drama.

> Its central theme is the idea of the Atonement as a Divine conflict and victory; Christ – Christus Victor – fights against and triumphs over the evil powers of the world, the 'tyrants' under which mankind is in bondage and suffering, and in Him God reconciles the world to Himself.[1]

It was this idea, Aulén claims, that dominated in the period of the New Testament and early church. It was taught by many, including Irenaeus (c. 130–c. 200), and continued to exercise an influence until the Reformation. Martin Luther revived it in his vigorous language about the gospel, especially in his catechisms and hymns. Luther's successors, however, reverted to the idea of atonement as a satisfaction for sin, which can be traced back to a Roman root in the writings of Tertullian (c. 160–220) and Cyprian (c. 200–258), and which was articulated most clearly by Anselm (c. 1033–1109).

The background to this 'classic' view lies in dualism: that is, that God is opposed by hostile powers and, in Christ, engages in a conflict with them which leads to their defeat. In the life, death and resurrection of Christ the drama of our atonement is played out as a continuous act of God. In Aulén's view, neither the objective nor the subjective theories of the atonement took the unfolding drama of salvation sufficiently into account. The 'objective' (satisfaction) idea of the atonement isolated the death of Christ from this continuous divine act, and 'subjective' (moral-influence) views did not sufficiently measure up to the real change that takes place between God and the

---

[1] Aulén, p. 20.

world through this drama.[2] The focus of the 'classic' view is on the work of Christ as a work of atonement, not just of salvation.

It is important, above all, at this point to see clearly that the work of salvation and deliverance is at the same time a work of atonement, of reconciliation between God and the world. It is altogether misleading to say that the triumph of Christ over the powers of evil, whereby He delivers man, is a work of salvation but not of atonement; for the two ideas cannot possibly be separated. It is precisely the work of salvation wherein Christ breaks the power of evil that *constitutes* the atonement between God and the world; for it is by it that He removes the enmity, takes away the judgment which rested on the human race, and reconciles the world to himself, not imputing their trespasses (2 Cor. 5:18).[3]

In support of his assertion that this is 'the' New Testament interpretation of the cross, Aulén looks to 1 Corinthians 15; 2 Corinthians 5:19 and Colossians 2:14 for support. He also interprets the central atonement argument of Romans (chs. 4 – 7) and references in Galatians 3:10–13, regarding the curse of the law, so as to present the law as an enemy, one of the hostile powers defeated by Christ.[4] Outside of Paul, Aulén calls a number of other passages into play, the most convincing of which are those that come from the imagery of the Lamb in the book of Revelation.[5]

Aulén's views have been the subject of a number of justifiable criticisms. John McIntyre speaks for many in saying that although this view of the atonement has a legitimate claim to be *one* of the New Testament models, the pre-eminence Aulén gives it is unwarranted, and 'it is a case of a brilliant idea being over-stated'.[6] Colin Gunton[7] fears that Aulén owes more to Origen than to the New Testament, and that he presents the atonement as a cosmic drama akin to the mythical stories of gods at war, rather than as a real and earthly story in which a human Christ battles against temptation and continuously wins victories over the demonic. The cross, Gunton says, is not so much a divine drama as a divine *and* human drama. Furthermore, Aulén's view errs on the side of triumphalism, for the battles continue to be fought by real humans who have come to believe in Jesus. Gunton's conclusion is that while the Bible certainly uses the metaphor of

---

[2] Ibid., pp. 20–22.
[3] Ibid., p. 87.
[4] Ibid., p. 84.
[5] Ibid., pp. 89–91.
[6] McIntyre, p. 43.
[7] Gunton, pp. 54–82.

victory, 'the language of victory does not then give us a theory, something final and fixed for ever, but one way into the many-sided reality'[8] of the cross.

While Aulén's argument has not succeeded in persuading many that this is the 'classic' view of the atonement, he has succeeded in resurrecting a neglected insight that does have some secure basis in the New Testament. Throughout the New Testament the cross is seen as a triumph, not as a defeat. It is spoken of with joyful confidence and in terms of victory. That, of course, as John Stott observes, is a matter of surprise, for 'any contemporary observer, who saw Christ die, would have listened with astonished incredulity to the claim that the Crucified was a Conqueror'.[9] Yet that, most emphatically, is what the early Christians claimed of the Christ of the cross.

One key passage where the theme of victory is found is Colossians 2:8–15, which, in many ways, is the heart of the letter to the Colossians. It begins with a warning as Paul alerts his readers to the hostile forces that seek to take them captive (8). It then introduces Jesus as God's answer to those hostile forces (9–12), and comes to a climax as it presents his work on the cross as the definitive answer to our sin and a decisive defeat for our enemies (13–15).

1. The hostile forces that want to enslave us (2:8)

a. The Colossian situation[10]

The sheep-farmers, crop-raisers and wool-dyers of Colosse lived in a precarious world. Not only did they lack any protection against hostile economic forces or natural disasters, but they were subject, or so they thought, to the activity of supernatural forces which populated the unseen world and caused them either to prosper or to suffer misfortune. Much of their religious life, therefore, was designed to ward off evil, to placate malevolent spirits, to call good spirits and angels to their aid and to secure good fortune. A whole armoury of religious weapons was available to obtain protection and prosperity: purity regulations, humiliating rituals, magic rites, mystery cults, worship of angels and so on. These practices were to be found not only among the pagans in Colosse but, the evidence suggests, among the Jews who worshipped in the synagogue as well.

Many of those who had converted to Jesus Christ would have imbibed this atmosphere deeply, whether directly from the Gentile pagan religions or indirectly from the Jewish synagogue. And, without reading much between the lines in Colossians, it is evident that even

---

[8] Ibid., p. 62.
[9] Stott, *Cross of Christ*, p. 227.
[10] The picture of Colosse drawn here is derived from Arnold, *Colossian Syncretism*.

though they had come to believe in Christ they had not left behind these attitudes and practices as they should have done. They still gave too much credence to the influence of these invisible powers and authorities (1:16; 2:15). They still sought to placate them by worshipping angels (2:18) and engaging in the typically syncretistic religious practices we have described, while simultaneously tying themselves up in all sorts of religious rules and regulations (2:16–23).

In doing so, they had entirely misunderstood the status of Christ. They recognized him to be one of the rulers and powers in the invisible world, but not as the supreme and pre-eminent one (1:18) around whom the whole of creation, past, present and future, revolved (1:15–20), and in whom 'all the fulness of the Deity lives in bodily form' (2:9; cf. 1:19). They knew that he occupied a place in the hierarchy of supernatural beings which dominated their world, and believed him to possess a measure of deity. But they put him alongside others somewhere in the pecking order rather than believing him to be unique. Clinton Arnold refers to a prayer excavated in Egypt but illustrating the syncretism of Asia Minor. In it, the name of Jesus is invoked alongside angels and pagan deities as if he were merely one of them. 'Hor, Hor, Phor, Eloei, Adonai, Iao, Sabaoth, Michael, Jesus Christ. Help us and this household. Amen.'[11] Paul therefore writes with a degree of urgency to instruct his readers in the truth about Jesus.

As a result of their confusion about the nature of Christ, they were failing to derive the full advantages of his work and still living in unnecessary fear of evil spirits. So the emphasis of Paul's letter is to encourage them 'to appropriate the benefits of union with the exalted Christ as a means of overcoming evil'.[12]

b. The captivating powers

Who were these powers that quite illegitimately threatened to hold the Christians in Colosse in bondage? They are described as 'thrones or powers or rulers or authorities'.[13] Paul identifies them further by describing the strategies they use to seduce people under their authority and to enforce their control. They entice people *through hollow and deceptive philosophy, which depends on human tradition and the basic principles of this world rather than on Christ* (8). Unfortunately their nature (indicated by their titles) and their methodology are subject to various interpretations.

First, what is the nature of these powers of which Paul speaks on more than one occasion (1:16; cf. 2:15)? Since the Second World War many scholars have declined to see them as powerful personal intel-

---

[11] Arnold, *Colossian Syncretism*, p. 242.
[12] Ibid., p. 102.
[13] Rom. 8:38; 1 Cor. 2:6, 8; 15:24; Eph. 1:21; 3:10; 6:12.

ligences devoted to evil purposes, preferring to demythologize them and see them as social realities embodied in human power structures: governmental, economic, military and other corporate institutions, together with the values, traditions, conventions and laws that shape them. They operate within the world, unlike traditional 'demons' who come from outside to determine the course of human existence.[14] According to this view, to exercise any sort of power, whether psychological or social, as though it were absolute, is to use it in a demonic way.[15] One can readily understand how such an interpretation arose in the face of Nazism, which seemed to incarnate the forces of evil in a world where the existence of demons and spirits no longer seemed plausible. This interpretation has some powerful advocates, including, most recently, Walter Wink.[16]

But in the context of the ancient world, as well as the particular contexts of the letters in which Paul speaks of these powers, there can be little doubt that he had personal demonic intelligences in mind – in other words, the devil and all his minions, including demons, fallen angels, and evil and astral spirits. No other interpretation does justice to the historical context of the letters, where belief in a spiritual realm populated by spiritual beings was commonplace.[17]

The conclusion that Paul has demonic beings in mind does not rule out their ability to work through corporate institutes and to organize structural evil in order to achieve their aims. The book of Revelation, to name but one, teaches us that they are quite capable of doing just that. In the contemporary western world, as distinct from other times and cultures, this may well be the principal way in which they work. But we must reject any identification of these principalities and powers with sociopolitical or socioeconomic structures, and allow for the fact that they may work directly or indirectly and through a range of strategies and institutions to produce evil at every level of society.

In using a variety of terms to describe these beings, Paul does not seem to be advocating any particular hierarchy of beings or trying to distinguish one sort of evil being too sharply from another. As Peter O'Brien says, 'the different terms point to the same reality, and any attempt to rank them is pure speculation'.[18]

Secondly, if we grant that Paul is referring to personal spiritual intelligences, how does he envisage that they work? Their primary strategy in Colosse would appear to be to entice Christians into a trap,

[14] See J. Ellul, *The Ethics of Freedom* (Eerdmans, 1976), p. 152.
[15] Gunton, pp. 70–73.
[16] See J. R. W. Stott, *The Message of Ephesians*, BST (IVP, 1979), pp. 267–275; and for an overall survey and critique of Wink (e.g. *Naming the Powers*, Fortress, 1984) see Arnold, *Powers*, pp. 167–209.
[17] O'Brien, *Ephesians*, p. 469.
[18] Ibid., p. 468.

so that they follow empty philosophies originating in *human tradition and the basic principles of this world* instead of continuing to trust in Christ alone.

Paul's use of the word *philosophy* does not refer to any particular school of thought. It may well have been the word the false teachers, who were unsettling the Colossian Christians, used to describe their own teaching. But, in any case, it carried a wide range of meanings. Paul is not dismissing philosophy in general as futile, but only those philosophies that are a hollow sham. His qualifying phrase *which depends on human tradition* is fairly inclusive, since both Jews and Gentiles regarded their 'philosophies' as sacred traditions preserved by succeeding generations of their disciples. Only the verses that follow (16–23) can tell us more precisely what the content of this philosophy or tradition was. They indicate that although the false teaching had a close relationship to the synagogue, it was syncretistic. Paul seems to engage in a deliberate play on words early in the verse: the word translated *takes ... captive* (*sylagōgōn*) is like the word for 'synagogue' (*synagōgē*), suggesting that that was in his mind. One thing was sure, however: Paul was certain that what they were being encouraged to follow did not originate with God but with human beings. It was not a divine revelation but a human invention.

The next phrase, which the NIV translates as *the basic principles of this world*, is really problematic, as all commentators indicate.[19] It is possible to take it in many different and incompatible ways. It was used of the physical elements of the universe – earth, fire, water and air – but that does not seem relevant here. By extension, it came to mean the heavenly bodies, the planets and stars, which were thought to govern the lives of human beings. Some have taken it to mean something like 'elementary knowledge' or the basic elements of religious teaching. But the use seems more personal here, and it is probably right to see it as another reference to the invisible, personal and spiritual forces, active in the heavenly realm, which had a major impact on life in the physical realm. These were really the source of the hollow philosophy, mediated through human traditions, that was unsettling Paul's original readers.

The Colossian believers were in danger of losing the freedom Christ had won for them because they continued to fear evil spiritual forces and sought to appease them. They had not yet broken free from the syncretistic religious atmosphere in which they lived. It led them to have too low a view of Christ and to minimize both his person and his achievement on the cross. They had no confidence that their God reigned supreme, and he alone. Behind the human philosophies to which they were attracted lay the very evil beings they sought to

[19] See especially the helpful discussion in O'Brien, *Colossians*, pp. 129–132, and Dunn, *Colossians*, pp. 148–151.

placate. As Clinton Arnold says, 'Paul's polemic would have startled his readers as they realized that he was actually denouncing their "philosophy" as inspired by the same malicious powers from which they were seeking protection.'[20]

2. The divine Christ who wants to deliver us (2:9–12)

In leading up to his great declaration of the victory won by Christ over all powers and authorities that stand in opposition to God, Paul lays a sure foundation, instructing his readers about the nature of Christ in whom they trust, and its implications for their Christian experience.

a. Who Christ is

Christ is unique. Unlike the other powers and authorities that trouble them, and to which they attribute some elements of divinity, he alone is the one in whom *all the fulness of the Deity lives in bodily form* (9; cf. 1:19). The other spiritual beings may have some supernatural powers or measure of deity in them,[21] although, if they have, it will be severely distorted and twisted since they have become the agents of Satan and sought to function independently of God. But even if they have, they are not in the same league as Jesus. For, in him, God is in residence. The plenitude of deity is embodied in him, meaning not that God temporarily adopted Christ as his home for the purposes of saving the world, but that the Christ himself is God come in bodily form. Christ is not less than God, but fully and uniquely God come as a human being. How different he is from the supernatural beings before whom they cringe! Any other power is massively inferior to him, and any other supposed route to God is a cul-de-sac. He alone is the one who can make the divine connection and bring about our reconciliation with God.

Eugene Peterson expresses the sense of Paul's words in a graphic way. 'Everything of God gets expressed in him, so you can see and hear him clearly. You don't need a telescope, a microscope, or a horoscope to realise the fulness of Christ and the emptiness of the universe without him.'[22]

b. What this implies

The connection between Paul's statements about Christ (9) and about the Colossian believers (10) is seamless. The fullness of deity was in Christ, so believers are filled in him. Christ came in bodily form, so believers form his continuing body, of which he is the exalted head. The fullness the believers experience is spoken of in the perfect tense

---

[20] Arnold, *Colossian Syncretism*, p. 190.
[21] Cf. 1 Cor. 8:5.
[22] E. Peterson, *The Message* (NavPress, 1993), p. 499.

and the passive voice: they have received it, but it remains their continuing present possession and experience. It is a gift they have been given by God, not a state they have achieved by their own efforts.

Paul does not define what sort of fullness it is that believers experience. Elsewhere he talks of being filled with 'joy and peace'[23] or with 'the fruit of righteousness'.[24] Earlier in Colossians he had prayed that they might be filled 'with the knowledge of his will through all spiritual wisdom and understanding' (1:19). Here it may refer to 'fullness of life'. But it is more likely that he is really saying: 'Since you have everything you need in Christ, how mistaken you are to think you need to top up your means of securing protection from principalities and powers by recourse to strategies other than trusting him. All that you need, and more besides, you have in Christ.' The Christ who was full of Deity fills us too. So there is no room for other 'powers' in our relationship with God.

c. How it works

Having made his claim, Paul now explains to them a little more how the fullness of Christ translates into the fullness of believers. The key lies in their union with him. Believers are incorporated into Christ. By way of explanation, Paul turns to the language of circumcision (the means by which Jewish male infants were incorporated into the covenant community of Israel) and of baptism (the means by which Christian believers are incorporated into the new-covenant community of Christ).

First, there is the analogy of circumcision (11). Just as eight-day-old Jewish boys underwent circumcision, so now another and more radical circumcision has taken place to enable believers to enter the new covenant. The Jewish boy has a tiny piece of his flesh stripped away. This new Christian circumcision involved stripping off the whole 'body of flesh'.[25] The original Greek leaves it open as to whether this circumcision, this stripping away of the flesh, is something Christians undergo as they strip off their *sinful nature* (as in NIV) and divest themselves of their alienation from God, or whether it is something that Christ underwent on our behalf. If the latter is correct, it refers to his violent death: the stripping off of his physical body. It is a difficult call. Peter O'Brien, on balance, prefers to see it as a reference to Christ, but admits that this is not without difficulty.[26] This interpretation prepares the way for what Paul is going to teach in the next paragraph about the cross. N. T. Wright, however, suggests another meaning. He

[23] Rom. 15:13.
[24] Phil. 1:11.
[25] This is the literal translation of the phrase the NIV renders *sinful nature*.
[26] O'Brien, *Colossians*, p. 117; Dunn, *Colossians*, p. 157.

points out that 'body' can refer to the body of the family, and says that when converts came for baptism 'the solidarities of the old life, the network of family and society to which, until then, he or she has given primary allegiance' are left behind.[27]

Regardless of Paul's exact meaning, the thrust of his teaching is clear. Just as Jews entered the covenant through a literal circumcision of the flesh, so uncircumcised Gentiles can gain entry to the new covenant through another kind of circumcision, which is a symbolic expression either for their own putting away of a life dominated by self and sin, together with all the sin-orientated networks in which they have been enmeshed, or for the gruesome death of Christ.

Secondly, there is the analogy of the death, burial and resurrection of Christ (12).[28] Here, Paul is perfectly clear. As converts are buried in water and rise from it again, the death, burial and resurrection of Jesus Christ are dramatically re-enacted. Believers initiated into the Christian life have died his death, have been buried with him (just as he was laid to rest in a tomb to prove that a real death had occurred), and have been raised to a new life with Christ through faith in the power of God. All these events are history. When these believers put their faith in Christ, they died to their former way of life. They buried it, and put away once and for all its old loyalties, habits, influences and lifestyle. Now they have been raised to experience the life of the Spirit and to walk in new ways that please God.

If, for the moment, their experience leads them to think they are not complete in Christ, and that something more than him is needed to give them a full life, free from the constraints of their present earthly lives (as the false teachers were suggesting), Paul urges them to understand that they already have been raised with Christ (cf. 3:1). The resurrection was an act of God's power – a power they have begun to experience, at least in part, in their own lives here and now. One day they will enter into its full reality. In the meantime, some aspects of their lives remain a mystery and do not add up. Their lives are 'hidden with Christ' (3:3), rather than fully revealed. The important thing is that they continue to hope exclusively in him, concentrating on his priorities for them and resisting any temptation to deviate down the path of other teachings.

The Colossian believers no longer need to feel oppressed by supernatural powers, for the one in whom the fullness of God himself dwells has come to their aid and given them all they need. So closely have they identified with him in his death, burial and resurrection that they have been joined to him. Since he is risen, victorious over all the authorities they credit with power, why do they still fear them?

---

[27] Wright, *Colossians*, p. 106.
[28] Rom. 6:1–4.

3. The amazing cross that liberates us (2:13–15)

Paul circles over the same ground once more but, this time, on an even higher plane, so that they may see more clearly the marvel of what Christ has achieved for them on the cross. He reminds them of what they were like in their uncircumcised state. They were anything but alive to God, and stuck in their state of sin, with no way of dealing with it. When they were unable to help themselves (for there is nothing so helpless as a corpse), God stepped in and, through the death of Christ, accomplished something that has made a dramatic difference to them. Again, Paul resorts to two images to help explain the work of Calvary. First, he speaks of the cross as cancelling our debts and, secondly, of it routing our enemies.

a. The cross cancels our debts

The perilous condition in which people stand before putting their faith in Christ is due to sin, and this is the problem the cross both addresses and cures. Sin is pictured as a debt we owe. It was a common practice in the ancient world for a debtor to write a note acknowledging the sum he owed and his obligation to pay it. Paul uses that as an illustration. But what exactly is the nature of this *written code* (14) that records the debt we owe because of sin?

Again, several possibilities suggest themselves. The note could be a document of indictment that records our guilt when we break the law. This seems an obvious interpretation, since Paul speaks of a *written code, with its regulations, that was against us and that stood opposed to us.* The Mosaic law, with all its legal demands and decrees, would soon ensure that a large list of offences was entered in the balance sheet, leaving us in debt to God. In any spiritual court it would not be difficult to throw the book (of the law) at us.

Peter O'Brien refines this view.[29] He points out that when Israel entered into the covenant with God, they contracted to obey the law and accepted that there would be penalty clauses if they failed to deliver. Not only had the Jews broken the covenant, with its just demands and regulations, but, he says, Paul would have assumed that the Gentiles were equally indebted to God and his law. In their case, their consciences would have obligated them to his moral law, and they would have been just as guilty of breaking it as were the Jews. So Jew and Gentile alike have an undischarged debt of obligation to God.

A second interpretation suggests itself to others, however. James Dunn thinks Paul probably borrowed an earlier Jewish idea: that of a book of the righteous kept in heaven.[30] Moses referred to it when

---

[29] O'Brien, *Colossians*, p. 125.
[30] Dunn, *Colossians*, p. 164.

pleading for God's mercy on Israel following the dreadful incident of the golden calf, 'Please', he cried, 'forgive their sin – but if not, then blot me out of the book you have written.' And God replied, 'Whoever has sinned against me I will blot out of my book.'[31] During the period when apocalyptic thinking became common, Judaism developed this idea, and believed that the angels kept books in heaven in which people's deeds, both good and evil, were recorded and kept for the future day of judgment.

It is unlikely that Paul was trying to be as precise in his use of this metaphor as either of these interpretations suggests, and we must be careful that such discussions do not distract us from his obvious message. What is abundantly clear is that sin costs, and that the debt of sin, which we are too impoverished to pay ourselves, is met in full by the cross of Christ. For there Christ did three things. He *cancelled* our debt (*exaleipsas* literally means that he wiped the slate clean), he *took ... away* the *written code ... that was against us ... nailing it to the cross* (14). If it was a bill of indictment, it was revoked. If it was a bill of obligation, it was paid by another. If it was a document of evil deeds kept in heaven, it was rendered void. All record of our debt was removed. The wonderful news of the cross is that the IOU of sin has been cancelled. The debt we owe to God has been eradicated once and for all by being nailed to the cross.

Centuries before, the prophet Isaiah had recorded God as saying, 'I, even I, am he who blots out your transgressions, for my own sake, and remembers your sins no more.'[32] Now God's promise has been fulfilled through his Son's cross.

People have read all sorts of ideas into this metaphor. It is frequently claimed that in Paul's world a bond was cancelled by crossing it through with an X – an obviously appropriate symbol for the cancellation of our debt with God on a cross. But that is a bit too neat, and Paul certainly does not draw attention to the shape of the cross here. Others have talked of the way in which debts were cancelled, when paid, by being impaled on a nail. Unfortunately, there is no evidence of such a practice.[33] There may be an allusion to the indictment nailed above the heads of victims of crucifixion so that the public could see why they were being executed. If so, Paul is saying that although Pilate claimed that Christ was being crucified as 'king of the Jews',[34] the accusation on the charge sheet should really have read, 'This is Jesus, who dies to pay the price for the people's sins.' But this metaphor, like any other, should not be pressed too far. The key issue is

---

[31] Exod. 32:32–33.
[32] Is. 43:25.
[33] O'Brien, *Colossians*, p. 126.
[34] See Matt. 27:37; Mark 15:26; Luke 23:38; John 19:19.

that 'this is a vivid way of saying that because Christ was nailed to the cross our debt has been completely forgiven'.[35]

Sin always has its price tag. We frequently begin to pay the debt run up by our sinful behaviour as we bear its consequences, but whether we bear them in this life or on judgment day, the debt we owe God because of sin is awesome. But what great news sounds forth from the cross! The debt we cannot possibly meet from our own meagre and tainted resources has been fully met by another. When Christ was nailed to the cross, so was our bond of debt. God declared it irrevocably cancelled.

b. The cross defeats our enemies

The cross deals with the problem of our sin. But that still leaves the problem of our enemies who, in continuing to exist, go on pestering us and, for all we know, may well yet succeed in winning the battle. The cross not only had to cancel out the works of Satan, but to deal with Satan himself and his subordinates too.[36] What, if anything, did the cross achieve in respect of them? How does the cross help Colossian believers, or any other believers, living in fear and feeling oppressed by forces too strong for them?

Paul's answer is that the cross settles that problem too, and in a decisive, audacious manner, brilliant in its conception and design. Christ did not remain safe in heaven while our enemies were on the loose, but entered our world and met the opposition head on. Tom Smail describes it vividly:

> Christ comes to the cross as the fireman comes to the fire, as the lifeboat comes to the sinking ship, as the rescue team comes to the wounded man in the Alpine snow. They have what it takes to help and deliver, but they must come to where the fire burns, the storm rages, the avalanche entombs, and make themselves vulnerable to the danger that such a coming involves.[37]

So Christ, *having disarmed the powers and authorities ... made a public spectacle of them, triumphing over them by the cross* (15). In the death of Jesus they have been rendered powerless, reduced to being captives themselves, and totally defeated.

Here is a wonderful irony. The unseen principalities and powers of the universe sought to do away with Christ and allied themselves with

[35] O'Brien, *Colossians*, p. 126.
[36] Wallace, p. 29.
[37] Smail, *Once and for All*, p. 106. Smail relates the pictures to Christ's coming to 'where the Father in his holy wrath has handed over the sinners to the consequences of their sin', but it fits equally well here.

the powers of the world to achieve their end. If they had succeeded, it would have meant the overthrow of God's good power, and the triumph of evil, unchecked, would have led the world down the path to total destruction. These allied powers left nothing to chance. Political and religious powers combined with the supernatural powers in a carefully staged drama to ensure Christ's death. He would be reduced to a state of utter weakness and degraded in complete humiliation. They ensured that he was powerless and without any chance of fighting back. And yet, paradoxically, in submitting to their abuse he gained the victory and overpowered them. It was the powers themselves that, rather than trapping and disarming him, were caught and vanquished.

As N. T. Wright puts it:

> The 'rulers' and authorities of Rome and Israel – the best government and the highest religion the world of that time had ever known – conspired to place Jesus on the cross. These powers, angry at his challenge to their sovereignty, stripped *him* naked, held *him* up to public contempt, and celebrated a triumph over *him*.

He goes on to explain that in that event, 'God was stripping *them* naked, was holding *them* up to public contempt, and leading *them* in his own triumphal procession – in Christ, the crucified Messiah'.[38]

Having done their worst, they overreached themselves. Having played their trump card, they were trumped. The cross means that the enemies have been outwitted and conquered.

Paul conjures up the picture of Christ as a victorious Roman general leading his troops into the city on a victory parade. The cross is like the chariot on which the victor rode in triumph.[39] Plutarch describes one such occasion, which lasted three days. The streets were crowded with jubilant people. On the first day the captured works of art were displayed in a procession of 250 chariots. On the second day, 'the finest and richest of the Macedonian arms were borne along on many wagons', followed by silver from their ransacked treasury. On the third day, led by trumpeters and a multitude of garlanded oxen that were to be sacrificed later in the proceedings, the defeated Perseus and his family were 'led along as slaves'. At the climax of the procession came the victorious general himself, Aemilius, 'wearing a purple robe interwoven with gold and holding in his right hand a spray of laurel'. He was accompanied not only by his victorious soldiers but by 'paeans of victory and hymns in praise' of his achievements. He was 'gazed upon and admired by all'.[40] If that was the way they celebrated

---

[38] Wright, *Colossians*, p. 116.
[39] Dunn, quoting Scott, in *Colossians*, p. 168.
[40] I owe this to L. Williamson, 'Led in triumph', *Int* 22 (1968), pp. 322–323.

Aemilius' victory over Perseus, how much more should we celebrate Christ's victory procession as he leads in his train a defeated Satan, all his entourage, and every other enemy that conspires against us, such as law and death!

Paul's claim is bold in the extreme – first, because it stands on its head our normal way of seeing the world. We usually think it is military power and political force that can put down enemies. But God does it through weakness. We boast of success, but in the cross Christ embraced defeat. We eschew pain, but Christ willingly accepted it. And through the weakness, shame, pain and apparent defeat he achieved a real and unsurpassable victory.

Secondly, for the Colossians, as for many subsequently, these oppressing powers still seemed to be at loose within our world and exercising power over people. How can we say, then, that they have been defeated? The cross guarantees their defeat and takes much further God's programme, which will culminate in our full experience of their defeat, made evident to all, when Christ returns in glory. But we have not yet reached its completion.

John Stott has set out God's six-stage programme like this:

Stage one is *the conquest predicted*, from Genesis 3:15 onwards.

Stage two is *the conquest begun*, in the ministry of Jesus.

Stage three is *the conquest achieved*, in the death of Jesus.

Stage four is *the conquest confirmed*, in the resurrection of Jesus.

Stage five is *the conquest extended*, through the church of Jesus.

Stage six is *the conquest consummated*, by the return of Jesus.[41]

We are currently at stage five, when the gospel must be announced but during which the powers will not concede their defeat. They pretend that their fictitious strength is unaffected and, even in their death throes, they continue to hold unbelievers captive and to hassle believers. They have no right to do so, but they are so practised in the art of deception that they do not even realize that they have been vanquished. It is for this very reason that we must announce the gospel. We must let people know that the Christ has opened the prison doors and taken our would-be jailers captive. We must announce the triumph of Christ to unbelievers and believers alike, so that the former may come into an initial experience of the liberating power of the cross and the latter may continue to experience the fullness of the liberation Christ brings. Here, Paul has the latter particularly in view. Believers lacked the confidence to shake off these hostile powers. Did they not realize that 'The unseen powers and invisible forces that had dominated and determined so much of life need no longer be feared. A greater power and force was at work, which could rule and determine their

---

[41] Stott, *Cross of Christ*, pp. 231–239.

lives more effectively – in a word, "Christ". Triumph indeed!'[42]

There are a staggering number of powerful images about the cross in these verses. It is a spiritual circumcision, a body of flesh stripped off, the way to burial and resurrection with Christ, a means of being made alive while dead because of sin, a wiping clean of the record of sin, and, supremely, a means of defeating our enemies and holding them up to public humiliation and shame. Most significant of these are the last two, the ones Paul has been working towards. On the cross Christ pays the enormous debt of our sin and defeats all our enemies.

Here is a victory to celebrate and announce with confidence, even now that we have become suspicious of triumphalism. The diffidence and mediocrity of much Christian living today may, indeed, be precisely due to our lack of teaching and believing that Christ really has *already* defeated our enemies through his cross. It is not a victory he has yet to win, but a victory he has won. It is not a victory in which he requires our assistance, as we engage in fighting the enemy, but one he could and did win on his own, and through which he offers assistance to us. It is a victory not just to celebrate but to experience, as, taking shelter in the cross of Christ, we resist our enemies and walk in freedom.

It was a victory indeed, but a tragic one, since it demanded that Jesus should pay an ultimate price and experience an unbelievable defeat. The Christ who is *Christus Victor* is also *Christus Crucifixus*.

---

[42] Dunn, *Colossians*, p. 170.

PART 4
THE CROSS APPLIED

Hebrews 10:1–18
15. Once for all

1. Is Hebrews still relevant?

At first sight the letter to the Hebrews seems remote from the concerns of the contemporary world. It was obviously written to people to whom Jewish religious rituals would have meant much. Furthermore, the readers would have been familiar with the intricacies of midrash, that is, the way in which the Jewish rabbis engaged in interpreting the biblical text, often finding something new and unexpected in it. The book's preoccupation with sacrifice is not shared by the modern world, at least in the West. Distant memories of the practice are only occasionally projected into our consciousness as a news story reports the killing of a sacrificial animal by a minority religious group whose practice causes alarm to the tender minds of 'civilized' human beings. But such a reaction betrays a very western-centric and modern view of the world.

Much of the non-western world continues the practice of offering sacrifices of one sort or another, however, and still ascribes importance to priests, temples and religious rituals. The letter to the Hebrews has an obvious apologetic value in those areas, as well as among those with a Jewish heritage. And it still speaks among contemporary western men and women. The concerns of Hebrews persist, albeit in new guises and apparently cut loose of their religious roots. Four of its relevant themes might be briefly mentioned.

First, the idea of sacrifice is still much admired.[1] While the practice of animal sacrifice might be consigned to a barbaric and primitive past, we still look with admiration on those who sacrifice themselves for others. The heroic rescuer who dies while saving the life of another, the soldiers who gave their lives for the cause of freedom, the brave woman who donates a kidney so that her brother may live, the generous benefactor who gives beyond his means to a good cause, all still provoke

---

[1] Gunton (pp. 115–117) argues that there is something inherent in the human condition to which it continues to appeal.

respect. Though devoid of any thought of atonement, the idea of sacrifice is still upheld as noble.

Secondly, the role of the priest is still necessary today. The priest stood as the mediator between God and people, relieving them of sin through offering sacrifices and providing wise guidance on how to live wholesomely in God's world. Our world is full of secular priests who, having renounced the significance of God, still seek to relieve people of guilty consciences and offer wisdom for living. Therapists and secular confessors abound. They often act in a mediatorial role, seeking to repair the damage of the past or to restore broken relationships. The secular priest acts as a mediator who puts clients in touch with themselves, their feelings, their true identity or their forgotten past.

Having marginalized the religious priest, contemporary people resort wholesale to the booming counselling industry. They seek peace in the private confessional of the therapist's clinic, or even in the public confessional of the chat show, like that of Jerry Springer. But what is offered is a hearing without any atonement.

Thirdly, the desire for access to the divine is evident. The quest for contact with deity is manifest in numerous places, not least within the various branches of the New Age movement, which teaches that the divine is within us. Its concept of God is far removed from the God who has revealed himself in Christ, and the route by which one can supposedly encounter and be intimate with divinity is anything but Christian. Nevertheless, the desire suggests that the same human quest for a meaningful relationship with deity that lay behind Hebrews persists today.

Fourthly, there is the concept of covenant, or rather its absence. Contemporary society's thinking has moved from relationships based on covenant to those based on contract. The sacred covenant of marriage (which binds a couple together 'for better, for worse ... until death do us part') has been replaced by the secular contract of marriage (complete with prenuptial agreements should the relationship go wrong). The same shift could be illustrated in any number of areas, from education and medicine to the employment of football managers. It lies behind the megashift from the traditional communities in which people once lived to the large, impersonal societies we now inhabit. According to Jonathan Sacks, Britain's Chief Rabbi, this profound change in our understanding of personhood can account for many of our society's ills.[2] So, while the concept of covenant, so vital to Hebrews, may not be uppermost on people's minds today, its implications for our way of living are profound.

These issues suggest that even in our very different world the message of Hebrews is still relevant, with points of contact that enable

[2] J. Sacks, *The Politics of Hope* (Jonathan Cape, 1977), *passim*.

us to build bridges from it into contemporary culture and then lead people back across them to encounter the most relevant truth of all, namely, the cross of Christ.

2. The cross in Hebrews

Apart from chapter 11, no chapter in Hebrews fails to mention the cross. 'It is', says Morna Hooker, 'the most sustained piece of writing on the subject [of the atonement] in the New Testament.'[3] A multitude of equivalent phrases and expansive pictures are to be found within the book, usually relating in some way or another to the work of the tabernacle and temple. The reason for the Son's coming was to provide 'purification for sins' (1:3). Jesus is 'crowned with glory and honour because he suffered death' (2:9). The 'author of ... salvation' was made 'perfect through suffering' (2:10). 'By his death' he destroys 'him who holds the power of death' (2:14). Jesus, the Son, was 'faithful to the one who appointed him' (3:20).

He is the 'great high priest' who is able to dispense mercy and grace 'to help us in our time of need' (4:14–16). He 'became the source of eternal salvation' because of his 'reverent submission' and his having 'learned obedience from what he suffered' (5:7–9). Jesus has gone before us, entering 'the inner sanctuary behind the curtain' (6:19–20). He is a priest after the order of Melchizedek, who sacrificed for sins once for all and, unlike other priests, 'is able to save completely' (7:17; 25, 27). He is the priest of the new covenant, which has rendered the old one obsolete (8:6, 13). He achieved purification from sins and the cleansing of people's consciences by offering his own blood (9:12). This priest, who *offered for all time one sacrifice for sins*, now reigns in majesty in heaven (10:12).

He enables us to come and offer joyful worship on Mount Zion because of his 'sprinkled blood that speaks a better word than the blood of Abel' (12:22–24). The penultimate picture, in an obvious reference to the scapegoat, introduces the new thought that Christ 'suffered outside the city gate to make the people holy through his own blood' (13:12). The final reference is found in the benediction, which again returns to the theme of the blood of the covenant offered by the 'great Shepherd of the sheep' (13:20–21). Each of these suggests a rich and varied understanding of the cross.

3. The purpose of Hebrews

Before looking at one particular passage on the cross, it will be helpful to gain an overall perspective on the book, from which we may

[3] Hooker, *Not Ashamed*, p. 112.

interpret the special emphasis it brings to our understanding of Christ's death. Several suggestions have been made about why Hebrews was written.[4] From its rhetorical structure and its spoken rather than literary style, it seems to have been a sermon rather than a letter, and is 'rabbinical in design, Christian in content and heroic in length'.[5] Its purpose is pastoral and it aims to persuade faltering Christian believers to remain faithful. Several reasons for their instability are proposed, and are worth exploring – even though there is surely no need to choose between them, since there was no doubt more than one issue on the agenda.

a. The question of apostasy

The letter is peppered with warnings against giving up and encouragements to persevere.[6] It alludes to the fact that the readers had suffered for their faith (10:32) and were currently experiencing the discipline of God (12:1–13), and that some of them were in prison, presumably for their faith in Christ (13:3). Perhaps their leaders had even paid with their lives for their faith in Christ (13:7). The writer encourages them to make a clean break from their former contacts in the synagogue and to remain true to the superior way of Christ (13:13). The danger that the readers might apostatize is widely accepted, but is not necessarily the only reason for the letter.

b. The question of weariness

Recently, Thomas Long has pointed out that the readers seem to be suffering from the sheer weariness of being Christians. He makes a credible case that this is the central theme of the letter, which, he says, comes to a climax in 12:12–13: 'Therefore strengthen your feeble arms and weak knees! "Make level paths for your feet," so that the lame may not be disabled, but rather healed.' Long summarizes his position and relates it to the contemporary world like this:

> The Preacher is not preaching into a vacuum; he is addressing a real and urgent pastoral problem, one that seems astonishingly contemporary. His congregation is exhausted. They are tired – tired of serving the world, tired of worship, tired of Christian education, tired of being peculiar and whispered about in society, tired of the spiritual struggle, tired of trying to keep their prayer life going, tired

[4] Some argue that trying to identify the 'readers' of the letter or the 'hearers' of the sermon is both speculative and unnecessary. They see Hebrews not as a letter or sermon but as an exposition of the majestic superiority of Jesus Christ, the climax of the Old Testament Scriptures, the truths and application of which are relevant for all.

[5] Long, p. 2.

[6] Heb. 3:6; 4:11, 14; 5:11 – 6:12; 10:19–25; 12:25–27.

even of Jesus. Their hands droop and their knees are weak (12:12), attendance is down at church (10:25), and they are losing confidence. The threat is not that they are charging off in the wrong direction; they do not have enough energy to charge off anywhere. The threat here is that, worn down and worn out, they will drop their end of the rope and drift away. Tired of walking the walk, many of them are considering taking a walk, leaving the community and falling away from the faith.

We recognise the problem, of course, but the Preacher's response may astound us. What is most striking about Hebrews is that the Preacher, faced with the pastoral problem of spiritual weariness, is bold enough, maybe even brash enough to think that Christology and preaching are the answers. The Preacher does not appeal to improved group dynamics, conflict management techniques, reorganisation of the mission structures, or snappy worship services. Rather he preaches – preaches to the congregation in complex theological terms about the nature and meaning of Jesus.[7]

c. The problem of a troubled conscience

The third suggestion, that of Barnabas Lindars, is that the problem is one of post-baptismal sin. He draws attention to the stress on the conscience which comes, for example, in 9:14: 'How much more, then, will the blood of Christ, who through the eternal Spirit offered himself unblemished to God, cleanse our consciences from acts that lead to death, so that we may serve the living God!' He argues that the work of Christ is particularly applied to those who seem to have over-sensitive consciences and find themselves unable to break free from perpetually nagging feelings of inadequacy and guilt. The writer strongly encourages the readers to 'draw near to God with a sincere heart in full assurance of faith' (10:22; cf. 4:16).

The readers' confidence in their faith, Lindars explains, has been undermined by a continuing sense of sin. When they suffered like this in the old days, they could always go to the temple and offer a sacrifice. Performing some practical ritual like this was a great therapy and served to ease the pain they felt in their consciences. But in their new faith, there was no equivalent ritual practice for them to undertake. The sacrifice had been offered once and for all, and they could not repeat it. So the old purification rituals retained a certain attraction for them.

Old answers to this dilemma had not been convincing up to now, says Lindars, so new arguments had to be produced. Step by step, the old Jewish customs had to be undermined, and the author 'must show in detail how the sacrifice of Christ applies in the present to meet their

[7] Long, p. 3.

need'.[8] So, in Hebrews, we are given 'a creative new development of the original contribution, a striking and original presentation' of the gospel.[9] In this way the author secures attention, overcomes resistance and provides the most imaginative, yet soundly based, exposition of the cross. It shows that we have a perfect high priest, superior to any who had gone before, and continuing to work for us now in heaven. It shows that we have the ultimate sacrifice, which exceeds the standard set by the Day of Atonement. And it shows that we have entered a new covenant, far superior to the old covenant after which the readers are tempted to hanker.

Whether the problem was apostasy, weariness or an uneasy conscience, the answer is always the same: it is Christ. The threefold exposition of his work as an effective sacrifice, the offering of a superior high priest and the establishing of a new covenant occurs time and again in the letter. It begins to be expounded in 5:1–10 and, after the author digresses to offer a strong warning in 5:11 – 6:19, is picked up again in 7:1 and developed right through to 10:18. Verses 1–18 of chapter 10 reach the climax of the argument and summarize what has gone before, making this a suitable passage for study here.

4. The cross of Jesus provides an effective sacrifice (10:1–10)

The thinking of the writer of Hebrews has been totally shaped by the Old Testament regulations for worship. He takes it as axiomatic, therefore, that 'without the shedding of blood there is no forgiveness' (9:22). He looks to see how Jesus' death not only meets but surpasses the standard set by the blood sacrifices of the Old Testament. In particular, the Day of Atonement,[10] which became the yardstick by which all other sacrifices were measured, forms the background to his writing about Christ's sacrifice.[11] On that day all the sins of the people were removed from them, and unless Jesus can match and exceed the achievement of that sacrifice, he has nothing to offer.

While it is clear that the author has the Day of Atonement in view, he uses it selectively. Surprisingly, he makes no mention of the scapegoat, and chooses to dwell instead on the sacrificed goat whose blood was sprinkled in the Most Holy Place. There is a reason for his silence about the scapegoat. His concern is with blood sacrifice, and to have drawn attention to the scapegoat, would have blurred the focus. The scapegoat, after all (as Lindars claims), signifies only 'the removal

---

[8] Lindars, p. 60.
[9] Ibid.
[10] Lev. 16. Ellingworth (p. 493) rightly comments that, while the Day of Atonement is primarily in view, the writer does not exclude the daily sacrifices.
[11] Lindars, p. 54.

of sins already atoned for by the blood ritual'.[12] What is really important is that Jesus was a sacrificial victim whose blood was shed.

But the writer's real interest is not in the similarity but in the difference between the death of Christ and the Day of Atonement, which only goes to prove the superiority of the sacrifice offered by Christ. So he establishes the inadequacy of the former blood sacrifices before turning to the effectiveness of Christ's sacrifice.

a. The inadequacy of the former sacrifices

Within a few concentrated verses, 1–4, the writer engages in a detailed critique of the Jewish sacrificial system as epitomized by the Day of Atonement. Philip Edgcumbe Hughes[13] draws from these verses four facts that make that system ultimately ineffective and therefore inadequate.

First, its character is insubstantial. The *law*, which embodies the ceremonial regulations of the Day, *is only a shadow of the good things that are coming – not the realities themselves* (1). The law is like a signpost that points to a reality some distance away, but is not itself the destination. Similarly, the Day of Atonement points to the reality revealed in the sacrifice of Christ. No traveller would confuse the sign with the destination, nor should a person seeking intimacy with God confuse the shadow of Old Testament ritual with the substance of Christ's atoning cross. In saying this, the writer is picking up an idea he used earlier but developed differently. In 8:5 he wrote of the earthly tabernacle as a 'shadow of what is in heaven'. The comparison there was between sanctuaries, but here is between sacrifices. Yet the point is the same. The manual typewriter, we might say today, was a shadow of the modern word processor. Useful though it was in its day, it was extremely limited compared with what is currently available. Why, then, stick with the early forms, which merely foreshadow later excellence, when the real thing is freely available?

Secondly, its nature is repetitive. The Day of Atonement was inadequate because it had to be *repeated endlessly year after year* (1). The writer seems to pile up the words for emphasis. To say it had to be *repeated* would suggest it did not adequately fulfil its purpose; but to add the word *endlessly* emphasizes its inadequacy, while the addition of *year after year* rubs salt into the wound. The most the Day of Atonement could achieve was cleansing for the past year. But twelve months later the same ritual was needed all over again, year in and year out. This, too, is a point the writer has made before, but in a different way. In 7:27 and 9:25, he observes that the high priests of Israel had to offer their sacrifices over and over again, day after day, year after year.

[12] Ibid., p. 92.
[13] Hughes, *Hebrews*, pp. 389–394.

Their work was never finished. How different is Jesus!

Thirdly, its achievement is inadequate. In view of what has already been said, how could it be otherwise? But the writer still has more to say about the ineffectiveness of the old sacrifices. They *can never ... make perfect those who draw near to worship* (1). In fact, they have the reverse effect, for far from transforming individuals they *are an annual reminder of sins* (3), that is, of their failure to transform people. They never absolve people's consciences; they only prolong their agony.

Thomas Long expresses the problem vividly:

> In fact, the whole Day of Atonement ritual, repeated annually, is like a sledgehammer to the human spirit, pounding away year after year with its constant battering away at the theme of sin. In other words, it doesn't work to heal; it works only to drub it into us that we are sinful, sinful, sinful – guilty and unacceptable to God.[14]

Sometimes, Long remarks, going to church can have exactly the same effect today. In reality, many preachers are better at reminding us that we are sinners than that God is gracious. They signal that people do not measure up. They don't give enough, pray enough, witness enough, come enough, serve enough, care enough, praise enough, or whatever the pastor's burden is. It's never enough. And the worshippers are left to bring their flimsy 'works' to God in the hope that they will be acceptable.

> Over and over we make these offerings, but it does not work. It is never enough, never adequate, so we keep our distance from the Holy of Holies, leave with a guilty conscience, and come back next week with another basket of good intentions and deeds to place on the altar – or we stay away altogether.[15]

It is all too easy to slide rapidly back from proclaiming a new-covenant gospel to trying to obey an old-covenant law. But what a betrayal of the cross of Christ that is!

Fourthly, its materials are invalid. The sacrificial element of the old covenant was *the blood of bulls and goats* (4), but how could they possibly be adequate as substitutes for human beings? Hughes lists their deficiencies. They have no volition, no rationality and no comprehension of what is happening to them. They are passive and inarticulate sacrifices. 'A brute beast, by its very nature, is unqualified to serve as a substitute to man, the crown of God's creation.'[16] Hebrews

[14] Long, p. 101.
[15] Ibid., p. 102.
[16] Hughes, *Hebrews*, p. 392.

tells us not that in principle they might be able to take away sins if they were good enough, numerous enough or offered regularly enough, but that in principle *it is impossible* (4) that they could ever serve as effective substitutes for sinful human beings. Wilful sinners need a wilful substitute to cleanse them through sacrifice. Here is what Paul Ellingworth calls 'perhaps the author's strongest negative statement about the Levitical sacrifices'.[17]

Put together, these four negative comments on the Day of Atonement, and, by default, on all the other sacrifices of the Old Testament era, totally demolish the supposed effectiveness of the sacrifices some of the readers are tempted to think are more effective than the work of Christ.

b. The effectiveness of Christ's sacrifice

Having offered a fourfold critique of the old sacrificial system, the writer now offers a fourfold case for the superiority of Christ's sacrifice. While it does not counter the defects of the old arrangement point by point, it does so implicitly, and builds a much more positive picture of the superiority of the cross than a more limited rebuttal would do. The work of Christ is effective because of how he lived, what he established, whom he affected and what characterizes it.

First, how he lived: he offered an obedient life (5–9). What was it that made the sacrifice of Christ effective? It was that what he offered up on the cross was a life of total moral obedience to God which had embodied the fulfilment of the law. The writer engages in a meditation on Psalm 40:6–8, largely in the Septuagint version but making a few changes to it, especially in the last line. As F. F. Bruce remarked, however, if he had used the Hebrew wording 'it would have served his purpose almost as well'.[18] The psalm is one of several texts where there might be seen to be some opposition between obedience and sacrifice.[19] By putting the words of the psalm into the mouth of Jesus, the writer makes the point that the tension between the two is perfectly resolved in him. What had so often been an obstacle in the old covenant, as people offered sacrifice without the corresponding obedience, was settled once and for all in him. He fulfilled to the letter the psalm's vision of human vocation. His life was one of total obedience, which enabled him to be the perfect sacrifice. His incarnation issued in the logic of the cross, for it was the same total obedience he demonstrated in his life that led him to make his way to Calvary.

Twice before, the writer has connected Christ's obedience and his

---

[17] Ellingworth, p. 497.
[18] Bruce, *Hebrews*, p. 232.
[19] E.g. 1 Sam. 15:22; Pss. 50:8–14; 51:16–17; Is. 1:11–17; Jer. 7:21–26; Hos. 6:6; Amos 5:21–24; Mic. 6:8.

suffering (2:10; 5:8). Now he brings the thought to a climax. The total availability of the Son to do the will of the Father, which results in his crucifixion, introduces an unprecedented form of sacrifice. Here, at last, is 'the new obedient man, the first fruits of a new kind of humanity that at last obeys God's commandment, reflects back God's holiness and fulfils God's covenant from the human side'.[20] In Jesus, as Tom Smail claims, 'Sacrifice is re-defined as obedient self-offering: not therefore simply the obedience of particular acts but the obedience expressed in the self-giving of a whole person.'[21] Because the writer sets out the sacrifice of Christ in these terms, we can immediately see its superiority to any sacrifice that had ever been offered before.

Secondly, Christ's work is effective because of what he established: he inaugurated a new covenant (9). After expanding a little on the perfect obedience and self-giving of Christ, the author makes his next point sharply. Christ *sets aside the first to establish the second.* The old order is abolished and the new is introduced. The work of Christ is not more of the same, with perhaps some minor improvements to the existing sacrificial system, but a radical new beginning. The old sacrifices have become obsolete and have been replaced by the vastly superior way of Christ. The readers cannot hedge their bets with a little trust in Jesus mixed with continuing dependence on old rituals. Either they belong to the old order of things or they have entered into the new age of Christ. From now on, intimacy with God, the forgiveness of sins and the cleansing of our consciences do not depend on our offering sacrifices, but on the sacrifice he has already offered in our stead.

Thirdly, it is effective because of whom he affected: he creates a holy people (10). The prophet Haggai[22] once told a somewhat obscure parable which seems to have been designed to reinforce the general Old Testament teaching that, while it is possible to be made unclean by touching something that is defiled, it is not possible to be made clean by touching what was holy. The old covenant erred on the side of the negative. It sought to prevent what was already defiled from spreading by isolating it or even by destroying it.[23] But it was powerless to make the unclean clean. It could recognize and celebrate when the transformation happened, but it could do nothing to bring the transformation about. By contrast, the members of the church *have been made holy through the sacrifice of the body of Christ.* Through it, believers are cleansed from sin, sanctified in Christ and set apart to serve as God's exclusively owned people. The cross does what the law could never do. Through it, Christ provides the status, relationship and transformation

[20] Smail, *Once and for All*, p. 111.
[21] Ibid.
[22] Hag. 3:10–14.
[23] Lev. 13 – 14.

that earlier sacrifices could never provide.

Fourthly, his sacrifice is effective because of what characterized it: he completed an unrepeatable act (10). All this was done *once and for all*. There is no need to go back annually and repeat the sacrifice, still less to offer a blood sacrifice daily. The sacrifice of Christ needed to be offered only once. The singular event of his death, on a hill overlooking Jerusalem, was to have universal and ongoing repercussions, but need never happen again. Dorothy L. Sayers points out how extraordinary that claim is. 'He is the only God', she writes, 'who has a date in history ... there is no more astonishing collocation of phrases than that which, in the Nicene Creed, sets these two statements flatly side by side: "Very God of Very God ... He suffered under Pontius Pilate."'[24]

How different this is from the emphasis we find in some present-day approaches to the atonement! There is no need for the Son of God to be offered repeatedly in the Mass. And we even need to be cautious about some teaching that at first sight appears quite acceptable. Salvation is a present experience, but atonement was achieved once for all. So when Paul Fiddes writes, 'Salvation happens here and now. It is always in the present that God acts to heal and reconcile, entering into the disruption of human lives at great cost to himself, in order to share our predicament and rescue us from it',[25] we must be careful. Salvation 'happens' in the here and now only because of the event that happened there and then. We dare not make our experience of penitence or of the Spirit central and imply that somehow salvation does not 'happen' until we experience it, lest we fall into the danger of displacing the completed work of Christ from its pre-eminence. Hebrews joins the other New Testament voices in a ringing endorsement that our salvation happened at Calvary and is already accomplished on the cross. We may personally appropriate it now through repentance and faith, but that does not mean that salvation is brought into being in the here and now. Anything we experience of God's grace is because of what he did for us some two thousand years ago. His work there was finished, once and for all.

Through both exposing the weaknesses of the Levitical sacrificial system and establishing the superiority of the sacrifice of Christ, then, Hebrews points out how foolish it would be for believers to turn their backs on Jesus and think they will find a more effective answer to their sin and guilt elsewhere.

5. The cross of Jesus displays a superior high priest (10:11–14)

The argument of Hebrews 10 now shifts its fluid imagery from the

[24] Quoted in P. Yancey, *The Jesus I Never Knew* (Marshall Pickering, 1995), p. 200.
[25] Fiddes, p. 14.

sacrifice that is offered to the priest who offers it. Jesus is both the perfect sacrifice and a superior high priest. The superiority of the priesthood of Jesus has already been set out in 7:1–28 and is only briefly recapitulated here. But, using the same approach, first undermining the value of the old and then establishing the value of the new, the writer once again sets out the key issues in a highly condensed fashion.

a. The ineffective priests of the past

Verse 11 delivers two knock-out punches to the Aaronic priesthood. However valuable its service in the past, and however useful its role in pointing to the superior high priest who was to come, it was ultimately incapable of finally dealing with sin. First, there was the problem of the repetitive nature of their task. *Day after day ... again and again*, they were compelled to offer their sacrifices. It never got them anywhere. They could never claim to have dealt with sin or to have finished their task. What they did today had to be repeated tomorrow. Theirs was a never-ending task. Secondly, there was the problem of the ineffective result of their work. Their endless sacrifices were ultimately futile, for they could *never take away sins*. It dealt with them at one level, but not fundamentally. They pointed forward to the perfect sacrifice that was to come, and their symbolism had value in anticipating the sacrifice of Christ. But only the sacrifice of Christ could *take away sins*. Any value they possessed derived from the sacrifice he was one day to offer.

b. The effective priest of the cross

The writer now switches attention from those priests to *this priest* (12), by whom he means, of course, Jesus. In a couple of verses he rattles off the headline facts about him, assuming that we shall be able to unpack the story in more detail from what he has written earlier, especially about the work of the priest in 4:14 – 5:10 and 7:1 – 8:6. We can allude to this fuller teaching only briefly as we look at these verses.

Who is *this priest*? He is a priest after the order of Melchizedek (7:17), which pre-dated the Aaronic priesthood and was superior to it. Its superiority is easy to prove. First, Abraham, the great patriarch of Israel, humbly received a blessing from Melchizedek and honoured him with his tithe (7:1–2).[26] Secondly, Melchizedek was appointed to the task directly by God and not because of his family connections. He was without 'father or mother, without genealogy, without beginning of days or end of life' (7:3). He has neither predecessors nor successors, and is the only member of the order.[27] Furthermore, his priesthood is eternal and built on 'the power of an indestructible life' (7:16). So there

[26] Gen. 14:18–20.
[27] Lindars, p. 75.

is no need for heirs. Melchizedek prefigures Jesus. All in all, his priesthood demonstrates that Jesus is in a class of his own.

But we may be tempted to think that such a priest could not sympathize with our condition and would be ill-suited to help us sinful and finite human beings. It is evident that he is well qualified to represent God, but is he well qualified to represent us? The writer is careful to balance the magnificent uniqueness of this priest with his sympathetic humanity. He points out that Jesus entered into our humanity and was made 'a little lower than the angels' (2:7, 9), was subjected to the full experience of temptation without giving in to it (4:15), and was exposed to weakness (5:2). His tears in the Garden of Gethsemane, followed by his submissive obedience to God's will, were particularly pertinent (5:7). He was honed and perfected through suffering for the task of priesthood. So from one angle, what qualified him to represent us to God was not his divine status but his proven humanity. In the normal world of leadership, businesses and politicians look to appoint 'successes', people whom they know will show no sign of weakness and will be impervious to suffering. But it is precisely his experience of weakness and suffering that made him fit to be our representative before God.

What did this priest do? Unlike every other priest, this one only ever offered one sacrifice. But it was the sacrifice to end all sacrifices. One sacrifice, if offered by *this priest*, was sufficient to abolish the whole Levitical system at a stroke. The sacrifices of the Old Testament were like batteries with a limited life. Their effect lasted until the next day, until the next sin or, at most, until the next year. The sacrifice Christ offered for sin, however, will never run out. It was 'for all time'. Not only is it definitive and unrepeatable, but it has a remarkable and transforming effect. It succeeds in doing what the sacrificial system never achieved, for through this *one sacrifice he has made perfect for ever those who are being made holy* (14). To be *made perfect* is to enjoy the blessings of the salvation of the new age.[28]

At first sight, it seems that the writer is just repeating the point he made in verse 10. But that is not quite so. There he used a perfect tense to stress the unrepeatable nature of the death of Christ as the means by which people were set apart from God. Here he uses a present participle, in the passive voice, to speak of the ongoing effect of the cross in the lives of God's people.[29] There his point was that Christ's sacrifice conferred a status of 'perfection' on those who availed themselves of it. Here it is that having become the people of God, they are able, in spite of their sin, to have continuous fellowship with him. Their intimacy with God need not be spoiled by post-baptismal sin,

[28] Seifrid, p. 276.
[29] Bruce, *Hebrews*, p. 241.

because the sacrifice of Christ has dealt with sin once for all. It goes without saying that there is no encouragement here for believers to continue in sin,[30] but there is the assurance that sin, when it occurs, has been fully and finally dealt with by Christ. The troubled conscience is silenced by the cross of Christ.

Where is this priest now? Having completed his work on the cross, *he sat down at the right hand of God* (12). Following his death, which was in perfect accordance with the will of God, he is vindicated by God through his resurrection and his exaltation in heaven. Although he continues to exercise his ministry as a priest, interceding for his people, he does not continue to offer sacrifices. That aspect of his work is done. So what is he doing? The writer tells us that *he waits for his enemies to be made his footstool* (13). If he is exalted, why haven't all his enemies immediately been subdued and placed under his feet? Why the wait? The wait, in Chrysostom's words, is 'for the sake of the faithful that would afterward be born'.[31] Christ waits, not because he is powerless to drive his victory through to its logical conclusion, but to prolong the day of grace so that in God's mercy more might turn to him in repentance and benefit from his salvation.

F. F. Bruce summarizes the passage at this point like this:

> Three outstanding effects are thus ascribed to the sacrifice of Christ: by it his people have had their conscience cleansed from guilt; by it they have been fitted to approach God as accepted worshippers; by it they have experienced fulfilment of what was promised in earlier days, being brought into that perfect relation to God which is involved in the new covenant.[32]

It is the covenant on which the writer now focuses.

6. The cross of Jesus creates a new covenant (10:15–18)

The theme of the covenant has already been explored in 8:6–13 and 9:15–22. To take the latter passage first, in 9:15–22 Christ is presented as 'the mediator of a new covenant', and the idea of the covenant is explored with reference to a will. The writer is making use of a play on words, since the one Greek word *diathēkē* means both 'covenant' and 'will'. Building on the metaphor, he points out that a will does not come into force until the person who has written it dies. The new covenant came into existence because Christ died. The writer thus moves from presenting the cross as a sacrifice of atonement, as set out in the

---

[30] The problem Paul addressed in Rom. 6:1–23.
[31] Quoted in Hughes, *Hebrews*, p. 402.
[32] Bruce, *Hebrews*, p. 241.

early chapters of Leviticus, to presenting it as a sacrifice that inaugurates a covenant, as set out in Exodus 24:5–8. The cross performs an indispensable role in the inauguration of the new covenant.

In the earlier passage, 8:6–13, the idea of the new covenant is expounded with reference to Jeremiah's prophecy about it.[33] The old-covenant arrangement had failed because of the people's disobedience, and God, in order to be true to his desire (expressed in that covenant) to redeem a people for himself, sought a new way to fulfil his covenant commitments. So Jeremiah envisaged a new day in which the covenant would bring about a decisive and inward change in God's people, enabling them to fulfil their side of the agreement. Surprisingly, this is a new idea in the New Testament, as Hebrews takes up what others have overlooked. Even those writers who had alluded to the gospel as a new covenant had not related it to the prophecy of Jeremiah.[34]

It is this aspect of the covenant-making work of the cross that the writer returns to briefly in 10:15–18. Previously he had quoted the whole of Jeremiah's vision of the new covenant (8:8–12). Now, by way of a reminder, he quotes only selected extracts. But they are carefully chosen to highlight the crucial issues. The new covenant brings about an inward change in people's lives. *'I will put my laws in their hearts, and I will write them on their minds'* (16). It is no longer a question of superficial, even grudging, obedience to an external law. Because the new covenant has worked an inner transformation in people's wills, obedience is now a matter of willing and voluntary submission to God's law. If the cross brought about an inward change, it also brought about a decisive change. *'Their sins and their lawless acts I will remember no more'* (17). The cross has dealt with them. They are forgiven. There is, then, no need for the sensitive conscience to be dragging them up again and again as if they continued to matter. Still less is there any need to offer further sacrifices for sin. The one offered has done all that was needed. Any more would not only be superfluous but, being nothing more than a cheap imitation of the real thing, would be an insult to the cross of Christ.

The cross, then, not only atones for past sins but initiates a new covenant. The atonement focuses on the past; the new covenant 'inaugurates a permanent arrangement for the future'.[35] As a sacrifice of atonement, the cross brings us into a state of forgiveness before God. As a sacrifice of covenant, it keeps us in a place of relationship with God.

The cross is central throughout the letter to Hebrews, and especially to its major themes of sacrifice, priesthood and covenant. Viewed from these perspectives it shows the crucified Christ to be an effective

[33] Jer. 31:31–34.
[34] Lane, *Hebrews*, pp. cxxxii–cxxxiii.
[35] Lindars, p. 95.

sacrifice which abolishes the need for any other sacrifice, a superior high priest who eclipses all priestly predecessors, and the initiator of a new covenant that surpasses all other covenants. Jesus, 'the apostle and high priest whom we confess' (3:1), is quite simply 'better' than any other. And the cross has made it so.

In the verses that follow 10:18, the author drives home the practical and pastoral implications of his teaching. If the cross has indeed accomplished all that he has claimed, believers can draw near to God with confidence (10:19–22), hold on to faith with determination (10:23), and encourage each other in hope (10:24–25). There can be neither reason nor excuse for going back on following Jesus.

1 Peter 1:2, 18–21; 2:13–25; 3:18–22
16. To this you were called

The apostle Peter's reflections on the cross of Christ are of special interest. No New Testament writer had a closer or more painful involvement with Christ's passion than he. And since he was the chief apostle of the early church, it is especially important to see what prominence and meaning he gives it.

In Leon Morris's view, 'For a short writing, 1 Peter has an astonishing amount to say about the atonement. Most of the Epistle bears on the problem in one way or another, for Peter is concerned throughout with the salvation that God has wrought in Christ.'[1] The cross is indeed central in the letter, and Peter's approach to it is noteworthy. References to it are scattered throughout the letter and, says James Denney, 'are all the more impressive because of the apparently incidental manner in which they present themselves to us'.[2] Unlike Paul, Peter does not discuss a complex theology of the atonement or elaborate any great apologetic scheme for it. To Peter, the message of the cross 'is not a theorem he is prepared to defend; it is a gospel he has to preach'.[3]

Peter writes as a simple pastor to encourage a group of Christians under attack for their faith. He reminds them of truths they already know but are not applying to their situation. He encourages them not only to look to Christ for help but also to imitate his example, especially in their suffering. To Peter, the cross forms the framework of our Christian discipleship; it is the chassis on which the whole vehicle of the Christian faith rests and which gives shape to our whole Christian experience. The cross is at the centre of the Christian's calling.

The letter shows that Peter is 'held and fascinated by the cross'.[4] He returns to it frequently and reflects on it deeply. He sets out not only its

[1] Morris, *Cross in the New Testament*, p. 316.
[2] Denney, p. 63.
[3] Ibid., p. 60.
[4] Ibid., p. 58.

exemplary role but its redemptive significance. His language is unusual and carefully selected to suit his ends. He speaks not of the cross, or of the crucifixion, but of *the sprinkling by his blood* (1:2), of the blood of *a lamb without blemish* (1:19), of Christ's suffering *on the tree*, of *his wounds* (2:24), and of his being *put to death in the body* (3:18). It is on the total passion of Christ that he meditates, with a view to making his readers more fully aware of their calling in Christ.

It is not true to say, as some have done, that there is little theology in Peter's letter. There is profound pastoral theology here which connects with the real-life experience of his readers. From a sound theological basis he shows them how they ought to conduct themselves. He does not leave theology behind as he addresses their problems, but approaches them from the standpoint of the cross, of which he speaks in the opening greeting and then on three other occasions within the letter (as noted above). All in all, he gives us a very wide-ranging picture of Christ's person and of his work on the cross.

1. The cross cements covenant loyalties (1:2)

Immediately after the customary opening, which records the writer's name, Peter identifies his readers and describes them in terms of the wonderful trinitarian blessing that has come into their lives. They have been chosen by the Father and set apart by the Spirit *for obedience to Jesus Christ and the sprinkling by his blood*. Right at the start, then, the cross is uppermost in his thinking.

His choice of vocabulary, however, is interesting. *Blood* witnesses to the fact that Christ's death was violent. At the same time, it opens a window on to the vista of the Jewish sacrificial system, where the shedding and manipulation of blood played such a significant part. One of three different facets of the blood rituals might have been in Peter's mind.

First, Peter may have been thinking of the role of sprinkling in purification. People with infectious skin diseases, once healed, had to undergo blood cleansing before being readmitted to the community.[5] Those who had defiled themselves by contact with a corpse had to be cleansed by a mixture of ashes and water that was sprinkled on them.[6] Furthermore, in the sacrificial rituals, the primary purpose of sprinkling blood on the altar, curtain or mercy seat was to enable sinful, 'unclean' people to approach their holy and pure God.[7] If this is the background to Peter's thought,[8] he is saying that his readers have been purified from

[5] Lev. 14:6–7.
[6] Num. 19:1–22.
[7] Lev. 1:5, 11; 3:2, 8, 13; 4:6, 17; 5:9; 16:14, 15, 19; 17:6.
[8] See Michaels, *1 Peter*, p. 12.

uncleanness by Christ's death and now have access into the very presence of the living God for themselves.

Secondly, blood was sprinkled on Aaron and his sons during their consecration as priests of the Lord.[9] If this was what Peter was thinking of, he would have been telling his readers that they too had been set aside to be priests and consecrated to serve God. This certainly fits with the other half of the phrase, which speaks of their being called *for obedience*, and it would anticipate his development of the theme of the church as a royal priesthood in 2:9.

The problem with both these interpretations, however, is that they would refer simply to the beginning of the Christian life, whereas Peter mentions the sprinkling of blood after talking about the sanctifying work of the Spirit, thus seeming to imply that he has the ongoing nature of the Christian life in view.[10]

A third Old Testament use of sprinkled blood provides us with the most likely background for what Peter means here. The phrase recalls the scene at Sinai when God entered into a covenant with Israel.[11] Edmund Clowney reminds us that

> At an altar of twelve pillars, sacrifice was offered. Half of the blood was sprinkled on the altar. Moses read again the words of God's covenant, and the people vowed their obedience. Moses sprinkled the people with the rest of the sacrificial blood, saying, 'This is the blood of the covenant that the LORD has made with you in accordance with all these words.'[12]

At Sinai, God and Israel entered into mutual obligations – he to be their God and they to be his people and obey his law – through a covenant sealed with blood. When Moses descended from the mountain and spoke to the people, their response was, 'Everything the LORD has said we will do.'[13] Since the note of obedience is closely associated with the sprinkling of blood in Peter's greeting, it is almost certainly this picture that he intends to borrow.

Peter tells the scattered believers, whose experience leads them to feel like strangers and exiles in the world, that they are, in reality, God's own covenant people. They are the ones who have entered into the new covenant envisaged by the prophet Jeremiah[14] and are members of the new people of God. This covenant brings into being a radically

[9] Exod. 29:21.
[10] Grudem, p. 53.
[11] Exod. 24:8.
[12] Clowney, p. 35, quoting Exod. 24:8.
[13] Exod. 24:3.
[14] Jer. 31:31–34.

different form of community, even though obedience is still high on the agenda. But they are no longer preoccupied with the observance of external legalities. Instead, they enjoy the privilege of an inner compulsion to please their God. The experience of his grace puts them in a radically different camp from that of religious legalists. It makes them secure in a world falling apart, and hopeful in a world rapidly descending into despair.

Like the covenant of old, this covenant relationship has been entered through the sprinkling of blood. On this occasion, though, the blood was not that of an animal but of a person. It is the cross of Jesus that has brought the covenant into being and made possible the inclusion of these Gentile readers. The sprinkled blood of Christ confirms the new-covenant agreement and its obligations.

2. The cross achieves effective redemption (1:18–21)

Peter's readers are engaged in a bitter struggle for their faith. Their neighbours are attacking them with 'a barrage of verbal abuse designed to shame, defame, demean, and discredit [them] as social and moral deviants endangering the common good'.[15] In the face of this opposition, it would not have been surprising if some had wanted to give up and return to a more comfortable, less controversial relationship with their neighbours. Peter encourages them not to give in to such pressures, but rather to *prepare* their *minds for action*, to *be self-controlled* and to *set* their *hope fully on* the goal of their faith, namely, *the grace* they will receive *when Jesus Christ is revealed*. They must strive to be *obedient* and continually to progress towards perfection. Whatever they might suffer on this earth will be worth it. Rather than fearing fellow human beings, they should show *reverent fear* of God, who is, in fact, their real judge.

His primary incentive for them as they continue on the path of holiness, however, is not fear but gratitude. He invites them to remind themselves of what God has done for them through Christ's death and to contemplate the value of the price he paid for their redemption. Within the space of a few concentrated sentences, Peter outlines a concise theology of redemption.

a. The fact of redemption

Redemption is an accomplished fact: *you were redeemed* (18). In our day, 'redemption' has become 'an impersonal term, used of the exchange of coupons for goods, the recovery of items from the pawnshop

---

[15] J. H. Elliott, 'Disgraced yet graced: the gospel according to 1 Peter in the key of honour and shame', *Biblical Theology Bulletin* 25 (1995), p. 173.

and the like'.[16] It was anything but impersonal in Peter's day, however. It was a vivid, as well as appropriate, metaphor for salvation in both the Jewish and Roman worlds. The Jewish law made provision for the redemption of the firstborn and of other people or possessions dedicated to the LORD.[17] It also provided for those who had fallen into poverty or slavery to be redeemed by their nearest male relative.[18] This wonderful concept of the kinsman-redeemer (gō'ēl) is beautifully illustrated in the story of Ruth, for whom Boaz assumes responsibility after she had been set adrift through bereavement, without any means of support.[19] In the Roman world, slaves could purchase their freedom with a ransom price deposited in the temple as a theoretical payment to the gods. In theory, the manumitted slave would then become the property of the gods, while in practice he would be free in relation to society.[20] Isaiah had pictured God as the Redeemer of Israel.[21] Now Peter says that God fulfilled his role for his readers through the payment of his Son's life as the ransom price.

b. The need for redemption

What was it that held us captive and from which we needed to be freed? Peter answers in a somewhat surprising way. He tells us we have been redeemed, not from sin, but rather from *the empty way of life handed down to you from your ancestors*. 'Futility' was the verdict the prophets passed on the way of life of those who worshipped impotent idols instead of the living God.[22] Thirteen times in the first two chapters alone, the Septuagint translation of Ecclesiastes uses the same Greek word (*mataios*) as Peter does to describe the emptiness, meaninglessness and banality of life. Paul too dismisses Gentile thinking outside Christ as futile.[23] Peter's concept of futility, then, refers primarily to the ancestral worship of idols his readers used to practise, and encompasses the whole style of life, including the ethical value systems, customs and culture, associated with it.[24] Christ has released them not only from the power and penalty of sin but from the burden of serving worthless idols as well.

Idolatry robs modern men and women of their freedom as much as it robbed the inhabitants of the ancient world, albeit in a less simplistic and obvious way. Almost fifty years ago, Joy Davidman commented:

---

16 Marshall, *1 Peter*, p. 56.
17 Exod. 13:13; Lev. 27:1–25.
18 Lev. 25:25, 47–53.
19 Ruth 4:1–12.
20 Michaels, *1 Peter*, p. 64.
21 Is. 41:14; 43:14; 44:24; 47:4; 48:17; 49:7, 26; 54:5–6; 60:16.
22 E.g. Jer. 2:5; 8:19; 16:19.
23 Eph. 4:17.
24 Morris, *Cross of Jesus*, p. 41.

'The house devours the housewife, the office rots the executive with ulcers, and canned entertainments leave us incapable of entertaining ourselves. Have our idols done us no harm?'[25] That sounds quaint now. But though the form of idolatry has changed, the problem itself shows no sign of abating. One has only to read psychologist Oliver James's book *Britain on the Couch*.[26] He asks how it can be that although the British are so much wealthier than they were a few decades ago, they are so much less happy, as evidenced by the massive rise in the incidence of depression. Similarly, Jonathan Glover's 'moral history of the twentieth century', entitled *Humanity*,[27] details the litany of cruelty and nationalism to which the world was subjected during those decades. Such facts make us realize that idols are still alive and well, and being worshipped by contemporary human beings. For many, the latest version of idolatry comes in the shape of the computer. But it comes in no single form. Evidence of its power still to subject people to lives of futility is seen wherever one looks.

The cross of Christ releases us from the prison of futility and introduces us to the God and Father of the one who is the origin, purpose and goal of the whole of creation, as well as of our existence.[28] In Christ, God releases us to enjoy our full inheritance. As Edmund Clowney says: 'In contrast with the empty life of "hollow men", Christians are given faith and hope in God. Meaninglessness evaporates in the glory of ultimate meaning: the eternal plan and purpose of God.'[29]

c. The cost of redemption

A ransom demand means that a price must be paid to enable the transaction to occur. It is extraordinary how little emphasis the Old Testament usually places on the value of the ransom.[30] In Isaiah 52:3, for example, God tells Israel that they will be ransomed from the exile 'without money'. Peter emphatically reverses this trend of indifference to the price. His focus is on the value of the sacrifice that has secured our redemption. His fundamental point is that the cost of our freedom was so great that we dare not throw it away, no matter how hard the going may sometimes be for the disciples of Christ. *It was not with perishable things such as silver and gold*[31] *that you were redeemed*, he writes, … *but with the precious blood of Christ, a lamb without blemish or defect* (18–19).

Several strands of thought are woven together here. Peter draws on

---

[25] Quoted in ibid., p. 38.
[26] Published by Century, 1997.
[27] Published by Jonathan Cape, 1999.
[28] Col. 1:15–20.
[29] Clowney, p. 72.
[30] Michaels, *1 Peter*, p. 63.
[31] Cf. Acts 3:6.

the image of the Passover lamb from Exodus 12:5, and more widely on the repeated references to the need for the sacrificial lamb to be perfect[32] if it was to prove acceptable to God. Perhaps with a hint of Isaiah 53 thrown in too, Peter says that Christ led a sinless and unblemished life when he was sacrificed to God as the ransom price that secured our release.

A slave would have saved for years to scrape together the ransom price. God has far exceeded any price sinners could possibly have afforded, and he had been working towards it since *before the creation of the world* (20). This was no cheap, last-minute arrangement, cobbled together by God without real cost, almost as an afterthought. This ransom was the most costly and the most perfect; it was planned before time and offered in history during the governorship of Pontius Pilate, and is effective for all men and women, before or since, who avail themselves of its benefit through faith.

Peter's reflections must have been shaped by the memorable words that fell from the lips of Jesus during their time together: 'For even the Son of Man did not come to be served but to serve, and to give his life as a ransom for many.'[33] If he failed to understand Jesus' meaning at the time, now, after the cross and resurrection, it had become clear. Jesus was the ransom price who alone could release people from their slavery, something that had proved impossible by human means.

d. The effect of redemption

The fact that, after his crucifixion, Jesus was both raised and glorified, leaves us in no doubt that the ransom price God provided was sufficient. The power of his life burst the chains that sought to bind him in death and that subjected us to futility without any possibility of escape. Consequently, we believers are now a people of hope, not meandering through a senseless wasteland, but journeying through this world with a sense of direction and destiny. We have faith and hope in a God who showed evidence of his power and trustworthiness in an empty tomb. Here is confidence that should enable us to endure hostility as we go on our pilgrim way and head towards the goal: the day when we shall be set free fully and for ever.

e. The purpose of redemption

In the meantime there is work to be done here. The purpose of our redemption is to release us to live a holy life. That is one of the great themes of Peter's letter. He writes about holiness on several levels, presenting it as a matter of personal character, of social behaviour and of community relationships. Here his emphasis is on holiness of char-

---

[32] Cf. e.g. Num. 6:14; 28:3, 9.
[33] Mark 10:45.

acter. Having experienced the purifying effect of Christ's blood through coming to obey the truth of the gospel, we now need to bear the fruit of redemption in our sincere love for one another (22).

Redemption is not designed for our personal convenience. Having had the penalty of our personal sin paid and having been set free from the prison of futility, we are not meant to indulge ourselves by a self-centred lifestyle. Our obedience to Christ must continue to express itself far beyond our initial response to the gospel. It continues as we move from self-directed to other-directed living and begin to serve others in practical, loving ways.

The cross redeems us in order to transform us, so that we live a life that will inevitably run counter to the wider society around us. When Peter returns to the theme of Christ's suffering, he again sets before his readers the same balance of teaching: wonderful grace flows from Calvary, but it causes us to handle life's circumstances and to react to its injustices in a totally counter-cultural way.

3. The cross models Christian discipleship (2:21–25)

Suffering hovers over 1 Peter. His readers are plagued by it. They are accused of doing wrong; they are insulted, maliciously slandered and considered deviant; and they find themselves on the receiving end of evil (2:12; 3:9, 16; 4:4). In a closely knit society, whose values revolved around honour and shame, their faith had cost them dear. How were they to handle this unjust situation?

Peter responds by first addressing the slaves (18), who, being treated as property rather than considered to have any rights as persons, would have borne the brunt of the opposition. But his focus soon takes in others and, by verse 24, he has moved from addressing 'you' to drawing out the implications of Christ's dying for 'us'.

a. The pattern of Christ's suffering

Peter takes it as axiomatic that their suffering is undeserved and unjust, He has no truck with those who suffer because they have done wrong (16, 19–20). It is not suffering in general that concerns him, but the prejudiced and unwarranted opposition they face because of their Christian faith. Nor is he discussing injustice in society generally and what steps Christians might appropriately take to correct it on behalf of others.[34] He is talking about unjust suffering that arises when followers of Christ are genuine about their discipleship. Such disciples are never going to be popular.

When they encounter that kind of injustice, he tells them, they have a particular calling to fulfil: to follow in Christ's footsteps (21). We

[34] See Marshall, *1 Peter*, pp. 87–98.

must be careful how we apply this. It is easy to think Peter means that the calling of every Christian is to suffer, and many take his words that way. But what he is really saying is that *when* suffering comes, *then* we must bear it with patience. 'When he says that they were called to *this*,' explains Howard Marshall, 'he means that they were called to the *patient* endurance of suffering.'[35] Peter's point is that they are not to respond to it as others might – with anger, by retaliating in like manner, by taking political action, with stoic resignation or by turning inwards in depression – but by accepting it in the same way as Christ himself did.

It is Christ's suffering that provides the model for Christians who suffer unjustly, and the incentive to bear it in this extraordinary way without retaliation. John Elliott compares Peter's exhortation with some advice given by the philosopher Plutarch. In his essay on *How to Profit by One's Enemies* he urges: 'If you wish to distress the man who hates you, do not insult him as lewd, effeminate, licentious, vulgar, or illiberal, but be a man yourself, show self-control, be truthful and treat with kindness and justice those who have to deal with you.'[36] But the comparison is unsatisfactory, as Elliott knows, for Peter is not offering a piece of general wisdom but giving them Christological motivation for bearing suffering with patience. And although Plutarch offered the advice, Christ lived it through bearing ultimate suffering himself. It is Christ who makes the difference to the way we handle our own suffering

Earlier in his letter, Peter's camera, as it were, captured Christ as the unblemished Passover lamb (1:19). Now he captures him as the suffering servant, using the words of Isaiah 53 as his filter. Christ is the flawless and faultless lamb who goes on his way to death. Each verse in the passage 2:22–25 is dependent on Isaiah 53. Verse 22 quotes Isaiah 53:9; verse 23 alludes to Isaiah 53:7; verse 24 includes words and phrases drawn unmistakably from Isaiah 53:4, 5 and 12; while verse 25 echoes Isaiah 53:6.[37]

Although he clearly reminisces about what happened at Calvary, Peter says nothing about the actual events. To have done so might have got in the way. He wants to get behind the events to highlight something of their relevance and significance for a suffering church. What he recalls most is Christ's uncomplaining, non-retaliatory acceptance of the injustice going on around him. When insulted, he was silent; when accused, he accepted it; when threatened, he submitted. It was not passive stoicism on Jesus' part. Rather, his reaction was a perfect model of active submission and trust. He had no need to fight back and

[35] Ibid., p. 92.
[36] Elliott, 'Disgraced yet graced', p. 171.
[37] Grudem, p. 129.

demand immediate justice, for *he entrusted himself to him who judges justly* (23). Peter's memory of Christ's passion is similar to Luke's account of it. Jesus was a trusting Son confident that vindication would follow. Therefore, in these most testing of all circumstances, Christ was able to put into practice his own teaching: he blessed those who cursed him and prayed for those who mistreated him.[38]

The passion of Christ, then, serves as a model for all believers who suffer for their faith. In this respect Jesus is to be their *example* (21). This word, *hypogrammon*, is used only here in the New Testament, but elsewhere it is applied to the way children copy letters as they learn to write the alphabet. Just as they carefully copy the writing set before them, so disciples must exercise the same care in imitating the example of Christ. If we do so, although the way may not be easy, we shall bear the suffering, trusting in God and believing that he will unquestionably avenge wrong and repay evildoers in his own good time.[39] Refusing to retaliate breaks the cycle of evil and overcomes evil with good.

b. The purpose of Christ's death

It is right to view Christ's passion as an example. But Peter is not content to leave it there. As he unfolds the exemplary model of Christ's passion, he cannot but simultaneously unfold its saving and redemptive significance as well. Howard Marshall aptly quotes James Denney's statement at this point in his commentary:

> It is as though the apostle could not turn his eyes to the cross for a moment without being fascinated and held by it. He saw more in it habitually, and he saw far more in it now than was needed to point his exhortation to wronged slaves. Is is not *their* interest in it, as the supreme example of suffering innocence and patience, but the interest of all sinners in it as the only source of redemption by which he is ultimately inspired.[40]

As Peter contemplates the suffering of Christ, he sees four further aspects of its purpose.

First, Christ died to bear our sins (24). Although Peter is alluding specifically to Isaiah 53:4 and 12 here, a wider Old Testament background is in view. This phraseology was a common way of saying that those who sinned must pay the price for it. It was in these terms that the children of Israel were sentenced to forty years in the wilderness because of their grumbling.[41] This is what Jeremiah and Ezekiel meant

---

[38] Luke 6:28.
[39] Rom. 12:19–21.
[40] Marshall, *1 Peter*, p. 91, quoting Denney, p. 57.
[41] Num. 14:33–35.

when they spoke of each individual's bearing the responsibility for his or her own sins, rather than passing on their consequences to others.[42] But in the mercy of God, under the new covenant, it is the suffering servant who bore the burden and consequences of sin in his own body and removes them far away from repentant sinners. This is possible only because in him a perfect substitute was found; being flawless, he had no sins of his own and no consequences to bear.

Peter speaks of Christ's death in an unusual manner, for he says Christ *bore our sins in his body on the tree* (24). Why *tree?* There were many other ways Peter could have chosen to speak of the crucifixion, and he does not choose the obvious word for 'cross' (*stauros*). His choice of 'tree' (*xylon*, wood, or an object made from wood) seems calculated to remind people of Deuteronomy 21:23. That verse speaks of hanging a body on a tree as a judicial punishment, and explains that 'anyone who is hung on a tree is under God's curse'. It is probably a deliberate reminder that, in bearing our sin when he died, Jesus suffered God's curse as a judgment on it.

His passion, then, is not only exemplary but redemptive.

Secondly, Christ died to renew our lives (24). He died *so that we might die to sins and live for righteousness*. The remission of our sins must lead to the renewing of our lives. In a classical Pauline way,[43] Peter explains that Christ's death is designed to accomplish more than the forgiveness of our wrongs. Through it we are joined with Christ and obligated to him to bear the fruit of righteousness.[44] Forgiveness must lead to a definitive reorientation of our lives away from sin towards living in a way that is right before God and others. His death is no 'cheap grace', which permits us to continue in sin because 'of course' we shall be forgiven. If we have understood the cost of his substitution for us, James Denney says, we shall see that it 'involves an immeasurable obligation to Christ and has therefore incalculable motivating power'.[45] We shall no longer want to sin.

Thirdly, Christ died to heal our wounds (24).[46] Sin brings a multitude of ills in its train, including pain and suffering, but his death secures a comprehensive cure for them all. The wounds inflicted on Christ lift our burdens and heal our wounds. We gain in direct proportion to his loss. 'Here, as Theodore said, is "a new and strange method of healing; the doctor suffered the cost, and the sick received the healing."'[47]

---

[42] Jer. 18:30; Ezek. 18:20.
[43] Cf. Rom. 6:1–23.
[44] Rom. 7:4.
[45] Denney, p. 60.
[46] We explored the implications of this statement when we looked at it in its original setting (Is. 53:5). See above, p. 116.
[47] Stibbs, *1 Peter*, p. 121.

Fourthly, Christ died to restore our relationship with God (25). Sheep have a tendency to stray. They wander off, oblivious to the dangers they face and indifferent to their need for guidance and protection from the shepherd. Human beings are exactly the same in relation to God. But through the cross, Christ seeks out the lost and brings them back home, restoring them to himself so that he may function as *the Shepherd and Overseer of* their *souls*. In him we recover our direction in life and are reconciled in our relationship with God.

In refusing to choose between Christ's death as exemplary and Christ's death as atoning, Peter achieves a balance that has eluded many subsequent generations of disciples. J. Ramsey Michaels notes:

1 Peter cuts through all the modern debates over whether the cross of Christ is an example of self-giving love or a divinely appointed means of reconciliation and redemption. Without question, it is both in this letter – with the two aspects not in tension. Each, in fact, requires the other. Christians can put sin behind them and follow in Jesus' footsteps because they have been redeemed by his death. Discipleship, therefore, demands more than a passive acceptance of the saving benefits of that death. It is nothing less than active participation in Jesus' death and all that led up to it.[48]

c. The appeal of Christ's death

We return, however, to the theme of Christ's passion and death as the model for believers, because evangelicals often understate it in their concern to champion the redemptive significance of the cross. *To this you were called, because Christ suffered for you, leaving you an example, that you should follow in his steps* (21). The example of Jesus is not just there to be envied – still less merely to be noted – but to be imitated. As his disciples, we share in his calling and we must walk in his footsteps, responding in the way he did to the injustices we suffer for his sake.

Martin Hengel has explored the nature of discipleship at the time of Peter's letter. Being a true disciple and following a master is, he says, 'in the first place unconditional sharing of the master's destiny, which does not stop even at deprivation and suffering in the train of the master, and is possible only on the basis of complete trust on the part of the person who follows; he has placed his destiny and his future in his master's hands'.[49] As disciples of Jesus we must follow where he leads and we should not be surprised if we arrive at a cross at some time or

---

[48] J. R. Michaels, 'Going to Heaven with Jesus: 1 Peter', in R. W. Longenecker (ed.), *Patterns of Discipleship in the New Testament* (Eerdmans, 1996), pp. 255–256.
[49] Hengel, *The Charismatic Leader and his Followers* (1968; ET T. and T. Clark, 1981), p. 72.

another. When we do, we must embrace it with the same willing submission that he had, knowing that it is through suffering that freedom comes, and through embracing injustice that evil will be defeated and good will one day triumph.

4. The cross proclaims total victory (3:18–22)

Peter returns to the cross of Christ once more in his letter, this time to rejoice in the total victory it has accomplished over all opposition to God.

a. The finality of Christ's death

Sounding a bit like the author of Hebrews,[50] Peter affirms that *Christ died for sins once for all* (18). His death, unlike the sacrifices offered by the priests of old, was a sufficient and a complete work of atonement. He has no need ever to die again, let alone repeatedly. 'Christ's suffering is over, its purpose fully accomplished,' comments Ramsey Michaels.[51]

Christ's death brought about a remarkable exchange, depicted by Peter's series of contrasts. Christ, the *righteous* one, stood in the place of the *unrighteous*, so that those who were far away from God might be brought near. He was *put to death* and then *made alive*. The former took place *in the body*, the latter *by the Spirit* (18).[52] The former occurred at the hands of men, and the latter by the powerful action of God. Polar opposites, then, are brought together, their tensions resolved by Christ's cross. Sinful people are reconciled to a holy God. Alienated people are brought into the presence of a reconciling God. The actions of wicked people who put Christ to death are transformed into the gracious actions of a God who intended the event to happen in order to save us. Death is overcome by irrepressible life. And the physical body, destined to perish, is replaced by an imperishable resurrection body that will live eternally. The cross bridges the gap between a righteous God and a sinful creation, once and for all.

b. The finality of Christ's victory

Peter is unable to separate Christ's suffering from his resurrection. They are both part of the one atoning act of God. Having introduced the

---

[50] Heb. 9:26, 28.

[51] Michaels, *1 Peter*, p. 202.

[52] Care is needed in contrasting the physical and the spiritual at this point. It is not a human flesh versus a human spirit that is being referred to, but a feeble body versus the powerful Spirit of God. The contrast is not between death in a physical body followed by the resurrection of the soul, but between the death of a physical body and the resurrection of a spiritual body. Christ rose with a new type of body through the powerful action of the Holy Spirit. Cf. 1 Cor. 15:42ff. See Michaels, *1 Peter*, p. 203–205.

thought of the resurrection, he now explores it more fully and draws out its pastoral implications for his readers. Unfortunately for us, he does so in some of the most difficult verses in the New Testament. His tortuous logic takes him from the resurrection to Christ's preaching to *spirits in prison* (19), who had been serving their sentences since the days of *Noah*, when they committed their offence (20). The thought of Noah takes him off on a new tack, or rather a couple of new tacks. In the ark only *eight ... were saved*; the rest were drowned in *water* (20). So the very water that drowned the many was the vehicle of salvation for the few who took shelter in the ark. Salvation, then, is the obverse side of judgment.

The mention of water reminds him of the water of *baptism*. Baptism still *saves* us (21) – not the physical washing, but what it signifies. It is *the pledge of a good conscience towards God* (21). Peter might mean that in baptism we promise that from now on we will live with a clear conscience in God's sight. Alternatively, since the word *pledge* (*eperōtēma*) can also mean 'request', he might be saying that in baptism we request God's forgiveness and his cleansing of our consciences.[53]

Having taken that meandering path, Peter finally reconnects with his starting-point. The risen Christ is now exalted at the right hand of God and reigns supreme over all the authorities and powers of the universe. That is, of course, precisely the point that Peter is making. To his readers, other authorities seem all too real and their power all too strong as they oppose the faith of Christ. But, in reality, Christ is the one who has conquered them. That is why he includes in his exposition the idea of Christ's preaching to the spirits in prison. Verses 19–20 are capable of a number of different interpretations, depending on what we decide about when Christ undertook his mission, to whom he preached, what he said, and where he went. The three main interpretations go like this.[54] The first says that Christ went and preached to the spirits of those who had been disobedient in Noah's day, either to announce his victory to them or to give them another chance of repentance. The second interpretation maintains that Christ entered into Noah and preached to the people of his day when the ark was being built, but they refused to listen to him. Or thirdly, Peter might mean that Christ visited the disobedient supernatural powers, imprisoned either down in Hades or up in heaven, to proclaim his resurrection and final victory over them and all other evil powers.

R. T. France's careful discussion of the verses leads him to adopt a version of the third view.[55] Peter says Christ's journey took place

---

[53] See Marshall, *1 Peter*, p. 131.

[54] Marshall, *1 Peter*, pp. 122–132, contains a very good and accessible introduction to the exegesis and the various interpretations of this passage.

[55] R. T. France, 'Exegesis in practice: two examples', in I. H. Marshall (ed.), *New*

through the Spirit, whom he has just mentioned as the agent of Christ's resurrection. It is logical, then, to understand that the journey took place after the resurrection *en route* to his exaltation in heaven – not between his death and resurrection, as some have understood it. Who was it to whom Christ preached? He preached to the disobedient *spirits* of Noah's day. This could refer to the departed spirits of those people who had caused God such grief in Noah's day, but is more likely to refer to the fallen angels of Genesis 6:1–4, who provoked human beings to sin at that time. The word *spirits* would usually mean supernatural beings of the sort Jesus frequently encountered during his ministry. Elsewhere we are told that they had been kept *in prison* awaiting final judgment.[56]

Where did this encounter take place? Peter actually gives us no indication. The Greek (*poreutheis*) simply tells us that *he went* (19). It does not tell us the direction he took. It may have been 'down' to Hades, the dwelling-place of the dead, as traditionally understood; but the text does not demand it. It might just as easily have been up to heaven, where, in one of the several layers of heaven in which the Jews believed, the evil spirits were held captive to await their fate. If this took place after the resurrection, as seems most probable, it makes more sense to think in terms of Christ going 'up' to the prison of disobedient spirits.

What did Jesus preach to them? There is no evidence that he preached a gospel of a second chance. Given the context of Peter's argument, one wonders what would be the point of his including it here if that was his message. Both the wider context of Scripture and the context of Peter's letter suggest rather that what Christ proclaimed was his victory over all the powers that stood in opposition to him. The resurrection proved that all his enemies had been routed. As R. T. France points out:

> And this was a theme of real practical importance to Peter's readers. They might be called to endure the worst that anti-Christian prejudice could inflict. But even then they could be assured that their pagan opponents, and, more important, the spiritual powers of evil that stood behind them and directed them, were not outside Christ's control; they were already defeated, awaiting final punishment.[57]

So Peter's final comments about the cross end on a note of victory.

Testament Interpretation: Essays in Principles and Methods (Paternoster, 1977), pp. 264–278. The view is also adopted by Michaels, *1 Peter*, pp. 205–220. See Grudem, pp. 157–162, for an alternative view.

[56] 2 Pet. 2:4; Jude 6.
[57] France, 'Exegesis in practice', p. 272.

The cross has conquered all who stand in opposition to God, including the very people who are making life difficult for his readers. Once more, in Peter's hands the cross proves to be good news, not just of salvation but of victory.

Two things stand out about Peter's treatment of the cross of Christ. First, he approaches it in a way that is perfectly consistent with the wider understanding of Scripture. He says nothing that is not to be found elsewhere. Indeed, he masterfully uses several images from the Old Testament sacrificial system to help his readers get a clear view of the meaning of Christ's suffering. And what he says resonates with the teaching of other New Testament writers too. Secondly, however, in his hands those old messages have a startling freshness about them. Like a skilled craftsman he takes what is familiar and shapes and polishes it until it looks quite new. In doing so, he exactly meets the practical and pastoral needs of his readers.

According to Peter, through his cross the suffering Christ became our covenant-maker, leading us to obedience; our ransom-provider, leading us to freedom; our sin-bearer, leading us to forgiveness; our supreme example, leading us to endurance; and our exalted Lord, leading us to victory.

1 John 4:7–14
17. God is love

For a man known for preaching love, the writer of 1 John has some remarkably sharp and uncompromising things to say about those who were leading the church into error. Three times he denounces them as 'liars' (2:4, 22; 4:20) and three times he attributes their ideas to the antichrist (2:18, 22; 4:3). Their teaching must have been seriously adrift to provoke such a reaction. Their error lay in their denial that God was incarnate in Christ. To them, flesh was evil, and it was inconceivable that God should enter in human form into our material world. Accordingly, they taught that Jesus was not really a human being but only *seemed* to be one; his human body was an illusion.

John rightly saw this as a heresy with the potential to undermine both vital Christian truth and genuine Christian living. If Christ has not come in the flesh (4:2), 'the reality of Christ's incarnation, atoning death and bodily resurrection'[1] must be called into question and we are left very uncertain as to what, if anything, God has done through him. We would certainly not be able to 'know'[2] God, or that we are his children and have received eternal life. Furthermore, 'false teaching always leads to false living',[3] and throughout his letter John is concerned with the practical outworking of the truth in his readers' lives.

John counters the false teaching by reminding them of his own eye-witness experience of the life of Christ (1:1–3). Others may be content with some inner illumination or secret revelation of divinity. Not John. The God he knows is the God who made himself known in the flesh-and-blood reality of the life and death of Jesus of Nazareth, and who did so openly for all to see. Knowing this God is not a matter of our subjective deduction, but of responding to his objective revelation in the person of Jesus. A crucial and indispensable piece of that revelation was given in the cross.

[1] Jackman, p. 15.
[2] *Know* is one of John's most frequent words; the Greek *ginōskō* occurs twenty-five times and the verb *oida* occurs sixteen times in his three letters.
[3] Jackman, p.15.

Finding one's way through John's first letter is difficult, for his approach is 'meditative and circular rather than argumentative and linear'.[4] Some struggle to see clear, logical pattern to his thinking, and regard it as a series of paragraphs connected by an association of ideas rather than by any analytical arrangement.[5] Many, however, see its argument as circular or, more particularly, 'in the form of a spiral, the same ideas being repeated several times at ever higher levels of discussion'.[6] This means that the death of Christ is mentioned not just at one point in the letter, but several times – in fact, no fewer than seventeen verses reproduce nine separate ideas about the cross,[7] using a variety of language – the language of blood, of sacrifice and of love.[8] Among those references, the passage 4:7–12, which we examine here, is arguably the fullest.

1. The cross reveals God's love

For John, the cross of Jesus supremely reveals the love of God for sinful humanity. In spite of his sharp condemnation of false teachers, it is the note of love, not of accusation, that dominates his letter. And the cross is the highest manifestation of God's love.

a. Who God is

This little letter contains two great statements that help us to penetrate the mystery of God's awesome and divine being. Early on, we read that 'God is light' (1:5). Later, we read that 'God is love' (4:8). This is the most profound revelation about the character of God. Love is not a quality that God possesses, but the essence of God himself.[9] It is not a minor attribute that characterizes God on occasions, but the very heart of God, his essential being. It is not a component part of God, but his very nature. Before God is anything else, he is love. In his love he created the world and brought people into being so that he might enjoy friendship with them. In his love he redeemed the world and re-creates people so that he may renew fellowship with them and restore the relationship severed by sin.

The love of which John speaks differs from human love as real, fresh fruit differs from artificial fruit flavours. The early Christians tended to avoid using the usual Greek word for love (*erōs*) when speaking of God's love, so as to avoid any possible misunderstanding. God's love is

---

[4] Eaton, p. 25.
[5] Marshall, *Epistles of John*, p. 26.
[6] Ibid., p. 22.
[7] R. E. O. White, *An Open Letter to Evangelicals* (Paternoster, 1964), p. 195.
[8] The principal places are 1:7; 2:2; 3:16; 4:9–10; 5:6.
[9] Jackman, p. 118.

agapē: love of an extraordinary kind, which gives itself in service to others to an unreasonable degree – even to the ultimate. Human love is usually *erōs*. It loves those who are worthy, lovable and able to love in return. It is characterized by desire, often a desire to possess.[10] *Agapē* loves the unworthy, and does so freely. So the love of God is not the human attitude we know as natural love. It is altogether new, and we shall never truly understand it if we just imagine human love, only magnified. His love differs from ours, not just in quantity, but in kind.

A word of caution is necessary. To say that 'God is love' is not to say that 'love is God'. To do so would be to commit a well-known logical fallacy. To say, for example, that 'all dogs are four-legged' is not the same as saying that 'all four-legged creatures are dogs'. The sentence is perfectly true when structured one way, but completely false when reversed. God is love, but not all love is therefore God. First, we must define what sort of love we are talking about, since, as we have seen, much love falls far short of God's love and fails even as a cheap imitation of his wonderful grace. Secondly, God is love, but he is much more than love. He is holy love, purposeful love, perfect love and redeeming love, as John, in his exposition of it, explains.

b. What God did

How do we know all this about God? What evidence is there that he is love? The answer is that we know God by what he does, and by his actions God has disclosed himself to us to be love. We have not imagined it, deduced it, wished it or assumed it. John says we have seen it. When we ask where he has revealed himself in this way, the answer is, 'In the cross.' Without the cross, our understanding of love would be deficient, for it is the cross that defines what love is. We might think of love as a nice warm feeling, as an emotion, or even as a commitment of the will. But the cross defines love as self-giving. 'This is how we know what love is: Jesus Christ laid down his life for us' (3:16). It is the cross that reveals to us, in the most convincing and irrefutable manner, that God is love. *This is how God showed his love among us: He sent his one and only Son into the world that we might live through him* (9). God did not love us just by feeling compassion towards us, or by just saying that he loved us. His love was demonstrated in action: he sent his most precious Son to live among us and to give himself for us. It was a tangible love. We are not left to discover it through some process of subjective illumination, as John's opponents were evidently teaching, but are shown it objectively on the cross.[11] On a day in history, on a hill outside of Jerusalem, the Son of God was crucified for us. What greater love could there be than this?

[10] Morris, *Cross in the New Testament*, pp. 339–340.
[11] Seifrid, p. 282.

> Here is love, vast as the ocean,
> Loving-kindness as the flood;
> When the Prince of Life, my ransom,
> Shed for me his precious blood.
> Who his love will not remember?
> Who can cease to sing his praise?
> He shall never be forgotten,
> Through heav'n's everlasting days.[12]

John Stott summarizes it like this: 'The coming of Christ is, therefore, a concrete, historical revelation of God's love, for love (*agapē*) is self-sacrifice, the seeking of another's positive good at one's own cost, and a greater self-giving than God's gift of His Son there has never been, nor could be.'[13]

c. How God works

Having told us that love is characteristic of God and is demonstrated by the cross, John now gives his teaching a more personal nuance. It is not only that 'God is love', or even that 'God showed his love among us', but that *he loved us* (10). From stating a basic truth about God and making an insightful comment about the cross, he comes to the point of personal application. When God sent his Son, it was to the world of real men and women, like us. And he loved us in the full knowledge of our sinful, rebellious, fallen humanity. We were not particularly lovable. We had shown little inclination to acknowledge our Creator with thankfulness, to follow him in faithfulness, or to walk with him in truthfulness. Instead, our fallen natures made us indifferent to his goodness, sceptical of his ways, and rebellious towards his laws. In fact, even if we had wanted to love him, our natures were so contorted that we were incapable of doing so in any sustained and meaningful way.

Yet, in the wonder of his grace, he did not wait for us to make the first move towards him, as, in his righteous majesty, he might have been justified in doing. Instead, he made the first move by seeking us, making known his love to us, wooing us and showering love upon us. *This is love*, writes John: *not that we loved God, but that he loved us and sent his Son* ... (10). Paul makes the same point, using different language, in Romans 5:6–10. God came seeking us in his saving love 'when we were still powerless', when we were 'ungodly', while 'we were still sinners,' and 'when we were God's enemies'. The initiative lay entirely with God. Like a smitten lover, God overcame every obstacle, set aside every disincentive and surmounted every impediment in order

---

[12] Hymn, 'Here is love', by William Rees and William Edwards.
[13] Stott, *Epistles of John*, pp. 164–165.

to woo us back into fellowship with himself. He did not wait for a step of recognition, a sign of reformation, a flicker of repentance, or a hint of response on our part before he took the risk of sovereign grace and demonstrated to us his forgiving love.

In the famous *Panorama* interview that the confused and hurt Princess Diana gave to Martin Bashir in November 1995, she commented, 'The greatest disease in the world is the disease of being unloved.' The cross tells us it is a disease from which none need suffer. For at the heart of our universe is one who not only loves us but has made his love known in the most unforgettable way. And when we protest that his love is not like that of another human being, we readily concede that it is not, for it is far superior to the love of any human being. The one who loves us in Christ is far more significant than any human. The love with which he loves us in Christ is far more amazing than any that we can ever receive from another human being. And the love he has demonstrated in Christ is far more sure than the love of another human being. Not one of his creation need suffer from 'the disease of being unloved'.

2. The cross propitiates God's wrath (4:10, 14)

a. The necessity of atoning love

Our view of love can easily degenerate into sentimentalism. When it does, we take it for granted that our heavenly Father loves us and that he will forgive us, as if it were the most predictable thing in the world and could occur without difficulty or cost. But sentiment is not true love. God's love is not a sentimental love. His forgiveness is not cheap grace. He does not 'love' us by ignoring what ruptured our relationship with him in the first place, pretending that it never happened. He loves us by dealing with the cause of our rift.

Writing in a similar vein about the fatherhood of God, P. T. Forsyth made the point like this:

> We put too little into the name Father, when we think no higher than natural fatherhood at its heavenly best. It was not by a father or all earth's fatherhood that God revealed Himself. That would have been but a manifestation, not a revelation. It was by a son and a cross ... What I mean is that we make too little of the Father when we do not rise beyond *love* to *grace* – which is holy love, suffering hate and redeeming it.[14]

John would agree. God's love is a holy love that deals with sin and atones for wrongdoing. The cross does more than influence sinners to

[14] P. T. Forsyth, *God the Holy Father* (1897; Independent Press, 1957), p. 7.

return to him by winning them over as they see how much he gave himself for them. It removes the barrier between himself and them and, in perfect justice, settles the problem of sin. It is crystal clear that, for John, the cross not only expresses God's love but atones for people's sin. The connection between Christ's death and people's sin was plain enough in John's Gospel, but it is 'unmistakable in the Epistle'. Leon Morris says there is probably no point at which the letter differs from the Gospel more than this: in establishing the connection between the cross of Christ and people's sin.[15]

The first indication of the importance of atonement to John comes early in his letter. In 1:7 he writes that 'the blood of Jesus, his Son, purifies us [that is, those who walk in the light] from all sin'. Not many verses later, the connection between his death and our sin is mentioned again. 'He is the atoning sacrifice for our sins, and not only for ours but also for the sins of the whole world' (2:2). As he orbits around his subject once again, John makes a further succinct statement which links together three things like sections of a telescope: one issues in another, which, in turn, issues in a third: *he loved us and sent his Son as an atoning sacrifice for our sins* (10). Section one says that God loves us. Section two says that Christ came for us. Section three says that Christ atoned for us. The means by which the love of a holy God is made available to sinful human beings is through the cross of Christ. It is precisely because God loves us that he does not ignore our sin, but rather confronts the reality of it, and offers his own Son as the answer to it.

'The depth of God's love', writes Howard Marshall, 'is to be seen precisely in the way in which it bears the wounds inflicted on it by mankind and offers a full and free pardon.'[16]

b. The nature of atoning love

John's letter spells out the means by which love overcame the problem of sin. Christ died on the cross *as an atoning sacrifice* (10). John's mind has been no less shaped by the Day of Atonement than was the mind of Paul. Blood is once again seen to be central to the process of cleansing and forgiveness, and the death of Christ is viewed essentially from a sacrificial perspective.

John, no less than Paul, speaks of the death of Christ as *hilasmos*, 'propitiation'. The same debate over the precise meaning of the word occurs in relation to John's letter as in relation to Paul's. The arguments over whether it means 'covering', 'expiation' or 'propitiation' will not be rehearsed again here.[17] Suffice it to say that John is very

[15] Morris, *Cross in the New Testament*, p. 348.
[16] Marshall, *Epistles of John*, p. 215.
[17] See above, pp. 195–197.

aware of God's moral purity (1:5–7) and of his future judgment (2:28), both of which imply that God will hold people, whom he created, accountable for their sin and for their failure to satisfy his righteousness. So there would seem to be every need to appease the just holiness of the divine judge if sinful people are to receive the gift of eternal life.

To those who argue that if God is love he needs no propitiation, R. E. O. White replies: 'what John teaches is that God is love and therefore provides the propitiation'.[18] Therein lies his love. It does not consist in sidestepping the just demands of his holiness or in suppressing his anger against sin, but in himself providing for us, through his Son, what we are unable to provide ourselves: the solution to our sinfulness. In a gracious and ultimately mysterious way, God's anger fell on Jesus instead of on us. So instead of being rejected by God, we are welcomed; instead of being punished by God, we are forgiven; and instead of being held captive to death, we are given eternal life.

It is here that John's special contribution to our understanding of the atonement lies. Although all New Testament writers connect the love of God to the act of propitiation, John does so more absolutely than any others. 'Propitiation and love become ideas which explain each other.'[19] James Denney continues:

> So far from finding any kind of contrast between love and propitiation, the apostle can convey no idea of love to anyone except by pointing to propitiation – love is manifested there; and he can give no account of propitiation but by saying, 'Behold, what manner of love.' For him, to say 'God is love' is exactly the same as to say 'God has in His Son made atonement for the sin of the world.' If the propitiatory death of Jesus is eliminated from the love of God it might be unfair to say that the love of God is robbed of all meaning, but it is certainly robbed of all apostolic meaning. It has no longer that meaning which goes deeper than sin, sorrow, death, and which recreates life in the adoring joy, wonder, and purity of the first Epistle of John.[20]

We fully, finally, truly know that God loves us only because Christ died for our sins.

c. The reach of atoning love

A few verses after making this great declaration of God's love for us,

[18] White, *Open Letter*, p. 205.
[19] Denney, p. 151.
[20] Ibid., pp. 151–152.

John seems to widen the scope of the atonement and declares Jesus *to be the Saviour of the world* (14). It is not the first time that he has written in an apparently inclusive and universalist style. It first occurred in 2:2, where he says that Christ's atoning sacrifice was 'for our sins, and not only for ours but also for the sins of the whole world'. What does he mean by this? Is he claiming that Christ's death has brought forgiveness to all, regardless of their faith in him?

The world is one of those terms that John keeps using. He uses it to refer not to Planet Earth but to the sinful people who live on it. His primary slant on the world is therefore a negative one. We are not to love the world, since it will pass away (2:15–17). The world does not love God and consequently does not love his followers either (3:1, 13). Its mindset is at odds with the believer's mindset (4:5). It is the home of false prophets and of the antichrist, and is under the control of the evil one (4:1, 3; 5:19). Yet this is the world to which Christ came, for which he died and over which he is victorious (4:4; 5:4–5).

In saying that Christ is the Saviour of this world, John is not saying that all men and women are automatically saved by Christ; but rather that Christ's death is sufficient to save all men and women, whoever they are, if they believe that Jesus is the Son of God, are born anew of God and live in him (e.g. 5:1–12). John's point is that, contrary to the dogma of the false teachers, people do not need esoteric illumination before they can be saved.[21] Christ's death was a public declaration of God's love for all and a sufficient instrument of God's salvation for all. Salvation is not reserved for an exclusive élite who are initiated into it through some secret and mysterious rite. Christ died openly, and whoever believes in him can be saved. In that sense he is *the Saviour of the world.*

3. The cross commissions God's people (4:11–12)

John has not finished with the cross yet. Having declared that it reveals God's love and propitiates his wrath, he now declares that it motivates God's people. *Dear friends, since God so loved us, we also ought to love one another* (11).

a. Love is an obligation

The love of God should never flow into our lives without also flowing through them to others. The cross not only affirms that God loves us, but insists that we must love others in turn. To have received the love of God in our own lives and then to refuse to share it with others is to turn God's free-flowing grace into a stagnant pool.

One of John's major concerns is to answer the question: 'How can

---

[21] Seifrid, p. 282.

we know that our faith is genuine?' He sets out three tests which he elaborates in three cycles of exposition.[22] The tests are, first, moral: the test of obedience; secondly, social: the test of love; and thirdly, doctrinal: the test of faith. It is with the second of these that we are concerned here.

John began by saying that love is required of us if we wish to live in the light. Without it we dwell in darkness (2:7–11). Then, using the illustration of Cain and Abel, he elaborated on this and uncompromisingly related hatred to murder (3:12). By contrast, he taught, God in Christ did not take another's life, but gave his own life for us, and in so doing gives us the ultimate illustration of love. Our love, he says, like God's, needs to be genuine, not fake, and expressed in action, not just words. How else but through action would we know that love was authentic? It is easy to say the right things, but much harder to deliver on what we say (3:11–18).

The focal point of his argument comes in 3:16. 'This is how we know what love is: Jesus Christ laid down his life for us. And we ought to lay down our lives for one another.' Within that single verse he speaks of the definition of love, the demonstration of love and the demand of love. It is because God has loved us in Christ that we are under an obligation to love others. And because he has loved us to the ultimate extent of dying on the cross, we are equally called to sacrifice ourselves even to the ultimate degree. God's love is not just a revelation to be admired but an example to be copied.[23]

When John returns to the issue, he not only reasserts the same truth – that believers have an obligation to imitate the self-giving of Christ – but adds a new depth and explanation to his exhortation. Loving means not only that we walk in the light and follow in the steps of Christ, but that we know God, for he is the source and origin of all true love: *God is love* (8). It is impossible to know God and yet fail to live a life of love. Not only is he love, but he has loved us. Though he had good cause to be angry at us because of our sin, love found a way to overcome sin and relate to us. We need to do exactly the same. When tempted to react with anger and impatience, selfishness or indifference to the needs of others, we must consciously choose the path of active love. Both who God is and what God has done provide us with powerful incentives to love others.

b. Love is a revelation

John then inserts a comment that at first sight seems irrelevant. *No-one*, he says, *has ever seen God* (12). True, God is Spirit and God is invisible, but even if we could see him, the sight of God, awesome and majestic

---

[22] The cycles are: 2:3–27; 2:28 – 4:6; and 4:7 – 5:5. See Stott, *Epistles of John*, p. 61
[23] Stott, *Epistles of John*, p. 147.

in his holiness, is more than men and women can bear. Moses asked for a sight of God's glory, but was told that no-one could see God face to face and live.[24] But now God can be seen, through us. Just as God was seen by John and others in the face of Christ, as John's Gospel testifies,[25] so now he can be seen in the love believers manifest when they actively serve others. To love is to provide the evidence that God lives in us just as once he dwelt in the tabernacle or the temple. When people want to see him, therefore, they should be able to see him in us. What a powerful evangelistic and apologetic tool love is! Christians do not need to feel intimidated by the arguments of the sceptical intelligentsia. One ounce of love outweighs a whole heap of philosophy. We love because we have seen God's *agapē* love, revealed in the cross, and also because it is the way to continue to reveal it to the world.

c. Love is a completion

A further puzzling phrase follows. God's love is not only revealed through us but is *made complete in us* (12). It is an astounding claim, so much so that some have tried to soften it by suggesting that John is no longer talking about God's love being perfected in us, but about our love for him being brought to completion. But, as John Stott argues, 'the whole paragraph is concerned with God's love and we must not stagger at the majesty of this conclusion'.[26] It is saying that God's love is completed only when it is reproduced in us. Unless it finds contemporary expression in the world, it remains incomplete. Love, by its nature, must express itself, and so it reaches out through us in order to have its full effect. For not only does love find its eternal origin in God's being and its historical manifestation in God's Son, but it is continuously, presently consummated in God's people.

This is no arcane, abstruse point made by an armchair theologian. As one would expect of John, the wise and elderly apostle of love, this has practical implications for the spiritual lives of God's people. What he is telling them in effect is that the false teachers who are troubling them have got it terribly wrong. They seek God in mystical experiences and in retreating from the world into tiny spiritual élites where they believe that they alone have private visions of God. They regard themselves as 'spiritual' when they escape the mundane world and the responsibilities of ordinary life and bathe themselves in the glow of extraordinary revelations. It is easy to see how they had reached such conclusions, since their ideas had some very faulty starting-points. They devalued the 'flesh' and argued that Christ had not been truly human. They were unlikely therefore to believe in a spirituality that was earthed

---

[24] Exod. 33:20.
[25] John 1:18; 14:6–11.
[26] Stott, *Epistles of John*, p. 167.

in the real world. Their spirituality was inevitably going to be world-rejecting and world-escaping. But, John insists, it is not by escaping the world that they will find the fullness of God's love. On the contrary, true knowledge of God is to be found in quite the reverse direction. God's love was to be most fully experienced in serving the world and in loving one's neighbours and enemies with the same sort of sacrificial, self-giving, down-to-earth service that could be seen in Christ.

Teaching similar to that which John opposes in this letter never leaves the church undisturbed for long. Today, there are versions of so-called 'evangelical spirituality' which contrast the spirit and the flesh in a quite unbiblical way, and imply that it is more spiritual to be caught up to the third heaven in worship, or to have some mystical experience of Christ, or to dwell on the mountain with the Lord, untroubled by the cares and problems around us, than to be caught up with practical service in our broken and mucky world. All these ideas need to be tested (1–3), and, when they are, many of them will be found wanting. For the basis of the Christian faith lies in the fact that God was incarnate in Christ (2), and that in human flesh he lived among us, served us and died for us. It is, then, in our ordinary, embodied life that Christians will bring God's love, manifest in the self-giving of Calvary, to completion.

Although, in some respects, the cross is not central to John's purpose in writing this short letter, it emerges as crucial to his argument and as anything but incidental to his theme. More than any other New Testament writer, John associates the cross of Christ explicitly with the love of God, and so with the very nature of God himself. It proves to be a love that is strong and pure, not a watered-down emotion or mere sentiment. It is a love that overcomes every obstacle to fellowship by bearing the cost of reparation and taking the destructiveness of sin into himself. It is a love that pays the ultimate price as Christ lays down his life as the atoning sacrifice for us. And it is a love that 'has proved no idle display, no spectacle for mere wonder and delight, but a transforming energy',[27] as God's people imitate his example by engaging in self-giving service. The cross tells us that God loves us, and that message should call forth our adoring worship. The cross tells us that God forgives us, and that news should call forth our penitent faith. But the cross also tells us that God commissions us to love his world as he loved it, and that charge should call forth our ready obedience.

It is too easy to lose sight of the wonder of God's love as we argue about the interpretation of the atonement or delight in theorizing about the cross. But John would bring us back to the heart of the cross. Put simply, it is there that we experience God's love for us.

---

[27] G. G. Findlay, *Studies in John's Epistles* (1909; Kregel, 1989) p. 353.

Revelation 5:1–14
18. Worthy is the Lamb

The book of Revelation provides a fitting climax for the Bible's teaching about the cross of Christ. It celebrates the triumph of God over all the forces of evil, in spite of the experience of harassed and persecuted Christians, to whom it sometimes looks as if evil is still in control. The reality is that God reigns supreme over all, even now, and one day will manifest his supremacy in the re-creation of all things. His victory is undeniable because the decisive battle is already won. It is beyond dispute because Christ, 'the faithful witness', conquered through dying and then rising to be 'the firstborn from the dead' (1:5). In the apparent defeat of an ignominious death lay the path to victory. From the very beginning of Revelation it becomes clear that the defeat of Satan and all his accomplices, including sin and death, has been brought about by the cross. It is by the blood of Jesus that people are released from their sins, and triumph over tribulation (1:5; 7:14; 12:11).

The image that dominates Revelation is one that takes us resolutely to the cross. It is that of the Lamb. There are twenty-nine references to 'the Lamb' in the book, and all but one refer to Jesus.[1] It is John's favourite title for Jesus. By comparison, he uses 'Jesus Christ' only seven times and 'Christ' four times.[2] The title is central to the whole book, which moves inexorably towards the final triumph of the Lamb and the consummation of history. In spite of all the forces of violence unleashed against him, the Lamb proves worthy of the worship offered to him, for he is the agent by whom the total rule of God is successfully established.

While the Lamb is shown to manifest wrath and mete out judgment (6:16; 14:10; 17:14), he is usually seen as the focus of the worship of the believing community. Standing in the control centre of the

---

[1] The exception is 13:11, where the beast of the earth had two horns like a lamb. Aune, pp. 366–367.

[2] D. Guthrie, 'The Lamb in the structure of the book of Revelation', *Vox Evangelica* 12 (1981), p. 64.

universe, worshippers rejoice in the salvation he has won for them (7:9–19; 15:3), look to him for protection and guidance (7:17; 14:4), keenly anticipate his wedding supper as he is joined for ever to his bride, the church (19:7–9), and confidently predict his future reign at the centre of the new creation (21:1 – 22:6).

The Lamb is first introduced in 5:6, a scene that discloses the worship offered to him in heaven, and that captures something of the depth of the image, especially in relation to the cross. In his vision, John has been overwhelmed by the dazzling sight of God on his throne (4:1–11), and, as his eye strives to take in the scene, it alights on a scroll, sealed with seven seals, written all over, at God's right hand. Then he hears an angel voice ask urgently, *Who is worthy to break the seals and open the scroll?'* (2). There seems to be no qualified candidate, and John is on the verge of despair. Then an elder directs his attention to one who is qualified to do so (5).

What is this sealed document which the assembled worshipping throng longs to see opened? Its description leads one to think in terms of a legal document.[3] George Caird mentions four possible interpretations of *the scroll*.[4] First, it could be the Lamb's book of life, and the writing on it the names of believers.[5] But this does not seem particularly relevant to what happens when the seals are broken. So it is unlikely to be that. A second interpretation, which makes much more sense of what happens subsequently, is that it describes the coming events which John is to witness and communicate to the churches.[6] But the right to open the scroll is very much connected with Christ's death, and that provokes the question: why did Jesus wait from AD 30 until the time of John's vision before opening the scroll? So some say, thirdly, that it is a scroll of Scripture, like the one Jesus read from in the synagogue in Nazareth.[7] This has the value of highlighting the fact that Revelation is 'a sustained meditation on the Old Testament in the light of the Christian gospel',[8] but it does not adequately explain much that happens as a result of opening the scroll, or indicate why the only one qualified to open it should be the Lamb who was slain. Caird, therefore, prefers a fourth view (and on balance I think he is right, even though the second interpretation has much to commend it): namely, that it contains 'God's redemptive plan, foreshadowed in the Old Testament, by which he means to assert his sovereignty over a sinful world and so achieve the purpose of his creation'. That plan was put

[3] Beasley-Murray, *Revelation*, pp. 120–123.
[4] Caird, pp. 70–72.
[5] Rev. 3:5; 13:8; 17:8; 20:12, 15; 21:27.
[6] This is the preferred view of Mounce, who points to Ps. 139:16 in support
[7] Luke 4:16–21.
[8] Caird, p. 72.

into effect through the death of Christ and his 'archetypal victory', which is why Christ alone is able to open the seals. Here is 'the world's destiny, foreordained by the gracious purpose of Christ'.[9] It is written on the back and on the front, Caird suggests, 'as an indication of the fulness and precision of the divine knowledge'.[10]

The opening of the scroll is going to prove crucial for the unfolding of Revelation. As each seal is broken, so new activity is initiated in the world until, finally, the seventh seal is opened (6:1 – 8:1) and the new symbolism of seven trumpets takes over (8:2 – 11:15). The sounding of the trumpets gives way, after an extensive interruption, to the pouring out of seven bowls of God's wrath (15:1 – 16:21). All of it moves towards the climax of God's triumph over his enemies and his reclamation of his fallen world. And all is set in motion by the Lamb.

Having been told by an elder that he need not fear, since there is one who has the right to open the seals of the scroll, John naturally looks to see who it is. It is then that the extraordinary image of the slain Lamb begins to emerge. His vision is recorded in detail, and every detail of it is significant.

1. The figure of the Lamb (5:1–7)

a. His titles

The elder describes the Lamb as *the Lion of the tribe of Judah, the Root of David* (5). Both titles are drawn from the Old Testament and both were used by the Jews as ready-made terms for the Messiah. The former alludes to Jacob's blessing on Judah at the end of his days:

> You are a lion's cub, O Judah;
>   you return from the prey, my son.
> Like a lion he crouches and lies down,
>   like a lioness – who dares to rouse him?
> The sceptre will not depart from Judah,
>   nor the ruler's staff from between his feet,
>   until he comes to whom it belongs[11]
> and the obedience of the nations is his.[12]

The second comes from Isaiah 11:1, which envisages the time when an ideal king will come from the blood-line of David and usher in an era of peace and rule the world in righteousness. At last, John is led to understand, the new age of peace and justice has commenced, and the

---

[9] Ibid.
[10] Ibid.
[11] NIV mg. reads 'or *until Shiloh comes*; or *until he comes to whom tribute belongs*'.
[12] Gen. 49:9–10.

one who has brought it about, the long-expected Messiah, has not only arrived but has accomplished his work.

b. His countenance

With such an introduction, John naturally expects to see a commanding military figure who has all the usual hallmarks of victorious generals and all the trappings of majestic splendour to go with it. Imagine his shock, then, when what he actually sees is *a Lamb, looking as if it had been slain* (6). Where the Lion was supposed to be standing, there is only a small, slaughtered Lamb. The word John chooses for *Lamb* is *arnion*, a diminutive, rather than the more usual Greek word *amnos*. Apart from John 21:15, in the New Testament it is used only in Revelation. Eugene Boring comments on how our familiarity with the image means that it does not have the effect on us that it would have had on John. 'This', he says, 'is perhaps the most mind-wrenching "rebirth of images" in literature. The slot in the system reserved for the Lion has been filled by the Lamb of God.'[13]

The stress is on the weakness and pathetic appearance of the Lamb. He looks as if he has been slaughtered. Far from being strong and virile, the Lamb is in a pitiful and lamentable condition. Francisco Zurbarán's moving painting of *The Bound Lamb* begins, for me, to capture something of the vulnerability of a lamb prepared for sacrifice. Against a dark and brooding background he sets a white lamb lying on a slab, its feet bound with rope, defenceless and dazed, and on its way to death. How much more pathetic would be the sight after completion of the sacrifice! How much more helpless the sight of the Lamb who has already been slain!

c. His posture

But there is an even more curious thing about the sight of this Lamb. Though it has been dragged through death, it is *standing* (6). Its throat may have once been slashed, but now it is alive and upright. We cannot expect John's imagery to be consistent, since that is not the way his visionary medium functions. Detail after detail may be hard to fit together, but every detail matters as a way of conveying insight and truth. So now, the fact that this Lamb is neither lying nor resting, as one would expect, but standing, testifies to its triumph. Though once slain, it is no longer dead, but alive again. 'The slain Lamb is the risen Lord.'[14]

d. His centrality

He is standing in *the centre of the throne* (6). He is no bystander or

---

[13] Boring, p. 108.
[14] Beasley-Murray, *Revelation*, p. 124.

secondary actor in the drama of heaven. He is the central figure on whom all attention is focused, to whom all eyes look and for whom all voices are raised in adoration.[15] He is encircled by the heavenly choir as the footballer who scores the winning goal is encircled by his team-mates in celebration, and as jubilant soldiers shower their victorious general with praise.

As the vision of Revelation unfolds, and the drama of judgment is played out until God reigns omnipotent in his holy grace, it is this Lamb who is key to it all. His person and his activity decide the course of history as it marches from the old age to the new era, and beyond it to the consummation of all things. It is he who defeats all who stand in opposition to God. He is the one who has put into effect God's great plan of redemption and who, now enthroned in heaven, will ensure that it comes to completion.

e. His features

This Lamb looks like no other anyone has ever seen. Gone are the usual two horns. Instead, *He had seven horns and seven eyes, which are the seven spirits of God sent out into all the earth* (6). Seven is the symbolic number for completeness, for perfection. Nothing is lacking when 'seven' is signified. The horn is a symbol of strength. *Seven horns* indicate an irresistible fullness of strength. Here is omnipotence. The eye is a symbol of knowledge or perception. *Seven eyes*, then, indicate a 'completeness of vision which leads to perfect knowledge'.[16] Here is omniscience. The eyes are further described as *seven spirits* (cf. 4:5), or, perhaps more accurately, the sevenfold Spirit,[17] the energies of the complete and adequate Holy Spirit which have been released by the risen Christ to accomplish his work on the earth. Here is omnipresence. No part of God's world is a no-go area to him. No country or institution, no power or ideology, can keep him out. The work of the risen Christ has ensured that he can penetrate his world whenever and wherever he chooses in order to reclaim it for himself.

It is obvious that we can never satisfactorily visualize the image of the slaughtered Lamb. Yet the message is clear. Through the death of this vulnerable creature, God has obtained a great victory. His enemies have been defeated and his conquest is proceeding apace until it reaches its consummation in his own good time. John is told to see a Lion (5) but actually sees a Lamb (6). They are not two different creatures. The Lamb does not eventually become a Lion. He is not a Lion to some and a Lamb to others. The Lion is quite simply the Lamb.

In a graphic, surprising and dramatic way John is being told to re-

---

[15] Hughes, *Revelation*, p. 79.
[16] Mounce, p. 146. Caird makes an interesting cross-reference to Zech. 4:10.
[17] As in NIV mg.

evaluate everything his Jewish heritage has taught him, particularly with regard to their nationalistic ambitions. He expects the conquest of evil to take place through a Lion, that is, a strong military power, with an impressive show of military strength. Instead, it takes place through a diminutive Lamb. John is being told, 'Wherever you are used to reading or thinking "Lion", read and think "Lamb".' For this is the way the almighty God chooses to work. As Caird puts it, 'Whenever the Old Testament speaks of the victory of the Messiah or the overthrow of the enemies of God, we are to remember that the gospel recognises no other way of achieving these ends than the way of the Cross.'[18]

2. The identity of the Lamb

The identity of the Lamb is in once sense patently clear. It is Jesus Christ. But where did such imagery come from? Can some knowledge of the background lend greater depth to our understanding of it? There have been two major ways of looking at the metaphor. It may refer either to a messianic ruler or to a sacrificial offering.[19]

a. A messianic ruler

Although the image of the Lamb does not seem to have been used as a metaphor for the Messiah in the Judaism of Jesus' day, there are a number of reasons to think of it as a picture of a strong ruler or liberating leader. Revelation itself emphasizes that the Lamb is enthroned (7:17; 22:1, 3) and receives worship. The Lamb is also shepherd (7:17; cf. 14:1–5), and 'shepherd' was a common metaphor in the ancient world for 'king'. The Lamb is a strong warrior (7:14), whose wrath is to be feared (6:16), and who exercises a role in judgment (13:8; 21:27). He is presented, then, in part at least, as a powerful warrior and mighty leader.

In apocalyptic literature, both Jewish and Christian, animals were often used to portray powerful world rulers. Lambs, in particular, were frequently chosen to represent kings and conquerors.[20] Much later, in the eleventh century, a tradition developed that depicted Moses as a lamb who would destroy Egypt and deliver Israel. On the basis of this, some have argued that the primary reference of the image is to a strong military leader who would deliver an oppressed people.

b. A sacrificial offering

More likely, however, the background to the image is found in the Old Testament teaching about sacrificial offerings. Even though there are

---

[18] Caird, p. 75.
[19] For details on which this section is based see Aune, pp. 367–373.
[20] Dan. 8:3–8, 20–21; *1 Enoch* 85 – 90.

several references to the strength and ferocity of the Lamb, the weight of the metaphor surely lies in the slaughter he has endured and the blood he has shed. John's choice of the unusual word *esphagmenon*, *slain* (6), emphasizes the 'violence and mercilessness' of the Lamb's execution. Only here is it used in reference to the cross.[21] The numerous New Testament references to Jesus Christ as a Lamb[22] and its many allusions to Isaiah 53[23] make this interpretation the primary one.

As before when we have encountered this metaphor, it is impossible to determine precisely which of the several Old Testament sacrifices was in the author's mind as he wrote. Was it the Passover lamb – as some strongly feel, since it fits the exodus theme so well?[24] Or was it the lamb of the burnt offering, or of the consecration offering, or of the purification offering? Was it the ram of the Day of Atonement, the lamb of Isaiah 53, or what? In all probability, we are not called upon to choose between them. One kind of lamb might merge into another in the minds of the New Testament writers, and they may be doing no more than using the 'general context in which the metaphor of a slaughtered lamb whose blood somehow effects redemption can be understood'.[25] They all have this in common: that atonement and deliverance come through offering the life of the sacrifice to God by shedding its blood.

This interpretation of the Lamb as sacrifice almost certainly has the edge over that which sees it as a messianic ruler. The Lamb who was slain fulfils and supersedes all the Old Testament sacrifices. Here is the ultimate sacrifice for sin, bringing complete atonement and liberation.

3. The achievements of the Lamb (5:8–10)

The song of the elders (9–10) declares the Lamb to be worthy to break open the seals of God's redemptive plan, and explains why. His worthiness here lies not so much in who he is but in what he has achieved.[26] Everything focuses on his death and what follows from it. That is what qualifies him for the role and permits him to set in train the events on earth that will culminate in the new creation. His once-for-all death on the cross has repercussions for world history which are still unfolding today, both in the theatre of our Planet Earth and behind the scenes in the heavenlies too. As John listens to the song of the living creatures and the elders, he hears much about the achieve-

---

[21] The verb *thyō*, from the same semantic domain, is used in 1 Cor. 5:7; Mark 14:12 and Luke 22:7 of the slaughtering of the Passover lambs. Aune, p. 361.

[22] E.g. John 1:29, 36; 1 Cor. 5:7; 1 Pet. 1:18–19.

[23] E.g. 1 Pet. 2:22–25.

[24] Beasley-Murray, *Revelation*, p. 125.

[25] Aune, p. 373.

[26] Mounce, p. 148.

ments of the cross. Three verbs are used of Christ's work, and a fourth spells out its implication: *you were slain, you purchased, you have made,* and, as a result, *they will reign.*

a. The purchase he made

'With your blood you purchased for God members of every tribe and language and people and nation' (9). Using the language of ransom, John updates God's plan, which all along had been to have a people he could call his own in a special way. From the calling of Abraham, through the exodus and the covenant at Sinai, and on to the prophecies of Jeremiah and Ezekiel, God's desire for a people to whom he could be faithful and who, in return, would be faithful to him, was evident.[27] Here, the staggering thought is that he has purchased such a people and paid for them with the blood of Christ. The thought is not exclusive to Revelation. Paul tells the Ephesian elders that the church of God was 'bought with his own blood'.[28] He tells the Corinthians that they have been bought at a price and therefore belong to God as their owner.[29] They are not free to do what they like with their lives. With a different nuance, Peter says that 'it was not with perishable things such as silver or gold that you were redeemed ... but with the precious blood of Christ, a lamb without blemish or defect'.[30] So it was a common enough idea among the early Christians.

As far as John is concerned, the emphasis is on God's ownership of his people. The blood of Christ, shed on the cross, not only set them free but purchased them for God. Therefore it is not for Satan to act as if he owns them and can do what he likes with them. Nor is it for them to choose whom they will serve. They belong irrevocably to one master, from whom they gain protection and receive a destiny, and whom, consequently, they should serve with unquestioning obedience.

Who are these people who belong to God? Unlike the earlier covenant people, they belong to no one race or nation. The people purchased by the blood of Christ are a great international throng from *every tribe and language and people and nation.* The new eschatological people of God have burst out of the narrow nationalism of Israel and foreshadow his universal reign.

b. The church he established

God had expressed his intention for Israel in the Sinai covenant. They were to be 'a kingdom of priests and a holy nation'.[31] Two ordinary

[27] Gen. 17:7–8; Exod. 6:7; 19:5; Jer. 24:7; 31:33; 32:38; Ezek. 11:20; 14:11; 37:27.
[28] Acts 20:28.
[29] 1 Cor. 6:19–20.
[30] 1 Pet. 1:18–19.
[31] Exod. 19:6.

words describing political entities – 'kingdom' and 'nation' – were transformed by the way they were qualified. The kingdom was to be populated by priests, and the nation was to be holy. The plan was that every member of the God-ruled kingdom should serve him in the world as priests. They were to mediate between God and the nations, serving as guides and intercessors and helping to bring sinful people who were far away from God back into a relationship with him. As a holy nation, they were set apart to follow him and to keep the stipulations of his covenant faithfully. It would result in their being marked out as a people different from any other nation.[32] But Israel failed in that calling. Rather than serving as priests for others, they needed priests themselves; and rather than being glad to be different from others, they tried to be just like them.

But what had failed under the old covenant came to fulfilment in the new. Christ's death, as king and priest, called into existence a 'kingdom of priests and a holy nation' who serve God steadfastly in the world and play a significant role in the coming of his universal kingdom. They possess no sovereignty or priesthood in themselves, but derive them from Christ himself. Their *raison d'être* is to continue his work on earth. In George Caird's words, 'John does not think of Christ as having withdrawn from the scene of his earthly victory, to return only at the Parousia. In and through his faithful followers he continues to exercise both his royal and priestly functions.'[33]

The role of the church, then, is to be a faithful witness and to take an uncompromising stand for God, even to the extent of its members' laying down their lives (12:11). The 'blood of the Lamb' which purchased them for God was not only shed in the one, historic event of Calvary long ago, but continues, in a derived sense, to be shed in the deaths of the martyrs.[34] When the Romanian church leader Joseph Tson was under arrest and being interrogated by Ceausescu's security forces, an officer threatened to kill him. Tson told the officer:

> Sir, your supreme weapon is killing. My supreme weapon is dying. Sir, you know my sermons are all over the country on tapes now. If you kill me, I will be sprinkling them with my blood. Whoever listens to them after that will say, 'I'd better listen. This man sealed it with his blood.' They will speak ten times louder than before. So, go on and kill me. I win the supreme victory then.[35]

[32] See e.g. Lev. 18:1–5; 1 Sam. 8:19–21.
[33] Caird, p. 77.
[34] R. Bauckham, *The Theology of the Book of Revelation* (Cambridge University Press, 1993), p. 75.
[35] *Leadership* 8.4 (1987), p. 47.

The officer sent him home. Tson was right. The supreme strategy of Christians against all the powers of evil is not to spill their enemies' blood but to point to their Saviour's, and, by extension, to shed their own if called upon to do so as they follow his example.

c. The victory he ensured (5:10)

The song of worship sung to the Lamb exudes a confidence which does not seem to tally with the actual circumstances of Christians who suffer under the oppressive measures of unjust regimes. The priests of the new covenant, it proclaims, *will reign on the earth* (10). Some of the Greek manuscripts put this in the present tense: 'they reign'. This would mean that even though the Christians appear to be despised and rejected, the truth is that they, not Caesar and his henchmen, are actually in control. But such a claim would be sheer fantasy. The future tense is surely correct. The song looks forward in hope to the day when Christ will reign over all, and they will reign with him.[36] As so often in Revelation, they are celebrating not the current but the ultimate reality. It is the end result that gives them cause to praise. Set before them is the vision that one day in the millennium (20:4) and in the re-created heaven and earth (22:5) they will be delivered from injustice and vindicated. They will receive redress, and reign with the Lord himself in triumph.

Such a vision strained credulity, and the heavenly choir might legitimately be asked: 'On what could you base such a hope? Their answer would have been unhesitating. It is because the Lamb was slain (9). The dying Lamb took on every evil power in the contest of his cross and, in ways that earlier chapters of this book have explored, roundly defeated them. Though for the moment they continue to parade their waning power, the final outcome is not in dispute. In the next act of the drama of world history, the devil will be banished and all his retinue and handiwork with him. The wise plan of God to defeat corrupt power by assuming abject weakness has paid off. And the resurrection is proof of it.

4. The worship of the Lamb (5:7–14)

John's teaching about the cross is implicit in his impressionist portrait of the choirs of heaven. It is as we linger over the details that we discern his meaning. The very act of worship, as well as its content, reveals much to us about the cross of Christ.

a. Who the worshippers are

The choirs of heaven are led first of all by a small number of representative voices, and swell until the whole of creation joins in his

---

[36] Mounce, p. 149.

praise. The first voices are those of *the four living creatures and the twenty-four elders* (8). The *four living creatures are described in 4:6-8.* Their station is immediately adjacent to God's throne, and they continually declare in song the holiness of his character and the eternity of his being. These alert and lively creatures represent the summit of his creation. The 'lion', the summit of the untamed animal kingdom, represents all that is noble. The 'ox', the greatest in the domesticated animal kingdom, represents strength. The 'human being', the crown of all creation, embodies wisdom. The 'eagle', the peak of all bird life, portrays speed. Status, power, wisdom and speed bow, then, in submission to their living and eternal creator.

The image of the twenty-four elders is not so easy to decode.[37] Some say they are the angels who form the heavenly court,[38] but these are not usually called 'elders'. Some say they are Old Testament worthies, akin to those listed in Hebrews 11. Others maintain that the number twenty-four suggests the twenty-four divisions in the Old Testament priesthood, all the heads of which had to be present for the great festivals of Israel.[39] Yet others view them as a combination of the twelve patriarchs of Israel and the twelve apostles of Jesus. Whether angelic or human, though, their task is to exalt God in his universe and reveal his supremacy over all the turmoil of earth. He is not embroiled in it, not because he is indifferent to it, but because he has already determined its outcome. He reigns victorious over it.[40]

The next choir to join in the praise is the choir of *many angels, numbering thousands upon thousands, and ten thousand times ten thousand* (11). John does not mean us to take the figure literally. He is telling us that vast numbers of angels, beyond our ability to count, are caught up in the praise of the Lamb. The angelic hosts of heaven looked on as Christ dwelt on earth and went to the cross. They understood, as the human participants in his crucifixion failed to do, just what it cost him and what it meant for him to die. Now that he is risen and exalted once again, they heap adulation on him as on a conquering hero on his return.

The choirs swell again until *every creature in heaven and on earth and under the earth and on the sea, and all that is in them* (13), are caught up in the worship of the Lamb. Of course, John knows that at this point there are elements in creation that are still hostile to his rule. But the cross has settled the matter. 'Such is his confidence in the universality of Christ's achievement', writes Caird, 'that his vision cannot stop short

---

[37] Sweet, p. 118.
[38] 1 Kgs. 22:19; Is. 6:1.
[39] 1 Chr. 24:4–18.
[40] Beasley-Murray, *Revelation*, p. 114.

of a universal response.'[41] With Paul, he knows that through the cross the entire universe will be reconciled to himself and that, as Robert Mounce says, 'the universality of Christ's achievement calls for a universal response'.[42]

The ever-widening circles of worshippers tell us that at the heart of our universe the achievement of the cross is celebrated by all that is best, all that is angelic and all that is human; no part of our created universe fails to join in the new song declaring the worthiness of the Lamb who was slain.

b. How the worshippers act

Besides their *loud* (12) and jubilant song of praise, we read of two other aspects of their worship. First, verse 8 records that the creatures and elders *fell down before the Lamb*. The final glimpse of the heavenly worship repeats the remark: *and the elders fell down and worshipped* (14). Confident though they are in his presence, and joyful as they are in their singing, their worship is still marked by reverence and humility before the Lamb. Their certainty of salvation has not led them to be over-familiar in their relationship. Rather, it has had the reverse effect. Such a great salvation calls us to prostrate ourselves in awe before the one who loved us so much that he set aside his power and endured the cross to break the power of our enemy and set us free.

Secondly, the creatures and the elders also hold *golden bowls full of incense, which are the prayers of the saints* (8). The connection between incense and prayer goes back to Psalm 141:2, so John is adopting a familiar image. What is remarkable at this point is that earthly realities are being introduced into the heavenly scene.[43] While the worshippers are taken up with acclaiming the Lamb, they do not do so in a way that cuts him off from the reality of the struggles and sufferings of earth. The Lamb they celebrate is not one who enjoys a cosy, detached, spiritual life up above the clouds, untouched by the real needs of his people still on earth. His high-priestly ministry of intercession continues in heaven and is not set aside as the choirs gather to celebrate his victory.

c. What the worshippers sing

The worshippers offer the Lamb a sevenfold acclamation. He is worthy *to receive power and wealth and wisdom and strength and honour and glory and praise!* (12). George Beasley-Murray suggests that in view of chapters 4 and 5, 'it would suit the context of the doxology here if its first four elements were to be viewed as expressive of the sovereignty

[41] Caird, p. 77.
[42] Mounce, p. 150.
[43] Sweet, p. 129.

exercised by Christ on behalf of God, and the last three that of the recognition accorded by the universe to the newly enthroned Lord'.[44] But he rightly adds that such a division cannot be pressed. Indeed, it is better to see each of the attributes mentioned as belonging to Jesus as much as to God.[45]

Elsewhere in the New Testament, as Robert Mounce points out, each of the qualities mentioned is ascribed to Jesus. It is no neutral list. The composer of this song did not consult a thesaurus for adulatory words and string them together, supported by a pleasant melody, before offering them for wider use. The words are carefully chosen, and they are both deeply subversive and deeply revealing. They are subversive because they ascribe to Jesus all the attributes that Roman emperors claimed for themselves. The homage offered to Rome, either voluntarily or under duress, rightly belongs to the Lamb, and to him alone. And he gained it not by might but by self-sacrifice.[46]

The words are deeply revealing because they ascribe to Jesus exactly the opposite of what any human being, unaided by faith, would see in the cross.[47]

Power. The cross speaks of defeat. The powers of the world moved to crush Christ and to do away with him, but, in reality, 'having disarmed the powers and authorities, he made a public spectacle of them, triumphing over them by the cross'.[48]

Wealth. The cross is the ultimate expression of poverty. The man who never owned a home of his own and had few, if any, possessions, was in the end stripped of everything, even his clothes, and was crucified naked. Yet the poverty of Christ crucified was to enrich our lives beyond imagination: 'For you know the grace of our Lord Jesus Christ, that though he was rich, yet for your sakes he became poor, so that you through his poverty might become rich'.[49]

Wisdom. The cross is the height of folly. No-one in his right mind would have put himself in a position to be crucified. The sophisticated world had devised it as a way of disposing of the foolish. Yet, in truth, the crucified Christ was 'the wisdom of God. For the foolishness of God is wiser than human wisdom ...'[50]

Strength. The cross epitomizes weakness. The powers of the world combined to subject Christ to total helplessness and defencelessness. He 'was crucified in weakness'.[51] Yet, in reality, it was God's power at work,

[44] Beasley-Murray, *Revelation*, p. 128.
[45] Sweet, p. 131.
[46] Ibid.
[47] I owe this to Mounce, p. 150.
[48] Col. 2:15.
[49] 2 Cor. 8:9.
[50] 1 Cor. 1:24–25.
[51] 2 Cor. 13:4.

for, to those whom God has called, Christ crucified is the power of God, and 'the weakness of God is stronger than human strength'.[52]

Honour. The cross represents shame. It was designed to degrade and humiliate its victims. It held Christ up to the mockery of the crowds and the ridicule of the priests. Yet, paradoxically, the cross was both his throne and the way to his resurrection from the grave, his ascension from the earth and his exaltation in the heavens. So now he occupies 'the highest place' and has 'the name that is above every name', so that one day 'at the name of Jesus every knee should bow, in heaven and on earth and under the earth, and every tongue confess that Jesus Christ is Lord, to the glory of God the Father'.[53]

Glory. The cross was a place of dark disgrace. It was hard to find any glory at Calvary. Melito, Bishop of Sardis in the second century, put it graphically in his *Homily on the Passion*:

> O unprecedented murder! Unprecedented crime!
> The Sovereign has been made unrecognisable by his naked body
> and is not even allowed a garment to keep him from view.
> That is why the lights of heaven turned away,
> and the day was darkened.[54]

Yet shining through the gloom came the irrepressible glimmer of glory. John testified that 'The word became flesh and made his dwelling among us. We have seen his glory, the glory of the One and Only, who came from the Father, full of grace and truth.'[55] He also testified that the hour of his greatest glory was seen not in his miracles or in his unanswerable teaching, but in his cross.[56]

Praise. The cross stood for a curse. People who ended up nailed to crosses were to be blamed, not blessed. The law said that 'anyone who is hung on a tree is under God's curse'.[57] But God had so arranged it that 'Christ redeemed us from the curse of the law by becoming a curse for us'.[58] So now he has become the object of our praise, which, as William Barclay says, 'is the one gift that we who have nothing can give to Him who possesses all'.[59]

What the evil powers of the universe and the unredeemed powers of the world viewed as a symbol of defeat, poverty, folly, weakness, shame, disgrace and cursing was transformed by the gracious action of God

---

[52] 1 Cor. 1:25.
[53] Phil. 2:9–11.
[54] Quoted in Hooker, *Not Ashamed*, p. 10.
[55] John 1:14.
[56] John 12:23; 13:31–32.
[57] Deut. 21:23.
[58] Gal. 3:13.
[59] Quoted by Mounce, p. 150.

into an instrument of power, wealth, wisdom, strength, honour, glory and blessing. And the focal point of it all, the slain Lamb, is worthy to receive our worship *for ever and ever!*

It would be hard to conceive of a more fitting metaphor than that of the 'slain Lamb', chosen by John under the inspiration of the Holy Spirit, as the climactic expression of Christ's work on the cross. It encompasses so many of the themes earlier preachers and writers had used. It balances the awful violence inflicted on the sacrificial victims – the lambs led to the slaughter – with the awesome triumph of the warrior king. It captures the profound mystery that God chose to conquer evil not by force and might but by self-giving and self-sacrifice. It tells us that the Lamb, who paid the cost with his own life, and still, in the very throne-room of God, bears the marks of his crucifixion, reigns victorious over the world.

Salvador Dali's painting of *Christ of St John of the Cross* is perhaps the most celebrated religious painting of the twentieth century. It is a startling portrayal of the crucified Christ hovering above the world, close yet transcendent, suffering yet somehow triumphant. The cross bursts out of the canvas as if reclaiming the world once and for all for God. And that, of course, is exactly what the cross accomplished.

Study guide

The aim of this study guide is to help you get to the heart of what Derek Tidball has written and to challenge you to apply what you learn to your own life. The questions have been designed for use by individuals or by small groups of Christians meeting, perhaps for an hour or two each week, to study, discuss and pray together.

The guide provides material for each of the sections in the book. When used by a group with limited time, the leader should decide beforehand which questions are most appropriate for the group to discuss during the meeting and which should perhaps be left for group members to work through by themselves or in smaller groups during the week.

In order to be able to contribute fully and learn from the group meetings, each member of the group needs to read through the section or sections under discussion, together with the passages of Scripture to which they refer.

It's important not to let these studies become merely academic exercises. Guard against this by making time to think through and discuss how what you discover *works out in practice* for you. Make sure you begin and end each study by focusing on God in praise and prayer. Ask the Holy Spirit to speak to you through your discussion together.

Introduction: The cross in evangelical spirituality and theology today (pp. 20–34)

1 What do you make of the suggestion that the cross 'no longer occupies the central place that once it did' in evangelical spirituality (p. 21)?
2 To what extent is Christianity for you 'the religion of a sinner at the foot of the cross' (Charles Simeon; p. 22)? What would you say lies at the heart of your faith?

'Every living experience of Christianity begins at the cross' (Campbell Morgan, quoted on p. 22).

3 How would you answer the claim that evangelical spirituality is unhelpfully 'word-centred' (p. 22)?

4 What positive consequences of a 'crucicentric' evangelical spirituality does Derek Tidball highlight on pp. 24–26?

5 'The Christian life is cruciform' (p. 26) What does this mean? Is it true of you?

6 What possible dangers of a cross-centred evangelical spirituality are highlighted here (p. 26)? How may they be avoided?

7 What is the difference between 'worthlessness' and 'unworthiness'? Which do you feel describes you? Why is it so important to make this distinction (p. 26)?

8 What evidence is there that the 'cross is being displaced from the centre of evangelical spirituality today' (p. 26)?

9 Is there any reason to think that 'Calvary has been replaced by Pentecost' (p. 27) in your experience of the Christian faith? What problems does this lead to?

10 What potential danger does Derek Tidball see in Celtic spirituality (p. 28)? How may this be overcome?

11 Do you agree that 'there is a need to restore the cross to its central position among evangelicals' (p. 28)? Why?

12 What is the 'classic evangelical position' (p. 29) concerning the interpretation of the cross?

13 What does 'penal substitution' mean (p. 31)? Why is there a degree of unease with this doctrine (pp. 31–33)? To what extent do you think this is justified?

'Our preaching of the cross ... must faithfully represent the revelation of our God rather than gratify the fashions of society' (p. 33).

14 What 'shifts in current evangelical thinking' (p. 33) about the cross does Derek Tidball identify? How should these be weighed?

15 What caution does Derek Tidball advise as we explore 'new avenues of understanding and new depths of interpretation' (p. 34)? Why?

PART 1. THE CROSS ANTICIPATED

Genesis 22:1–19
1. The Lord will provide (pp. 36–50)

1 What is exquisite and 'shocking' about this story (p. 36)?
2 How does the writer of Genesis underline the extent of the ordeal facing Abraham (pp. 37–38)?
3 How are we to explain why God told Abraham to do something as 'repulsive' (p. 38) as sacrificing his son?
4 Why is this in fact 'a particularly suitable test' (Claus Westermann, quoted on p. 39)?
5 How does the text demonstrate the totally trusting nature of Abraham's obedience (pp. 39–41)?

'Delay is the craftiest net of Satan ...' (Henry Law, quoted on p. 40).

---

6 What was the probable purpose of this story for Israel? What particular relevance would it have had (pp. 41–42)?
7 Why do we need to 'exercise care' in reading Christian meanings back into the Old Testament (p. 41)? What guidelines are we offered here?
8 In what ways is Isaac presented as 'an unmistakable picture of Christ' (p. 43)? What is 'the most remarkable point of similarity' between Isaac and Jesus here (p. 45)?
9 What is so 'scandalous' for our world (p. 47, Brueggemann's word) about the claim that God is 'the Lord who provides'?

'The promises of God, which were always certain, have been strengthened by Abraham's own obedience' (p. 48).

---

10 What is the significance of the location of this incident (pp. 48–49)?

Exodus 12:1–51
2. It is the Lord's Passover (pp. 51–67)

1 Why does Derek Tidball describe the way the exodus story is

sometimes used as 'dangerous' (p. 51)?

2 'Above anything else the Passover story is a self-disclosure of God' (p. 52, citing John Stott). What does it reveal about him (pp. 52–53)?

3 What is the relationship between the exodus and the Passover that precedes it (p. 54)?

4 What 'five distinct yet related outcomes' of the Passover are set out here (pp. 57–64)?

5 'Our image of God does not permit us easily to think in terms of his anger' (p. 58). Is this true of you? How does what Derek Tidball says help?

6 In what way were the plagues inflicted on Egypt a demonstration of 'God's power' (p. 59)?

7 In what ways does the story of the Passover and exodus point forward to the death of Christ? How do the writers of the New Testament bring this out (pp. 64–67)?

'... all that happened through the Passover lamb in Israel's experience happens now through Jesus in our experience' (p. 65).

Leviticus 16:1–34
3. 'This day atonement shall be made for you' (pp. 68–84)

1 What in this passage serves to highlight the importance of the Day of Atonement (p. 68)?

2 Why do the preparations for the Day need to be so rigorous? What is being underlined here (pp. 69–71)?

3 How does Leviticus 16 help us to understand the meaning of sin (pp. 71–74)?

'Whether by unintentional spiritual neglect, more conscious spiritual indifference or outright spiritual rebellion, sin drives God out of his world ...' (p. 72).

---

4 How would you answer someone who suggested that sin is primarily about a broken relationship with God and that thinking in terms of legal categories is not so helpful (pp. 72–73)?

5 What are the four aspects of the atonement ritual which 'require attention' (pp. 74–81)?

6 What does the shedding of blood signify – the release of the victim's life or the victim's death (p. 76)? Why?

7 Why do some people object to the use of the word 'substitute' in talking about sacrifice for sin? What truths does this idea safeguard (pp. 76–78)?

8 What exactly does 'atonement' mean? What do you make of the respective merits of the three alternatives (pp. 78–79)?

9 How do the details of the scapegoat ritual further help our understanding of atonement (pp. 79–81)?

10 In what ways was the sacrifice of Christ one of 'infinite superiority' compared with the rituals prescribed for the Day of Atonement (pp. 81–84)?

'[Christ's] single death was the ultimate act in the drama of atonement and won for us a permanent forgiveness' (p. 83)

Psalm 22:1–31
4. 'My God, my God, why?' (pp. 85–99)

1 What 'massive tension' is highlighted in verses 1 and 2 of this psalm (pp. 86–87)? What experience have you had of this?

2 In what way is the psalmist's initial plight reinforced by the reactions of other people? How does he express this (pp. 87–88)?

3 What third dimension to his suffering does the psalmist highlight in this psalm (p. 88)?

4 'Battling with the dominant, haunting melody of trouble is the irrepressible music of trust' (p. 89). Which particular truths about God does the psalmist focus on here (pp. 89–91)?

5 What is the dramatic shift that occurs from verse 22? How might we account for it? What are its consequences (pp. 91–93)?

'What began as a personal song of praise … moves out in ever-increasing circles until the whole world is caught up in worship' (p. 93).

---

6 In what ways is Psalm 22 such an 'apt' and 'accurate' portrayal of the suffering of Christ (pp. 94–96)?

7 What difference should we note between the experience of the psalmist and the experience of Jesus (p. 97)? Why is this so significant?

8 In what way does this psalm hint at the resurrection of Jesus (pp. 97–98)?

'Jesus alone perfectly fits the words [of this psalm] and completely fulfils their meaning' (p. 99).

Isaiah 52:13 – 53:12
5. Man of sorrows (pp. 100–116)

1 What is 'daringly new' about what this passage says about God (p. 100)?
2 What is the 'enigma' of the servant (pp. 102–104)? How is it expressed in 52:13–15?
3 How do those who view the servant explain the reason for his suffering? What have they failed to consider in arriving at this conclusion (pp. 104–105)?
4 How would you answer someone who claimed that 'the full extent of God's purpose was to bring sinners to repentance by influencing them through the example of the servant' (p. 108)?
5 How do you respond to the idea that you are part of the 'we' in verse 6 (p. 109)?
6 How does the writer of these verses underline the voluntary nature of the servant's suffering (pp. 109–110)? Why is this so important?
7 What is 'difficult' about verse 9 (pp. 111–112)? How can this be resolved?
8 In what ways is verse 11 'one of the fullest statements of atonement theology ever penned' (Alec Motyer; p. 114)?
9 Are Christians justified in seeing this passage as pointing most clearly to Jesus (pp. 115–116)? Why?

PART 2. THE CROSS EXPERIENCED

Matthew 26:1 – 27:56
6. Crucified Messiah (pp. 117–134)

1 The Gospel writers appear to say little about the interpretation of the death of Jesus. How then do they show what his death means through what they write (pp. 117–118)?
2 Do the differences between the Gospel accounts bother you? How are we to account for them (pp. 118–119)?

3 In what ways does the 'shadow of the cross' fall across the whole of Matthew's Gospel (p. 119)?

4 What are the 'five themes', which emerge in Matthew's passion narrative (pp. 120–133)?

'No aspect of the drama of the death of Jesus is there by chance' (p. 122).

---

5 What aspects of the death of Jesus does Matthew's use of the Old Testament serve to convey (pp. 120–124)?

6 What 'three dimensions' are involved in the symbolism of blood in Matthew's account (pp. 124–126)?

7 In what ways does the description of Jesus as a 'martyr' fall short of the whole truth? How does Matthew bring this out (pp. 126–130)?

8 How does Matthew indicate that Jesus remained in 'sovereign control' of events (pp. 130–131)?

'The cross is no tragedy passively endured but an action deliberately undertaken and successfully completed' (Tom Smail, quoted on p. 131).

---

9 What is significant about the way Matthew ends his account of the crucifixion of Jesus (pp. 132–133)?

Mark 14:1 – 15:47
7. Suffering servant (pp. 135–150)

1 What is distinctive about the approach Mark takes in his Gospel (pp. 135–137)?

2 What 'four significant themes' does Mark bring out in connection with the cross (p. 137)?

3 How would you answer someone who questioned the suggestion that Jesus alludes to Isaiah 53 in Mark 10:45? Why is this verse a 'key statement' in the Gospel (pp. 137–139)?

4 What might we miss that is 'obvious' in what Jesus says about his suffering as the servant (p. 138)? How does this amplified in Mark's Gospel? Can you think of ways in which this applies to you?

5 In what ways is Jesus 'portrayed as somewhat passive' in Mark's account? How is this significant (pp. 138–139)?

6 How does Mark convey the redemptive effectiveness of the suffering of Jesus? Why is such redemption necessary (pp. 139–141)?

'... the way to freedom was found in Jesus' voluntarily surrendering to those same forces he came to defeat, and through his weakness he brought their power to an end' (p. 140).

---

7 What 'two competing and ultimately complementary themes vie with each other ... throughout Mark's Gospel' (p. 141)? How does Mark bring out the theme of the sovereignty of Jesus (pp. 141–144)? What particular help would this have been to the first readers of the Gospel?
8 Who recognizes the kingship of Jesus? And who fails to recognize it? Why (pp. 142–143)?
9 Why is 'Mark's view of the cross often considered to be the grimmest'? How is this brought out in what he writes (pp. 144–148)?
10 What remarkable 'paradox' is revealed by Jesus' cry of abandonment on the cross (pp. 146–148)? What does this say to us about human suffering today?

'... there are no depths of experience to which men and women can sink to which he has not already plunged. Christ is able to share with us the pain of desertion, the loneliness of suffering, the darkness of depression, the bewilderment of circumstances and the agony of death ...' (p. 147)

---

11 How does Mark bring out the truth that the suffering and death of Jesus serve as a 'model for believers' (pp. 148–151)?
12 'Disciples today are still called to bear the cross' (p. 149). How does this apply to you?

Luke 22:1 – 23:56
8. Compassionate Saviour (pp. 151–167)

1 In his account of the passion story, what does Luke choose to omit? And what does he include which Matthew and Mark leave out? What distinctive perspective does Luke bring to these events (pp. 151–152)?

2 How does Luke draw attention the fact that Jesus was a 'deliberate victim' rather than 'an unfortunate victim who got caught in the cross-fire' (p. 152)?

3 'The eternal God had decreed that through this historic event of the sacrifice of his Son, the salvation of the world should be accomplished.' Why must we be 'careful when speaking in these terms' (p. 153)?

4 What is so encouraging about the role of Satan in the events leading to the death of Jesus (p. 154)?

'Satan ... was unaware that in playing his dangerous game he was paradoxically fulfilling God's plan and simultaneously overreaching himself and spelling his own defeat' (p. 154).

---

5 Who are involved in the 'alliance of guilt that let Jesus die' (p. 155)? In each case, what lies behind their involvement (pp. 155–159)? To what extent do you recognize these things in your own life?

'The cross demonstrates that only losers succeed in Christ's kingdom' (p. 156).

---

6 In what ways might your religion be 'getting in the way' (p. 157)?

7 Can you think of ways in which your 'instincts towards self-preservation' (p. 158) lead you into sin?

8 'The picture of guilt built up by Luke suggests that no human escapes some measure of blame for Jesus' execution' (p. 159). Where do you see yourself in this scenario?

9 What is the 'most outstanding feature of Luke's portrait of the death of Jesus' (p. 159)? How does Luke bring this out (pp. 159–163)?

10 What is so 'outrageous' about the grace Jesus showed to the dying thief who sought mercy from him? In what way is this thief the 'model for us all' (pp. 161–163)?

'... on the cross, Jesus embraced the greatest outsider of all and promised him a place in paradise' (p. 162).

---

11 What 'two further things are worth noting' from what Jesus says to the dying thief (p. 162)?

12 How does what Luke writes about the suffering of Jesus 'reveal the special relationship between Father and Son'? What two reasons for Luke's emphasis does Derek Tidball highlight (pp. 164–169)?

13 How is the theme of Christ as 'coming king' brought out in Luke's Gospel (pp. 164–165)? Why is this aspect so important for us today?

John 18:1 – 19:42
9. Glorious life-giver (pp. 168–183)

1 What is it about John's portrait of Jesus that makes it a 'fitting climax' to the Gospel accounts (p. 168)?

2 How would you answer the suggestion that John underestimates the importance of the crucifixion (p. 168)?

3 'The Christ John presents is in control …' In what different ways is this brought out in John's account of the passion (pp. 169–175)?

4 What is 'remarkable' about the conversation between Jesus and Pilate (pp. 171–172)? How does this highlight John's distinctive theme?

5 How can Jesus' journey to the cross be described as a 'coronation procession' (p. 173)?

6 'Even in his death, this king who sought to reach out to all was to prove profoundly unsettling to those who had a tunnel-vision picture of what royalty, especially divine royalty, was like' (p. 174). How do you think of divine royalty? Does what John sets out here unsettle you?

7 What does John mean when he describes Jesus as being 'lifted up' on the cross (pp. 174–175)?

8 In what ways does John underline the reality of the humanity of Jesus? Why is this so important (pp. 175–176)?

9 'Jesus died not just as a solitary individual but as a representative human being' (pp. 176–177). What does this mean? How does John bring out this truth?

10 How does John develop his initial description of Jesus as 'the Lamb of God, who takes away the sin of the world' (1:29; pp. 177–180)?

11 What does 'glory' mean? How is it that Jesus could describe the cross in terms of glory (pp. 180–183)?

'… in the reverse economy of God, Jesus' death was the supreme manifestation of his glory' (p. 182).

PART 3. THE CROSS EXPLAINED

Romans 3:21–26
10. The cross as undeserved righteousness (pp. 184–199)

1 How do we know that 'the message of the cross' was so important to Paul (p. 185)? How central would you say the cross is for you? Why?
2 Why is it so important to insist that the gospel begins, not 'with the needs of people, but with the righteousness of God' (p. 185)?
3 'The key question is: what does Paul mean by the phrase *righteousness of God*?' What does he mean by it? How does it fit in what God has already revealed about himself (pp. 186–188)?
4 How in this passage does Paul set out the twofold nature of the problem the cross is intended to resolve (pp. 188–192)?

'The harlot, the liar, the murderer are short of [God's glory]; but so are you. Perhaps they stand at the bottom of a mine, and you are on the crest of an Alp; but you are as little able to touch the stars as they' (Handley Moule, quoted on p. 189).

---

5 'Many today are hesitant to speak of the wrath of God' (p. 189). Are you? Why? How does what Derek Tidball says here help?
6 What 'three metaphors' does Paul use to explore the 'mysterious wonder of God's grace to us through the cross of Christ'? How do these images contribute to our understanding (pp. 192–196)?
7 What is the difference between forgiveness and justification (p. 193)?
8 What options are suggested for the meaning of the word *hilastērion* (pp. 194–196)? Which do you find most persuasive? Why?
9 In this context, what does it mean to have *faith in Jesus* (3:26; p. 197)?

'... justification by faith alone ... "advances the true glory of Christ and beats down the vain glory of man"' (Cranmer, quoted by John Stott on p. 197).

---

10 What does Derek Tidball mean when he states that 'The justice of God stands in the dock of humankind' (p. 197). How does the cross demonstrate God's justice?

11 'The cross functions retrospectively as well as prospectively' (p. 199)? What does this mean? Why is it important?

1 Corinthians 1:18 – 2:5
11. The cross as wise folly (pp. 200–215)

1 In what ways have you noticed the cross to be 'offensive' (p. 201) in our culture?

2 What was so 'foolish' about the message of the cross in Paul's day? Why would everyone, Jews, Romans and Greeks alike, have responded so negatively to it (pp. 201–204)?

3 'The truth was that the reality of the cross was entirely different from how they saw it' (p. 204). Why are people – then and now – so wrong in their assessment of the significance of the cross?

'While the world functions on the basis of self-centredness, God functions on the alternative basis of self-denial' (p. 206).

---

4 How can Paul be so sure that popular opinion is wrong and that the cross reveals God's wisdom (pp. 204–206)?

5 Other than salvation, what consequences of the cross does Paul weave into this passage (pp. 206–209)?

6 Of all the possible ways to categorize people in our world, what is 'the most significant division of all' (p. 206)? What is the practical impact of this for the Christian believer?

7 'God can be known only through the cross ...' (p. 207). How do you react to this statement?

8 In what ways does the cross challenge 'the illusory "wisdom" of our age' (pp. 208–209)?

9 Why is it such a good thing to glory in or be 'obsessed by' the cross (p. 209)?

10 How did 'the composition of the church in Corinth [mirror] the message of the cross' (pp. 210–215)? Where would your church fit in at this point?

11 What does it mean in practice for the Christian community to be 'characterized in its day-to-day life by the ... cross' (p. 212)?

12 How was Paul's medium shaped by his message? How did he differ from other communicators of his day (pp. 213–214)? What lessons are there here for us today?

'Modern Western evangelicalism is deeply infected with the virus of triumphalism ...' (D. A. Carson, quoted on pp. 213–214).

13 'The Corinthian church had been called into being by the cross as a sign of the age to come, but was still too affected by the conventional thinking of the world' (p. 214). In what ways could this be said of you?

2 Corinthians 5:18–21; Ephesians 2:11–22; Colossians 1:19–20
12. The cross as fatal reconciliation (pp. 216–231)

1 How do we know that the concept of reconciliation is so significant to Paul (pp. 216–218)?
2 Do you agree that 'the interpretation of the cross as reconciliation is one of the most dominant today' (p. 218)? Why is this?
3 Why is reconciliation 'no easy goal to achieve' (p. 219)? Can you think of examples in your own life and in the world more generally?
4 Why does Paul insist that the initiative for reconciliation comes from God rather than us (pp. 220–222)? How does he get this across?
5 God 'could not simply decree reconciliation by fiat ...' (p. 222). Why not?
6 How exactly does the cross of Christ bring about reconciliation (pp. 222–224)?

'What Christ gives in return for sin to those whom he relieves of it is the right standing before God which he alone deserved' (p. 223).

7 What 'misunderstanding of this doctrine' does Derek Tidball deal with here (pp. 223–224)?
8 How would you answer someone who suggested that 'God was engaged in a process of universal reconciliation which takes place automatically in the lives of all' (p. 224)? What then needs to happen for reconciliation to take place? Why?
9 What does 'peace with God' mean (pp. 224–225)? In what ways do you experience it?

10 How does Paul understand the role of an ambassador? Why is it vital for us to 'imitate Paul's method as well as to proclaim his message' (pp. 225–226)?

11 What 'demonstrated that [the Christians in Corinth] had not really grasped the meaning of reconciliation' (p. 226)? Can you think of ways in which you might be in the same boat?

12 How does Paul develop the idea of reconciliation in 'two wonderfully new ways' (pp. 227–231)?

' ... the wooden stake erected centuries ago on a hill opposite Jerusalem was set up not merely for the salvation of individuals but for the transformation of ethnic relations too' (p. 228).

---

13 What does Paul mean when he writes about God reconciling *all things* (Col. 1:19), as distinct from reconciling repentant and believing sinners (pp. 228–230)?

14 What questions does this 'bold claim' raise? How may they be answered (pp. 230–231)?

'[Reconciliation] is the one means by which God brings the total creation into harmony with himself' (p. 231).

Galatians 2:20; 5:24; 6:14; Philippians 3:10–11
13. The cross as present history (pp. 232–246)

1 What biblical truth have 'recent evangelical preaching and teaching ... tended to neglect'? Why is this so serious (p. 232)?

'Holiness is impossible unless the death of Christ becomes a present experience as well as a past event' (p. 233).

---

2 What do you think it means to live a 'cruciform way of life' (p. 233)? What shape is the way you live your life?

3 What is the context in which Paul writes about being 'crucified

with Christ' in Galatians 2:20? Why is it so important to bear this in mind when interpreting this text (p. 235)?

4 How can Paul say both that we have died with Christ and that we need daily to crucify the flesh? What does this mean? How do we do it (pp. 237-238)?

5 How do you respond to the call to 'mortification'? Why do you think there such an 'uneasy silence' about it (pp. 238–241)? What, in practical terms, does it mean for you?

'... daily self-mortification is an indispensable requirement if we are to pursue holiness' (p. 240).

---

6 In what ways are Paul's comments in Galatians 6:14 so relevant to us and our contemporary world (pp. 241–242)?

7 What two observations will help us better to understand what Paul says about suffering with Christ in Philippians 3:10 (p. 243)?

8 How is that Paul is able to embrace suffering so joyfully (pp. 243–244)? What impact does this have on you?

'We have the immense privilege of bearing the shame of the cross and walking the way of the cross to Calvary, in the footsteps of Jesus himself' (p. 244).

---

9 What would you say to a Christian who felt guilty because his or her 'circumstances do not seem to lend themselves to persecution' (p. 245)?

10 'We must do something about the cross, and one of two things only can we do – flee it or die upon it' (A. W. Tozer, quoted on p 246). Which option will you go for?

Colossians 2:8–15
14. The cross as tragic victory
(pp. 247–261)

1 What is meant by the so-called 'classic' idea of atonement set out by Gustav Aulén? What 'justifiable criticisms' may be directed at his views (pp. 247–249)?

'Throughout the New Testament the cross is seen as a triumph, not as a defeat' (p. 249).

2 What features of the situation faced by the Christians in Colosse serve to illuminate what Paul says in Colossians 2:8–15 (pp. 249–250)?

3 What exactly does Paul mean by the *powers* and *authorities* of which he writes in this passage? Why is it misleading to see them simply as 'social realities embodied in human power structures' (pp. 250–251)?

4 What strategies of evil does Paul describe here (pp. 251–253)? Can you think of examples of these at work in the world today?

5 What lies behind the transforming difference Christ makes to this situation (p. 253)?

6 How exactly does the reality of who Christ is translate into the lives of those who believe in him? What does Paul's use of the analogy of circumcision contribute to our understanding (pp. 254–255)?

7 What are the 'two images' that Paul uses to describe further the freedom that we have in Christ? How do these help our grasp of what the cross means (pp. 256–261)?

'What great news sounds forth from the cross! The debt we cannot possibly meet from our own meagre and tainted resources has been fully met by another' (p. 258).

8 How does the cross help believers who are living in fear and feeling oppressed by forces that are too strong for them (pp. 258–261)?

9 What is so 'bold' about Paul's claim in Colossians 2:15 (pp. 258–260)? How does this work out in practice for us?

10 'The diffidence and mediocrity of much Christian living today may, indeed, be precisely due to our lack of teaching and believing that Christ really has *already* defeated our enemies through his cross' (p. 261). What difference would believing this more fully make to your life?

PART 4. THE CROSS APPLIED

Hebrews 10:1–18
15. Once for all (pp. 262–277)

1 What four 'relevant themes' from Hebrews does Derek Tidball mention (pp. 262–264)? What do these tell us about the likely benefits of studying this letter?

2 What are some of the issues this letter was written to address (pp. 264–267)?

'What is most striking about Hebrews is that the Preacher, faced with the pastoral problem of spiritual weariness, is bold enough, maybe even brash enough, to think that Christology and preaching are the answers' (Thomas Long, quoted on p. 265).

---

3 What features of the Old Testament system of sacrifices 'make it ultimately ineffective and therefore inadequate' (pp. 268–270)?

4 'In reality, many preachers are better at reminding us that we are sinners than that God is gracious' (p. 269). What experience have you had of this? Why do you think it happens?

5 By contrast with Old Testament sacrifices, what is it about Christ that makes his work so much more effective (pp. 270–272)?

6 'We ... need to be cautious about some teaching that at first sight appears quite acceptable' (p. 272). What is Derek Tidball referring to here? Why is this so important?

7 What 'two knock-out punches to the Aaronic priesthood' does the writer of Hebrews deliver here (p. 273)?

8 How does the writer show that the priestly ministry of Jesus is so much better than that found under the old covenant (pp. 273–275)?

9 'Hebrews is careful to balance the portrait of the magnificent uniqueness of this priest with his sympathetic humanity' (p. 274). Why is this so important for us?

10 What does it mean to be *made perfect* by the sacrifice of Christ on the cross (10:14; p. 274)? How does this help those with a troubled conscience?

'... there is no encouragement here for believers to continue in sin, but there is the assurance that sin, when it occurs, has been fully and finally dealt with by Christ' (p. 275).

---

11 What is meant by the phrase 'new covenant'? In what ways does it differ from the 'old covenant'? How does the imagery of making a will help our understanding of what the writer is saying (pp. 275–277)?

1 Peter 1:2, 18–21; 2:18–25; 3:18–22
16. To this you were called (pp. 278–293)

1 'The apostle Peter's reflections on the cross of Christ are of special interest' (p. 278). Why is this the case?

2 What is particularly significant about Peter's 'choice of vocabulary' in his reference to the death of Christ in 1 Peter 1:2? What is this intended to communicate to his readers (pp. 279–281)?

3 What is the 'concise theology of redemption' which Peter outlines in 1 Peter 1:18–21 (pp. 281–285)?

4 'Idolatry robs modern men and women of their freedom as much as it robbed the inhabitants of the ancient world ...' (p. 282). What examples can you think of? What 'idols' are you tempted to serve?

The cross of Christ releases us from the prison of futility and introduces us to the God and Father of the one who is the origin, purpose and goal of the whole of creation, as well as of our existence' (p. 283).

---

5 What effects of redemption does Peter highlight here (p. 284)? To what extent do you experience these in your own life?

6 What is the 'purpose of our redemption' (pp. 284–285)? How does this work out in practice?

7 Why must we 'be careful how we apply' what Peter says about following in the footsteps of Christ (p. 286)?

'Refusing to retaliate breaks the cycle of evil and overcomes evil with good' (p. 287).

---

8 Apart from serving as an example for Christians to follow, what other aspects of the purpose of Christ's suffering does Peter highlight here (pp. 287–289)?

9 What 'balance that has eluded many subsequent generations of disciples' does Peter achieve (p. 289)? Why is this so important?

10 What do 'evangelicals often understate ... in their concern to champion the redemptive significance of the cross' (p. 289)? How does this work out in practice for you?

11 In what ways does the cross proclaim the total victory of Christ (pp. 290–292)?

12 Why are 1 Peter 3:19–22 'some of the most difficult verses in the New Testament' (p. 291)? What do you think Peter means?

13 What 'two things stand out about Peter's treatment of the cross of Christ' (p. 293)?

1 John 4:7–12
17. God is love (pp. 294–304)

1 What was the false teaching circulating among John's readers, which he tackles in this letter? Why does he react so strongly to it (p. 294)?

2 What does the cross of Jesus supremely reveal for John (p. 295)?

3 In what ways would our understanding of God 'be deficient' without the cross (p. 296)?

'Like a smitten lover, God overcame every obstacle, set aside every disincentive and surmounted every impediment in order to woo us back into fellowship with himself' (pp. 297–298).

---

4 'We take it for granted that our heavenly Father loves us and that he will forgive us, as if it were the most predictable thing in the world and could occur without difficulty or cost' (p. 298). What is wrong with thinking like this? What more needs to be said about the way God's love deals with sin?

5 What is 'John's special contribution to our understanding of the atonement' (p. 300)?

6 In saying that Christ is *the Saviour of the world* (4:14), how can we be sure that 'John is not saying that all men and women are automatically saved by Christ' (p. 301)? What is he saying, then?

7 'The cross not only affirms that God loves us, but insists that we must love others in turn' (p. 301). Why is this? How does it work out in practice for you?

'It is impossible to know God and yet fail to live a life of love' (p. 302).

8 In what way is love a 'powerful evangelistic and apologetic tool' (p. 303)? How have you experienced this?

9 What is so astounding about the claim that God's love is not only revealed through us but also *made complete in us* (4:12)? What 'practical implications for the spiritual lives of God's people' (pp. 303–304) does this suggest?

10 'Teaching similar to that which John opposes in this letter never leaves the church undisturbed for long' (p. 304). What examples of this can you think of? What test for assessing the genuineness of Christian teaching does this suggest?

Revelation 5:1–14
18. Worthy is the Lamb (pp. 305–319)

1 In what ways is Revelation a 'fitting climax for the Bible's teaching about the cross of Christ' (p. 305)?

2 What is so 'extraordinary' about the image of the slain Lamb in Revelation 5 (pp. 307–310)?

3 What is implied by the fact that the Lamb is *in the centre of the throne* (5:6; pp. 308–309)?

4 What message is 'clear' from this picture of the Lamb (p. 310)?

'Whenever the Old Testament speaks of the victory of the Messiah or the overthrow of the enemies of God, we are to remember that the gospel recognises no other way of achieving these ends than the way of the Cross' (George Caird, quoted on p. 310).

5 What 'two major ways of looking at the metaphor' of the Lamb have been explored? Which is more likely to lie behind John's vision (pp. 310–311)?

6 What does the opening of the seals on the scroll represent? Why is only the Lamb worthy to do this (p. 311)?

7 'The blood of Christ, shed on the cross, has not only set them free but purchased them for God' (p. 312). What implications does this have for you?

8 What does heaven's worship reveal about the cross of Christ (pp. 314–318)?

9 What is 'deeply revealing' about the seven-fold acclamation offered

STUDY GUIDE

by the worshippers to the Lamb (pp. 317–318)?
10 Why is the image of the slain Lamb such a fitting metaphor for summing up the work of Christ on the cross (p. 319)?

341